Terror and Greatness

Terror & Greatness

Ivan & Peter as Russian Myths

Kevin M. F. Platt

Cornell University Press
Ithaca and London

First published 2011 by Cornell University Press

Printed in the United States of America

Library of Congress Cataloging-in-Publication Data

Platt, Kevin M. F., 1967–
    Terror and greatness : Ivan and Peter as Russian myths / Kevin M.F. Platt.
        p. cm.
    Includes bibliographical references and index.
    ISBN 978-0-8014-4813-3 (cloth : alk. paper)
    1. Russia—Historiography.   2. Ivan IV, Czar of Russia, 1530–1584.   3. Peter I, Emperor of Russia, 1672–1725.   I. Title.
    DK38.P57 2011
    947'.043072—dc22

                                                            2010047917

Cornell University Press strives to use environmentally responsible suppliers and materials to the fullest extent possible in the publishing of its books. Such materials include vegetable-based, low-VOC inks and acid-free papers that are recycled, totally chlorine-free, or partly composed of nonwood fibers. For further information, visit our website at www.cornellpress.cornell.edu.

Cloth printing   10 9 8 7 6 5 4 3 2 1

for Kasia, Dasha and Poli (who are just great)

Can the link between document and narrative,
between life and history, ever be broken?
Benedetto Croce

CONTENTS

ACKNOWLEDGMENTS

I could not have written this book without the help of many colleagues and collaborators who have patiently read drafts, offered criticism, and suggested sources and avenues for further investigation. Work with David Brandenberger on our articles and coedited book on the historical revisionism of the Stalinist period was instrumental in forming my views at an early stage of research. David also generously read drafts at many stages of completion of the project. Patented no-holds-barred critique from the Penn Works In Progress group—Barbara Fuchs, Maurice Samuels, Emily Steiner, and Paul Saint-Amour—has improved every chapter. Andrei Zorin made crucial interventions into the project upon reading its first drafts, engaged with various intermediate versions, and read and commented on the entire finished manuscript. Among his other important suggestions, Arden Reed advised against rushing to complete the project too soon. Liliane Weissberg and Jerome Singerman offered important advice as the project was nearing completion. My research assistant, Maksim Rappaport, was a great help in organizing bibliography and other resources. Anna Shulgat and Konstantin Polivanov helped me gain access to archives in Russia. Among the many others who have read drafts or responded to my presentations, I must thank in particular: Konstantin Bogdanov, John Bender, Oksana Bulgakowa, Katerina Clark, Aleksandr Dmitriev, Caryl Emerson, Terence Emmons, Alexander Etkind, Lazar Fleishman, Gregory Freidin, Hans Ulrich Gumbrecht, Peter Holquist, Ilya Kukulin, John Mackay, Laurie Manchester, Benjamin Nathans, Joan Neuberger, Serguei Oushakine, Konstantin Polivanov, Stephanie Sandler, Andrey Shcherbenok, Peter Steiner, William Mills Todd III, Elizabeth Kridl Valkenier, Ilya Vinitsky, Andrew Wachtel, and Danny Walkowitz. I thank as well the participants in the graduate seminar History, Memory, Trauma that I taught in fall 2004 who aided me in working through key concepts for this book.

I have also benefited from many forms of institutional support while working on this book: a Short-Term Research Grant at the Kennan Institute for Advanced Russian Studies, a Fellowship at the Davis Center for Russian Research at Harvard University, a Fellowship at the Stanford Humanities Center, and a Weiler Faculty Research Fellowship from the University of Pennsylvania School of Arts and Sciences. Thanks are due as well to many libraries, archives, and their staffs in Moscow, St. Petersburg, Riga, and Washington, DC, and at Stanford University, the University of Pennsylvania, Harvard University, Princeton University, and Pomona College. My research was also made possible in part by grants from the International Research and Exchanges Board (IREX), with funds provided by the National Endowment for the Humanities and the U.S. Department of State, which administers the Russian, Eurasian, and East European Research Program (Title VIII). Support was also provided by a Fellowship Grant from the National Council for Eurasian and East European Research, under the authority of a Title VIII Grant from the U.S. Department of State.

I have presented aspects of the arguments contained in this book in the journals *Ab Imperio*, *Common Knowledge*, *Novoe literaturnoe obozrenie*, and *Stanford Slavic Studies*, as well as in the book, *Epic Revisionism*, which I co-edited with David Brandenberger, and in *Violence in Russian Literature and Culture*, edited by Marcus Levitt and Tatyana Novikov, both published by the University of Wisconsin Press. I thank all those journals and presses for their support for my work. In the final stages of my writing, the editorial interventions of John Ackerman at Cornell University Press aided me immensely in discovering the book's proper scale and proportion and in taming unruly sentences. I also thank editor Candace J. Akins and my wonderfully deft copyeditor Carolyn Pouncy, as well as the many others at the Press who will have contributed their energies to editing, design, and production of this volume. Yet my most crucial support during work on this book has been from my family: my two daughters, whose greatness is unadulterated, and my closest friend and collaborator, Karina Sotnik.

NOTE ON TRANSLITERATION

The transliteration of Russian terms, titles, surnames, and geographic locations in this volume follows a modified form of the standard practiced by the Library of Congress, in which I have omitted diacritical marks to improve readability (Solovev, not Solov'ev; Kazan, not Kazan'). In the interests of scholarly precision, however, I have preserved all diacritical marks in bibliographical entries. Exceptions to these general rules occur in quotations taken from other sources and in instances when contradicting existing practice would create unnecessary ambiguity (Eisenstein, not Eizenshtein; Meyerhold, not Meierkhol'd; Chaliapin, not Shaliapin).

Terror and Greatness

Toward a Cultural Historiography of Russia

> Now one Hero speaks to the other:
> "It was not in vain that we toiled,
> Not in vain was our joint deed,
> That made the whole world fear the Russians.
> By our efforts our realm has extended far
> To the north, west, and east.
> Now Anna is triumphant in the south
> Sheltering her subjects with this victory."
>   —Mikhail Lomonosov, "Ode on the Taking of Khotin"
>   (Oda na vziatie Khotina), 1739

Ivan the Terrible and Peter the Great

In the concluding stanzas of the *Ode on the Taking of Khotin*, a work canonized as nothing less than the cornerstone of modern Russian literature, Mikhail Lomonosov entertains a historical fantasy in which Ivan the Terrible (1530–84, grand duke of Muscovy from 1533, crowned tsar in 1547) and Peter the Great (1672–1725, tsar from 1682, emperor from 1721) appear on the battlefield of Russia's victory over the Turks in 1739.[1] In the lines above, Emperor Peter explains to Tsar Ivan that the genealogy of Russian rulership links the two of them, the creators of Russia's empire, to the reigning Empress Anna, whose military triumphs continue their project of territorial expansion. With these lines, Lomonosov collapses Russia's history into his own time, bringing figures of vastly disparate eras into a moment of simultaneity in order to place the present into the stream of time and to bring the origins of the Russian state and of Russian literature into synchronicity. This telescoping of chronology grants the status of superhistorical fate to certain features of the Russian political and social experience: awesome rulers imposing transformative policies, the grand impulse of imperial extension from west to east, the insignificance of human suffering in the face of *raison d'état*—all marshaled by Russian cultural institutions in support of a teleological vision of history that culminates in the achievements of the present. In Lomonosov's vision, the past and the present

---

1. Lomonosov, "Oda na vziatie Khotina," in his *Polnoe sobranie sochinenii*, 8:23.

are hypostases of a grand, mythical pattern of recurrence that achieves its fulfillment in his own articulation of modern Russian experience.

Yet despite the aspiration to the timelessness of myth, Lomonosov's creative
anachronism around the figures of Ivan and Peter is itself just the beginning of
a long and complex history—not only of modern Russian cultural life but also
of this rhetorical strategy with regard to the past. In epochs subsequent to Lomonosov's, Russian literary, political, and historical discourse returned again
and again to these same "prototypical" autocrats, placing them into equivalence with virtually all later rulers of Russia, viewing the triumphs, injustices,
and traumas of each new epoch through the lens of those long past reigns, and
exploring the logic of historical and political life that they represent in ever
new circumstances.

The present book examines this relationship to Ivan the Terrible, Peter the
Great, and—through them—to the ever-present past and frequently archaic
present in Russia. I seek to discover the implications of this peculiar conception of politically charged time and space. Why did Imperial Russian and
then Soviet political culture adopt despotic rulers, responsible for extraordinary violence, as heroic figures and avatars of social identity? What has been
the consequence of this fixation on traumatic periods of history as scenes of
collective becoming? What does it mean to live the present as a reiteration of
the deep past? How may we understand the strange interrelationship of the
historical myths of these two figures, and the corresponding intertwining of
stories of heroic redemption and traumatic suffering, of greatness and terror,
in the Russian historical mind? Finally, what can such an investigation reveal
about the relations of Russian cultural and other discursive institutions to
political power, about the production and use of history in Russia, and in
history writing in general? It is my hope that by tracing over the long term
the representations of these specific figures, we can see the currents that carry
visions of the past from one re-vision to the next and that contribute to
the development over time of historical discourse—whether in the form of
common-knowledge views of the past, popular amusements, or a scholarly
consensus. Peter and Ivan serve in my study as something like the arrays of
floats researchers drop into the oceans—by watching the progress of the floats
through the world's waters, one can reconstruct the circulatory system of the
seas.

Why study representations of Ivan IV and Peter I together? Despite many
distinctions between the historical actualities of their reigns and between later
interpretations of them, these two figures are the most prominent examples
drawn from the deep national past of an important category in Russian historical thought: the ruler who is alternately lionized for his heroic, great
achievements and condemned for his extraordinary violence and despotism.
Very often, the two have been compared, either as similar or contrasting figures, and from the middle nineteenth century a well-defined, if seldom dominant, school of history in Russia viewed their reigns as analogous moments

of state building and transformative social change at the command of a prescient leader.[2] This view reached an apogee in the startling elevation of both Ivan and Peter, among other tsarist figures, as heroic predecessors, models of leadership, and touchstones of Soviet collective identification during the Stalinist 1930s and 1940s. The tradition of connecting these figures, however, serves only as an initial motivation for my study, in which I approach representations of the history of Ivan and Peter as "myths," bringing to light the ways in which they have illustrated and explained collective selfhood in Russia. I view the divergent interpretations of the two rulers as a dynamically interrelated but unstable and fluid system of historical myths that has over time formed a persistent symbolic reserve, shaping and serving the changing needs of Russian political and cultural life. This symbolic system has taken shape in a convoluted history of use, reuse, exchange, and circulation of these myths across many different social institutions. To trace this history of development, I have shaped this study as a "cultural historiography"—that is, a chronologically organized series of close analyses or thick descriptions of key texts ranging from scholarly histories to works of fiction, drama, film, and visual art.

Ultimately, my analyses reveal that the extraordinary variability of interpretations of Ivan and Peter reflects a deeper mechanism whereby they have served as crucial sites in Russian articulations of the relationships between coercion and social progress and between trauma and collective identity. In Russian conceptions of national history each of the two functions as a chronological and civilizational boundary figure, overseeing transitions between premodernity and the modern, and marking the geographical and cultural borders between Russia and its imagined others to the east and west. Generally dominant interpretations of the two have tended to represent Ivan as a figure for terror and historical trauma and Peter as one of greatness and historical triumph, relegating the corresponding counterinterpretations of Peter's terror and Ivan's greatness to a secondary position. Study of the two figures together, however, uncovers the relationships between the traumatic and heroic interpretive stances that have been applied to each, revealing the intimate connection between greatness and terror in Russian historical mythology and in Russian political practice. As becomes apparent below, the political and cultural function of historical "greatness" in modern Russia has been, at base, founded on the experience, disavowal, and reinscription of "terror."

---

2. In the early 1980s, the Soviet cultural historians Aleksandr Panchenko and Boris Uspenskii published one of the most extensive and interesting comparisons of Ivan and Peter, arguing that programs of the two figures represent efflorescences of a single cultural logic, that of the revolutionary "first monarch." Beyond the impressive erudition of this essay, one cannot help but wonder to what extent the authors intended their scheme of analysis to extend to unmentionable twentieth-century revolutionary "monarchs" (Panchenko and Uspenskii, "Ivan Groznyi i Petr Velikii").

My book contributes to a number of scholarly subfields and builds on the work of many predecessors.[3] In terms of method, I rely on, among other models, the "history and memory" studies of Pierre Nora and his school; Hayden White's rhetorical analysis of historical texts; Eric Hobsbawm and Terence Ranger's work on the "invention of tradition"; Reinhart Koselleck's conceptual history; and the extensive literature on memory and trauma.[4] I have also followed the precedent of works on similar problems in other national traditions. Thus, the historical mythology of conflict between Saxons and Normans, which has been the subject of brilliant treatments by Asa Briggs, Christopher Hill, and others, is in many ways comparable to the long and varied process of historical mythmaking regarding Ivan IV and Peter I in Russia.[5] Yet my own method of cultural historiography represents a substantially new approach, particularly in its attention to the dynamic interrelationships of differing cultural, political, and scholarly social institutions and the complex process of use and reuse of historical myths over the long term. A common oversight of studies of historical knowledge is that they forget a step, placing historical representations in direct relation to historical "events." Instead, I study the intervening history of historical representations as they wend their way through time in their own contingent unfolding. In short, I have sought a thoroughgoing historicization of the histories of Ivan the Terrible and Peter the Great.

Materials and Methods

The most striking feature of my material, at first glance, is the sheer variability of representations of Ivan IV and Peter I. The reigns of each have commonly been considered scenes of radical social transformation, state building, con-

---

3. Studies of the representation of each ruler, individually taken, include many articles and two monographs regarding representations of Peter: the first of these, by Gasiorowska, is a focused account of historical fiction about the first emperor; and the second, by Riasanovsky, is a detailed, encyclopedic account of the "image" of Peter in Russian thought and history (Gasiorowska, *Image of Peter the Great*; Riasanovsky, *Image of Peter the Great*). With regard to Ivan, Maureen Perrie has published a monograph on the Stalinist rehabilitation of the tsar (*Cult of Ivan the Terrible*). Natal'ia Mut'ia's recent book tracing the evolution of representations of Ivan in Russian culture appeared too late for me to refer to it while working on my own book (*Ivan Groznyi: istorizm i lichnost'*).

4. Nora, ed., *Realms of Memory*; White, *Metahistory*; Hobsbawm and Ranger, eds., *Invention of Tradition*; Koselleck, *Futures Past*; Koselleck, *Practice of Conceptual History*; Caruth, *Unclaimed Experience*; LaCapra, *Writing History, Writing Trauma*.

5. Briggs, "Saxons, Normans, and Victorians," in his *Collected Essays*, 2:215–35; Hill, *Puritanism and Revolution*, 46–111; Pocock, *Ancient Constitution and the Feudal Law*; Simmons, *Reversing the Conquest*. A comparable problem in the Russian tradition, that of the history of representations of the thirteenth-century prince Aleksandr Nevskii, has been treated in an exhaustive recent monograph by Frithjof Benjamin Schenk (Shenk [Schenk], *Aleksandr Nevskii v russkoi kul'turnoi pamiati*).

quest of empire, and modernization, achieved at the cost of extraordinary political conflict and bloodshed. Their fundamental significance as transitional figures has lent itself to any number of interpretative stances. Over the course of the last two centuries, each has been viewed by some as a cruel monster and by others as a heroic leader, at times as a demonstration of the necessity of bloodshed for collective progress, and at others as an illustration of the inhuman and morally compromised nature of modernization or the ironic inseparability of violence and power in Russia. A facile response to the enormous range of competing views might conclude that it reflects simply the arbitrariness of historical interpretation itself—illustrating Hayden White's metahistorical dictum that "any historical object can sustain a number of equally plausible descriptions or narratives of its processes."[6] Yet Reinhart Koselleck's remark that "in the course of research, all metahistorical categories will change into historical statements" reminds us that representations of history, no matter how arbitrary they appear in relation to "events," are themselves always historically conditioned.[7] The many and divergent visions of Ivan and Peter are no exceptions— each was contingent on the needs of a particular time and audience, and each built on and responded to prior representations. Perhaps more important, the specific mode of variability germane to historical accounts of Ivan and Peter— the regularities and constraints of interpretation's development—has itself been contingent on the political, intellectual, and cultural purposes to which such accounts have been put. Historical knowledge of these figures, in this sense, has itself always been locked in history, trapped in an irresolute, dialectical relationship with its own historical unfolding.[8]

How, then, may we approach the witches' brew of arbitrariness and contingency presented by the history of representation of Ivan IV and Peter I? Pierre Nora has remarked that the touchstones of collective memory in modern societies that he terms "*lieux de memoire*"—a category that includes monuments, battlefields, historical texts, and national heroes—"only exist because of their capacity for metamorphosis, an endless recycling of their meaning and an unpredictable proliferation of their meanings."[9] Eric Hobsbawm illustrates this process in his description of how May Day celebrations have been appropriated by diverse states and political movements, often with utterly opposed ideologies.[10] Similarly, Hill shows how multiple revisions of the theory of the Norman Yoke have served the political aims of diverse times and places.[11]

---

6. White, "The Politics of Historical Interpretation: Discipline and De-Sublimation," in his *Content of the Form*, 58–82, here 76.

7. Koselleck, "On the Need for Theory in History," in his *Practice of Conceptual History*, 1–19, here 3.

8. Platt, "History and Despotism."

9. Nora, "Between History and Memory," 19.

10. Hobsbawm, "Mass-Producing Traditions: Europe, 1870–1914," in Hobsbawm and Ranger, eds., *Invention of Tradition*, 263–307, esp. 283–87.

11. Hill, *Puritanism and Revolution*, 46–111.

My work builds on the example of these scholars, yet cautiously. These studies have generally presented such "usable pasts" as being entirely contingent on
the political needs of each successive moment—as a species of fallen historical thought, completely unmoored from history itself. A certain scholarly irony
commonly inflects such studies, communicating the researcher's dismissal as
spurious of the historical representations under investigation. However, if we
allow national symbols such as Ivan IV and Peter I to retain their aura of ancient
solidity and weightiness, we must ask: what happens to this specific gravity
when these figures are repeatedly reinvented as symbols for political and social
identification, and in the service of such radically different ideologies as the Official Nationality of Nicholas I and the National Bolshevism of Stalin? How do
prior deployments of historical myth, no matter how tendentious or specious,
exert influence on later ones? Do consecutive iterations of historical myth, as in
Levi-Strauss's account of the operations of myth more generally, each add to a
perpetually evolving and accumulating significance?[12] Alternatively, might some
representations of Ivan or Peter, in the past or future, break free from all prior
ones to renovate history entirely?

As my study demonstrates, the answers to these essentially theoretical questions oblige us to investigate specific historical circumstances. In general, scholars regard themselves and their own historical moment as uniquely capable of
critically reflecting on prior traditions in historical imagination and seldom
consider whether this privileged, metahistorical position has had previous
occupants.[13] In contrast, I strive to comprehend the extent of the metahistorical
consciousness of the historians, painters, and party hacks of the past and to investigate how their reinterpretations of the Russian past actively coped with the
influence of prior ones, with this "unpredictable proliferation of meanings," in
order to continue to generate specific, necessary meaning in a given moment. I
have sought to explain, for example, how Stalinist cultural figures capitalized
on, circumvented, and managed the legacy of tsarist mythmaking around Ivan
IV and Peter I. In general, I describe the history of representation of the Russian
national past as a process of continuous accumulation over time of new interpretations and new twists on old interpretations, but not a blind or undirected
accumulation. As the penumbra of competing representations has grown, so
too has the complexity of managing the meaning of new ones.

Among the chief contexts conditioning this feedback loop between the histories of Peter and Ivan and the history of those histories have been ongoing attempts to define and shape collective identity in Russia. With increasing
frequency over the past several decades, scholars have linked problems in the
representation of history to the study of collective self-representation, and espe-

12. Levi-Strauss, "Structural Study of Myth."
13. Nora's program statements go so far as to make reflexive self-critical thought on the
generation of historical knowledge one of the central features distinguishing the *lieux de mé-
moire* from historical scholarship devoted to their study ("Between History and Memory").

cially national identification.[14] One must note at the outset that questions of collective identity are uniquely complex in Russia—forever the multiethnic center of multinational empires, unions, and federations, which despite much intellectual and political ferment around the idea of the nation has never been ruled by a fully nationalist regime or, some argue, developed a full-blown sense of national selfhood. Students of nationalism share a broad consensus regarding the status of national identification as a prima facie modern phenomenon that, especially where it coincides with a high degree of ethnic and linguistic commonality, as in Europe, has paradoxically sought to ground itself in the aura of the ancient and the primordial.[15] Out of the tension between the relatively recent efflorescence of nations and the nationalist drive to celebrate an ancient history arises the need to discover or invent a glorious past. Scholarship devoted to the study of how national communities have called their present identities and past histories into being illustrates how complex and varied this process can be, depending on where, when, and by whom it is carried out.[16]

In modern Russia, questions of collective identity have from the start been distinguished by efforts to subordinate the "collective" to autocratic authority, resulting in a paradigmatic case of "official nationality."[17] One of the chief complexities of the Russian case is the problematic status of the national idea in an

14. In light of Rogers Brubaker's and Frederick Cooper's critique of the term "identity" as compromised by its contemporary political significance and its overly broad range of connotations, in the present work I attempt to use some of the more precise terms they recommend to discuss problems of collective selfhood. I opt most frequently for "collective identification" as an umbrella term for the processes by which conceptions of group selfhood are generated and maintained. As the need arises, I apply other terms, such as "collective self-representation" and when warranted "collective identity." See Brubaker and Cooper, "Beyond 'Identity.'"

15. The imagined communities of modern nations are the emergent effects of a convergence of economic (the rise of capitalism), social (the development of standard, shared languages and modern communications media), and political (the fading of traditional sources of authority with accelerating secularization) factors. Nationalist ideological formations, especially in Europe, have commonly derived their own authority and charismatic appeal from the "natural" self-evidence of homogenous communities rising from the mists of a primeval past. See Benedict Anderson, *Imagined Communities*; Hobsbawm, *Nations and Nationalism*; Hroch, "From National Movement to the Fully-formed Nation."

16. English nationalism emerged from the political struggles of the seventeenth and eighteenth centuries as a conceptual field dispersed among classes and political actors. Central European national identities were largely articulated in the nineteenth century by intellectuals in search of a novel political idiom. Nations have been created by colonial powers, subsequently to be coopted or rejected by subaltern political movements, and they have arisen as a result of the Soviet Union's pursuit of the Marxist-Leninist theoretical imperative that nations must form before they can disintegrate into a stateless, classless, and postnational society. See Duara, *Rescuing History from the Nation*; Greenfeld, *Nationalism*; Hroch, *Social Preconditions of National Revival*; Martin, *Affirmative Action Empire*; Slezkine, "USSR as a Communal Apartment."

17. Benedict Anderson, *Imagined Communities*, 83–111; Wortman, *Scenarios of Power*, 1:379–404; Riasanovsky, *Nicholas I*.

imperial context, which led to its consistent political and conceptual attenuation in order to justify a Russian tsar's reign over a multinational empire and its subsequent cooptation in the Stalinist era in what has sometimes been termed an experiment in "National Bolshevism."[18]

As the first two chapters of this book demonstrate, the distinctive, extreme variability of historical visions of Ivan and Peter reflects the conceptual and practical complexities of collective identification in Russia, which called for a past that was as multivalent as the political contexts that it would be made to serve. Ivan and Peter, both of whom in their own characteristic manner straddle the physical and symbolic borders of nation and empire, of the modern, and of political belonging, were in unique fashion suited as mythic forebears of a community that positioned itself as never only Russian, not fully or only modern, and never completely settled politically. For the same reason, however, their significance for formulations of collective selfhood became uniquely variable and unstable. Drawing on classical anthropological work on ritual and identification, I rely on the term "liminal" to describe this feature of Ivan and Peter as myths in (and of) motion.

The liminal potential of Ivan and Peter served collective identification in diverse ways. In some contexts, one or the other's story of collective and personal transformation served as a heroic focus for the celebration of "becoming Russian"—as a ritual exemplar of stepping into the collective being. In periods of consolidation of collective identity, such as the first half of the nineteenth century, or mobilization in the face of war, as in the 1930s and 1940s, these figures served as rousing symbols of collective unity and pride. Yet seen from other angles or in other moments, the violence and mayhem of the reigns of these same figures served to define collective selfhood by negative example. It is a tricky business to apply a term relating to individual psychology such as "trauma" to matters of collective experience or reminiscences of long-past events. In full recognition of the partly metaphorical nature of this application, I suggest that representations of history are as much about present experience and identity as they are about the events of the past, and they gain relevance for individuals as means of making sense of personal experience that may be broadly shared but is no less personal for that reason. The modern periods I treat in this study are all too frequently scenes of collective suffering. Indeed, works such as Pushkin's *Bronze Horseman* demonstrate how the "trauma" embedded in the story of Peter I's construction of Petersburg, for example, has been for later generations as much violence at the hands of later regimes as a memory of the sufferings of the dead.[19]

---

18. Brandenberger, *National Bolshevism*; Martin, *Affirmative Action Empire*; Miller, *Romanov Empire and Nationalism*; Slezkine, "USSR as a Communal Apartment."

19. Similarly, Andrey Shcherbenok has recently argued that the ongoing process of coming to terms with memory of the mass violence affecting the Soviet Union during the twentieth century has as much to do with the historical experience in question as with the traumatic

Recent studies have shown how collective identification may be predicated on a common narrative of historical suffering, or a "chosen trauma," often comprising distant and mythologized historical events that enter into complex allegorical relationships channeling contemporary events, conflicts, and experiences—the Battle of Kosovo in modern Serbian constructions of national selfhood, for example.[20] In contexts where Ivan and Peter have appeared as a despots rather than heroes, their reigns have sometimes been cast as such chosen traumas, serving to define a community of survivors and witnesses of ancient violence. Yet these two figures have served *both* as avatars of collective greatness and as the architects of mass trauma. The implications of this mythic overdetermination have played out in a surfeit of unintended consequences and ironic effects. Since the nineteenth century, successive authoritarian regimes have found it expedient to exalt Ivan and Peter as historical prototypes demonstrating the necessity of a violent imposition of authority to achieve national greatness. In this vision of history, greatness has been predicated on overlooking or disavowing traumatic violence. Ironically, however, the disavowal of trauma, a process that enlists society in the support of a patriotic collective identity, is itself a form of symbolic violence—a violence against memory in which all members of society are called to participate. Moreover, such patriotic celebrations of the ruler's heroism and the consequent disavowal of the trauma they inflicted have frequently been accompanied by new violence in the service of collective greatness. In this manner, the regimes that have mobilized Ivan and Peter have written their own eras into history as analogical eras of heroism, purchased at the price of mayhem and bloodshed. Just so have the eras of Nicholas I and later of Joseph Stalin come to be remembered not only as later images of durable national glory but also as scenes marked by the resurgence of ancient trauma. In sum, as I demonstrate in the present work, Peter and Ivan have been central elements of a dynamic system of historical symbols and political practices that has persisted across two centuries, through wars and revolutions, and that has confounded all attempts to redirect the significance of these figures.

Terror and Greatness

The chapters that follow trace Russian visions of Ivan IV and Peter I from the start of the nineteenth century, when Russian historical writing first achieved prominence in cultural and political life, through the 1950s, when the Stalinist adoption and modification of tsarist historical myths faded into the background

---

experience of the post-Soviet era. I refer to his presentation at the roundtable on "The Soviet Past as the Traumatic Object of Contemporary Russian Culture" at the American Association for the Advancement of Slavic Studies (AAASS) National Convention, Boston (November 2009).

20. Volkan and Itzkowitz, "Modern Greek and Turkish Identities."

of Soviet political life. A brief conclusion touches on the resurgence of these myths in the late twentieth century and points to their relevance for collective identification in contemporary Russia. I do not attempt in this book to offer a "complete" catalogue of representations of the two tsars, which number in the thousands. In place of such an encyclopedic mode, I examine closely a smaller subset of materials and episodes. My analyses are grouped into six chapters, chronologically organized, each of which takes on a focused set of historically significant and theoretically interesting concerns in the context of the given period's historical thought. Chapter 1, "Liminality," investigates how Ivan and Peter served during the first half of the nineteenth century to articulate conceptions of collective selfhood in foundational texts of Russian historiography—Nikolai Karamzin's monumental *History of the Russian State* and Nikolai Ustrialov's textbook *Russian History*—as well as in the historical novels *The Last Novice* by Ivan Lazhechnikov and *Prince Serebriannyi* by Aleksei K. Tolstoi. As I explain, although dominant conceptions of Russian history of this period adopted Peter as a transcendent, heroic "father of the fatherland" and Ivan as a depraved tyrant, each ruler functioned in his own way as a liminal figure, serving to demarcate the boundaries of collective selfhood in Russian ideological formulations. Chapter 2, "Trauma," examines how during this same period unofficial and countertraditional representations of Russian history charted subterranean relationships between the tsars and between the conceptions of collective greatness associated primarily with Peter and of historical trauma tied to Ivan's name. As the historical writings of Hegelians such as Konstantin Kavelin and as Aleksandr Pushkin's masterwork *The Bronze Horseman* each reveal, in the historical thought of Official Nationality Peter's greatness is predicated on a disavowal of the mayhem and trauma of his reign; analogously, Ivan may just as easily be viewed as a hero as a tyrant, with the worst excesses of his reign recast as historically necessary bloodshed. In sum, the two figures were from the start of the century used to construct collective identity on a base of disavowed trauma.

Chapter 3, "Filicide," turns to middle and late nineteenth-century traditions in representations of the two rulers. Here, I focus in particular on stories of intergenerational conflict and violence that served as allegories for contemporary politics and social life in this era, obsessed as it was with problems of "fathers and children." As I show, late nineteenth-century Russians debated the achievements and costs of coerced modernization through contemplation of the deaths of Ivan's son Ivan and Peter's son Aleksei at the hands of their respective fathers. Interestingly, while the death of the Tsarevich Aleksei was largely a topic of historical analysis by the leading historians of the day—including Mikhail Pogodin, Sergei Solovev, and Nikolai Kostomarov—Ivan's inadvertent killing of the Tsarevich Ivan (or of fictional children), was most prominently the subject of plays and operas—by Aleksei K. Tolstoi, Lev Mei, and Nikolai Rimskii-Korsakov, among others. The conclusion of this chapter investigates how the portrayals of these father-son confrontations in two historical paintings by Nikolai Ge and Ilia Repin offer not only an additional treatment of violence and power in Russian history but also a metahistorical reflection on the tension between the divergent approaches of historiography and cultural life to the Russian past.

Chapter 4, "Prognostication," considers Silver Age representations of Ivan and Peter, with particular focus on Dmitrii Merezhkovskii's historical novel *Antichrist (Peter and Aleksei)* and Pavel Miliukov's *The Outlines of Russian Cultural History*. By the start of the twentieth century, the reigns of the two rulers had come to serve as the primary foundational myths of Russian political and social life. The ambivalence of these myths between stories of greatness and stories of terror, rather than diminishing their capacity to provide meaningful explanations of Russian history, had rendered them "all-purpose" instruments for interpreting political experience, capable of explaining any event and "predicting" any outcome. Ultimately, these qualities of multivalence and ubiquitous utility ensured that even after the revolutions of 1917, the historical myths of Ivan and Peter were to retain their relevance for later generations and formulations of collective identity.

The final two chapters are devoted to Stalinist historical revisionism, which in the 1930s and 1940s "recycled" Ivan IV and Peter I as vehicles for Soviet mass culture and political myth—as transparent doubles of contemporary events and figures. Chapter 5, "Rehabilitation," traces the emergence of Stalinist historical revisionism from the 1920s to the 1930s, analyzing in detail the central place of Ivan the Terrible and Peter the Great in the *Short Course in the History of the USSR*, edited by Andrei Shestakov. Although the historiography and public discourse of the 1930s announced the new approach to the Russian national past as a complete break with both the prerevolutionary tradition and the historiography of the 1920s associated with the name of Mikhail Pokrovskii, Stalinist visions of the past are in fact best understood as an inheritance from imperial historiography, mediated by Pokrovskii's work. Furthermore, while articulation of the new historical orthodoxy of the 1930s was managed by party elites, it was not simply as imposed "from above" on Soviet public culture. Instead, it emerged from and responded to the exigencies of the historical imagination of the 1920s, which continued to see the present through the lens of Russian history and through the allegorical figures of Ivan and Peter.

The book's sixth and final chapter, "Repetition," analyzes representations of the two rulers in the cultural life of the 1930s and 1940s, in particular Aleksei N. Tolstoi's novel *Peter I* and Sergei Eisenstein's uncompleted film trilogy *Ivan the Terrible*. Although each of these works, in its own way, may be seen as an orthodox contribution to Soviet mass culture, each also commented on, managed, and critiqued Stalinist revisionist historiography's efforts to reduce the myths of Ivan and Peter to a single, final, and maximally "useful" interpretation.

In sum, my book offers a history of specific historical myths with great significance for political and cultural life in Russia over the course of the last two centuries. It may also help us assess and comprehend Russia in the here and now. The unfolding of the historical mythology of Ivan the Terrible and Peter the Great, both in Russia and in the West, is not over—witness Zurab Tsereteli's 196 ft. monument to Peter the Great, erected in central Moscow in 1996, or the recent "election" in the "Name of Russia" Internet and television competition of both figures among the twelve most "valuable, remarkable, and symbolic personalities of Russian history," or Pavel Lungine's recent film about the terrible tsar.[21] The political culture and visions of collective identity articulated through the figures of Ivan and Peter in many ways still lie at the basis of contemporary conceptions of what it means to be a Russian. Although my work, as represented in this book, leads me to view aspirations for "escape" from this tradition in historical thought as naïve, I nevertheless hope that study of the myths of Ivan and Peter, their genesis and transmission from one generation to the next, can yield beneficial insight into their implications for the Russian political experience today.

21. See the results of the "Name of Russia" project at "Imia Rossiia," www.nameofrussia.ru (accessed March 26, 2009). For the description of the project cited in my text "O proekte," see www.nameofrussia.ru/about.html (accessed March 24, 2009).

CHAPTER ONE

Liminality

The Russian people deserve to know their history.
—Alexander I, in a communication to Nikolai Karamzin, c. 1803

The noisy protest of the liberals affected the Historiographer—all the more so, since he had to mix with these wailers in high-society salons. To reconcile them with his history, he threw them the disfigured, dismembered corpse of Ivan the Terrible.
—Sergei Solovev, on Karamzin's *History of the Russian State*, c. 1870

We visited the Armory, monasteries, and museums with Kostia [Grand Prince Konstantin Nikolaevich], who not only owned [Karamzin's] *History of Russia* but also knew it well. He was a marvelous cicerone and impressed everyone with his insightful questions and comments. But he was also mischievous: he tried on Peter the Great's boots, sat on Ivan the Terrible's throne, and would have put on the Crown of Monomakh if [our chaperon] Litke had allowed.
—from the memoirs of Grand Princess Olga Nikolaevna, c. 1900

I will tell you here of my most private idea: the history of the last *ten years* has revealed to us the secret of Peter's great, great grandson—of Him, Who ascended the throne *exactly one hundred years later* (1725–1825). We know *Who* is reincarnate in *Him*.
—Nikolai Polevoi, remarks concerning Peter I and Nicholas I, 1836

Liminal Heroes

In 1803, Emperor Alexander I personally appointed Nikolai Karamzin official historiographer of Russia, launching the respected author on the project that would occupy him for the rest of his life: his *History of the Russian State* (Istoriia gosudarstva rossiiskogo, 1818–26). As Aleksandr Pushkin quipped, Karamzin was the "Columbus of Russian history," and it is with his "discovery" of the Russian past that I begin this cultural historiography of Russia. Now, I do not mean to claim that Russians had no conception of Ivan IV and Peter I in prior eras: as my introduction's epigraph from Lomonosov's "Ode on the Taking of Khotin" illustrates, a great deal of important writing concerning the two rulers had appeared during the preceding century.[1] Yet that body of literature

---

1. Lotman made the point that the comparison of Karamzin to Columbus was apt precisely in that the latter "was not the first European to reach the shores of America, and his

was a prelude to the far more intensive, self-reflexive and continuous traditions of representation of these figures that began during the reign of Alexander I (1801–25) and continued under Nicholas I (1825–55). It was in these years that Ivan and Peter gained their significance as touchstones in Russian thought about the relationship between rulers and ruled, between the exercise of coercive power and the content of the collective being, and between traumatic historical experience and political greatness. The traditions that began with Karamzin have retained their significance without interruption (although with unpredictable transformations and revisions) up to the present day.

The appearance of these novel but enduring conceptions of Ivan IV and Peter I was a part of the rise of the reading and writing of history to cultural prominence in Russia, which was itself a special case of the common European apotheosis of history during this period. In a corollary to the rapid spread of nationalist thought during the Romantic era, the representation of history became a key tool for the articulation of collective selfhood. We may take the case of postrevolutionary France, at the leading edge of these social and political transformations, as emblematic.[2] In the words of Lionel Gossman, the "Romantic remake of the history of France" involved "the discovery and substitution of the people for the royal dynasty as the hero of the piece," in the service of "a larger ideological program designed to legitimate the postrevolutionary nation and—more particularly—the postrevolutionary bourgeoisie."[3] From this era onward in Europe, the intertwined problems of political experience and collective identity would be refracted through the historical imagination. Note, however, that at this same moment in Russia—an unreformed dynastic empire comprising immense ethnic and regional differentiation—the role of nationalism was equivocal; bourgeois society had yet to appear, let alone produce politically dominant elites; and conceptions of popular sovereignty were nearly meaningless. Nevertheless, there, too, the representation of history came to play a crucial role in concepts of collective identity and political legitimacy. Russian thought of the early nineteenth century, rather than laboring to set the national being on historical foundations, instead used history as a tool to negotiate the problematic interrelationship between imperial and national frames of reference and between dynastic and national principles of political life. And in this fraught negotiation Ivan and Peter played a special role. These

---

journey was made possible only thanks to the experience of his predecessors." Iurii Lotman, "Kolumb russkoi istorii," in his *Karamzin*, 565–87. Other important works on Ivan and Peter from the eighteenth century include a number of odes by leading poets, the works of aristocratic historians and chroniclers such as Ekaterina Dashkova and Mikhail Shcherbatov, Voltaire's *History of the Russian Empire under Peter the Great* (Histoire de l'empire de Russie sous Pierre le Grand, 1759–63), Mikhail Kheraskov's epic poem on Ivan's conquest of Kazan, the *Rossiiada* (1779), and Jacob von Staehlin's and Ivan Golikov's extensive collections of historical anecdotes about Peter.

2. See Barzun, "Romantic Historiography"; Samuels, *Spectacular Past*, 1–17, 44–47.
3. Gossman, "History as Decipherment," 31.

were "liminal" historical figures, whose stories bridged geography and epochs, and for this reason they were ideally suited to give purchase on difficult questions such as that of Russian identity in the imperial era.

Before working out in full the concept of liminal historical figure, let us observe that in this foundational moment for historical myth, Russians did not often link Ivan and Peter as comparable rulers. Indeed, it would be more accurate to say that they presented a study in contrasts: absence and plenitude, respectively, or terror and greatness. During the reigns of Alexander I and Nicholas I, Peter was everywhere: invoked at nearly every court ritual; the subject of countless pamphlets, articles, brochures; represented in the most prominent monuments (see fig. 1) and toponyms (most obviously, St. Petersburg).[4] In step with his prominence in patriotic rhetoric, he was also central in this era's cultural life, which produced an endless series of historical and literary representations of Russia's first emperor. In this plethora of writing and representation there were a few who considered Peter in a negative light, such as the Decembrist Petr Kakhovskii, who wrote to Nicholas I in 1826 from his prison cell that Peter had "murdered everything national in the fatherland."[5] Pushkin's canonical poem, *The Bronze Horseman*, is famously ambivalent about Peter's role in history. Yet in the main and in official and culturally dominant views, Peter the Great was a hero—an ideal ruler who presented a mythic exemplar for all who came after.[6] Nikolai Polevoi's suggestion that the first emperor was reincarnate in Nicholas I presents a fine example of Peter's cultish significance.[7] Or consider the Moscow University historian Mikhail Pogodin's 1841 announcement:

Contemporary Russia, that is, European Russia—diplomatic, political, military, commercial, industrial, educational, and literary Russia—is a creation of Peter the Great. [. . .] We cannot open our eyes; we cannot make a move; we cannot turn in any direction without encountering him: at home, in the street, church, school, court, regiment, at leisure. He is

4. St. Petersburg, of course, is named for Peter's patron saint, not for Peter. And it must be noted that the semiotic function of this name is not only aimed at a linkage to Peter himself but also to one of the models of the new imperial capital, the prototype of all sacral and imperial centers, Rome. See Iu. M. Lotman and B. A. Uspenskii, "Otzvuki kontseptsii 'Moskva—tretii Rim' v ideologii Petra Pervogo," in Lotman, *Izbrannye stat'i*, 3:201–13.

5. Petr G. Kakhovskoi, letter of February 24, 1826, to Emperor Nicholas I, in *Iz pisem i pokazanii dekabristov*, ed. Borozdin, 3–18, here 11.

6. In Nicholas Riasanovsky's words, he was the "patron saint of Imperial Russia" (*Nicholas I*, 115).

7. From a communication to chief of the secret police Aleksandr Benkendorf concerning a proposed history of Peter the Great. As the journalist expanded on this theme elsewhere in the same document: "*Peter was the Son of the Fates.* [. . .] All the preceding history of Russia was a preparation for the era of Peter, and all subsequent history up to Nicholas was the further development of the era of Peter. Today, this development has reached its limit. God has sent us another son of the fates, who has begun a new era." Cited in Lemke, *Nikolaevskie zhandarmy*, 100–102, emphasis in the original.

Figure 1: Monument to Peter the Great (The Bronze Horseman),
St. Petersburg, 1768–82, sculptor Étienne Maurice Falconet.
Picture postcard c. 1900. LOC LOT 13419, no. 107.

everywhere, every day, every minute, at every step. We wake up. What
day is it? 1 January 1841. Peter the Great ordered us to number years
from the birth of Christ. Peter the Great ordered us to take January as the
first month. Time to get dressed—our clothing is sewn in the manner Peter
the Great prescribed, our uniforms according to his design. The fabric is
woven at a factory that he founded; the wool is shorn from sheep that he
bred. Our gaze falls upon a book—Peter the Great introduced this alpha-
bet and carved this type himself. You begin to read—Under Peter the First
this language became a written, literary one, supplanting the earlier
church language. The newspapers are brought in—Peter the Great
founded them.[8]

Pogodin works this odic vein for many more paragraphs, the excesses of which
illustrate the degree to which Russian elites felt that Peter bounded and defined
their existence—if it were any less fervent, Pogodin's vision of Peter's omni-
presence could be described as claustrophobic.

By contrast, in elite culture of this period Ivan the Terrible was far from
prominent—by comparison with Peter, he was nearly invisible. Although the
first half of the century brought several important treatments of him, there can
be no comparison of this minimal cultural presence with Peter's looming one.
Furthermore, nearly all representations of Ivan from this period depict him as

8. The passage is drawn from Pogodin's essay "Peter the Great," which was published in
the first issue of his ardently patriotic journal *Moskvitianin* and enjoyed overt official sanction and the approval of the emperor. See Barsukov, *Zhizn' i trudy M. P. Pogodina*, 6:5–8,
22–23.

a cruel despot. He is at his most sympathetic in Mikhail Lermontov's *Song about Tsar Ivan Vasilevich, the Young Oprichnik, and the Valiant Merchant Kalashnikov* (1837), where he appears as a capricious and violent, yet not wholly unjust, ruler.[9] In the 1840s and 1850s, Westernizer critics and State School historians, inspired by Hegelian historical thought, would renovate Ivan into a heroic transformer and prototype for Peter. Yet the single most influential representation of Ivan from the first half of the century was the ninth volume of Karamzin's *History* (1821), which shocked Russian society with its frank portrayal of the tsar as a bloodthirsty "tormentor." This work branded Ivan as a villain who was never to be rehabilitated into a positive element of the official genealogy of Russia and who would remain up until 1917, at least in the rhetoric of court and state, a shameful family outcast, mentioned as little as possible—a bloody "corpse" whose periodic exhumation never failed to shock.[10] Dedicated some forty years after Karamzin's revelations, Mikhail Mikeshin's monument to Russian history (see fig. 2), in celebration of the millennial anniversary of ancient Rus in 1862, showed nearly every other notable figure of the Russian past, including even contemporaries of Ivan such as his advisor Aleksei Adashev (credited with guiding the tsar during an early period of wise rule), and the Cossack conqueror of Siberia, Ermak—yet the terrible tsar himself was conspicuously absent.[11]

Ivan's few real appearances at the center stage of Russian cultural life were shocking scandals—not only because of the sensationally bloody nature of the myth of the Terrible Tsar, but also because they violated the de facto taboo on discussion of him. The reception of Karamzin's work set the precedent here, too: although the volume on Ivan was intended, as was the *History* as a whole, to legitimate and instruct present rulers (in this case by means of a negative example, contrasting with enlightened modern autocrats), official responses were anything but positive. The future tsar Grand Duke Nikolai Pavlovich is rumored to have pronounced Karamzin "a scoundrel, without whom the people would never have figured out that among tsars there are tyrants."[12] Casting doubt on the officially sanctioned principle that "the Russian people deserves to know its history," Metropolitan Filaret, recalling many years later Karamzin's first public reading of his work on Ivan in 1820, wrote that "the reader and the reading were delightful, but what was read was terrifying. At the time I thought, 'wouldn't history have fulfilled her calling satisfactorily if she illuminated the better part of the reign of Ivan the Terrible, and threw a shadow over the rest, rather than articulating its many

---

9. For discussions of this poem, see Serman, *Mikhail Lermontov*, 98–125; and Powelstock, *Becoming Mikhail Lermontov*, 213–20.

10. Solov'ev, *Izbrannye trudy*, 329.

11. The absence of Ivan on the monument was undoubtedly related as well to its location in Novgorod, the site of one of Ivan's most storied and violent suppressions of regional resistance to autocratic rule.

12. This is an anecdote of uncertain veracity, cited in Lotman, "Kolumb russkoi istorii," 583.

Figure 2: Monument to the Russian Millennium, Novgorod, 1862, sculptor Mikhail Mikeshin. LOC LOT 13254, no. 23.

striking, gloomy features—that are so painful to see attributed to a Russian tsar.' "[13]

It is only when one turns to the matter of Russian collective identity that these two dissimilar figures appear to share some common features. The term "collective" must be qualified before application here. In contrast to the great modern publics that had already taken shape in western Europe, the Russian cultural milieu was intimately scaled—composed of a few tens of thousands of men and women of elite society, clustered around the twin capitals of Moscow and St. Petersburg. For these few decades this tiny, privileged society, which nevertheless saw itself as representative of a vast many-peopled empire, constituted a laboratory or hothouse, producing the novel cultural and political ideas that would develop into the more broadly shared traditions to come.[14]

13. The pronouncement concerning the Russian people, taken as epigraph to this chapter, is drawn from a royal commendation granted by Nicholas I to Karamzin on May 13, 1826. Nicholas attributes the phrase to his predecessor Alexander I. See Eidel'man, *Poslednii letopisets*. Filaret is cited in Lotman, "Kolumb russkoi istorii," 583.

14. The best representation of Russian cultural and intellectual life of the period is Todd, *Fiction and Society in the Age of Pushkin*, 45–105. In some ways, the situation is similar to

So how did conceptions of social belonging respond to the novel ideological conditions of the new century, as older modes of legitimacy and collective self-representation that had served the Romanov emperors and their courts for generations—dynastic tradition, divine right, imperial allegiance—faced the rising challenge of the national idea? As Richard Wortman has explained, beyond the incompatibility of popular will with the autocratic principle, the national imagination was fundamentally at odds with the rhetoric of the Russian court. For centuries, the authority of the Russian ruler had been cast as a superior, external force imposed on obedient subjects. In the new century, Wortman writes: "the people's involvement in the imperial scenario threatened the tsar's image as a superordinate force, whose title came from outside or from above, from divine mandate, or the emanations of reason. In social terms it was impossible to present the people as a historical agent in a scenario that glorified the monarch's authority as the idealization of the ruling elite."[15] In a sense, the emperor had hitherto been imagined as not really sharing in any collective Russian being at all. The result for the political imagination was, in the words of Monika Greenleaf and Stephen Moeller-Sally a "crisis of identity."[16]

It is in this context that Ivan the Terrible and Peter the Great gained their modern significance as crucial instruments in formulations of Russian collective selfhood. This is not to claim that Russians saw these two tsars as representatives of some essential core of shared identity—as the above suggests, Russian thinkers were often in disagreement about the significance of each figure considered in isolation, let alone as symbols of some shared deep essence. In this light, it may seem counterintuitive that either of them would play any role at all in formulations of collective identity. In national contexts collective identification commonly focuses on figures who occupy a place of honor at the heart of the collective being: George Washington, Shakespeare, Jeanne d'Arc, Goethe, Elizabeth I, and so on. In Russian historical myth there are figures who correspond to these in their unequivocal "Russianness": Prince Vladimir, Aleksandr Nevskii, Minin and Pozharskii, and Lomonosov, for example. Yet Ivan and Peter contributed in a different way to the especially complex process of collective identity formation in Imperial Russia. As Peter Stallybrass and Allon White observed some decades ago, "cultural identity is inseparable from limits, it is always a boundary phenomenon and its order is always constructed around the figures of its territorial edge."[17] Stallybrass and White were concerned with the formation of bourgeois class identity through the transgressive poetics of

---

the political ferment among intellectual and cultural figures of eastern European national movements, who articulated the conceptions that later generations of national activists would disseminate broadly as the basis for collective identities. See Hroch, "From National Movement to the Fully-Formed Nation."

15. Wortman, *Scenarios of Power*, 1:221. Also see Suny, "Empire Strikes Out," esp. 41–44.

16. Monika Greenleaf and Stephen Moeller-Sally, "Introduction," in their *Russian Subjects*, 1–17, here 1.

17. Stallybrass and White, *Politics and Poetics of Transgression*, 200.

carnival, romanticism, or modernism. Yet in the different circumstances that concern us here, the figures of Ivan and Peter made possible a similar discursive mechanism, which by "forcing the threshold and interrogating the liminal position" acted out and produced Russian collective being.[18]

At base, Ivan's and Peter's significance as borderline figures was founded on shared fundamental interpretations of their reigns as transitional epochs, separating the premodern and modern eras. Depending on one's frame of reference, this transitional role could hold any number of implications: by some, one or the other was seen as architect of a new social order, "father of the fatherland," a creative force behind modern Russian selfhood. Others viewed one or the other as responsible for the downfall of an ancient social order or as an apostate who betrayed a truer collective being.

Yet the liminal significance of these figures extended beyond narrative schemes to matters of geography, conceptions of rulership, systems of cultural value, and more. Rather than standing as unequivocal symbols at the center of a common identity, Ivan and Peter hovered on the edges and demarcated its boundaries, occupying an eccentric and often paradoxical position. Their reputations as conquerors of new territory to east and west allowed them to represent both the national territory that gave them birth and the empires they created. Because of their suppression of old elites and promotion of new ones, they could stand both as representatives of potent autocratic authority and as champions of the people.

In this way, both inside and outside, in step with and ahead of the collective being, they illustrated both the essential identity of ruler with ruled and the traditionally superordinate, transcendent character of the autocrat. Yet just as surely, their borderline position could also render one or another alien to the collective being. In short, their liminal character made Ivan and Peter rhetorically useful to the point of overdetermination: ripe for exploitation in any number of conflicting formulations—but also unstable, so that each at times could "reverse polarity" and leap from the heights of heroism to the depths of villainy or back again, unexpectedly appearing in a new light or in a novel role.

The term "liminal" is derived from anthropological analysis and has particular relevance for rituals associated with group identity.[19] My treatments of Ivan and Peter in the first half of the nineteenth century enable comprehension of the literary, political, and educational discourse in which Peter and Ivan were invoked as rituals of becoming, in which Russians traced the outlines of, and stepped into, their collective being. Yet ritual is often a messy business, and so were the reigns of these two figures. All deployments of Ivan and Peter as tools to define collective identity also had to contend with the violence of their epochs. And so these affirmative civic rituals also frequently led to an

18. Ibid., 200.
19. For a classic anthropological work on ritual and the liminal, see Turner, *Ritual Process*.

intentional or unintentional contemplation of the bloody roots of Russian political life—of historical trauma and its latter-day legacies.

In the past two decades, much scholarship has been devoted to the study of collective trauma, casting particular light on the difficulties presented by events of extreme violence for historical recollection—trauma is, in this sense, that which neither historians nor individuals are capable of fully representing or rendering meaningful, which for this very reason persists in memory and history as an unsolved problem or an unhealed wound. As Dominick LaCapra has put it, trauma leads to a condition in which one is "possessed or haunted by the past, whose ghosts and shrouds resist distinctions. [. . .] Indeed, in post-traumatic situations in which one relives (or acts out) the past, distinctions tend to collapse, including the crucial distinction between then and now."[20] This critical lens enables investigation in the current chapter of how representations of Ivan and Peter labored at times to exhume and examine ancient bloodshed and the modern trauma that is allegorically linked to it and at other times to conceal and disavow this trauma. In both modes, the historians and authors I consider strove to achieve closure or to lay the memory of bloodshed to rest. Ironically, however, their writing often resulted merely in the attachment of new episodes of trauma to mythic precedents, blurring Ivan's or Peter's violence together with that of Nicholas and giving shape to a mechanism of inherited consciousness of collective victimhood.

Ultimately, however, the historical myths of Ivan and Peter illustrate how historical trauma may present not only psychic and rhetorical pitfalls but also "productive" opportunities for political culture. As other work on trauma has shown, some representations of historical violence and cataclysm contribute to the construction of collective identities. At times, distant historical violence may serve to generate a modern sense of shared experience and interests—as is the case, for example, with the memory of the Battle of Kosovo in Serbia or of the "conquest" of Greece by the Ottoman Empire in modern Greek collective identities. Such cases have been described with the term "chosen trauma," referring to representations of events in which segments of a population are made "to feel victimized, humiliated by another group, and to suffer losses," and which that population or its descendants may "chose, consciously as well as unconsciously, to [. . .] mythologize" in order to "define its identity."[21]

The application of this concept in the Russian case is a tricky matter. The histories and novels examined in the present chapter endeavored to cast Ivan's reign as such a chosen trauma, calling forth a modern community of witnesses and heirs to ancient victimization. In contrast, the patriotic and official nationalist representations of Peter examined here celebrated his reign as a transformative rise into true Russian being, justifying any violence incurred in the process. Yet each of these projects was beset by difficulties, for in distinction to

20. LaCapra, *Writing History, Writing Trauma*, 46.
21. Volkan and Itzkowitz, "Modern Greek and Turkish Identities," 232.

cases such as the Battle of Kosovo, Ivan and Peter, the very sources of traumatic suffering for Russians, were also their divinely ordained rulers. As will
become apparent, in their curious, doubled-over nature as both objects of proud
patriotic identification and as figures of collective victimhood, the deployment
of these two liminal rulers in a tidy rhetoric of either heroic redemption or
traumatic violence proved no easy task.

History and Identity: Nikolai Karamzin and Nikolai G. Ustrialov

For Russian society in the first decades of the nineteenth century, the publication of Karamzin's *History of the Russian State* was among the most important catalysts of novel conceptions of collective selfhood. Appearing in the
years after the Napoleonic Wars, this work confirmed the uniqueness of the
Russian people and its history, as well as the present world-historical role of
the empire and emperor.[22] As Petr Viazemskii put it: "Karamzin was the equivalent of Kutuzov in 1812—he saved Russia from the onslaught of oblivion,
called her to life, showed us that we have a fatherland, precisely reiterating the
lesson we learned in 1812."[23]

But in contrast to the general shape of Russian historical consciousness during this period, in which Peter the Great overshadows all other figures, it is he
who is absent and Ivan who plays a special and prominent role in Karamzin's
History. For the ninth volume of the *History*, published in 1821, presented a
sensational account of the bloodshed of Ivan's reign that became the foundational text for a rich tradition of subsequent representations. One cannot over-
emphasize the innovative nature of Karamzin's depiction of Ivan: to the eighteenth-
century Russian historical imagination, Ivan had been known as a severe but
pious ruler, who had earned much glory by his conquests. Karamzin, relying
on previously little-known sources, created the modern tradition in which Ivan's
name was synonymous with unbridled despotism.[24] Compounding the impact
of this fundamental revision of the material, the ninth volume of Karamzin's

---

22. On "Russianness" during the Napoleonic Wars, see Zorin, *Kormia dvuglavogo orla*,
239–66; Suny, "Empire Strikes Out," 42; and Wortman, *Scenarios of Power*, 1:215–43.

23. Cited in S. O. Shmidt, "Nikolai Mikhailovich Karamzin," in *Portrety istorikov*, ed.
Sevost'ianov and Mil'skaia, 25–37, here 25.

24. Although there were earlier sources that presented Ivan in a negative light, these did
not form the basis for a productive modern historical tradition prior to Karamzin. Edward
Keenan has argued that many of these "anti-Ivanian" sources are fabrications relating to
later, seventeenth-century political contexts. See Keenan, *Kurbskii-Groznyi Apocrypha*; and
Keenan, "Putting Kurbskii in His Place." An exception to the trend in historiography prior
to Karamzin toward a neutral or glorious representation of Ivan's rule is Gerhard Friedrich
Müller's explicit account of Ivan's violent sack of Novgorod. Gratuitous details notwithstand-
ing, however, Müller suggests that Ivan had good reasons to punish the city and refrains from
negative judgments regarding Ivan's reign in general. See Miller [Müller], "Kratkoe izvestie o
nachale Novagoroda," esp. 138–41.

history deployed a completely new mode of historiographic narrative as well—one that, as Caryl Emerson has explained, presented historical actors as psychologically complex but archetypical figures who could be the objects of readers' sympathy and moral judgment.[25] Its admirers celebrated the canonical authority and emotional impact of this new interpretation: "in our day, blessed by a government firm in virtue and in the love of the nation, the Russian Caligula found his Tacitus, who, with the same sacred hatred of vice as the great Roman historian, presented the tyranny of Ivan in all of its revolting nakedness: 'Let all who see it tremble!' "[26]

Now, there is nothing surprising about Peter's absence in the *History*, for that work was devoted to premodern Russian history, which Karamzin saw as the essential basis of patriotic sentiment. Note, however, that the historian's critical views of Ivan in certain ways corresponded to his conceptions of Peter. In contrast to the majority of Alexander I's advisers, Karamzin espoused an aristocratic conservatism staunchly opposed to reform projects that might threaten cultural continuity or political stability, although at the same time he considered social progress and enlightenment as among the chief duties of Russia's throne, state, and gentry. In his view, Russia needed strong rulers but could do without radical reform, state-imposed or otherwise; autocracy was defined by bonds of council uniting ruler and gentry, as well as bonds of religion and custom uniting ruler and people; and Russian identity itself depended on the integrity of a gradual evolution. Such views help explain the historian's at times far from celebratory opinion of Peter I.[27] In a private memorandum of 1811 to Alexander I, *A Note on Ancient and Modern Russia* (Zapiska o drevnei i novoi Rossii), Karamzin condemned Peter's cultural reform projects and by analogy critiqued certain of Alexander's as well. After praising Peter's accomplishments in enlightenment and conquest, the historian bluntly stated that the first emperor's "passion for new customs exceeded the bounds of reason." As he explained:

> Peter did not wish to comprehend the truth that the moral might of states, which is just as necessary for their stability as physical might, is founded on the people's spirit. This spirit and faith saved Russia during the times of the pretenders; it is nothing other than an attachment to what is our own,

---

25. Emerson, *Boris Godunov*, 43–46.
26. Shul'gin, *Izobrazhenie kharaktera i soderzhaniia istorii*, 144–45.
27. At other times and in other contexts, Karamzin expressed quite opposite views of Russia's first emperor—as, for instance, in his *Letters of a Russian Traveler* (Pis'ma russkogo puteshesvtennika), where he names Peter as a "ruler who has no equals anywhere," and explains: "The Germans, French, and English were in advance of the Russians by at least six centuries. Then Peter moved us with his potent hand, and we nearly caught up to them in just a few years." See Karamzin, *"Pis'ma russkogo puteshesvtennika,"* in his *Izbrannye sochinenii*, 1:77–601, here 1:416–18. On the variability of Karamzin's politics, see Lotman, "Kolumb russkoi istorii," 567–78.

nothing other than respect for our national dignity. By uprooting ancient customs, by presenting them as absurd, and by praising and introducing foreign ways, the sovereign of Russia humiliated Russian subjects in their very hearts.[28]

In Karamzin's view, Peter's cultural innovations had cut Russia's elites off from the masses and their own past and had occasioned much of the violence of Peter's reign. Now, although this vision of Russia's first emperor is reminiscent of the sentiments of the Decembrist Kakhovskii, Decembrist circles in general had expressed little but disdain for Karamzin after the publication of the first eight volumes of the *History*, which expressed his basic conservatism and loyalty to the autocracy. Yet strangely enough, even though the ninth volume of the *History*, with its nightmarish vision of Ivan, derived from this same outlook and was intended to bolster the authority of beneficent rulers such as Alexander, the Decembrists and their sympathizers celebrated this new installment of Karamzin's project as but one step removed from an open condemnation of autocracy. In such ideological irresolution, we may begin to grasp the complex implications of the figure of Ivan for Russian political rhetoric.

To unravel this knot, let us take a closer look at the exemplary horror of Karamzin's Ivan. So that no one will mistake his didactic purpose, the historian places the tyrant in stark and explicit contrast with a list of ideal modern rulers, including Peter (portrayed in this public document in a rather different light than in the historian's confidential *Note*): "armed only with prayer and patience, Russia endured this destroyer for twenty-four years, in order to see, in better times, Peter the Great and Catherine II (history avoids referring to the living)" (9:258).[29] In Karamzin's vision, Ivan was a fallen god of Russian history and a negative example to all rulers who would stand against, rather than with, their subjects. Adorned with great literary and spiritual gifts, the future tsar is corrupted in his orphaned youth by grandees:

[They] attempted to bind Ivan to them by fulfilling all his childish desires. They ceaselessly entertained him, amusing him in his palace with rowdy games and in the field with the hunt, fostering his tendencies to gluttony and even to cruelty, not guessing at the consequences. For example, with his

28. Karamzin, *Zapiska o drevnei i novoi Rossii*, 32. The *Note*, composed at the behest of Grand Princess Ekaterina Pavlovna, was intended as a memorandum to Alexander I, rather than as a published treatise. It was not known to broader circles of Russian elites until about 1835, when manuscript copies appeared in many hands. Published in considerably censored form in 1837, it was published in full only in Naumberg in 1861. See Lotman, "'O drevnei i novoi Rossii v ee politicheskom i grazhdanskom otnosheniiakh' Karamzina—pamiatnik russkoi publitsistiki nachala XIX veka," in his *Karamzin*, 588–600; and Pipes, *Karamzin's Memoir*.

29. Karamzin, *Istoriia*. Karamzin's remark in parentheses acts to include the reigning emperor Alexander I in the series of "good" monarchs. References to this edition are given in text.

fondness for the hunt, he was enamored not only of killing wild animals but also of torturing domestic ones by throwing them from his high balcony onto the ground below—but all the Boyars would say was "let the master have his fun!" (8:49)

Despite these corrupting influences, during the first thirteen years of Ivan's reign, supported by his ideally moral first wife Anastasia and his wise advisers the priest Silvestr and the boyar Adashev, Ivan became a model sovereign who achieved significant diplomatic and military ends—chief among them the conquest of Kazan, successes in the early phases of the Livonian War, and the compilation of the *Sudebnik* of 1550, an important legal codex. Yet with the death of Anastasia in 1560, "Ivan lost not only his wife but also his virtue" (8:188). With this event begins Ivan's descent into a depravity of grand dimensions. This transformation of Ivan from heroic ideal to anathema constitutes the symbolic border that Karamzin's narrative exploits in his construction of ideal rulership and collective identity.

The historian represents Ivan in his mature savagery as a deviation from the positive norms of behavior in every way. Most important, Ivan repeatedly transgresses the moral law of Orthodox Christianity, which is central to every formulation of Russian collective identity. For Ivan's reprisals against real and imagined political enemies Karamzin names him a "baneful Angel of Darkness for Russians, red with the sacred blood of the innocent" (9:156), and he offers a running commentary on the ever-increasing certainty of his personal damnation.

This motif reaches a climax with the tsar's accidental killing of his son and heir in a fit of rage in 1581: "Thus the justice of the Avenger on High at times punishes giants of inhumanity in this world more in order to provide an example than to spur them to rectification. For it seems that there is a limit in evildoing, beyond which there is no true repentance and there is no free and decisive return to the good. Instead, there is only torment, the onset of the torments of hell, without hope or change of heart" (9:209).

Ivan's transgression of limits is also evident in his unbridled sexual appetite. Each of the tsar's six marriages after his first to the virtuous Anastasia presents a further departure from moral purity by a tsar, "insatiable in murder and lust" (9:162). Karamzin describes with particular consternation how even as the aged tsar lay on his deathbed, his daughter-in-law, the wife of Tsarevich Fedor, had to "flee in disgust from his shameless lewdness!" (9:257). Ivan's sexual appetites are matched by his love of feasts and unruly revelry, "games and amusements in which sobriety, solemnity and propriety itself were considered improper" (9:9)—all adding to the evidence of Ivan's gross, sinful gluttony.

Yet by far the most extreme of Ivan's perversions is his indulgence in bloody and lawless violence. The young tsar's delight at torturing animals grows by his maturity into a true sadism, fed by psychotic paranoia. Violence is a grand leitmotif, a constant refrain, achieving considerable rhetorical effect through repetition and accumulation. Time after time, Karamzin exploits the simple device of listing the names of the executed, presenting readers with a dizzying stream of senseless murders. Again and again, the historian offers detailed descriptions of inhumanly cruel punishments, as for example in his description of the 1570 sack of Novgorod:

> Thus, Ivan and his son imposed their judgment: every day from five
> hundred to a thousand or more Novgorodians were brought before them.
> They were beaten, tortured, and burned with some kind of flammable
> mixture, tied by the neck or the legs to sleighs, dragged to the banks of the
> Volkhov, where the river does not freeze over in the winter, and thrown
> from the bridge into the waters—whole families, wives with husbands,
> mothers with infants at the breast. The Moscow soldiery would take boats
> out on the Volkhov with spears, boat hooks, and poleaxes: if anyone swam
> up out of the waters, they would stab and slice him apart. (9:88)

In the description of a mass execution on Red Square that same year the historian offers a horrific narration of Ivan's apparent pleasure as his victims are beheaded, tortured, boiled alive, and torn limb from limb. At the conclusion of this last episode, Karamzin relates how the tsar finished his day of bloodshed with rape:

> Having ridden round the square and inspected the piles of corpses, Ivan,
> sated with murder, still had not had his fill of human despair. Desiring to see
> the unfortunate widows of Funikov and Viskovatyi, he rode to their houses
> and laughed at their tears. He tormented the former, demanding treasures,
> and wanted to torment her wailing and sobbing fifteen-year-old daughter
> but instead gave her to his son Tsarevich Ivan. Afterwards he committed her,
> along with her mother and Viskovatyi's widow, to a nunnery, where they
> died of grief. (9:94).

In such passages, Karamzin's description of Ivan's tyrannical violence becomes gothic in its overheated excess and lurid detail.

Ivan's sadistic excesses achieve sublime heights in their ingenuity, echoing the motif of "inventive punishment" associated with Ivan and other legendary tyrants in folklore.[30] Karamzin reports that, "Ivan supposedly compelled the young Fedor Basmanov [his former favorite—K.M.F.P] to kill his own father, and at about the same time he forced Prince Nikita Prozorovskii to put his own brother, Prince Vasilii, to death" (9:94–95). In another episode, Karamzin relates how when Nikita Kozarinov-Golokhvastov takes monastic orders in old age, the tsar orders him tied to a barrel of explosives, laughing that "monks are angels and should fly up in the air" (9:95). Karamzin's rhetoric renders violence as the most extreme aspect of Ivan's physical gluttony—as is illustrated

30. Rosovetskii, "Oral Prose," esp. 21–25; Ia. S. Lur'e, *Povest' o Drakule*, 65–66; Perrie, *Image of Ivan the Terrible*, 96–101, 179.

best in the tsar's tendency to punctuate his wild banquets with painful punishments for his feasting companions or to rush from the table directly to the dungeons for a dessert of torture. In the historian's account, the Russian people are overwhelmed by Ivan's violence, paralyzed with dread, reduced to a sickness and lethargy that destroy the economic life of Muscovy and catalyze epidemics and starvation. Russians "wander like shadows" (9:99) and even resort to cannibalism. Nevertheless, they do not rebel:

> It may be that Ivan did not surpass all others in the tortures he inflicted, but the people certainly surpassed all others in their patience, for they considered the tsar's power as God's power, and every opposition to be an act of lawlessness. They attributed Ivan's tyranny to heavenly anger and repented of their sins. . . . They died, but they preserved the might of Russia for us, for the strength of the people's obedience is the strength of the state. (9:98)

In sum, Ivan's reign charts a path from righteousness and propriety into a despotic violence so extraordinary that the realm itself is preserved only by a similarly extraordinary miracle of popular faith and obedience.

Yet strangely, for all this, Karamzin's Ivan is not a pure antitype but rather a gray figure of indeterminacy: "Even the tyrant must be given his due: Ivan, in the greatest extremes of evil, is a peculiar specter of a great monarch—zealous, tireless, often acute in his political activity" (9:260) This distorting-glass relationship of Karamzin's representation of Ivan to the ideals of Russian rulership is especially apparent in the imaginary geography of his reign. Karamzin gives Ivan credit for his tentative efforts to deal with the cultural and territorial challenges presented by the west: his reign saw increased diplomatic contact with western states, the initiation of commercial ties with England, significant enlightening activities such as the introduction of book printing and attempts to import technical specialists. The historian presents the Livonian War as an effort "to gloriously anticipate Peter's great project, to gain seaports for commercial and diplomatic relations with Europe" (9:206). Yet these efforts ended with Ivan's capitulation of all the gains of the twenty-four year conflict in the "disgraceful" Peace of Yam Zapolsky (1582).[31]

Much more pronounced than these weak strivings toward the west, however, is the oriental motif that colors Karamzin's representation of Ivan and his depravity. In several places the historian is explicit in this regard. He characterizes Ivan's love of luxury, feasting, and display of wealth as evidence of his taste for "Asiatic grandiosity" (9:278). In contrast to his Russian first wife, Anastasia, who restrained his tyrannical impulses, Ivan seeks a second wife "in Asian lands" and finds her in Mariia Temriukovna, a converted Circassian princess, who "wild in temperament, cruel in spirit, reinforced Ivan's evil tendencies

---

31. Karamzin pronounces this treaty "less glorious for Batory [the king of Poland] than shameful for Ivan, who in the peculiarities of the war demonstrated all the weaknesses of a soul debased by tyranny" (*Istoriia*, 9:206).

even further" (9:20, 26). But in a more general assessment of Karamzin's rhetoric, Ivan's sexual appetites, his cruelty, love of bloody, "witty" punishments, irrationality, unpredictability, and habit of debasing his subjects all project an image of oriental despotism familiar from European political discourse.[32]

If we turn from imaginary to actual geography, whereas Ivan's western expansions of his realm did not hold, he retains the titles of conqueror of Kazan and first Russian ruler of Siberia—accomplishments that, to be sure, illustrate his prosecution of the interests of Orthodox Christendom, but which also physically insinuate Ivan into the depths of Asia. If Ivan's Asian conquests are the culmination of the long story of Muscovy's struggle for dominance over successors to Mongol power in the east, Karamzin's language also several times aligns Ivan's reign with Tatar-Mongol domination as comparable calamities: "Among other heavy burdens of her fate, beyond the misfortunes of the *udel* [the old Russian appanage system—K.M.F.P], beyond the Mongol Yoke, Russia had to endure the disaster of an autocrat-tormentor" (9:258).

In sum, Karamzin's *History* charted a trajectory out from the center of the collective self to a location beyond all its boundaries. Degenerating from a brilliant model ruler into a tyrannical mass murderer, a moral and sexual deviant, and a victim of alien, eastern influences, Ivan served, as a photographic negative is used to project a positive image, to demonstrate the ideals of rulership that Karamzin held dear: wise rule in consultation with elite advisers, close identification with the people's interests, spiritual values and culture, and the ability to control both personal passions and the weaknesses of subjects.

Ivan's extreme deviance from the positive norm enabled Karamzin to demonstrate the most important characteristic of the Russian people: their identity as humble subjects, devoted to their divinely ordained ruler. As Karamzin puts it: "Russia [. . .] withstood the autocrat-tormentor with love for the Autocracy, for she believed plagues, earthquakes, and tyrants are sent by God" (9:258). Ivan's reign was a trial of suffering that enabled Russians to discover the depth of their own essential nature against the foil of their ruler's perversions. In this manner, by renouncing the despot completely, Karamzin enlisted all his excesses in the cause of collective identity, making use of ancient pain as a chosen trauma—a common wound that calls into being a corresponding community of sufferers. Ivan's reign allowed Russians to recognize their present blood kinship by witnessing a long-past flow of Russian blood.

Yet the use of Ivan's considerable negative potential to define positive ideals of rulership and collective identity was not without complications. Karamzin's efforts, state-sponsored though they were, were not welcomed by all as a masterwork of loyalist rhetoric, for Ivan's story left a problematic rhetorical and historical residue. Most basic, of course, was the matter of accounting for Ivan in the first place—of addressing the grand duke's objection that Karamzin had

---

32. For a critically acute discussion of oriental despotism, see Perry Anderson, *Lineages of the Absolutist State*, 462–549.

let slip that "among tsars there are tyrants." The historian's assertion that Ivan's mayhem had been ordained by providence provided at best a partial explanation for why a people that had already had its fair share of pain inflicted by external enemies should also be condemned to suffer at the hands of its own tsar. As the historian himself announces at the crucial moment of Ivan's conversion to evil following the death of Anastasia: "Despite all speculative explanations, the personality of Ivan, hero of virtue in his youth, savage bloodsucker in his maturity and old age, is a riddle for the mind" (9:259).

After Karamzin, Russian court and official patriotic culture preferred simply to pass over this riddle in silence, but other voices were prepared to solve the historian's conundrum. Ivan's foreignness to his own subjects, which Karamzin intended as a warning to Russian rulers of the need to rein in base passions and remain true to people and state, could easily be seen as a revelation of the fundamental, violent truth behind traditional representations of the emperor as a conquering foreign power. For opponents of the throne, the tsar's place at the eye of an "alien storm, somehow sent from the depths of hell to plague and torment Russia" (9:11) was completely consistent with the age-old estrangement of the autocracy from the suffering Russian masses. The Decembrist Ryleev, on reading this volume of Karamzin's history, promptly penned a meditative poem on Ivan's political opponent Andrei Kurbskii, depicting him as a Russian patriot, tormented by his exile from a fatherland ruled by a tyrant.[33] Several years later, the same volume was brought to the Decembrist Mikhail Bestuzhev, awaiting judgment in prison, who wrote: "Why was I brought precisely the ninth volume? Could it have been because fate desired to acquaint me in advance with the subtle whims of despotism and prepare me for what lay in store for me?"[34] For these readers, the traumas of the deep past were genealogically and allegorically linked to the cruelty of the contemporary state and to their personal experience of its violence. As we shall see, the oppositional potential in the history of Ivan's reign would surface again and again in histories, operas, paintings, and plays that variously sought to suppress or unleash its energy.

—⁂—

Karamzin's *History* laid the historical foundations for Russian collective identity yet left much to be accomplished. Perhaps the most important aspect of this project still to be addressed at the end of the reign of Alexander I was the creation of an authoritative history of Peter the Great—a task that was to plague Russian historians for decades to come. Compared with the more remote eras of the Russian past, Peter's epoch was a fresh memory—nearly contemporary in terms of its dynastic, political, cultural, and even familial significance. The transformations in Russian political life that ensued from the failed Decembrist uprising further complicated the situation in the early years of the new reign. Taking to heart the lessons of the mutiny, Nicholas I and his

---

33. Ryleev, *Polnoe sobranie sochinenii*, 458.
34. Cited in Eidel'man, *Poslednii letopisets*, 174.

ministers energetically set out to create mechanisms for policing the nascent sphere of Russian public discourse, with the overt intention of controlling dangerous ideas and inculcating proper ones. One area of their concern was education, and it is in educational materials that an officially sanctioned myth of Peter was most completely formulated.

In 1843, Minister of Education Sergei Uvarov wrote in his general report to the emperor—summing up the preceding ten years of activity: "Everywhere there was a need for a textbook which, on one hand, might attract the attention of the young to study, and on the other, could introduce them carefully and safely to the main results of national history. This problem [. . .] was solved by [Nikolai G.] Ustrialov's book."[35] Uvarov's career was founded on his role as chief ideologue of what later came to be called the "Official Nationality" of the reign of Nicholas I.[36] He is most commonly remembered as the inventor of the tripartite formula that served to define the official vision of Russian imperial culture during this period and in subsequent revivals: Orthodoxy, autocracy, and nationality. The book that he praised so highly in his 1843 report was the university textbook *Russian History*. Its author, Nikolai G. Ustrialov, was the state spokesman on history under Nicholas I: a professor at St. Petersburg University, the historian laureate of the empire, he was later to compose the standard but never completed six-volume history of Peter the Great. During Uvarov's tenure as minister of education, Ustrialov's textbook became the only officially sanctioned tool for university instruction in the field, and it went through five editions from its first publication in 1837 until the end of Nicholas's reign eighteen years later.

Ustrialov reveals the goals of his historiographical activities in the 1836 essay "About a System of Pragmatic Russian History":

> There is perhaps no other people that can look on its past with more satisfaction or that can derive from it greater value than can we Russians. On one hand, we may say with legitimate pride that our forefathers, repeatedly faced with unprecedented misfortunes that many other nations would not have withstood, survived—and not by virtue of good fortune or foreign aid but by their own efforts. That they managed to extricate themselves from the most difficult situations with honor and glory. That the pages of our history are filled more with deeds of virtue than of vice. And finally, that only our own history includes the accomplishments of Peter the Great. On the other hand, following European education's decisive influence on us, when there has finally awakened thought of nationality, which promises such enviable fruits in the future, from where else other than from history

---

35. Uvarov, *Desiatiletie Ministerstva narodnogo prosveshcheniia*, 97.

36. The term "Official Nationality" was devised by the historian Aleksandr Pypin in the late nineteenth century to describe this ideological formation. It was not used by Uvarov or his contemporaries. See Riasanovsky, *Nicholas I*, 73–183; and Zorin, *Kormia dvuglavogo orla*, 339–74.

may we learn of the content of our nationality or of the fundamental principles from which our social, civic, and family life developed? Lastly, Russian history must resolve in the most decisive manner the great contemporary question concerning Poland and western Russia, which was once under her power. (1:405–33)[37]

Ustrialov's textbook set out to place Official Nationality firmly onto the foundations of history: to create a narrative from which students could learn the "content" of their collective being. The core of this narrative, as the passage makes plain, is the difficult passage of the people through unusual, painful trials, culminating in the historical figure of Peter the Great, whose accomplishments are one of the chief wellsprings of Russian collective pride, as well as its culmination. Although readers, following Karamzin's revelations, might have been tempted to imagine the reign of Ivan among the "unprecedented misfortunes" of the Russian past, Ustrialov's textbook does not in fact revisit the scene of collective trauma in Ivan's day in any detail. In this, the work reflects the overall tenor of official patriotic and court rhetoric of history under Nicholas I, which simply ignored the bloody image of Ivan, while washing Peter clean of blood and elevating him in glory.[38]

Before further examination of Peter's place in Ustrialov's story, consider certain peculiarities of Russian historical myth under Nicholas I revealed in the passage cited above. Above all, the main competitor of Russian national consciousness is "European education," the influence of which has until this point been "decisive." Herein lies one of the central quandaries of collective identity projects in early nineteenth-century Russia: for a century and a quarter, imperial policy and elite society, identifying historical and cultural progress with European norms, had labored to assimilate Russia to a common European civilization with little regard for cultural principles that would appear authentically Russian in the age of nationalism that followed. In the first half of the nineteenth century, this legacy could not be simply ignored: in pragmatic terms, Russia's rulers hardly wished to turn away from industrial, military, and technical modernization, which were seen as basic to the maintenance of Russia's great-power status but were firmly identified with Europe. In cultural terms, Russian elites could not exit the circle of European language, literature, art, fashion, and manners, which

---

37. The essay was included as an appendix in later editions of Ustrialov's textbook: N. G. Ustrialov, "O sisteme pragmaticheskoi russkoi istorii," in his *Russkaia istoriia*, 405–33. References to this edition are given in text.

38. That Ustrialov devotes only a few pages to Ivan's depredations in his *Russian History* is hardly surprising. Ustrialov's work was intended as a triumphal dithyramb—an instrument for celebrating the historical achievements of the Russian nation, not for critiquing the inessential or problematic pages of the past. The historian limits himself to succinct statements of Ivan's deviance from the positive norms of behavior and identity: "in his maturity he was more of a threat to his subjects than to enemies of the fatherland"; "he did not comprehend his high calling or the true needs of the state" (*Russkaia istoriia*, 1:224, 227).

were fundamental to the lives of the Russian gentry. Uvarov himself was a passionate admirer of the Enlightenment, a friend and interlocutor of Madame de Staël and Charles-Joseph Prince de Ligne, and preferred to write in French and German rather than in Russian (ironically, the original formulation of the tripartite mantra of Official Nationality was drafted in French and translated by the minister's staff into Russian).[39] For him, and for many other elite Russian men and women, any literal-minded attempt to return to the authentic national life by growing beards and dressing up in Russian "folk" costumes (as some Slavophiles did later in Nicholas I's reign) appeared undignified, possibly subversive and rather barbaric.[40]

Ustrialov concludes the passage above by noting that his historiography takes up as one of its main tasks "the great contemporary question concerning Poland and western Russia." Here the historian recognizes the other complicating factor in Russian collective identity projects: the empire. As discussed above, during this era nationality and empire were potentially contradictory ideological principles, both of which appeared necessary for the continued legitimization of state and autocracy. Any formulation of historical myth promulgated by the representatives of the court needed to justify the continued subordination to the throne of groups who ranged broadly in their degree of differentiation from Russian linguistic, cultural, and political norms. Some, of course, were viewed simply as cultural inferiors subject to paternalistic domination: Jews, Muslim, Buddhist, and pagan ethnic groups of the Caucasus, Central Asia, and elsewhere.[41] Yet others were seen as ripe for integration into the imperial social, cultural, and political core.

For centuries, Muscovite and imperial society had assimilated with little difficulty non-Russian elites—foreign servants to the imperial throne or princes of conquered territories who accepted Orthodox Christianity. We should also note, however, that during the period in question many of the national movements of eastern Europe were themselves just taking shape, and those at the center of the empire had no reason to exclude any of the patchwork of Slavic ethnicities of the western territories—in what is today Ukraine, Be-

39. Zorin, *Kormia dvuglavogo orla*, 341.

40. On the Slavophiles, national dress, and official responses, see Barsukov, *Zhizn' i trudy M. P. Pogodina*, 10:238; and Wortman, *Scenarios of Power*, 1:400–402. For an example of Uvarov's struggle with the content of "Russian" civilization, consider his attempt to define "nationality" (*narodnost'*): "With regard to nationality, the chief problem is in the harmonization of ancient and new conceptions. But nationality does not demand that we halt or move backward; it does not require an immobility of ideas. The composition of the state, like that of the human body, changes its external appearance in correspondence with age: features change with the passing years, but physiology must not change. It would be improper to work in opposition to the periodical nature of things" (*Desiatiletie Ministerstva narodnogo prosveshcheniia*, 3–4).

41. Becker, "Russia and the Concept of Empire"; Hosking, "Mozhet li Rossiia stat' natsional'nym gosudarstvom?"

larus, and eastern Poland—from a shared, quasi-national imperial collective identity.[42]

For these reasons, Russian elites of the period often imagined the collective being in uniquely "capacious" manner. Uvarov, for instance, formulated the goals of educational policy in "returned" territories (i.e., those claimed as a part of Russia proper in the course of successive partitions of Poland), as an effort "to smooth out, as much as is possible, those extreme characteristic features that differentiate the Polish youth from the Russian, and in particular to suppress any thought of a separate nationality among them; to bring them closer and closer to Russian conceptions and customs and to transfer to them the general spirit of the Russian people."[43] Uvarov's policy, however, begs the question of what could possibly constitute the "spirit of the Russian people," given the contradictory demands of European cosmopolitanism and the nebulous limits of Russia itself.

The answer to this question was found in Peter I. In the concluding passage in his treatment of the first Russian emperor, Ustrialov writes:

> To [Peter] belongs the glory of the creator of Russia. Our civic life arose from principles established for the most part by Peter. Not one of its aspects escaped his attention, and to each aspect he imparted motion toward a single elevated goal, which governed all his actions: toward the transformation of our half-Asiatic life into a European one, without, however, any harm to the basic principles of nationality. Peter supported, strengthened, and ennobled everything that was sympathetic to this goal; everything that was contradictory to it he destroyed without mercy, replacing the old with the new. In this manner, he preserved and strengthened the basic elements of our nationality—autocracy, Orthodoxy, the mutual relations of the estates [sosloviia], language—everything that our ancestors could be proud of, that was fused with Russian life. But he was a determined foe of traces in Russia of Mongol rule, of all that took root in her as a result of civic disorder, or of ignorance. (2:80)

Here, in a passage that exemplifies Peter's "liminal" characteristics—a passage shot through with edges and borders of many sorts—the utility of the first emperor for the official nationalist project becomes clear. Ustrialov's Peter created the Russian present, yet he did not create it *ex nihilo*. Rather, he "destroyed without mercy" certain features of the Muscovite existence while "preserving and strengthening" certain others. The elements that he preserved were none other than a version of Uvarov's nationalist trinity.[44] The elements that he eliminated,

42. Suny, "Empire Strikes Out"; Miller, *Romanov Empire and Nationalism*, 139–59; Weeks, "Russification."

43. Uvarov, *Desiatiletie Ministerstva narodnogo prosveshcheniia*, 39.

44. Ustrialov replaces the term "nationality" in Uvarov's formula with the "relations of the estates"—shorthand for the supposedly benevolent "patriarchal" relations of the gentry

however, are the "traces of Mongol rule" that rendered pre-Petrine Russia "half-Asiatic."

As Ustrialov explains in the chapters of his work devoted to the "Mongol Yoke," under Tatar rule the Russians "became used to slavery, stagnated in silent ignorance, and with superstitious fear looked on their state of servitude as providentially ordained" (1:140). In his view, the backwardness of Russian industry, the vices of bribery and dissimulation before the powers-that-be, torture, the custom of holding noble women in seclusion in the *terem*, the waste and self-indulgence of "Asiatic luxury," a military culture given to "crushing the enemy by sheer force of numbers and laying waste to enemy lands" with no thought of "art or glory"—all these vices were an Asian imposition on the a priori European Russian national culture, which Ustrialov traces in his opening chapters to the so-called Norman influence of Russia's early Varangian rulers (1:185–93; 2:39, 41).[45] Note the radical nature of Ustrialov's divergence from other contemporary considerations of Russian history, such as Karamzin's, which saw Peter's reforms as an attack on the authentic Russian being in the name of European ways. In a brilliant orientalizing sleight of hand, Ustrialov's Peter becomes the genius of national continuity, who restored to Russia its rightful identity as a part of Europe.

This novel rendering of Russia's "eastern" affiliations is matched in the historian's innovative views on her western borderlands. For Ustrialov, many of the Slavs of eastern Europe—the occupants of today's Ukraine and Belarus—were subjected to depredations no less harsh than the Tatar Yoke.[46] He portrays this "Polish Yoke" as inimical to Russian culture and identity, responsible for persecution and the attempted conversion of Orthodox Christians to Catholicism and the pollution of the Russian language with Polish words and literary forms (1:195–200). By casting western Slavic peoples as Russians fallen victim to an illegitimate Polonization, Ustrialov reconceived the expansion of the Russian Empire in eastern Europe from the middle seventeenth until the late eighteenth centuries as a restoration of the original configuration of Russian territory, collective identity, and statehood.[47] Peter, of course, was the visionary who comprehended the need to reclaim Russia's ancient western territories and to cow Poland into submission.

---

to the serfs—and with language—a necessary element in Romantic formulations of national identity. Unsurprisingly, these last two categories, taken together with Orthodoxy, are the same features of the national being that the historian describes earlier as unaffected by Tatar rule (Ustrialov, *Russkaia istoriia*, 1:192–93).

45. On the "Norman theory" in Russian historiography, see Riasanovsky, "Norman Theory"; and Mazour, *Modern Russian Historiography*, 9–34.

46. Ustrialov writes: "Western Rus remained until the end of the sixteenth century under the dominion of the Lithuanian princely family of Gediminas, but just as did eastern Rus, she retained her faith, her language and her civil order" (*Russkaia istoriia*, 1:12).

47. See Miller, *Romanov Empire and Nationalism*, 145.

In Ustrialov's hands, Peter offers the solution to the conundrum of Russian imperial identity. Precisely by virtue of his borderline position in the historical and geographical orders, straddling the divide between past and present, between east and west, and between nation and empire, he served as a sort of rhetorical filter—as both a conduit, connecting the imperial present with the wellsprings of Russian selfhood in the ancient past, and a barrier, preventing the corruption of Russia's fallen "middle ages" from disfiguring the present. In this, Ustrialov's representation exploits the liminal figure in a manner precisely opposite to Karamzin's treatment of Ivan, tracing a path from a corrupt condition into a purified modern identity. What appeared to some as the westernizing tendencies of a tsar who preferred European civilization to his own instead took shape as a reclamation of kinship with the European homeland.

The versatility of the borderline figure is apparent in Ustrialov's manifold use of Peter. At times, the historian projects Peter's occupation of temporal and geographical boundaries as a lesson in discontinuity—to expel the threatening cultural contamination of the Orient and the archaic from the Russian character. At other times, liminality serves to bridge disparate elements and bind together the new (but also primordial) cultural whole.

Yet one must also suspect here that Peter's function as a generator of collective identity, like Ivan's, is unstable: who is to dictate whether his passage through any given border is trangressive or constructive? Ustrialov consistently stages Peter's reign as the moment when all ancient historical trauma, all divisions and lacerations of the collective being, were healed. Yet this recovery from the pain of the past came at considerable human cost, by means of violent suppression of unrest and endless war abroad. As the introductory passage cited above makes plain, although there is no room for lament in Ustrialov's celebratory rhetoric, modern Russia would not have come to be if Peter had not "destroyed without mercy" all that opposed him—and he found a great many men and women in his path. Simply put, Peter's status in Ustrialov's history as the genius of national wholeness rested, paradoxically, on the fragmented nature of a ruler who himself had one foot in the east and one in the west—who had blood ties and bloody confrontations both with the Muscovite past and the imperial future.

The Historical Novel as Ritual: Ivan Lazhechnikov's *The Last Novice* and Aleksei K. Tolstoi's *Prince Serebrianyi*

Karamzin's history and Ustrialov's textbook were intended to transform subjects of the throne into Russian patriots. Uvarov explicitly aimed to render education as a form of civic initiation: a symbolic passage into a new understanding of personal and social identity. Other realms of public life offer alternative, complementary forms of civic ritual. Although historical narratives can impart a precisely calculated dose of historical myth, neither monumental histories nor officially approved history textbooks are surefire means to stimulate patriotic exhilaration. Literature, in contrast, while it may present more conceptually muddied waters, is rich in the empathetic and symbolic possibilities that can ignite political sentiment. In her account of a much later literary tradition, Katerina Clark has applied the term "history as ritual" to the Soviet novel, explaining: "rituals personalize abstract cultural meanings and turn them into comprehensible narrative. [. . .] The subject of the ritual 'passes' from one state into another, well-known examples being the progression from boyhood to manhood or from foreigner to citizen."[48] In the novels that Clark examines, the protagonists undergo personal transformations that mirror in miniature the revolutionary social transformations of the day, so demonstrating to readers the path to Soviet social identity. European historical novels of the nineteenth century, following the literary fashion initiated by Walter Scott, were functional precursors to the Soviet novel. In many instances, they relate narratives of personal becoming in lockstep with national historical transformations, enacting a ritual passage into national identity. One thinks of Scott's *Ivanhoe*, which models the creation of modern English national identity in the fusion of primordial Anglo-Saxon and Norman roots, or even Lev Tolstoi's *War and Peace* (Voina i mir, at a considerable remove from the Romantic conventions of Scott's novel), which tells the story of Russian national awakening during the Napoleonic Wars.[49]

In distinction from historical narrative proper, the historical novel presents a clear point of empathetic contact for the reader—a fictional "everyman," whose personal story, usually a love plot, interlocks with a larger tale revolving around the nonfictional events and figures of the nation's past. Through identification with a protagonist like Scott's Ivanhoe or Tolstoi's Pierre Bezukhov, the reader discovers the imbrication of the most intimate aspects of personal identity with the grand story of the national being.

In 1829, at the age of twenty-three, the future historian and critic Stepan Shevyrev wrote in his diary: "Each evening certainly, and sometimes in the mornings too, I assign it to myself as an unfailing duty to read the life of Peter the Great and everything related to him. Be such a man as Christ, be such a Russian as Peter the Great."[50] A few years later, in 1832, Nicholas I used similar terms in banning Pogodin's play *Peter I* (the historian also tried his hand at dramaturgy): "The person of Peter the Great should be an object of love and veneration for every Russian. To represent him on stage would be tantamount to blasphemy."[51]

48. Clark, *Soviet Novel*, 9.

49. On *Ivanhoe* and the idea of the nation, see Ragussis, "Writing Nationalist History"; on *War and Peace* and the idea of the nation, see Feuer, *Tolstoy and the Genesis of "War and Peace,"* 135–206.

50. Cited in Riasanovsky, *Nicholas I*, 105.

51. Markov, *O teatre*, 1:46; Drizen, *Dramaticheskaia tsenzura*, 22–23.

Statements like these reveal the extent to which Peter played the role of demiurge of Imperial Russian identity for elites during this period. Here, perhaps, my application of the anthropological term "liminality" to Peter may gain a bit more of its technical meaning. For Nicholas, Shevyrev, and countless other educated Russians, Peter was a mythic, divine model who held out the possibility of secular salvation through collective identity in the same manner that Christ held out the possibility of spiritual salvation. Peter, the first modern Russian—who recreated himself, his people, and his state through an act of inspiration and will—was commonly and explicitly promoted to the status of idol, presiding over civic rituals of becoming.

In his hunger for reading material that would help him follow the "way of Peter," Shevyrev almost certainly came across Ivan Lazhechnikov's novel *The Last Novice, or the Conquest of Lifliandiia in the Reign of Peter the Great* (Poslednii novik, ili zavoevanie Lifliandii v tsarstvovanie Petra Velikogo). Written in the first years of Nicholas I's reign and published in parts in 1831–33 to critical acclaim, the novel was one of the earliest fruits of the craze for historical fiction in the manner of Scott.[52] Lazhechnikov's work is one among a great many more or less forgotten historical novels dedicated to the era of Peter and composed in the first half of the nineteenth century—a partial list of which could include equally or perhaps more readable titles such as Rafail Zotov's *The Mysterious Monk* (Tainstvennyi monakh, 1834), Nestor Kukolnik's *Two Ivans, Two Stepanyches, Two Kostylkovs* (Dva Ivana, dva Stepanycha, dva Kostylkova, 1844), Mikhail Zagoskin's *Russians at the Beginning of the Eighteenth Century* (Russkie v nachale osmnadtsatogo veka, 1848), as well as far less impressive works of literary art such as Konstantin Masalskii's *Love of Beards* (Borodoliubie, 1837) and Faddei Bulgarin's *Mazepa* (1833–34).[53] Lazhechnikov's novel serves us here as an example of a burgeoning industry of middlebrow Petrine historical fiction, rather than as a canonical great work of literature.

The setting of *The Last Novice* itself reveals the author's interest in Petrine history as a story of transformation. As the author himself points out in an introduction, it may appear curious that a patriotic Russian novel should be set at the edge of the Russian Empire, in one of the two principalities comprising present-day Latvia—"Lifliandiia, the name of which alone rings foreign." In explanation, he writes:

52. Lazhechnikov's work enjoyed immediate critical success as "the best Russian historical novel yet to have appeared," as the influential critic Orest Somov wrote. It was reprinted in several editions during the 1830s and earned its author the title of "first Russian novelist," in the opinion of the young Vissarion Belinskii. Cited in N. G. Il'inskaia's notes in Lazhechnikov, *Sochineniia*, 1:540. References to this edition are given in text. For a detailed analysis of the relationship of Lazhechnikov's novel to the example of Scott's historical fiction, see Al'tshuller, *Epokha Val'tera Skotta*, 132–43.

53. For critical consideration of a number of these works, see Gasiorowska, *Image of Peter the Great*.

No other land in Russia presents the nation's novelist with a more pleasant or advantageous setting. [. . .] Other territories in Russia are poor either in history or in locale, yet in the picturesque mountains and valleys of Lifliandiia, in the ruins of her feudal castles, on the banks of her rivers and of the Baltic Sea, the Russian has imprinted the ineradicable traces of his might. This region witnessed the infancy of our military glory, of our commerce and our power [. . .]; from this land came the woman whose miraculous and deserved fate it was to become the wife and inseparable companion of the creator of our fatherland [. . .]; so much here speaks of the incomparable Peter. And this is what drew me to Lifliandiia. Errastfer, Gummel'sgof, Marienburg, Kantsy, Lust-Elan. These names are now unfamiliar to Russians, yet they were the sites of the great events I have mentioned here. I want to lay a fresh path to these regions; so that those who are moved by our national glory will point them out with pride to foreigners; so that Russian hearts will beat faster repeating these names. The feeling that holds sway in my novel is one of love for the fatherland. In a foreign land, this feeling burns more brightly. Among the crowd of foreigners, in the sphere of heavy Germanic influence, the Russian national physiognomy is more visible. . . . Everywhere [in my novel], the name of our native land rings triumphant. (1:36–37)

There are a number of interesting slippages in this passage, beginning with the description of Lifliandiia both as a "territory in Russia" and a "foreign land." It is both, depending on what era you have in mind, or whether you are speaking of Russia proper or of the Russian Empire. And the novel is located on the cusp in both of these respects, recounting events that take place during the conquest of this imperial borderland in the course of the Northern War (1700–1721) against the Swedish Empire. As his explanation makes clear, Lazhechnikov, like a belated foot soldier in Peter's armies, intends to lay a "fresh path" to these regions in order to uncover the "Russian national physiognomy" by studying its borders: temporal (Muscovite and Imperial Russia), geographical (Russian and foreign) and personal (Peter I and Catherine I—the latter was born in Marienburg and "conquered" in the process of the Northern War). One also senses the symbolic complexity of the novelist's undertaking: Lazhechnikov promises his Russian readers that they will be moved by the names "Errastfer, Gummel'sgof," and so on. Yet note that these Germanic names, like Lifliandiia itself, ring foreign to the Russian ear. To accomplish his task, Lazhechnikov must somehow fill foreign words with Russian meaning— binding together for his readers the imperial periphery and the national heartland, the Russian past and the cosmopolitan present.

The main character of the novel, the "last novice," is himself a creature of the borderlands; and his story is a study in the resolution of a fragmented identity. "Valdemar" first appears as a wandering minstrel, thought to be a spy in the service of the Swedish forces in Lifliandiia. As the reader soon learns, he is in fact the Russian Vladimir. As a child, he was the beloved page and "last novice" of Peter's half-sister and rival for the throne, Tsarevna Sophia.[54] Aligned with the "old Russian" camp of Sophia, Vladimir was the instrument of a failed assassination attempt against Peter during the last days of Sophia's regency, but he miraculously eluded execution and escaped into exile in Sweden. Ironically, in the ten years that have elapsed since his exile, he has assimilated to the western culture he hated in his youth. Vladimir, physically and emotionally, is stranded on the defining boundaries of modern Russian identity—between past and future, east and west, Muscovy and the empire. As it turns out, he is no instrument of Swedish espionage. Childhood memories of onion domes and the simple village life combine with his respect for Peter's modernizing genius, impelling Vladimir to seek pardon for his crimes by delivering intelligence to the Russians as they prepare to invade Lifliandiia.

Peter the Great himself makes only a few cameo appearances, yet as the demiurge of modern Russia, his spirit permeates Lazhechnikov's novel. Reflecting their political sympathies, the novel's characters offer eulogies or denunciations of the emperor on what seems like every other page. Vladimir himself is bound by history and fate to Peter. The two are roughly the same age. Like the future emperor, as a child Vladimir organized his playmates into military formations. Yet whereas Peter's "play army" eventually matured into a force that ensured his ascent to the throne, Vladimir's was in imitation of the *Streltsy*, the military caste that supported Sophia's claim to power. At one point, Peter offers Vladimir a commanding position in his own play formations, but he proudly refuses: "Let Germans play in your games—I am a Russian and would rather be the lowliest servant of the lawful tsarevna than the first boyar under you" (1:470). During his youth, he even entertains fantasies of ultimate power himself. In short, the young Vladimir is a doppelganger, a Muscovite mirror image of the reforming tsar.

Now, before examining Lazhechnikov's resolution of Vladimir's identity crisis, consider its resonance with the conflicted political identities of Russian readers in 1833. During this first decade of Nicholas's reign, one could hardly fail to recognize in Vladimir's story of treasonous rebellion, punishment by execution or exile, and hope of clemency an allusion to the fate of the Decembrists. In this, it may be compared to the celebrated poem *Stanzas* that Pushkin addressed to Nicholas in 1826, comparing that tsar's suppression of the Decembrist mutiny to Peter's suppression of the *Streltsy*, and calling on Nicholas to further emulate his great forebear by being merciful to his defeated opponents. Potentially, by rehabilitating Vladimir, *The Last Novice* communicates a plea for justice toward the exiled Decembrists. Yet the novel is addressed not

54. Although Vladimir's parentage remains mysterious, Lazhechnikov hints that he may have been the love child of Sophia and her favorite, Vasilii Golitsyn, who together oversaw his upbringing and entrusted his education to the Old Believer leader Andrei Denisov—a historical figure who was among the founders of the Vyg Old Believer community in present-day Karelia. The designation "last novice" itself has little historical meaning.

to the tsar but rather to the general readership, and it is concerned less with influencing the psychology of the Russian autocrat than with examining that of the Russian patriot. Note that the historical analogy of Peter's rebels with Nicholas's places Old Russian conservatives like Vladimir into a peculiar equivalence with progressive Decembrists. This odd collapse of political categories is a reflection of the overdetermination of Peter himself, who could serve both as the foundational figure of Nicholas's absolute autocracy and as the model for its continued revolutionary modernization—and therefore as the symbolic object of resistance or point of identification from either end of the political spectrum. An inverse reflection of this same historical and political incoherence may be glimpsed in a passage from the Decembrist Aleksandr Bestuzhev's letter to Nicholas, written from the Peter and Paul Fortress: "I am convinced that in You the Heavens have granted us a second Peter the Great"; in this, the Decembrist was expressing his hope that Nicholas would initiate reforms modeled on those of his forebear, yet the new emperor's resolution of the fate of the Decembrists and the subsequent history of his reign demonstrated the tsar's fulfillment of a different Petrine legacy—a legacy of despotism.[55] The quandary of Russian political elites after the suppression of the Decembrist revolt, like that of Vladimir, is the age-old problem of Russian historical thought: how to derive a whole identity from a history that is cut in half? On one hand, in the 1830s Peter appeared to hold the key to social progress "from above"—a reconciliation of the real power of the autocracy with the desire for continued enlightenment and cultural advance. In this key, some could enlist Peter's multivalent features both to integrate the fragments of the Russian past and to bridge the country's present political chasms, as did Ustrialov. Yet other devotees of the reforming tsar stumbled on his tendency to slide unpredictably from one significance into its opposite—from enlightener to bloody despot.

So how does Lazhechnikov resolve the riddle of Russian identity? *The Last Novice*, like Ustrialov's textbook, employs Peter and his epoch as mediating figures to cobble fragments together into new wholes. The main action of the novel describes Peter's successful conquest of the Baltic region. In the process, the characters of this borderland are sorted into the social and political framework of the new Russian Empire. The work's epilogue is set years later in Moscow, where many of the novel's Baltic characters—intellectuals and nobles formerly on the staff of the Swedish army—have become exemplary members of Russian society. The most important such success story is that of the humble Baltic maiden Katerina Rabe, who has ascended the Russian throne as Empress Catherine I.[56] Others who experience such an imperial rebirth include Peter's military commanders, who are drawn from lands ranging from France

55. A. A. Bestuzhev, letter to Emperor Nicholas I, in *Iz pisem i pokazanii dekabristov*, ed. Borozdin, 35–44, here 44.

56. Lazhechnikov, following the historiographical tradition of the era, transforms the historical personage Marta Skavronska—a commoner who was taken by the Russians as a

and Germany to the reaches of Asia, and who guarantee victory by a mating of Teutonic know-how and Mongol abandon. Rounding out this array of national types are the limiting terms of Lazhechnikov's political imagination—characters who cannot fit in the Petrine "big tent": corrupt Baltic nobles, representatives of a hypertrophied Germanic aristocratism; and Jews, portrayed in ham-fisted caricatures as greedy and craven "orientals." In sum, *The Last Novice* renders the Petrine epoch as a moment of social fusion that produced Russian imperial identity by the inclusion of certain key, counterpoised elements drawn from Europe and Russia, east and west, and the exclusion of other undesirable dimensions of these same terms.

Yet the denouement of the last novice's own story suggests rather different conclusions. Although he ultimately earns clemency in absentia from Peter for his services to the empire, his life ends tragically. In one of the novel's final, melodramatic scenes, Vladimir murders Andrei Denisov—the Old Believer leader who claims to be his father and who represents his blood ties to the reactionary resistance. Following this crime, in a semiconscious daze Vladimir stumbles into the company of Peter the Great himself, who is leading a raid on the nearby Swedish outpost of Neinshants on the Neva River. Not suspecting Vladimir's identity, Peter warms him with his own coat, saving the last novice from death from exposure. Ultimately, Vladimir wanders to Moscow and enters a monastery to devote the remainder of his life to prayer for forgiveness for the murder of Denisov. Neinshants is the site of the future capital St. Petersburg, the founding of which Lazhechnikov effusively describes in passing. These telling conversions of Vladimir's path with the story of the Russian Empire serve to remind us again that Vladimir is a peculiar, inverted double of Peter. His story is a prism, refracting interpretational possibilities for Petrine history itself. Despite Lazhechnikov's loving eulogy of Petersburg and Peter, and despite the "happy endings" of many of the novel's characters, in the distorting mirror of Vladimir's story it seems that St. Petersburg was founded on a crime: on the bones of the past and on a ritual killing of the father that cannot be simply buried and forgotten.

Although Lazhechnikov's stated purpose was to construct a collective identity on the firm foundations of a celebratory Petrine history, his novel ultimately demonstrates how unwieldy Russia's first emperor could be as a symbol of common social being. The equivocal fate of the last novice and the unmistakable echoes of the Decembrist revolt suggest that Peter's epoch constituted not only a wellspring of collective identity but also a sinkhole, a scene of social division that prefigures and calls forth modern resurgences of ancient bloodshed. In this interpretational reversal, Lazhechnikov's civic pilgrimage to the sites of Peter's conquests in an effort to "be such a Russian as Peter the Great" begins to resemble more a rite of atonement for Petrine violence that inscribed historical

---

war trophy and by an accident of fate passed up the chain of command to the emperor himself—into a noblewoman trained by Glück to love Russia and its emperor.

and geographical fissures into the Russian heart. The instability of the Petrine myth, as formulated by Lazhechnikov, was reflected in the inconstancy of official response to the novel. Despite success with a patriotic readership in its serial publication and separate editions in the 1830s and 1840s, a volte-face on the part of the censorship—its sensitivity heightened into near paranoia following the revolutions of 1848—halted republication of the novel during the 1850s. As the censor's report concluded:

> The main protagonists of the novel, Patkul and the Novice, respectively, are a traitor to his sovereign who has assumed leadership of the rebellion of Lifliandiia and a murderer-mutineer who has made an attempt on the life of Peter the Great. Each of them is presented as a victim and evokes involuntary pity. The first is a victim of his love for his unjustly oppressed homeland, and the second of his boundless loyalty to Tsarevna Sophia, who had been his just ruler.[57]

In Lazhechnikov's seemingly unintended slide from a celebration of empire and the creation of collective identity to a rehearsal of ancient violence and victimization we may discern characteristic features of the legacy of collective trauma: the compulsion of victims to return to the scene of violence, matched by the tendency of traumatic historical experience to resist explanation and closure.

—∾—

As in the case of Lazhechnikov's rendition of Peter the Great, the representation of Ivan the Terrible in the Romantic historical novel illustrates the problematic significance of the liminal figure, heavy with the twin burdens of the Russian collective self-imagination, on one hand, and of past and present traumatic violence, on the other. In this case, the very history of the composition and publication of Aleksei K. Tolstoi's novel *Prince Serebrianyi* (Kniaz' Serebrianyi), much of which was derived directly from Karamzin's *History*, perfectly illustrates the disavowal of the violence of Ivan's reign during Nicholas's era of Official Nationality.[58] Although the work was first published in 1862, six years after the coronation of Alexander II, it demands to be read as something of a "return of the repressed" from the preceding reign. Tolstoi conceived his novel in the late 1840s and had completed what was likely a full draft version by the early 1850s. The delay does not imply that Tolstoi ran afoul of the censor—as a highly placed member of the court and party to the official convention of silence surrounding Ivan, the author seems to have simply refrained from publishing his work until different circumstances obtained. A frame of metatextual commentary precisely places the novel in this regard. In the dedication to Em-

---

57. Cited in Il'inskaia's notes in Lazhechnikov, *Sochineniia*, 1:541.

58. Tolstoi signals his dependence with an epigraph from Tacitus (as illustrated above, Karamzin was commonly referred to as the Russian Tacitus, esp. for his depiction of Ivan) and by means of numerous obvious borrowings from Karamzin and, in one instance, a direct page-long quote of Karamzin's description of Ivan's palace in Aleksandrova Sloboda.

press Mariia Aleksandrovna, Tolstoi writes: "Your Majesty's name, which you have permitted me to place at the start of this tale of the times of Ivan the Terrible, serves as the finest demonstration that an impassable abyss separates the dark events of our past from the radiant spirit of the present era."[59] The novel's final paragraphs expand on its relationship to contemporary times:

> Let God help us expel from our hearts the last traces of that awful time, the influence of which was to pass from generation to generation for many years like an inherited disease. Let us forgive Tsar Ivan's sinful soul, for the responsibility for his reign is not his alone. He was not unaided in establishing arbitrary rule [*proizvol*], tortures, executions, and informants—all of which subsequently entered into our habits and even duties. The way was paved for these troubling phenomena in still earlier times—the land, which had fallen so low that it could look on such abuses without indignation, itself created and perfected Ivan. [. . .] Each deed, each word, and each thought grows like a tree—and much of the good and evil that exists unexplained today in Russian life hides its roots in the obscure depths of our past. (2:388)

The contradiction between the triumphal dedication and the critical notes in this final passage regarding the survival of ancient vices in latter-day Russia is only an apparent one. The "radiant" present of the dedication is the Epoch of the Great Reforms of Alexander II, whose sweeping transformation of Russian society captured the imagination of the vast majority of educated Russians in the late 1850s. The conclusion's evocation of "arbitrary rule, tortures, executions and informants" is a transparent reference to the universally condemned ills of Nicholas's reign—"arbitrary rule" in particular was a term commonly applied to the paternalistic repressions and abuses of the 1830s and 1840s.[60]

When Tolstoi speaks in his dedication of an abyss separating the past from the present, he is therefore referring to the chasm that separated the rule of Alexander II from that of his predecessor. In this critical projection of the traumas of the deep past onto the political experience of his own day, Tolstoi makes his most significant departure from his model, Karamzin, for whom the incomparable moral superiority of Russia's modern rulers to Ivan was axiomatic. Note, too, that whereas Karamzin lauded the Russian people for their patient endurance of Ivan's depredations, Tolstoi saw submission to terror as a form of complicity. In the context of the early 1860s, this conviction resonated with the common sense of hope for the novel civic organizations and limited self-governance instituted by the era's reforms. Yet it would be a mistake to take Tolstoi as heir to the Decembrists' reading of Karamzin as a critique of autocracy in toto: the novelist stops short of anything like an equation of Nicholas's era, in its petty despotisms, with Ivan's reign of terror. Instead, the excesses

---

59. A. K. Tolstoi, *Sobranie sochinenii*. References to this edition are given in text.
60. See Platt, *History in a Grotesque Key*, 66–75.

under Nicholas appear as a last, weak echo of the ancient vices of Ivan's day—vices that will be eradicated in the glorious reign of Alexander II.

Following Karamzin, Tolstoi viewed Ivan as a monstrous deformation of the ideals of rulership and of the Russian collective being, who therefore projects an inverted image of the true features of ruler and ruled. *Prince Serebrianyi* is a conventional example of its genre, borrowing stock episodes and characters from the works of the acknowledged master Scott as well as from his Russian epigones.[61] The plot revolves around the opposition of the virtuous yet rigidly moralistic Prince Nikita Romanovich Serebrianyi, an idealized national type, and the despotic Tsar Ivan. The work centers on the basic moral/political question of the relationship of ruled to ruler when legitimate power is wielded in a patently unjust manner. The prince, returning victorious from the Livonian War, filled with joy at the meadows and forests of Russia, finds that his beloved tsar has been transformed from an ideal young ruler into a bloodthirsty despot. Serebrianyi is cast by the vagaries of the plot into the company of a band of honorable robbers led by Vania Persten, who ultimately is revealed to be Ivan Koltso, a historical Cossack ataman who participated in the conquest of Siberia.[62] This topsy-turvy situation, where virtue is found in the company of thieves, is mirrored in Ivan's palace, where vice and lawlessness are found at the seat of divinely ordained power. In Aleksandrova Sloboda, at a symbolic remove from the true seat of power in Moscow, Ivan holds his *oprichnik* court, composed of unambiguously evil men who spend their days in feasting and depraved violence, punctuated by a hypocritical regimen of prayer. In the opposition of noble thieves and a despotic tsar, then, the novel exemplifies the poetics of a world-upside-down, which as Stallybrass and White have explained, is a basic tool of cultural forms that generate identity by means of symbolic inversions that serve as a dramatic reinscription of the original system of values.[63]

The novel's erotic plot concerns the triangle among Serebrianyi, his fiancée Elena, and the love-crazed *oprichnik* Viazemskii. In Serebrianyi's absence, Elena has married the righteous old boyar Morozov in order to ward off Viazemskii's

61. The most important Russian model is Mikhail Zagoskin's *Iurii Miloslavskii*, set in the Time of Troubles. Among Scott's novels, *Prince Serebrianyi* shares particular affinities with *Ivanhoe* and *Rob Roy* but also, given the formulaic nature of the genre, with many other works. On *Prince Serebrianyi* as an imitation of both Scott and his earlier Russian followers, see Dalton, *A. K. Tolstoi*, 54; and Al'tshuller, *Epokha Val'tera Skotta*, 270–72.

62. "Persten" and "Koltso" are nearly synonymous Russian words for "ring." Persten, a.k.a. Koltso, is obviously modeled on Scott's representation of Robin Hood in *Ivanhoe*, who also "hides" under a pseudonym for most of the plot and whose loyalty to the "true" bases of English nationality legitimates his opposition to a corrupt prince.

63. See Stallybrass and White, *Poetics and Politics of Transgression*, 13–16. Hans Ulrich Gumbrecht has also noted the conservative implications of binary inversion. See "Laughter and Arbitrariness, Subjectivity and Seriousness: The *Libro de buen amor*, the *Celestina*, and the Style of Sense Production in Early Modern Times," in his *Making Sense*, 111–32.

advances. Tolstoi renders the religious and sexual law plain via the contrast between Serebrianyi and Viazemskii—the former respects the matrimonial vows that make his love for Elena impossible, whereas the latter descends on Morozov's house with a force of arms to take Elena by violence (rape is prevented only by a fortunate turn of the plot).[64] Another element in the erotics of the novel amplifies an important aspect of Ivan's historical mythology. Serebrianyi is straight in every sense of this word (to the point of dullness, really).[65] Yet Tolstoi baldly implies a liaison between the tsar and the beautiful, "feminine" (ii, 124) and overtly homosexual *oprichnik* Fedor Basmanov, who is rumored to have dressed as a girl for the tsar's amusement. In one scene, Serebrianyi is outraged by Basmanov's provocative invitation to join him in his bath, where there are "peasant girls for the choosing and boys—all younger than twenty" (ii, 285).[66] In contrast to such illustrations of the "deviant" sexuality of the tsar's court, the merry camaraderie of the robber camp presents a model of noneroric male intimacy. In fact, the novel's positive heroes seem to be utterly desexualized— Serebrianyi loves no one but the forbidden Elena; Elena and Morozov (who is described as "an old man") have a white marriage; and when Morozov is executed, Elena retires to a monastery, leaving Serebrianyi forever loveless. With this prudishness, Tolstoi's novel ritually rejects the filth of sexuality to represent the clean and decent body of Russian collective being.[67]

Much like Karamzin, Tolstoi's exploration of Ivan's negative potential relies on orientalist categories. The tsar's deviancy is represented in the clearly recognizable key of Asiatic despotism, characterized by unchecked absolute power, irrational unpredictability, and taste for sensual pleasures. The theme of illicit homosexual eroticism, a commonplace of images of eastern rulers, supports

64. The theme of rape or threatened rape of married women by *oprichniki* is a commonplace of representations of Ivan, found in Karamzin and in many other historical and literary portrayals of Ivan and his reign. Tolstoi probably borrowed his subplot from Mikhail Lermontov's *Song about Tsar Ivan Vasilevich, the Young Oprichnik, and the Valiant Merchant Kalashnikov,* in which an enamored *oprichnik* assaults the wife of Kalashnikov, who then avenges himself on Ivan's lawless henchman.

65. Tolstoi was himself aware of the dullness of Serebrianyi's character. See his letter to S. A. Miller of December 13, 1856, in his *Sobranie sochinenii,* 4:324.

66. Accounts of Ivan's reign by the German soldier Albert Schlichting and the Italian soldier Alessandro Guagnini are apparently the main historical sources of rumors of Ivan's relations with Basmanov. In his account of Muscovy, Guagnini claims that Ivan had Dmitrii Ovchinin-Obolenskii executed in 1564 for accusing Fedor Basmanov of having intimate relations with Ivan. Karamzin, who referred to Guagnini's work a number of times, shied away from reiterating the accusation of homosexuality in print. In the footnote where Karamzin reproduces other aspects of Guagnini's account of Ovchinin-Obolenskii's death the historian makes no mention of the sexual innuendo and finds it necessary to remark that "one can't be certain of the truth of everything Guagnini relates about events in Moscow." See Karamzin, *Istoriia,* 9:9–10, n. 34. On Schlichting and Guagnini, see Poe, *A People Born to Slavery,* 131–33.

67. In this connection, see Richard Wortman's discussion of "family values," the royal family as a moral exemplar, and the production of Russian collective identity (*Scenarios of Power,* 1:247–95).

Ivan's "Asian" profile as well. But the texture of Tolstoi's prose itself contributes most to the orientalized image of the tsar. Ivan's "magical palace" at Aleksandrova Sloboda is presented as an architectural explosion of colors and forms, irrationally multiplied in a profusion of luxurious details with no order other than the rule of excess:

> It is difficult to describe the variegated splendor of this residence. No window resembled any other, and no column was similar to any other in its decorative designs and colors. A multiplicity of domes crowned the structure, crowding each other, piled one on top of another, jutting out and bursting forth. Gold and silver and colorful tiles, like the scales of a fish, covered the palace from top to bottom. When the sun illuminated it, from a distance it was impossible to say whether it was indeed a palace, or rather a gigantic flowering plant or a dense flock of phoenixes, which had alighted on the earth and unfurled their fiery plumage. (2:122)

Tolstoi devotes a similarly purple passage to the tsar's daily banquet, where exotic foods are piled in an improbable array reaching the ceiling of a hall that holds seven hundred guests. Richly dressed servants, who change their costumes with each appearance, bring a never-ending stream of new dishes, each more amazing than the last. Reigning over this scene of "Asiatic splendor," Ivan inspires his guests with fear and awe, unpredictably granting royal favor to some, symbolized by a goblet of wine sent from the tsar's table, and death to others, by means of poison placed in just such a goblet. The theme of irrational sensual excess associated with the tsar is brought to a climax in a chapter that describes a mass execution in terms derived from Karamzin's portrayal of the public executions of 1570. Tolstoi's rendering of Ivan's obscene violence, like the historian's, plainly evokes earlier descriptions of feasting and gluttony: finally, Tolstoi's rhetoric makes Ivan's "Asian" nature plain. As Serebrianyi himself comments, in another echo of Karamzin, "the *oprichniki* rape and pillage the land worse than the Tatars!" (2:175).

The plot of the novel turns on the confrontation of the opposed categories of the fickle and vice-ridden Asiatic despot and the incorruptible and steadfast Russian Prince Serebrianyi. At times, Tolstoi tantalizes readers with the vague hope that virtue will triumph. The case of Fedor Basmanov is instructive in this regard. In Serebrianyi's chief encounter with the tsar's young erotic companion, whom he has earlier seen from a distance, the prince and the *oprichnik* join forces in attacking a marauding Tatar army. At first, the prince does not recognize Basmanov, who shows no trace of his previous effeminacy and appears on the battlefield as a "handsome young man" who "cuts a swath to the right and left." Serebrianyi's comrade remarks that: "It's him all right, but he seems like a different person. It's shameful to even think it, but he's been known to dance like a girl in a dress. But now it seems like he's been inspired: he raised the peasants and serfs and has attacked the Tatars. The Russian spirit must have given voice in him" (2:282).

But this surprising transformation is short-lived. After the battle, the prince finds the *oprichnik* lounging in his "Persian tent": "Lying on silk cushions, Basmanov, already combed and perfumed, was admiring himself in a mirror held by a young valet kneeling before him" (2:285). Basmanov's surprising transformation is catalyzed by battle with the "true" Asian enemy—the Tatars, which enables him to overcome, for a time, the internal enemy of depravity.

In the larger plot of the novel this transformational mechanism appears to operate as a general principle. Ultimately, Serebrianyi and Persten's band of robbers, who have all been condemned to die for resistance to Ivan's reign of terror, earn clemency from the tsar for their part in defeating the Tatars. In the epilogue, which jumps forward ten years to the end of Ivan's reign, Vania Persten reappears as Ivan Koltso at the tsar's court to announce the conquest of Siberia by Cossack mercenaries in the employ of the Stroganov merchant family. In this episode, not only do the Cossacks receive the tsar's pardon for their past crimes, but Ivan himself is apparently transformed by these new triumphs over the east: "He seemed somehow less gloomy, as though the news brought by the Stroganovs had lifted his spirit, and a smile even appeared on his lips, when he spoke to Godunov" (2:378). For Tolstoi, it seems, the history of Russia was a battle with the Asian other both on the internal battlefields of the soul and in the actual expanses of the landscape, a battle that led through bloodshed and sacrifice to the achievement of a purified collective being.

Ultimately, however, *Prince Serebrianyi* fails to resolve either the political conundrum of the unjust ruler or the categorical tensions that drive the novel's action toward the promise of a better future. Although Basmanov can access the "Russian spirit" in combat, he lapses back into perversity; and whereas Ivan rises to moments of reconciliation with his subjects when confronting his Asian enemies, he returns to mad, bloody persecutions soon enough. Resolutely loyal, despite the insane injustice of Ivan's reign, Serebrianyi's own solution to the riddle of the crowned despot is to resist the iniquities of the *oprichniki* and to speak truth to power in an artless manner. This dumbly virtuous approach lands him on the scaffold, condemned to die for treason, to be saved only by another lucky twist of the plot.

At the conclusion of the novel, rather than accept the tsar's invitation to join the *oprichnina*, Serebrianyi rides off to die in battle in the east. Boris Godunov, who tries to persuade Serebrianyi to remain in Moscow and join efforts to reform the tsar or at least temper the violence of his rule, presents a counterexample in stark contrast with the prince's principled resistance to injustice. A trusted advisor who is himself alien to the perverse violence of the tsar, Godunov manipulates Ivan both to minimize the deranged ruler's evildoing and to advance his own ends. However, Godunov's calculating maneuvers are suspect from the start, and Tolstoi spells out in his epilogue that the necessity for compromise with evil eventually damages his moral fiber, "transforming a man of superlative qualities into a criminal" (2:378), who would eventually arrange the murder of Ivan's heir Dmitrii to clear his own path to the throne.[68]

Like Karamzin before him, Tolstoi portrayed Ivan's reign as a site of chosen trauma, an ancient trial that could occasion the emergence of a purified collective being from under the rubble, and positioned the despot as a negative example for beneficent modern rulers. The novelist's vision crystallizes stock features of Ivan's historical myth that would echo in future representations: homosexuality, a tendency to introspective examination of his own sins, and the mechanism of contamination by violence that affects all who surround the tsar. Offering his vision of the tsar to a qualitatively different political era than had Karamzin, Tolstoi attempted to draw the traumatic vision of Ivan out into a political allegory concerning the necessity of resistance to evil—even enthroned evil.

Like Karamzin, Tolstoi sidestepped key implications of his exploration of Russia's past. Eschewing any actual struggle with autocratic authority, *Prince Serebrianyi* offers no program by which to extract a pure Russian identity from the dross of a bloody history other than to take cover and wait it out, as the prince did in deciding to quit the tsar's court. Tolstoi's deferral of publication of his novel, with its implied critique of the reign of Nicholas I, until that tsar was safely consigned to history himself, illustrates this strategy of duck and cover perfectly.[69]

Critics were quick to note how the novel's belated appearance robbed it of both political and literary punch. The leading liberal journalist Mikhail Saltykov-Shchedrin, for instance, writing in the voice of a "retired teacher of Russian literature," penned a parodic eulogy to a historical novel that itself belonged to history:

> I have grown young again! I read and do not believe my eyes! You have plunged your brush into the living waters of fantasy and have allowed me, an old man, to experience firsthand "the deeds of days of yore"—bravo! But even greater accolades for your resurrection of my youth, for you have returned me to the days of the appearance of *Iurii Miloslavskii* and *Roslavlev* [historical novels of the 1820s—K.M.F.P.] . . . , to the first shy efforts of Lazhechnikov. That was a happy time indeed, o dear count—a time when writers knew how to "Speak truth to tsars with a smile."[70]

68. In accordance with the nineteenth-century historiographic consensus, Tolstoi believed that Godunov was directly responsible for the death of Tsarevich Dmitrii. For an account of changing views of the matter, see Vernadsky, "Death of the Tsarevich Dmitry"; and Emerson, *Boris Godunov*, 48–61.

69. Tolstoi was known to speak truth to power—only not to Nicholas I but to his far more restrained successor Alexander II, for whom the author had been a childhood companion. Tolstoi interceded with the emperor on behalf of a number of disgraced or suspect authors, including the radical author Nikolai Chernyshevskii following his arrest in 1862. See Zhukov, *Aleksei Konstantinovich Tolstoi*, 260–62; and Dalton, *A. K. Tolstoi*, 27.

70. The final words of the citation are quoted from Gavriil Derzhvin's poem *Monument* (Pamiatnik). M. E. Saltykov-Shchedrin [unsigned], review of *Kniaz' Serebrianyi, povest' vremen Ivana Groznogo*, by A. K. Tolstoi, *Sovremennik* 95, no. 3–4 (1863): 295–306.

Palpably, the critic's disdain extended as much to the novel's political tardiness as it did to its old-fashioned and epigonic generic features. But despite poor reviews, *Prince Serebrianyi* became an instant and enduring success with readers.[71] One may attribute this success to Tolstoi's lucid mobilization of the poetics of liminality to project present identity against the silhouette of the past, to trace the outlines of a positive Russian character against the edges of the anti-Russian Ivan, and to cement modern Russians together as survivors of the traumas and injustices inflicted by rulers ancient and modern.

—⁂—

In the first half of the nineteenth century, Russian cultural and educational discourse granted Peter and Ivan sharply distinguished historical roles, consistently cutting apart the opposed heroic and traumatic possibilities of the liminal figure in order to attribute the glories of the former to Peter and the tyranny of the latter to Ivan. Patriotic examinations of Peter and Ivan offered up a hymn to a Russian collective being in harmony with autocratic power and threw questions of the interrelationship of progress and violence into the shadows. The bloodshed and coercion of Peter's rule was minimized and legitimated, while that of Ivan was rendered axiomatic and rejected from the Russian political legacy as a compelling negative example, throwing the glory of model tsars into high relief. Peter and his reign were elevated as a glorious historical birth into the truly Russian, a myth of origins that could cement together the disparate elements of the collective being: imperial pretensions and national traditions, ancient native roots and modern European tastes. Ivan, in contrast, became an anti-Russian deviation whose reign was a traumatic trial that marked out the limits of identity as an object of collective renunciation. In this manner, the patriotic rhetoric of Russian history harnessed these multivalent historical figures to articulate a modern collective identity and a genealogy of Russian rulership. Here, the young Konstantin Nikolaevich playing at dress-up in Peter's boots and sitting in Ivan's throne in the Moscow armory illustrates the rituals of the age—both as a member of the royal family experimenting with exemplars of rulership and as a child exploring the boundaries of modern Russian collective identity.[72]

Yet related rhetorical pitfalls afflicted the superficially dissimilar mythmaking projects around the two figures, belying the logic that distinguished their opposed roles. In the case of Ivan, Karamzin's *History* and Tolstoi's *Prince Serebrianyi* were hard-pressed to reconcile the despot's ostensibly anti-Russian violence with the greatness, power, and identity with the people inherent in his high station: if his terror could aptly be portrayed as a chosen trauma, the

71. Within a quarter-century, literary criticism had anointed the novel as a canonical (if secondary) work. It has been reliably reissued at least once a decade up to the present; translated into German, French and English; reworked for the dramatic and operatic stage; and regularly adopted as a staple of school curricula.

72. See the third epigraph to the present chapter, drawn from Ol'ga Nikolaevna, "Son iunosti," 239.

explanation of why a divinely ordained ruler should inflict such suffering on his own people remained "a riddle for the mind." In a complementary manifestation of liminal instability, Ustrialov's textbook and Lazhechnikov's *Last Novice*, which strove to use the Petrine myth to integrate Russia's national character and historical development, could not conceal the disfigurement of the collective physiognomy wrought by Peter's age of coerced social transformation. Inexorably, visions of a despotic Ivan punishing his subjects raised the question of autocratic violence in general. This was a problem that patriotic treatments of his reign sidestepped, but that surfaced for their readers, from progressive noblemen seeking justification for rebellion, such as Ryleev, to Nicholas I and his representatives, who preferred to forget this reminder of their medieval institutional inheritance as they erected a modern system of coercion and surveillance. From another perspective, as Karamzin's *Note on Ancient and Modern Russia* illustrates, it was an open secret that Peter's brilliant accomplishments had come at the cost of immense suffering. Although many thought this "collateral damage" was justified by his great achievements, it proved difficult to dismiss, especially when the bill was still being paid by later generations subject to the same logic of state violence in the service of social progress. As we shall see, the echoes of legitimate power in Ivan's despotic terror and of trauma in Peter's heroism presented obvious starting points for other, fuller explorations of the interrelationship of terror and greatness in Russian history.

CHAPTER TWO

Trauma

> And should we hide from ourselves one other brilliant error of Peter the Great? I have in mind the founding of the new capital on the State's northern border, amid the swampy waters, in a region destined by nature for sterility and loss. [. . .] How many people died, how many millions and how much labor were exhausted in order to realize this plan? One may say that Petersburg was founded on tears and corpses.
> —Nikolai Karamzin, *A Note on Ancient and Modern Russia*, 1811

> The difference between the state institutions of Peter the Great and his temporary decrees is worthy of amazement. The first are the fruits of a broad mind, filled with good intentions and wisdom; the second are not infrequently cruel, capricious, and, it seems, written with a knout.
> —Aleksandr Pushkin, notes for a *History of Peter the Great*, 1835

Terror as Greatness

It is a striking and persistent irony that rather than any of the unequivocally triumphal representations of Peter I dating to the era of Nicholas I, Pushkin's *The Bronze Horseman* (Mednyi vsadnik, 1833), identified in critical common-place and in countless school essays as a thoroughly "ambivalent treatment of the legacy of Peter I," became a key text in modern rituals of Russian collective identity. The lines of the introduction to Pushkin's poem's commencing with "I love you, creation of Peter" (4:245), memorized by generations of Russian children, have for a century and a half been solemnly recited at every celebration of St. Petersburg, of Peter, and of Russian high culture with convenient obliviousness to their author's overt subversion of any straightforward, optimistic reading of these very lines.[1] For undeniably, in *The Bronze Horseman*, this superlative autocrat and the glorious civilization he created are, somehow, also the cause of a tragic spiritual degradation and physical destruction of the individual.

We can discern a not unrelated irony in the later fate of the theory of history articulated in the 1840s and 1850s by the Westernizer critics and State School historians Vissarion Belinskii, Konstantin Kavelin, and Sergei Solovev,

---

1. Pushkin, *Polnoe sobranie sochinenii*. References to this edition are given in text. All translations of *The Bronze Horseman* are my own.

who recast Ivan from a cruel despot to a heroic visionary and prototype for Peter. By an unpredictable twist of fate, the idea of Ivan as a heroic state builder, which originally promoted a conception of progressive liberal reform opposed to the stagnant dogmas of Nicholas I's Official Nationality, came a century later to serve the ideological purposes of a regime repressive beyond the wildest imaginings of either the dissenting intellectuals who authored the theory or the middling despot Nicholas.

Admittedly, my primary examples in this chapter make an odd pair: the canonical works of Russia's national poet, Pushkin, on one hand, and the writings of a largely forgotten historian, Kavelin, on the other. Yet as is the case with Ivan and Peter themselves, in studying this unlikely pair together we discover deeper principles linking together superficially distinct phenomena. As we have seen, in the first half of the nineteenth century, elite culture granted Ivan IV and Peter I opposed roles in narratives of Russian history—Ivan the bloody tyrant, and Peter the glorious hero. Nevertheless, patriotic authors like Ustrialov and Lazhechnikov were hard pressed to elide the legacy of historical violence in their heroic representations of Peter, while loyalists such as Karamzin and Tolstoi could never fully control the implications of a crowned tormentor in their portrayals of the bloodstained Ivan. The interrelationship of the tsars' heroic and traumatic aspects was a carefully managed but ultimately ungovernable rhetorical pitfall. In contrast, Pushkin's and Kavelin's works self-consciously explore the fuller potential of liminality, investigating the unseemly mating of terror and greatness. For this reason, these works achieve a more profound level of insight regarding Ivan and Peter, power and collective identity, in Russia, offering an avenue of critique of the representations of the two examined above. Yet for this very reason, these works, which maximally opened out the multivalence of these figures, also became maximally susceptible to later appropriations—unpredictable reversals of fortune in unanticipated future contexts.

In classic descriptions of the psychic legacy of trauma, the seeming impossibility of adequate representation of extreme suffering gives rise to uncontrolled, painful resurgences of memory. Recovery and treatment revolve around the search to express this experience that seemingly defies human understanding, thereby achieving closure and laying ghosts to rest. The phenomenon of chosen trauma, however, depends on recovery's failure. Subject to intentional or happenstance manipulation for political ends, chosen trauma capitalizes on the urgency of the memory of historical violence to generate collective identity out of a shared myth of victimization. As the texts examined above illustrate, the era of Ivan the Terrible was a problematic candidate as a site of chosen trauma because he was a crowned autocrat. Peter the Great, in contrast, presented difficulties as a heroic touchstone of collective identification precisely because of a troubling residue of unexamined historical trauma.

As will become apparent, however, it was just this concatenation of triumphal celebration and historical suffering that underlay, in both cases, the unique affective power of the Russian mythology of history. Whereas official ideology worked to construct firewalls between terror and greatness—in relation both to present experience of a regime founded on continuing violence and to the historical myths that supported this regime—it also capitalized on the subterranean flows that linked terror and greatness together. For truly, what could be more effective in rituals of collective identity than mythic examples who enact the bloody passage to a new state of being, in both its violence and its promise of rebirth? My examinations of Pushkin's and Kavelin's writings enable an extension of thought concerning the category of chosen trauma, illustrating that, whereas the equation of terror and greatness is indeed counterintuitive in political rhetoric, in anthropological perspective it appears fully comprehensible as the basis for ritual affirmations of the violence of a glorious state.

Aleksandr Pushkin's Petrine Project

Exiled from the Russian capitals for his youthful political and literary indiscretions, Pushkin was absent from St. Petersburg in December 1825, when the death of Alexander I and the ascent of Nicholas I set the stage for the Decembrist uprising. The bloody suppression of this attempted coup and the ensuing investigations, culminating in the execution of the conspiracy's leadership and the exile of all other participants to Siberia, deeply scarred the poet, who was tied by friendship and common political aspirations to many of the rebels. Until his death a decade later, Pushkin's attempts to work out the implications of these events—a trauma of both social and personal significance that was all the less susceptible to the poet's comprehension by virtue of his absence from the events—constituted one of the main drives of his creative output. Summing up this crucial focus of Pushkin's later writing, Iurii Lotman has argued that the poet sought to reconcile a historicist comprehension of the "objective" bases of state legitimacy in the reality of autocratic might with a humanist understanding of justice as a function of the well-being of the individual. For Pushkin, the key to this conundrum lay in a resolution of Peter's liminal ambivalences—of the tensions between the sovereign's inherited right to govern as he saw fit and his willful tendency to challenge all previous norms; between his solid, immobile pose as a founding figure and his protean role as an innovating revolutionary; between his creation of a liberating cosmopolitan Russian identity and the archaic cruelty with which he cut his subjects to conform to this new pattern. For Pushkin, these problematic ruptures held out the vague promise of joining together a divided political scene and forging a coherent identity for modern Russians, or at least of comprehending the impossibility of these projects.

The Petrine "originative scene" of Russian history concerned Pushkin abstractly, relative to modern Russian collective identity; politically, with regard to the relationship of individual and state; and personally, in terms of Pushkin's own dependency on the court and his genealogical interest in the Petrine epoch as the point of entry of his African forebear into Russia. In 1832, Pushkin remarked about progress on his history of Peter: "I have not yet been able to comprehend this giant and grasp him in one stroke of the mind: for us, in our myopia, he is too enormous [. . .]. But I will make something out of this gold."[2] The problem of Peter was the sheer abundance of interpretations—the impossibility of grasping him in a single image—and it is therefore not surprising that the poet had difficulty bringing work on the first emperor to a conclusion. Besides *The Bronze Horseman*, he composed a great many other Petrine works, most importantly the lyric poem *Stanzas* (Stansy, 1826), the epic poem *Poltava* (1828), the uncompleted historical novel *The Blackamoor of Peter the Great* (Arap Petra Pervogo, 1827–30) and the *History of Peter the Great*, which was still only in its initial stages when the poet met his death in 1837. Whereas in the earlier of these works, *Stanzas* and *Poltava*, his deployment of the myth of Peter resembles the affirmative civic rituals evident in the works of Lazhechnikov and Ustrialov, in the latter works one senses that Pushkin is exploring Petrine liminality itself. In a letter of 1834 to his wife concerning his history of Peter, Pushkin wrote that he would "cast a bronze monument which it will not be possible to drag from one end of the city to the other, from square to square, from alley to alley."[3] Clearly, the history was to be a completed, final statement on the first emperor, which would bring all historical tension to resolution. In contrast, *The Bronze Horseman* is a mobile monument: a maximally complex exposition of the uneasy mating of greatness and terror in Russia's first emperor.

The *Stanzas* of 1826 were written a year after the Decembrist debacle as an epistle to Nicholas I, who in September of that year had summoned Pushkin to St. Petersburg and pardoned his past indiscretions, returning him to Russian society. This short poem contains the seeds of Pushkin's thought concerning Peter the Great:

> In hope of glory and the good
> I look ahead without fear:
> The start of Peter's glorious days
> Was darkened by rebellions and executions.
>
> But he attracted hearts with justice;
> But he tamed custom with learning,
> And distinguished between
> An unruly *Strelets* and a Dolgorukoi.
>
> With an autocratic hand
> He boldly sowed enlightenment;

2. Dal', "Vospominanie o Pushkine," 260.

3. Letter of May 29, 1834, to N. N. Pushkina, in Pushkin, *Polnoe sobranie sochinenii*, 10:378–79. The comment has been discussed most memorably in Belyi, *Ritm kak dialektika*, 71; and Jakobson, *Pushkin and His Sculptural Myth*, 29.

He did not disdain his native land;
He knew its predestination.

At one moment an academic, at another a hero,
A navigator or a joiner,
With an all-encompassing soul,
He was an eternal worker on the throne.

Be proud, then, of your family likeness;
Be like your forebear in all things:
Like him, unfaltering and firm,
And like him, forgiving of past wrongs.
(2:307)[4]

Following in the tradition of Lomonosov and Karamzin, who offered coronation odes instructing earlier tsars to follow the example of Peter, Pushkin's
Stanzas renders Russia's first emperor an object of adoration and homage—a
mythic exemplar, the emulation of which grants the new tsar, Nicholas I, access
to his familial, political, and national heritage.[5] What sharply distinguishes Pushkin's poem from earlier examples of this poetic tradition is its direct representation of Peter in all his complexity, as the source of both social advancement
and of autocratic violence. Even before showing the emperor as an enlightener
and laborer for the common good, Pushkin boldly evokes the suppression of
the *Streltsy* revolt of 1698—one of the bloodiest episodes in Peter's reign, during which the emperor himself personally participated in mass executions of his
rebellious subjects. Although the poet names Peter's era as a whole as "glorious" (l. 3), he attributes the pall cast over its start not only to rebellions but also
to executions—suggesting a measure of critique aimed at the emperor himself
for his part in the affair. Even more audaciously, in Pushkin's poem the mythical identity of Peter and Nicholas rests on the initial congruence of the mutiny
and punishment of the *Streltsy* with Nicholas's suppression of the Decembrists—
still a fresh wound and a forbidden topic of conversation in 1826. Although the
poet announces optimistically, "I look ahead without fear" (l. 2), the reader
might well infer that the poet looks at the past somewhat differently—that is,
the line also evokes the atmosphere of dread that gripped elite society in the
aftermath of the uprising.[6]

All these gestures toward critique of either Nicholas or Peter are artfully
understated. More important, they are majestically overshadowed by the poet's

4. This translation is my adaptation of George Gutsche's version, published in his article
"Puškin and Nicholas," 188. On Pushkin's *Stanzas* and Nicholas I, see Riasanovsky, *Image
of Peter the Great*, 88.

5. Important readings of this poem include Scherr, "Poet and Tsar"; Gutsche, "Puškin
and Nicholas," 194–96; Blagoi, *Tvorcheskii put' Pushkina*, 127–33; and Meilakh, "Iz istorii
politicheskoi liriki Pushkina."

6. Gutsche, "Puškin and Nicholas," 189.

account of the mature Peter's genius and the anticipation that the reign of
Nicholas, begun in a similar moment of bloody conflict, will achieve similar
heights of scientific advancement and social progress. The example of Iakov
Dolgorukoi (l. 8), whose outspoken criticism Peter is known to have tolerated,
offers a happier model for the relationship between the ruler and his opponents
than the harsh punishment of the "unruly *Strelets*" (l. 7) and perhaps constitutes a metapoetic commentary, illustrating the position of respected, reason-
able adviser to which Pushkin himself aspired with this very poem. Note, too,
that the progression from armed uprisings at the start of Peter's reign to Dolgorukoi's articulate opposition demonstrates not only the success of Peter's efforts to ennoble and uplift his subjects, to attract "hearts with justice" (l. 5),
but also the progress of the emperor himself, who grew with his epoch into a
more just and tolerant ruler. As the third and fourth stanzas of the poem demonstrate, this other Peter rightly earned the epithet "Great," leading by example
in all areas of human endeavor with a seemingly superhuman capacity for labor. And so the disturbing, mythic concert of executions past and present in the
first stanzas serves as a motivating device for the poem, which rides out the
analogy of epochs to conclude by instructing Nicholas to emulate his great
forebear in service to the social good. Some of Pushkin's contemporaries and a
great many later commentators have viewed this poem as a toadying capitulation to a tsar who could only be viewed as a tyrant—indeed, the lion's share of
critical work on the poem has been devoted to a polemic between condemnation and defense, demonstrating once again the capacity of explorations of the
liminal emperor for countless interpretational reversals in future political contexts.[7] Undoubtedly, Pushkin intended *Stanzas* to exploit his new closeness to
Nicholas, who had recognized the poet's genius, forgiven his past offenses, and
assumed the role of his personal censor, and who the poet rightly or wrongly
hoped might become a force for progress. Certainly, too, the last line of the
poem, calling on Nicholas to be "forgiving of past wrongs" (l. 20), constitutes
a plea for clemency toward the exiled Decembrists and indulgence of Russian
liberal-leaning society in general. Yet the poet's strategy in *Stanzas* is a good
deal more complicated than simple abasement and supplication.

Levi-Strauss's discussion of myth's "two-dimensional time referent" provides
a useful lens for study of this complexity. According to the theorist, the mythic
exemplar consists of events organized according to the diachronic logic of historical, nonreversible time but also interconnected *across* time by a consistent
set of relations reflecting a synchronic and ahistorical temporality.[8] It is this
interpenetration of temporal modes that licenses Pushkin to adopt the stance of

---

7. Scherr, "Poet and Tsar."

8. Myth, Levi-Strauss wrote, is organized according to this "two-dimensional time referent which is simultaneously diachronic and synchronic, and which accordingly integrates the
characteristics of *langue* on the one hand, and those of *parole* on the other" ("Structural
Study of Myth," 212).

prophet, speaking as the voice of Russian history itself and projecting the Petrine originary scene forward into his own future. By linking Peter's enlightening activity back to the exercise of violence against his subjects, Pushkin establishes the necessity of Nicholas's pursuit of similar policies of enlightenment—for the poet's rendition of the Petrine myth renders the accomplishment of progressive goals the only path to redemption of state-sponsored bloodshed.

The poem's key rhetorical moment in this regard is the repeated conjunction "but" (ll. 5–6), which signals the narrative and ethical relationship between the emperor's cruel executions and his later service to the collective good—the latter qualifies and justifies the former. And while the later stanzas of the poem carry the reader's attention up from the coercive base of Petrine autocracy toward its noble and benevolent summit, the liminal amalgamation of the whole persists in the "autocratic hand" (l. 9) with which Peter sows enlightenment; in the untold breadth of his "all-encompassing soul" (l. 15)—one wants to add to the list of Peter's professions "hangman"; and finally in Pushkin's exhortation to Nicholas to be like his forebear "in all things" (l. 18)— that is, not only in the violent suppression of unrest but also in redeeming his reign through progressive advances. Nicholas, in short, must either follow the first emperor's example or risk falling out of the Petrine myth.[9]

Like the patriotic and official nationalist deployments of Peter that would become standard fare in subsequent decades, the *Stanzas* make use of the liminal potential of the first emperor to stitch together Russian history and identity. Yet to a far greater degree than Lazhechnikov or Karamzin, Pushkin explores Peter's full range of potential meaning. The *Stanzas* carefully manage his contradictory dualities, plotting a story of development from bloody conflict between the ruthless violence of an all-powerful state and the lawless resistance of the individual toward a triumph of state-imposed enlightenment that both legitimates power and benefits the individual. Both in Peter's epoch and, as Pushkin hoped, in his own, progressive accomplishments could justify and ennoble autocratic rule.

Despite its optimism, the poem's historical vision also raises the specter of less auspicious convergences of past and present, for Pushkin's neat organization of Petrine history ignored other possible stories in which terror and greatness would be less easily reconciled. The resurgence of archaic brutality in the executions of the Decembrists alone raises doubts concerning the efficacy of Russia's progress in justice and enlightenment under Peter: that collective transcendence of state violence, it seems, was itself temporary and unstable, a prelude to later eruptions of arbitrary cruelty. Furthermore, a poem that commemorates bloodshed as an insurance of future social harmony is an ironic illustration

---

9. This mode of exerting influence on the psychology of the tsar corresponds to Pushkin's general poetical/political strategy in the early post-Decembrist years. See, for example, Iurii Lotman's reconstruction of the poet's discussion with the tsar of September 8, 1826, in his "Neskol'ko dobavochnykh zamechanii."

of the resistance of historical violence to all ostensibly final analyses. Trauma is not easy to retell as a closed book.

Moreover, especially for later readings of the poem, Pushkin's incantatory use of Petrine history as a tool for prognostication and a lever on his own tsar's psychology did not bear its intended fruit. As the 1820s wore on and Nicholas's feeble enlightening activities proved an insufficient justification for his despotism, a rosy assessment of either Russia's past or its future became increasingly difficult to maintain; and Pushkin's first, redemptive formulation of the myth of Petrine autocracy was, one might say, obsolesced.

In *The Bronze Horseman* Pushkin explores the ruins of his earlier conceptions, articulating the chaotic implications of Petrine duality that he controlled so brilliantly in *Stanzas*: the difficulty of harmonizing Peter's aspects, the tragic eruption of trauma and bloodshed when least expected in both past and present, and the impossibility of resolving Russian history into a plenitude of meaning that might support collective identity and political harmony.[10] The reassuring breadth of the "all-encompassing soul" transforms into the riddle of the Petrine myth's impossible concatenation of extremes. To briefly recapitulate Pushkin's masterpiece, the work's introduction celebrates the godlike creative leap of the founder of St. Petersburg:

> On the shore of desolate waves
> Stood *he*, filled with great thoughts,
> And gazed afar. Before him broadly
> The river flowed; along it a humble boat
> Made its lonely way.
> On mossy, swampy banks,
> Here and there stood dark hovels
> Refuge of the humble Karelian.
> And the forest, unknown to the rays
> Of a sun hidden in mists,
> Rustled all around.
> And he thought;
> From here we will threaten the Swede.
> Here a city will be founded
> To spite our haughty neighbor.
> Nature has decreed that here
> We shall cut a window into Europe.
> (4:244)

---

10. Readings of *The Bronze Horseman* that have contributed to my own include Belyi, *Ritm kak dialektika*; Tomashevskii, "Istorizm Pushkina," and "Pushkin (monograficheskaia stat'ia)," in his *Pushkin: kniga vtoraia*, 154–99, 479–541; Jakobson, *Pushkin and His Sculptural Myth*; Lednicki, *Pushkin's "Bronze Horseman"*; Bethea, *Shape of Apocalypse*, 44–61; Lotman, "Zamysel stikhotvoreniia o poslednem dne Pompei," in his *Pushkin*, 293–99; and Evdokimova, *Pushkin's Historical Imagination*, 209–31.

The opening scene recalls the biblical *Genesis* with its imagery of the deserted waters of the Neva, covered with mist, and reference to Peter with a simple pronoun.[11] This divine figure inscribes Petersburg in a virtually empty space between Russia and Europe, past and future. Peter pronounces that his deeds are in harmony with nature ("Nature has decreed"), yet in the following lines, as Pushkin leaps forward a century, the city appears to be more properly a supernatural phenomenon—a teeming metropolis that has sprung fully grown from the mind of the emperor, to which the poet addresses his unqualified love and admiration in the well-known lines cited at the start of this chapter: "I love you, creation of Peter" (4:275). In short, the introduction of *The Bronze Horseman* (the only segment of the poem that could be published during the poet's lifetime) offers a contribution to the official nationalist cult of Peter. It envisions the construction of St. Petersburg as a metaphorical representation of the emperor's godlike, imperial recreation of Russian identity and of Russia as a whole: "Be beautiful, city of Peter, and stand, / Unshakable, like Russia herself." In its monumental firmness, this last image ascribes to a celebratory vision of the emperor precisely the interpretive solidity to which Pushkin aspired in his study of Peter.

Yet the body of the work presents a jarringly different vision—one that accords more with Karamzin's conception of the folly of building St. Petersburg on the Neva's swampy mouths.[12] Like a historical novel, the poem offers readers a fictional character as a point of affective entry into history, but in place of a plot set in the past, Evgenii is a modern character whose loss of his fiancée and his sanity in the 1824 flood of St. Petersburg is metaphorically transposed into an encounter with the Petrine legacy. The construction of Petersburg on the banks of an uncontainable river is revealed to have been in agreement with nature and the needs of the national being only from the perspective of an autocratic military and economic raison d'état. In contrast to the poet's euphoric experience in the introduction of a plenitude of Imperial Russian identity, modern Russia leaves a tattered and abused Evgenii with no identity at all:

So did he his unfortunate existence
Drag on, neither beast nor man,
Neither this nor that, not a dweller of the world
Nor a lifeless specter.
(4:285)

---

11. Lednicki, *Pushkin's "Bronze Horseman,"* 50, 80–81.

12. Karamzin, *Zapiska o drevnei i novoi Rossii,* 37. As Aleksandr Ospovat and Roman Timenchik explain, Pushkin intended to publish this passage from Karamzin's *Note on Ancient and Modern Russia* in a single issue of *Sovremennik* with the re-edited version of *The Bronze Horseman* (taking into account the objections of the "Highest Censor" Nicholas I). The poet's death prevented him from carrying out this plan. For an insightful reading of the unrealized dialogue between the poem and the *Note,* see Ospovat and Timenchik, *Pechal'nu povest' sokhranit',* 71–73.

For Evgenii, Petersburg is a fatally unnatural and spiritually damning place: a liminal city that transforms its citizens into liminal subjects. And the first mover in this hellish reality is Peter, who looms in the background—in the fabric of the capital city itself, in Petrine toponyms (Petrograd, Petropol, Peter Square, etc.), but most ominously in the figure of the bronze horseman, who oversees Evgenii's downfall. As Pushkin's repeated application of the epithet "idol" to the famous monument illustrates, the idea of Peter that animates the body of the poem stands at some remove from the divine Peter of the introduction. This vision of the emperor as a false god achieves its apotheosis in the poem's final scenes, where the horseman abandons his pedestal to pursue the madman through the streets of the capital—an image that, as David Bethea has observed, represents the unholy forces of innovation and revolution that challenge the unity and sanctity of the Old Russian world and recalls nothing so much as a rider of the apocalypse.[13] If the monumental rhetoric of the introduction signaled the reassuring solidity of the interpretation of history offered there, the grotesque image of the animate statue now projects the horror of a history prone to dissolve into interpretive flux.

The extraordinary range of Peter's liminal capacity is most fully expressed in this standoff of cosmic alliances, from the divine to the diabolical, which recapitulates the structure of eighteenth-century historical mythology concerning the first emperor. The elevation of Peter to the status of divinity was a commonplace from his reign onward. In his panegyric to Peter, Mikhail Lomonosov declared, "if you must find a man like unto God, according to our understanding, you will find none but Peter the Great," a sentiment that he redeployed in an oft-quoted 1743 ode including the line: "he was a God, he was your God, O Russia."[14] Gavriil Derzhavin exclaimed, "In him, did not a God descend from the heavens?"[15] Yet this rhetoric found its mirror image in the demonic conception of Peter current among Old Believer communities. The idea that Peter was in fact the Antichrist was a productive element of Old Believer thought up through the nineteenth century—adduced in apocalyptic treatises as a proof that all of Russia's subsequent rulers were also aligned with Satan and that the end of history was already nigh (or in process, or even past).[16] At base, this mythic duality is a corollary of Peter's political function as a "revolutionizing

---

13. Bethea, *Shape of Apocalypse*, 44–61; Bethea, "The Role of the *Eques* in Puškin's *Bronze Horseman*," esp. 115–18.

14. The panegyric is Lomonosov, "Slovo pokhval'noe blazhennoi pamiati Petru Velikomu," in his *Polnoe sobranie sochinenii*, 8:584–612 (611). The ode (cited in stanza 13) is his "Oda na den' Tezoimeninstva Ego Imperatorskogo Vysochestva Gosudaria Velikogo Kniazia Petra Fedorovicha 1743 goda," in his *Polnoe sobranie sochinenii*, 8:103–10 (109).

15. From Derzhavin, "Petru Velikomu," in his *Sochineniia*, 1:221–25.

16. See Platt, "Antichrist Enthroned"; Cherniavsky, "The Old Believers and the New Religion," in *The Structure of Russian History*, ed. Cherniavsky, 140–88; Chistov, *Russkie narodnye sotsial'noutopicheskie legendy*, 91–112; Uspenskii, "Historia sub specie semioticae"; Riasanovsky, *Image of Peter the Great*, 76–85; and Gur'ianova, *Krest'ianskii anti-*

tsar," who uses his own divinely sanctioned authority to challenge the institutional and cultural bases of that same spiritually reinforced authority. And the paradoxical image of a crowned ruler whittling away at the legs of his own throne is complemented by the ironic convergences of those who adorned Peter in the costume of earthly god with those who saw in him an enthroned demon—one Old Believer tract, for instance, adduces the very Lomonosov eulogy just cited as evidence of the unholy nature of Peter, usurper of divine authority.[17]

In the *Stanzas* Pushkin had capitalized on the emperor's duality to bridge the divide between epochs and political principles, so deriving a coherent story of progress from traumatic violence to redemptive enlightenment. *The Bronze Horseman* disrupts this orderly myth, shaking ancient tragedy loose to haunt later eras. The horrible reanimation of the monument in Evgenii's hallucination gives a fixed form to the resurgence of unresolved trauma. Yet, as in Pushkin's *Stanzas*, the poem also deploys more precise allegorical linkages between past and present. The horseman's suppression of Evgenii's "revolt" on Senate Square vividly evokes Nicholas I, crushing the Decembrists in that same space.[18] Yet one must note that Nicholas's rebellious subjects themselves in fact massed around the monument to Peter, who symbolized for some the conception of social progress and modernization for which they had taken up arms. Then, too, Evgenii's pose in his crucial scene of crisis—frozen and staring out over the floodwaters, mounted on a statuary lion on the embankment—sets him up as a parodic double of the equestrian monument, and even of Peter, staring into the distance in the first lines of the poem.

In this, *The Bronze Horseman* renders Peter's allegorical significance with an ambivalence just as pronounced as in its treatment of his historical function or his cosmic alliances: the crowned revolutionary is as much a ritual prototype for the rebellious modern individual as he is for the later autocrat. The modern Russian identity that Peter constructed can at times simply cancel itself out, returning individuals like Evgenii to a pre-Petrine historical nullity. All these modern Russians are doomed to inhabit perpetually the ironically mismatched categories of Petrine history: the autocratic state that crushes its people in the name of their well-being, the rebel who seeks to overthrow the past but ultimately reenacts it, the individual who should be the beneficiary of cultural and political progress yet instead becomes its victim.

---

monarkhicheskii protest, 17–60 and 115–52. The last citation includes publications of Old Believer writings regarding Peter I.

17. See notes to Lomonosov's eulogy by T. A. Krasotkina and G. P. Blok in Lomonosov, *Polnoe sobranie sochinenii*, 8:901. For the particular Old Believer composition in question, see *Chtenie v Obshchestve istorii i drevnostei rossiiskikh*, 1863, no. 1, 3d pagination, 60–61.

18. For more extended treatments of this reading of Evgenii's revolt, see Lednicki, *Pushkin's "Bronze Horseman,"* 81; and Bethea, "Role of the *Eques*," 113–15.

How is one to resolve the paradoxical inconsistencies of this *Petersburg Tale*? The question misses the point: Pushkin's poem is constructed as an insoluble rebus of Russian history and identity. Perhaps the most precise, compact account of the intentional irresolution of *The Bronze Horseman* may be derived from Lotman's brief observation that Pushkin's thought on history in the latter portion of his career was characterized by a tripartite figural system:

> The first member of the paradigm could include anything associated in the consciousness of the poet at one or another time with an elemental, catastrophic eruption. The second position is distinguished from the first as something that is manufactured, which belongs to the world of civilization. From the first member of the paradigm, this second stands out as the conscious in opposition to the unconscious. The third position, in distinction from the first, is characterized by individuality (in antithesis to the impersonal) and contrasts with the second position as the living to the lifeless, as a person to a statue.[19]

Just such a figural system drives *The Bronze Horseman*'s unstable set of mobile oppositions and alliances. Pushkin captures three symbolic centers—Peter the Great, Evgenii, and the unruly force of the natural elements—in a complex choreography by which all coherent binary oppositions are pregnant with a third, destabilizing term, scuttling any attempt to reduce liminal complexity to a simple plot or conflict of principles. In the poem's introduction the figure of the godlike emperor stands in opposition to the wildness of untamed nature and external enemies, and in a positive relationship with the individual, who, in the person of the poet, benefits from Peter's progressive accomplishments. Here, civilization and the individual stand together in opposition to the elements. In the conclusion of the poem, Peter's state, as represented in Falconet's monument, appears in a less noble light, as the diabolical inhuman weight that crushes the individual, Evgenii. In this latter moment, civilization and the elements fall into alliance, each dealing death in its own way to the hapless clerk. Finally, looking back to the center of the poem, Evgenii's defiant challenge to the monument rests on yet a third configuration, in which the individual and the elements stand shoulder to shoulder in their wild rebellion against the constraints of civilization. Although diverse critical readings have sought to reduce the poem to one or another of these categorical oppositions, to identify heroes and villains in the poem's poetic structure, the work is intentionally configured to impede any attempt at a satisfying closure with unresolved residues of meaning. In the figural trap of *The Bronze Horseman*, all hope of bringing historical interpretation to rest is flummoxed by Russian history's excessive complexity.[20]

19. Lotman, "Zamysel stikhotvoreniia," 295.
20. For a fuller development of this reading of the tripartite structure of *The Bronze Horseman*, see my "Pushkin's *History of Peter the Great*."

The Bronze Horseman reveals the consequences of fixing the monument of collective identity to a fissured historical base. Peter is balanced on the border between Russia and Europe, between the divine and the satanic, between despotism and heroism, between historical memory and oblivion, and between the living and the dead. Rather than use the first emperor's border crossings as an opportunity to locate the boundaries of an integral Russian identity, Pushkin recasts Peter's epoch as an inauguration into a divided modern selfhood, uplifted by a great cosmopolitan civilization yet lacking in wholeness. The uncanny, demonic aspect of the animate monument conveys the tragic lack of resolution in this vision of history: the state that Peter built is both the savior and the tormentor of the Russian people. The perfected society that the emperor hoped to create can never leave behind the state-sponsored violence that continues to sustain it. Just as the inanimate monument comes to life to pursue Evgenii, the distant and buried past rises to crush later generations.

Bethea's reading of Pushkin's Peter as a figure for the threatening force of modernity, revolution, and antitraditionalism is compelling, but Peter also represents the archaic violence of Russia's traditions of absolutism. By this reading, Peter's reforms were damned at the outset by their ironic dependence on the unbridled power of the premodern autocrat. In Pushkin's notes for the unfinished *History of Peter the Great*, he wrote: "By ancient custom, when the people met the tsar they fell on their knees before him. In Petersburg, the muddy, swampy streets of which were not yet paved, Peter the Great forbade falling on one's knees. But since the people did not obey him, he forbade it *under pain of cruel punishment, so that,* Shtelin writes, *the people would not be smeared with mud*" (original italics; 9:83). Here, Peter's dependence on humiliation to uplift his subjects reveals Pushkin's conception of the self-defeating mechanisms of Russian history, where the effort to break with the past works to reinscribe that very past, which, like a case study in trauma, will rise elementally again and again with the floodwaters of the Neva.

Pushkin's dramatization of both Peter's greatness and his terror calls for a reconsideration of the psychic economy that tied these opposed terms together in Russian thought about the era of Alexander I and Nicholas I. Patriotic representations of Peter's reign like Ustrialov's textbook labored to exclude any hint of traumatic suffering from their heroic vision of history. Pushkin's works, in contrast, suggest that beyond the sheer utility of Peter's liminal features for patching political and social reality together, a deeper logic supported the election of a tyrant as father of the fatherland. The rhetorical force of history for Official Nationality, like the poetical force of Pushkin's "I love you, creation of Peter," derived in great part from the necessity to overlook the violence buried at the Petrine base of Russian history and its continuation in the modern autocracy. This disavowal of traumatic violence inheres in the very structure of Pushkin's poem, which calls readers to look past the legacy of Petrine violence to its triumphs but in so doing to recognize the cognitive dissonance of such a gaze—to join the poet in adoration of "Peter's creation" in spite of Evgenii's plight, in spite of the bloodshed of Peter's rule, and in spite of Nicholas' violent suppression of the Decembrists.

Ironically, such a disavowal is illustrated by the poem's own publication history—by the propagation of the introduction and the suppression of Evgenii's tale. More generally, as a critique of Petrine history, the poem exposes the act of disavowal inherent in historical representations such as Ustrialov's textbook. In short, the poem shows how misrecognition of the ongoing violence of the state was as much a part of the celebration of Peter as was admiration of his glory, how such a celebration was itself a form of violence against memory, and how participation in patriotic Russian identity therefore required a form of complicity in the state's coercive relationship to its subjects.

The traumatic irresolution of Petrine history imparted urgency to such rituals of modern Russian identity as Shevyrev's mantra to "be such a Russian as Peter the Great." In this regard, Peter's role in the rhetoric of Official Nationality calls for a more complex conception of chosen trauma, illustrating how the construction of collective identity may capitalize on open historical wounds not only by telling stories of common catastrophe, as in the case of Ivan, but also by passing over them in silence, as in the case of Peter. In short, Pushkin's poem suggests that Peter became an idol in rituals of Official Nationality not in spite of the trauma of his reign but in part because of it. No less than Ivan's reign, Peter's constituted a site of chosen trauma—a strategically submerged one that enabled men and women to become Russian subjects only by an act of self-abnegation.

Slavophiles and Westernizers

Pushkin's work on Peter presented a challenge to the official historical mythology of his age by discovering an open secret—that in the glorious figure of Peter lay trauma and bloodshed as extreme as in the proverbial despot Ivan. Yet this was not the only avenue to subversion or critical revision of histories in the key of Official Nationality. In subsequent years other Russian thinkers took precisely the opposite tack, exploring the element of the heroic inherent in the historical myth of Ivan the Terrible. This complementary discovery arose in the heated if suppressed intellectual ferment of the latter decades of Nicholas's reign. The progressive erosion of Pushkin's confidence in the Russian autocracy as a champion of enlightenment and, as a corollary, with Peter the Great as the epitome of this vision of Russian history presaged the common development of intellectual life under Nicholas. As the tsar and loyal supporters like Uvarov grew increasingly authoritarian in their preservation of the status quo, perfecting in the process the ideological edifice of Official Nationality, those members of Russian educated society who did not completely identify with the state were overtaken by a disillusionment that gradually transformed into political dissent. During these decades, Russia's educated society grew by many orders of magnitude, leading to the appearance by mid-century of a modern public sphere—a dynamic arena for the exchange of ideas, overseen by institutions of state censorship, to be sure, but driven by the autonomous social and economic impetus of professional authors working to satisfy the voracious appetites of a new generation of readers.

The conceptions of Russian history that were to prove decisive on this new social scene first came to the fore in a scandalous episode in 1836, when a mistake by the censor led to the publication of Petr Chaadaev's first "Philosophical Letter." This work, heavily influenced by German idealistic philosophy, blamed Russia's apathetic social and spiritual development on its total alienation from the great truths of European culture and history. Peter I appears in passing in this essay as the great leader whose attempt to correct this situation had in the end thrown only a "mantle" of civilization over Russian cultural vacuity.[21] Placed under house arrest and declared insane by Nicholas and his ministers, a year later Chaadaev penned his "Apology of a Madman," in which he brilliantly recast the social disease he had diagnosed as presenting a peculiar civilizational advantage. Here, Peter became the heroic ruler who: "found in his country only a blank sheet of paper; on it he wrote: 'Europe and the West.'"[22] According to Chaadaev, Peter had saved his people by giving them all the goods of Western civilization as their own. Even more, because modern Russians had no traditions or history to weigh them down, they were equipped to forge ahead on humanity's common path of enlightenment more rapidly than any others: "the past is no longer in our power, but the future is ours."[23]

In a dynamic exchange of ideas and writings over the next two decades, dissenting intellectuals would modify and revise Chaadaev's teleological historical vision, messianic imaginings and schematic dichotomies. The circles and journals of these thinkers quickly divided into the camps that came to be known as Slavophiles and Westernizers. Their standoff was a clash of alternative utopian ideals derived in precisely opposed fashion from Chaadaev's novel distillation of Russian history: the Slavophiles exalted the primordial past as the wellspring of religious values and a lost national soul, whereas the Westernizers fetishized modernization and political reform following western European models. Defining their positions chiefly through polemical engagement with each other (even the monikers Slavophile and Westernizer originated as derogatory stones cast by the opposed camps), their debates orbited around common wedge issues.[24] In the interpretation of history, the chief focus of argument was Peter the Great, whose position at the crux between the imagined ideal of an authentic Rus

---

21. Chaadaev, *Philosophical Letters*, 31–51, here 36. On Chaadaev, see Riasanovsky, *Image of Peter the Great*, 98–106; Wachtel, *Obsession with History*, 134–35; and Walicki, *History of Russian Thought*, 81–91.

22. Chaadaev, *Philosophical Letters*, 167.

23. Ibid., 175.

24. For extensive discussion of Slavophile and Westernizer views, see Walicki, *History of Russian Thought*, 92–151; and Riasanovsky, *Image of Peter the Great*, 122–151.

and the promise of modernity—as well as between Russian and European civilizations—demarcated the philosophical battle lines.

Westernizers saw in Peter the superlative hero of modernization and social progress—a view that the influential critic Vissarion Belinskii summed up in his 1841 announcement: "Peter the Great is the greatest phenomenon not only of our history but of the history of humanity. He is the divinity who summoned us to life, who with his breath blew a living soul into the colossal body of ancient Russia, which was mired in a deathly slumber."[25] As Belinskii's statement suggests, Westernizers regarded Peter with a reverence that rivaled the sacral place of the first emperor in the rhetoric of Official Nationality. Yet whereas Peter's liminal potential served in these official conceptions of history to suture Russia's diverse historical and geographical fragments into a whole, if static, collective identity, for the Westernizers Peter's borderline features themselves offered a model for continued innovation and progressive development. For thinkers like Belinskii, the fragmentary nature of modern Russian identity, which had so stymied Pushkin's visions of both the Petrine past and the present under Nicholas, translated into the essential incompleteness of the Petrine project: "Peter the Great is not only the creator of the past and present greatness of Russia, but he will also forever remain the guiding star of the Russian people, thanks to which Russia will always follow her true path toward the high goal of moral, human and political perfection."[26]

In short, Westernizers saw Peter the Great not simply as the creator of a new and better order of things but as an expression of the principle of historical unfolding itself. In their view, this Petrine principle represented the necessary antidote to the ills of their own period, in which they felt trapped by a reign opposed to progress in any form. In future years, this conception of Peter as a symbol and instrument of historical development would prove attractive to progressive and revolutionary thinkers of many different stripes.

In symmetrically opposed fashion, Slavophiles indicted Peter as the champion of harmful alien ideals and as the greatest enemy of the ancient truths of both Orthodox Christianity and Old Russian national culture. In an ironic twist of intellectual history, the Slavophiles revised certain commonplaces of German Romantic thought into a rejection of European civilization itself as essentially soulless, mechanistic, and rational, in contrast to the organic, spiritual, and intuitive culture of Russia. According to an 1838 essay by Ivan Kireevskii, Peter was a "destroyer of the Russian and founder of the Germanic," who through his efforts turned the educated classes into a rootless

---

25. Belinskii, "Rossiia do Petra Velikogo," review of *Deianiia Petra Velikogo, mudrogo preobrazovatelia Rossii*, by I. I. Golikov, 2d ed.; *Istoriia Petra Velikogo*, by Veniamin Bergman, trans. E. Alad'in, 2d ed.; and *O Rossii v tsarstvovanie Alekseia Mikhailovicha*, by G. Kotoshikhin, in his *Sobranie sochinenii*, 4:7–63, here 9.

26. Belinskii, "Kritika sochinenii Pushkina: Stat'ia piataia," in his *Sobranie sochinenii*, 6: 249–98, here 289–90.

"society within a society."[27] As the Slavophile author Konstantin Aksakov put it in 1851: "Peter stood for exclusive nationality, only not for his own but for western nationality; he destroyed every expression everywhere of Russian life, every Russian phenomenon."[28] Peter, according to this conception, was responsible for most of the ills of modern Russian society—its slavish and imitative cultural life, its oppressive form of statehood, and the alienation of the landed gentry from the truer national principles that still lived among the simple people. Yet all was not lost. According to the law of the dialectic, through a "negation of the negation"—that is, a return to the principles of Old Russian life—Russia could leap ahead on the path of universal human progress.

One of the greatest innovations of the era's debates over the interpretation of Peter lay not in these opposed conceptions of the first emperor himself, which in many ways simply refracted earlier traditions through new modes of historical thinking, but rather in the linkage of Peter to his predecessor Ivan the Terrible. This novel interpretive knot originated as a common point of reflection in both camps. In the essay just cited, Kireevskii posed the question of the preconditions of the Petrine reforms ("how was Peter possible?"). For an answer, he pointed to the era of Ivan the Terrible as the cradle of those vices that led to Russia's subsequent downfall, impeaching in particular the centralizing and standardizing church reforms of Ivan's era as the corrupting element that led to "*mestnichestvo, oprichnina*, slavery and [. . .] Peter."[29] The younger Slavophile thinker Aksakov at one point in his career had been inclined to see Ivan as an ideal expression of Old Russian civilization, but he subsequently adjusted his position to one more in alignment with Kireevskii's.[30]

Westernizers derived a rather different view of historical process from the linkage of the two rulers. Belinskii, in an 1840 discussion of Lermontov's stylized folk epic *The Song of Tsar Ivan Vasilevich, the Young Oprichnik, and the Valiant Merchant Kalashnikov*, articulated a moderately apologetic view of Ivan as "a great man, but one who appeared in Russia at the wrong time, too soon": "Perhaps there were boiling in him unconsciously all the forces necessary for the transformation of that repugnant reality into which he appeared

---

27. Kireevskii, "V otvet A. S. Khomiakovu," in his *Polnoe sobranie sochinenii*, 2: 109–20, here 119–20. For a more complete account of the views of both of these camps on Peter, see Riasanovsky, *Image of Peter the Great*, 86–151.

28. Aksakov, "Neskol'ko slov o russkoi istorii, vozbuzhdennykh istorieiu g. Solov'eva," in his *Polnoe sobranie sochinenii*, 1:42.

29. Kireevskii, "V otvet A. S. Khomiakovu," 120. For extensive analysis of Kireevskii's positions, see Christoff, *Introduction to Nineteenth-Century Russian Slavophilism*, 2: esp. 247–51.

30. For Aksakov's idealization of Ivan, see his "Neskol'ko slov o russkoi istorii," 1: 46–48. For his later discussion of Ivan, see his "Po povodu vi toma Istorii Rossii g. Solov'eva," in his *Polnoe sobranie sochinenii*, 1:125–72. On Aksakov's views of Ivan, see Christoff, *Introduction to Nineteenth-Century Russian Slavophilism*, 3:308–9.

so prematurely—a reality that did not so much triumph over him as break him down, and on which he then took his revenge so horribly for the rest of his life, destroying both it and himself in anguished and senseless rage."[31]

In an 1843 essay Belinskii developed these views, formulating a congruence between Ivan and Peter as equivalent figures cast into different epochs, and treating Ivan's reign as the beginning of those social transformations that would find their conclusion in Peter's exploits:

> The reign of Ivan the Terrible marks the conclusive formation of the physiognomy and spirit of Old Russia but also the beginning of the negation of both. This spirit of negation was expressed in the figure of Ivan. It would be unsupported speculation to think that a bad upbringing and the death of Anastasia rendered Ivan the scourge of Russia. In his nature, Ivan was a great man, and for him only two roles were possible—either Peter the Great or *Ivan the Terrible*. There were insurmountable barriers for the realization of the first potential, which arose both out of the alienation of Russia from Europe and from the chaotic condition of Europe itself. And so the grandson of Ivan III became not the transformer of Russia, but a terrible scourge derived from her eastern form of statehood.[32]

Belinskii goes on to give a brief account of the seventeenth century as an interlude during which the transformative energies first evident in Ivan's time gestated, awaiting a genius to bring them to fruition, concluding: "That genius was Peter, and he accomplished the revolution for which conditions had ripened and the time had come."[33] Inherent to all these polemically counterpoised voices, but perhaps expressed most precisely by Belinskii, was a rise in abstraction that brought into view the shared transitional significance of both figures. Rather than identifying the two tsars with specific images of Russian greatness that they either had brought into being or demolished, these thinkers now envisioned Ivan and Peter as the instruments and symbols of progress itself. This was a rise in abstraction that brought into view their dualistic function in the temporal order as figures of transformation and modernization. Catalyzed by the common background of these thinkers in German dialectical philosophies of history, this novel analysis of the national past enabled Slavophiles and Westernizers alike to see in the figure of Ivan the Terrible a mirror image of Peter the Great.

---

31. Belinskii, review of *Stikhotvoreniia*, by M. Iu. Lermontov, in his *Sobranie sochinenii*, 3:216–77, esp. 240. For another early statement on Ivan, see his review of *Borodinskaia godovshchina*, by V. A. Zhukovskii, and *Pis'mo iz Borodina ot bezrukomu k beznogomu invalidu*, in his *Sobranie sochinenii*, 2:109–18, esp. 115.

32. Belinskii, review of *Istoriia Malorossii*, by N. Markevich in his *Sobranie sochinenii*, 5:223–42, here 235. Belinskii's remarks in this essay represent the culmination of views that he began to develop as early as 1839.

33. Belinskii, review of *Istoriia Malorossii*, 5:235.

Belinskii's notion of Ivan as Peter's double, a servant of the same mechanism of historical transformation who was doomed to failure by his appearance too far ahead of his proper time, was to find its most complete articulation in the historical writings of Konstantin Kavelin, which made the new view a cornerstone in what would become a persistent if understated countertradition in Russian historiography. A seminal intellectual figure of his generation, Kavelin was among Russia's first professional historians, in distinction from the gentlemen authors of previous decades like Pushkin and Karamzin. Although educated in large part informally, in his early years Kavelin fell into the leading circles of the nascent intelligentsia of Moscow and St. Petersburg and dedicated himself to an academic career. In 1847, in the inaugural issue of a new journal that took its name from Pushkin's *Contemporary* [Sovremennik], Kavelin published his first major article, "A Consideration of the Legal Life of Ancient Russia," which served as a manifesto of Westernizer views on the Russian past and immediately became a lightning rod for critical debate. The article itself is of a polemical and rhetorical rather than a scientific character—leading one scholar to wonder at its "fairy-tale manner of recounting Russia's past," which backs up claims either inadequately or not at all.[34] (Kavelin draws conclusions about the basis of Old Russian society in clan relations from musings on such flimsy evidence as the habit of contemporary peasants to refer to just about anyone as brother, sister, mother, etc.) But it is precisely as a broad-stroke sketch that the article could represent national history so compellingly in ideological silhouette.

Following the earlier work of the German-born historian Johann Philipp Gustav von Ewers, Kavelin imagined Russian history as a progressive unfolding of social institutions from the primordial organizational principle of a stifling clan structure toward the "higher" good of the elevation of the free human personality, which in Russia had been achieved only by the reforming energies of the centralized state.[35] According to Kavelin, this historical *telos* was successively bringing Russia closer to western Europe, which was proceeding toward this same goal from the different starting point of a society organized according to confining, legalistic relationships that express the principle of individuality while subjecting it to degrading distortions. For Kavelin, the crucial juncture in Russia's modern historical development was none other than the era bounded by the reigns of Ivan the Terrible and Peter the Great, who had personally effected the greatest leaps forward along this path of development:

This transitional period—the dawn of a new epoch and the twilight of the preceding one, an ill-defined epoch, like all intermediary periods—is delimited from what preceded and followed it by the two greatest figures in

---

34. Christoff, *Introduction to Nineteenth-Century Russian Slavophilism*, 4:125.
35. Ewers had articulated the theory of the clan-based social structure of Kievan Rus in his *Das älteste Recht der Russen*. On Ewers, see Rubinshtein, *Russkaia istoriografiia*, 223–33.

Russian history, Ivan IV and Peter the Great. The former inaugurates the
transitional period, while the latter concludes it and initiates a new era.
Separated by an entire century, completely disparate in character, they are
marvelously similar in their aspirations and in the general direction of their
activity. Both pursue the same aim, and a certain sympathy binds them
together. Peter the Great deeply respected Ivan IV, called him his model,
and placed him higher than himself; and in fact, the reign of Ivan found its
continuation in the reign of Peter. The unfinished reforms of the former,
halted in midstream, were continued by Peter. (1:46–47)[36]

Here, Kavelin expands Kireevskii's and Belinskii's formulae of equivalence into a
lucid articulation of the shared liminal qualities of these transitional monarchs.

The detailed historical account introduced by this passage devotes far
more attention to Ivan than it does to Peter, for Kavelin's view of Russian
history was largely in consonance with the standard account of the first emperor as heroic transformer but necessitated a wholesale reevaluation of the
Terrible Tsar. Kavelin cast Russian history as a story of dialectical development—
the original unity of purpose of the primordial Slavic clan structure was progressively attenuated over centuries as the multiplication of diverse princely
families and the increasing distance between rulers and ruled led to intraclan
power struggles and failing social cohesion. This disunity set the stage for the
Mongol conquest. The rise to dominance of Moscow over all other princely
territories represented the advent of an individual representative of power
acting to negate the primordial clan structure out of devotion to "the idea of
the state." This renewal of social unity made it possible to cast off Mongol
dominance.

Even so, the original dialectical tension persisted in the conflict between
the state's interests, represented by the grand prince, and the clan interests of
his boyars and servants, expressed in the petty abuse of power, *mestnichestvo*,
and the passivity of the lower orders. Kavelin interprets Ivan's reign as a concerted but ultimately unsuccessful effort to reform these archaic social principles. The tsar's legal reforms extended state power and protected the lower
orders against their rulers' depredations; he advanced lowborn servants of the
state as scribes and officials to enact reform; the *oprichnina* itself was an attempt to eliminate traditional hierarchies by surrounding the throne with good
men of humble origins. Kavelin attributes the ultimate failure of Ivan's deeds
to the critical shortfall of any sense of individual and responsible citizenship
among those he promoted, who themselves adopted the self-interested and
corrupt practices of the boyars whom they had replaced. Whereas Russians of
Ivan's day saw only his failures, and subsequent commentators only "repeated
the words of the contemporaries who protested loudest, [. . .] one person

---

36. Kavelin, "Vzgliad na iuridicheskii byt drevnei Rossii," in his *Sobranie sochinenii*,
1:5–66. References to this edition are given in text.

understood [Ivan]—the great successor who was fated to complete his undertakings and bless Russia with a new path" (1:53), that is, Peter the Great.

Kavelin's model brings to light cryptic sympathies linking Ivan and Peter and yields a considerable explanatory payoff. Because of their prescient grasp of the progressive goals of Russian history, both monarchs were out of synchronicity with their own times, and this temporal displacement accounts for the complex, ambivalent features of each. In this manner, the historian explains both Ivan's fall from princely grace into horrific despotism—the transformation in character that Karamzin had seen as an incomprehensible mystery—and Peter's capacity for moral lapses and violence:

> Ivan was ultimately overwhelmed by the weight of the idiotic, semipatriarchal, and already pointless milieu in which he was fated to live and act. Locked in mortal combat with that milieu for many years without visible results, finding no support, he lost faith in the possibility of realizing his great plans. Then life became for him an unbearable burden, a perpetual torment, and he became spiteful, a tyrant, and a coward. [. . .] Peter, endowed with a fearsome will and astonishing pragmatic insight, lived a century later, when conditions had changed and much had been prepared for him. He had a predecessor—predecessors, even. With the confidence of a genius he plunged into his undertakings and had the rare good fortune to see them ripen and bear fruit. But Peter's character, too, was shaped in a severe, harsh form; he, too, needed loud diversions, in which he could lose himself; and he, too, experienced moments when his muscles grew weak and a heavy, anguished infirmity and spiritual exhaustion interrupted his tireless activity. (1:47–48)

Yet the linkage between these monarchs is not simply one of equivalence, for the force of Kavelin's model draws out the dissimilar features of the two tsars, as they were commonly viewed, in order to render the contradictory features of each monarch fully comprehensible. Peter's manifest greatness lifts up and legitimates Ivan, allowing his formerly unfathomable abuses to fall into place as a symptom of his progressive historical strivings: "Ivan fell so low precisely because he was so great" (1:47). Symmetrically, Ivan's axiomatic brutality renders Peter's troubling episodes of violence and despotism a vestige of the past, justified by an epoch that could be reformed only by harsh means:

> Monstrous were those times and that society, which could remake the noble character of Ivan IV into that of a moral degenerate, a reprobate, whose arbitrary rule knew no limits. It was the coarse, untamed, pitiful historical milieu itself, in which there was no trace of public opinion or of any shared spiritual or even material interests whatsoever, that made possible the transformation [of Russia in Peter's reign] in the manner in which it was accomplished, in all its harsh measures and violence. The justification of the epoch of reform is in its aims; its means were given it by ancient Rus itself. (1:59)

In this manner, the linkage of Ivan and Peter brings the liminal complexity of each figure under control by drawing out and mitigating those features that in other visions of the national past erupted as uncontrolled ironic excess.

Kavelin's theory of history is a polemical response—both to those such as Pogodin and Ustrialov, who saw in Peter the founder of a monolithic civilization and in Ivan a pure deviation from national principles, and to those who saw in either of the two tsars a destroyer of the true, primordial essence of the Russian nation, such as the historian's Slavophile opponents. Kavelin's strategy, following the gesture of Kireevskii and Belinskii to its logical conclusion, was to "step back" from the events of history as such in order to comprehend liminal complexity as a metahistorical function. From this vantage point, the essence of both figures was not in the fixed orders that they championed or opposed but in their embodiment of the progressive momentum of Russian history. Ivan and Peter were bound to Russia's past and future in dialectical fashion—as the leaders who resolved the contradictions growing in the bosom of the collective life: "Peter the Great left not a single living question that had arisen in ancient Rus without an answer" (1:60).

Responding specifically to Slavophile critiques of Peter's reign as the source of the self-alienation of modern Russians, Kavelin argued that in the wake of the Petrine reforms eighteenth-century Russians had experienced no sense of rupture in collective identity, for they had understood their epoch as the logical unfolding of what had preceded it. And in a neat corollary, the problematic sense of national inadequacy or wounding afflicting Kavelin's contemporaries called for a diagnosis different from that offered by those who blamed Peter for the later disintegration of the Russian being. For Kavelin, the principle of forward motion joined not only the ages of Peter and Ivan but pointed toward the future as well:

> They say that the epoch of transformation created an impassable, yawning chasm separating the old Rus from the new, making us into something neither here nor there, intermediate between Russia and Europe—human amphibians. But this is not so. [. . .] We became intermediate beings only later, when the epoch of reforms had come to an end, when society was formed and an unconscious demand for independent thought and action was born. Then, we began to ask questions of the past, present and future. [. . .] Everything became the subject of criticism and judgment, and while the results of this criticism had not been found and a definite view of things had not been worked out, doubt and indecision paralyzed thought and action. But this was a new phenomenon for Russia, not a consequence of the reforms, but the necessary prelude to a new order, which was then being conceived. (1:60–61)

Ostensibly, this passage refers to the late eighteenth-century transformations of the Russian social order, yet as an articulation of Kavelin's dialectics of Russian history it offered readers a surprisingly open call for reform in the present.

For the historian's formulation implies that the problematic gap between na-tional essence and historical reality reflects nothing other than the exhaustion of the transformative energies released in Peter's era and of any subsequent moment of forward progress. The resulting internal contradictions demanded a new era of transformation.

To Kavelin's contemporaries, this was a startling resolution of the Russian past. As Belinskii wrote to Aleksandr Herzen, "Kavelin's article is a milestone in Russian historical writing, inaugurating the philosophical study of our past. I was thrilled by the vision of Ivan the Terrible. Instinctively, perhaps, I always judged the Terrible Tsar positively but did not have the knowledge to justify my view."[37] In subsequent years, Kavelin's story of state-instituted progressive change was taken up and elaborated by the so-called "State School" of historians—a largely liberal and reform-minded group that took shape in the 1850s. Its most impor-tant member was Sergei Solovev, who beginning in 1851 and continuing until his death in 1879 produced the multivolume *History of Russia from Ancient Times* that superceded Karamzin's *History* as the authoritative comprehensive account of the Russian past.[38] Solovev's work is suffused by the Westernizer fascination with the state as the engine of progressive change. Yet whereas Ka-velin's work was inspired by Hegelian dialectics and schematic to the point of cartoonishness, Solovev shared with François Guizot a conviction that faith in providence could be confirmed by a scientific account of history's progressive movement and a dedication to painstaking archival research and analysis.[39] The introduction to Solovev's first volume throws down a thumbnail sketch of Russian history as a whole that, as in Kavelin's view, identifies the passage from an ancient clan structure to a united modern state championing material prog-ress and spiritual enlightenment as the "main event" of Russia's story of na-tional becoming and casts Ivan IV and Peter I in the starring roles in this dra-ma.[40] Volume 6 of Solovev's *History* (1855) presents a detailed account of Ivan's reign that consistently describes the first tsar as the bearer of the progres-sive, transformative seeds of Russia's future: a proponent of centralized state power in conflict with the archaic holdovers of clan-based princely power; a visionary who comprehended the progressive need to acquire western Euro-pean cultural and technological advancements and to conquer seaports to this end; a strong leader who was capable of implementing reform. Echoing Kave-lin, Solovev remarks that Peter revered Ivan for his desire to conquer the Baltic states and elevates Ivan to equivalency with Peter for his successful conquest of Kazan and Astrakhan: "We understand, therefore, how Ivan towered over his

---

37. Belinskii, letter of March 20, 1846, to A. I. Herzen, in his *Sobranie sochinenii*, 9:588–89.

38. On the "State School," see Rubinshtein, *Russkaia istoriografiia*, 289–342. For analy-sis of the "State School" qua school, see Hamburg, "Inventing the 'State School.' "

39. Ana Siljak, "Christianity, Science, and Progress."

40. Solov'ev, *Istoriia Rossii*, 1:55–59.

predecessors and how for Russians of the seventeenth century he was the grand-
est figure in national history, overshadowing all others, just as Peter would be
for Russians of the subsequent two centuries."[41]

Unlike Kavelin's vague gestures toward Ivan's deficiencies, however, Solovev does not diminish the terror of Ivan's reign. His narrative includes, for
example, a blow-by-blow description of the tsar's sack of Novgorod that recounts in as much detail as had Karamzin the gruesome murders of innocent
men, women, and children.[42] Like the first official historiographer, Solovev
saw the circumstances of the Terrible Tsar's upbringing as responsible for
Ivan's "terrible disease" of abnormal and vicious tendencies, overblown "sus-
ceptibility, passions, and capriciousness."[43]

Yet Solovev's history, in sharp distinction from Karamzin's, is not really concerned with the evaluation of Ivan's character or actions in psychological or
moral terms: "any confusion of the historical explanation of events with their
moral justification would be more than peculiar."[44] Instead, Solovev situates
such bloody episodes in a grand narrative that pits Ivan's progressive endeavors
against the archaic reaction of his contemporaries. In this manner, Solovev
largely looks past Ivan's deeds and his lamentably vicious means to envision
instead the lineaments of Russia's historical fate: "the age posed important
questions, and at the head of the state stood a man who was by his nature capable of moving decisively to resolve them."[45] Later, in the volumes of his history devoted to Peter the Great and in his celebrated public lectures during the
bicentennial of the emperor's birth, Solovev would reiterate his view of both
Ivan and Peter as champions of the progressive unfolding of the Russian state.[46]

Kavelin's rendering of Russian history found not only admirers and followers but also ardent critics. Immediately after publication, the "Consideration
of the Legal Life of Ancient Russia" attracted a firestorm of debate, the most
significant and representative critique being that of the Slavophile thinker Iurii
Samarin. As might be expected, given the nature of the era's intellectual de-

41. Ibid., 3:475.

42. Ibid., 3:560.

43. Ibid., 3:541, 712.

44. The phrase is redolent of Hegel's argument in the introduction to the *Philosophy of
History* that the violence of history must be seen as independent of the progressive dialectical unfolding that it serves.

45. Ibid., 3:707.

46. In subsequent decades, this vision of Ivan and Peter as heroes of progress was to become a prominent feature of Russian historical thought, reiterated in the works of a leading
historian of the subsequent generation, Konstantin Bestuzhev-Riumin (who was to write the
essay on Ivan the Terrible in the influential Brokgauz-Efron encyclopedia of 1890–1907).
See, for example, the final pages of Bestuzhev-Riumin's two-volume *Russian History*, published in 1885, where he discusses the "character of the Terrible Tsar": "In comprehending
his activity, one must be struck by the comparison with the tsar and epic hero of the eighteenth century. It was not without reason that Peter regarded Ivan as his predecessor, as the
legends tell us. They had common plans" (*Russkaia istoriia*, 2:315–19, here 318).

bates, Samarin's extended review focused chiefly on disputing Kavelin's dismissive evaluation of Old Russian society. Countering Kavelin's placement of clan at the nadir of a hierarchy of social organizational types, his critique argued that ancient Russians had lived in a communal society informed by timeless Christian moral values, which had been progressively attenuated, most decisively as a result of the Petrine reforms.

Yet Samarin devoted no little attention to Ivan as well, for doing so offered a lever by which to upend his opponent's argument. After citing Kavelin's "remarkable" comparison of Ivan and Peter, Samarin wrote: "We completely understand that this view derives naturally from the conceptions of the author concerning the meaning of the individual in history. [. . .] But if the only objection that could be raised to this theory were that it rendered the writing of these lines necessary, this alone would be enough to conclusively reject the theory."[47] Offering a dramatic list of the tsar's victims and misdeeds, Samarin repudiated the conception of history on which his opponent's views were based on the grounds that it justified bloodshed and violence in the name of progress and exonerated Ivan's great moral failings as a result of circumstance.

Samarin's neat reversal of Kavelin's positions demonstrates how smoothly the opposed interpretive potentials of these borderline figures can move in concert, like adjacent gears rotating in opposite directions. Turning Kavelin's history on its head to reread progress as degradation, Samarin's treatment of Ivan projected a mirror image in which the Terrible Tsar's reign constituted a watershed of immorality and vice presaging the corruption of subsequent centuries of modernization. And if Kavelin's mythic rendering of the national past and Solovev's majestic treatment of that same myth worked to lift eyes from the events of history toward a grand scheme of progress, Samarin's response insisted on recognition that such a view based collective greatness on the mayhem wrought by coercive regimes.

—⁂—

The works examined in chapter 1 constructed a historical mythology in which trauma and greatness, state-sponsored violence and progress, Ivan and Peter were conceptually cordoned off from each other. Pushkin's and Kavelin's works turned attention to the interrelationship of violence and social discipline in Russian history and uncovered the interdependence of aspirations to greatness and resurgences of trauma in Russian visions of the past and formulations of collective identity. Whereas officially sanctioned representations of the past utilized the ambivalent potential of Ivan and Peter for categorically distinct rhetorical ends, Pushkin and Kavelin study the fuller implications of the liminal figure per se—the deep structure that links together the traumatic and the heroic possibilities of interpretation. In *The Bronze Horseman*, Pushkin exposed the residue of trauma remaining in a history that can never be closed but

47. Samarin, "O mneniiakh *Sovremennika*, istoricheskikh i literaturnykh," in his *Sochineniia*, 1:61.

demands closure, a vision of social progress that is predicated on brutal violence, and a conception of collective identity in which the aspiration to greatness is based on complicity with and acceptance of a coercive state. In contrast, Kavelin recovered the hope of future progress from the bloodiest episodes of the Russian past, deriving from the equivalence of Ivan and Peter a principle of historical advance and dynamism that promised a future reconciliation of the fragmented present. Pushkin discovered terror submerged in greatness, whereas Kavelin discovered greatness inherent in terror.

Yet Kavelin's and Pushkin's historical visions, complementary though they are, each provide tools to critique the other. Kavelin's conception of progressive history recalls the views Pushkin articulated in the *Stanzas* of 1826. Violent rule—whether that of Peter, Ivan, or some later ruler—can and must be ennobled by enlightenment and social progress. Glorifying past eras' transformative accomplishments, no matter how marred they were by bloodshed, the historian, like a younger Pushkin, was able to "look ahead without fear" toward Russia's future. In light of Kavelin's progressive myth of history, the poet's critique of the autocratic state as incapable of carrying out social and political progress without unjustified violence in *The Bronze Horseman* could appear to be simply a sophisticated rationale for political apathy.

But by the same token, Pushkin's critical revision of the hopeful scheme of history he had earlier cherished may be extended into a critique of Kavelin's historical writings as well. As the poet's masterwork discovers, the Russian model of state-imposed social change ironically tended to reinscribe autocratic brutality in the very struggle to institute a better society. Though one must identify with liberals like Kavelin in their contempt for the stagnant political dogmas of their age, the historian's implicit endorsement of violent change modeled on that of Ivan or Peter as a solution can only seem naïve in light of subsequent Russian history.

By the end of Nicholas I's reign, Russian historical thought had built around Ivan IV and Peter I a tightly interrelated set of interpretive options, ranging from the celebration of foundational myths to the collective memory of despotic impositions of traumatic violence, the celebration of progressive transformation, and the realization of the tragic incompletion of history and modern Russian selfhood. As the Slavophile-Westernizer debates illustrate, these variations on a theme emerged together, as a unified field of interpretations balanced against one another and deriving explanatory force from their fugal interweaving.

Most striking in retrospect, and determinative of the future fate of these figures, is their political versatility. By a slight shift in emphasis these myths could shore up a regime or fuel oppositional fervor, always offering convenient focal points for repudiation by new generations of polemical opponents. As Pushkin's masterpiece demonstrates, these opposed conceptions of history are far more than a binary system of alternative options; they are a mobile system of oppositions and tensions, interpretations and metainterpretations, which could be reconfigured in any number of positions with equivalent rhetorical efficiency. It is this versatility that drove the future productivity of the historical myths of Ivan the Terrible and Peter the Great in unforeseen political contexts: Alexander II could embrace an idea of Peter that differed radically from the conception of the first emperor that figured in the court culture of his predecessor Nicholas, marking in this manner both the continuity of genealogy over the long term and the advent of a new political era. A similar logic was later to underwrite the Soviet claim to these same heroes. In this sense, the conservatism of the tradition in historical imagination and political rhetoric with regard to Ivan and Peter was ensured by their originally overdetermined character; for renunciation of the past never necessitated repudiation but could always lead instead to rewriting and reclamation in any of many available alternate keys.

As we shall see in subsequent chapters, this conservative tendency to revise and reclaim Ivan and Peter also ensured that their great potential for ironic slippage would never fade—Kavelin's liberal historical myth would transform into a Stalinist mobilizational tool; Pushkin's vision of historical ambivalence would be recast in the rituals of collective affirmation; and every other vision of the Russian past would remain open to rewriting and redeployment, potentially in a manner completely contrary to its prior significance and author's purpose. Before death brought his projects to a halt, Pushkin's work on the *History of Peter the Great* went only so far as a detailed series of chronologically organized notes.[48] In Pushkin's comments to Dal regarding the impossibility of grasping Peter's enormous figure "in one stroke of the mind" the poet remarked that "we are still standing too close to him—one must step away from him by two centuries."[49] The implication here for Pushkin and Dal—separated from the first emperor by only a hundred years—is that the vantage point from which Peter's accomplishments would appear distinct from their ironic foundations had not been reached, and that the poet in fact could not have brought his *History* to a final resolution.

Or perhaps one should conclude that the materials communicate Pushkin's view of history more effectively in their unfinished form, matching the incomplete nature of history itself.[50] Here I may apply Monika Greenleaf's formulation regarding another of Pushkin's great tragic works, *Evgenii Onegin*, which "allegorizes irony's refusal to give up, to synthesize, to privilege one perspective over the other."[51] Pushkin's work on Peter suggests that ultimately, the vantage

48. For an account of Pushkin's work on the history of Peter, see Feinberg, *Nezavershennye raboty Pushkina*. Although Feinberg holds that Pushkin's notes for the *History* present a late stage of work, it is clear that they are in fact very preliminary.

49. Dal', "Vospominaniia o Pushkine," 260.

50. On the ultimate irresolution of Pushkin's historical vision, see Evdokimova, *Pushkin's Historical Imagination*, 1–28; and Wachtel, *Obsession with History*, 66–87.

51. Greenleaf, *Pushkin and Romantic Fashion*, 207. Alexander Dolinin has defined the view of history animating Pushkin's *History of Pugachev* as a form of providentialism that he inherited from French Romantic historiography. According to Dolinin, by the 1830s

point that could redeem the failures and ironies of the Petrine legacy lay outside of history itself. The liminal character of Peter in the *History*, like Evgenii in *The Bronze Horseman* and like Pushkin himself, is essentially incomplete, mired in a temporal sinkhole that could be exited only in "eternity, or at any rate the future" (9:287).

From Pushkin's insight into the persistent incompleteness of a history founded on a liminal figure, one may derive a corollary to the productivity of the historical and rhetorical tradition around Ivan and Peter: the remarkable difficulty of future artists, historians, and political contexts to capture them in any aesthetic or pragmatic closure. From Ustrialov's uncompleted five-volume history of Peter to Lev Tolstoi's tens of attempts to write a historical novel set in Peter's day, Aleksei N. Tolstoi's uncompleted Socialist Realist historical novel *Peter I* and his unfinished dramatic trilogy on Ivan, and Eisenstein's scandalous unfinished film trilogy *Ivan the Terrible*, the history of representation of these figures is replete with fragments that, like Pushkin's *History*, may reveal more about Russian visions of the past as shards than they would in completed form. In closing this chapter, I offer that this same superordinate irony persists in subsequent generations' loving recitation of *The Bronze Horseman*—an apt foundational text in Russian culture *because* it commemorates the fractures marring the Russian collective being so well, the chosen but disavowed trauma of Russian history.

Pushkin had come to believe that history represents the workings out of the divine will, but that the movement of providence is incomprehensible to those whose lot it is to witness history ("Historicism or Providentialism," 307).

Figure 5: *Peter I Interrogates Tsarevich Aleksei Petrovich at Peterhof*, by Nikolai Ge, 1871, State Tretiakov Gallery (Moscow, Russia). Reproduced with permission.

Figure 6: *Ivan the Terrible and His Son Ivan, 16 November 1581*, by Ilya Repin, 1885, State Tretiakov Gallery (Moscow, Russia). Reproduced with permission.

CHAPTER THREE

Filicide

The fate that befell the Muscovite period of Russian history will without fail
come to pass with the Petersburg period as well. Just as the reforms of Peter
murdered the Muscovite order of things, the coming reforms will murder the
Petersburg order.

—Aleksandr Herzen, "Russia and Poland," 1860

[Ivan IV and Peter I] both recognized equally clearly the idea of the state and
were both its most noble and worthy representatives; but Ivan recognized it as a
poet, while Peter the Great did so primarily as a pragmatic individual.

—Konstantin Kavelin, *A Consideration of the Legal Life
of Ancient Russia*, 1847

Page versus Stage

The coronation of Alexander II in 1856 inaugurated the Epoch of the Great
Reforms, which brought sweeping changes to Russia. Serfdom was abolished,
institutions of limited self-governance were introduced, and both the legal system and the military were restructured and professionalized. Shaking off the
political, social, and cultural norms of the era of Nicholas I, Russia embarked
on a surge of modernization. In this new era, the myths of Ivan IV and Peter
I proved their resilience. Reconfigured, rather than discarded, they remained
linchpins in the story of Russian becoming. As in prior decades, both in frequency
of representation and in heroic significance Peter overshadowed Ivan, whom
most people still viewed as a bloody despot (see figs. 3 and 4). Yet the dominant
political rhetoric no longer celebrated Peter chiefly as founder of a monumental
imperial civilization. Influenced by the views of the Westernizer, statist historians
of the 1840s, the court and elite circles now came to emphasize the first emperor's
dynamism, promoting him as a model for state-led social progress.

Similarly, the Westernizers' view of Ivan's progressive role in state development and his status as Peter's predecessor had gained ground. The new take on
Ivan is evident in many of the era's historical, literary, and theatrical works,
but its broad dissemination is demonstrated most pointedly by a guidebook
produced for the Moscow Polytechnic Exhibition of 1872, which commemorated the bicentennial of Peter's birth. Although an engraved portrait of the Great
Reformer prefaces discussion of the exhibition, the frontispiece is a portrait of
Ivan the Terrible. The work's editor, Grand Duke Vladimir Dolgorukii, explained

Figure 3: "Tsar Ivan the Terrible at the Place of Skulls," illustration from a popular history-education pamphlet, *Russkaia istoriia v dvadtsati chetyrekh kartinkakh* (St. Petersburg, 1866).

his choice of illustrations with language cribbed from Kavelin: "In the one figure—Peter I—we see the ruler who accomplished the transformation of Russia; in the other—Ivan IV—we see a ruler who recognized the bankruptcy of ancient institutions and strove to transform them."[1]

Every generation must rework prior views of history. However, as a result of the integral nature of the complementary, interlocking stances toward Ivan and Peter worked out in the first half of the nineteenth century, their revision was to prove particularly problematic. For Russians of these years, the previous era's array of interpretational stances formed a cultural mechanism that could not be ignored. The total range of interpretations of the two liminal tsars—from the traumatic to the heroic—reached forward to inflect all later interpretations. For this reason the new era saw a proliferation of the formula

1. This formulation is followed by an account of Ivan's excesses that writes them off as directed mostly at the recalcitrant traditionalist boyar elite and as largely unremarkable for their era: "In the time of Ivan IV all these terrible tortures and executions—which are so striking to us, which cause our hair to stand on end—in those days they were an ordinary matter, and not even a slight departure from the everyday" (Dolgorukii and Anofriev, *Putevoditel' po Moskve i okrestnostiam*, iv, 1st pagination). The portrait of Ivan is on i, 1st pagination, and that of Peter is on i, 4th pagination.

Figure 4: "Peter the Great Celebrates the Peace of Nystad," illustration from a popular history-education pamphlet, *Russkaia istoriia v dvadtsati chetyrekh kartinkakh* (St. Petersburg, 1866).

"a survey of opposed views" in everything from critical essays like Nikolai Mikhailovskii's "Ivan the Terrible in Russian Literature,"[2] to poetic treatments like Apollon Maikov's 1887 poem, "At the Grave of the Terrible One" (U groba groznogo):

> Account has been given of his sins and crimes;
> Witnesses have been called; sentence pronounced,
> But something higher still delays the confirmation,
> The crowd is still filled with doubts,
> And this silent tomb remains clothed in mystery . . .
> [. . .]
> O, if he were to rise now, in his funeral robe,
> And address the people, as of old:
> He'd say "I created a state, and in the present day
> It is still standing still, for a fourth century . . .
> Judge me now!"[3]

2. Mikhailovskii, "Ivan Groznyi v russkoi literature," in his *Sochineniia*, 6:127–220.
3. Maikov, "U groba Groznogo," in his *Polnoe sobranie sochinenii*, 2:166.

Invested with enormous significance for political mythology, Ivan and Peter could not be ignored. Nevertheless, like Maikov and his reader, all who attended to the two tsars' voices in this period faced the problem of managing a contradictory interpretive inheritance.

While mindful of this problem of the "echoes" of prior conceptions of history, I here concentrate on a distinct and less easily grasped shift, which relates not to the content but to the form of historical myth. In 1847, Kavelin had defined the distinction between the tsars in terms of contrasting talents or disciplines—Ivan was a "poet," whereas Peter was a "pragmatic individual."[4] About a decade later, Konstantin Aksakov articulated a similar analysis of Ivan in a review of the sixth volume of Sergei Solovev's history of Russia: "Ivan IV had an artistic nature; he was an artist of life. He apprehended appearances and was drawn by their superficial beauty. He understood artistically the good, seeing its beauty, and appreciated the beauty of repentance and of valor. Yet he also was drawn to horrors by their terrible spectacularity."[5]

The historian Nikolai Kostomarov expressed similar views in 1872, noting that from an early age Ivan "found pleasure in the pictorial qualities of evil."[6] One might be tempted to dismiss these remarks as mere metaphors—and anachronistic ones, at that. Yet these pronouncements resonate in striking manner with the contrasting positions of the two figures in Russian cultural life during the second half of the nineteenth century. As in the reign of Nicholas I, Peter remained an idol of official political rhetoric and, as the century wore on, the most important object of professional historical research and debate. Ivan, in contrast, although he was still rarely mentioned in political discourse and remained far less prominent in historical research, emerged as one of the most frequently portrayed historical figures on Russian operatic and theatrical stages. This is not to claim that there were no histories of Ivan or that Peter was never the subject of dramatic treatments. In general, however, the most culturally significant representations of the two figures corresponded to these different institutional contexts, and their "public images" were identified with alternate modes of representation.

Let us first consider "Peter's realm" of political rhetoric and official historical mythology. As in Pushkin's day, Ivan's scant presence in political discourse

4. Kavelin, "Vzgliad na iuridicheskii byt drevnei Rossii," in his *Sobranie sochinenii*, 1:5–66, here 47.

5. Aksakov, "Po povodu vi toma Istorii Rossii," in his *Polnoe sobranie sochinenii*, 1:167.

6. Kostomarov, *Russkaia istoriia*, 457. Kostomarov was a prominent historian of the middle decades of the century who mixed romantic nationalism with populism. The citation is drawn from his popular *Russian History in the Biographies of Her Leading Figures* (Russkaia istoriia v zhizneopisaniiakh ee glavneishikh deiatelei)—one of the most damning portraits of Ivan ever written. Kostomarov was also the author of a historical novel titled *Kudeiar* (1874), after the legendary cossack brigand who is its main character, in which Ivan appears as the apotheosis of bloodthirsty tyranny.

derived from his bloody reputation, which even after his partial rehabilitation remained too negative to allow him to serve as a triumphal example in Russian court rhetoric or political symbolism. Peter, in contrast, occupied an indisputable prominence in imperial ritual and political life as the model for state-sponsored social transformation. From the start of the reign of Alexander II, Russian public discourse was rife with comparisons of him to Peter as analogous reforming tsars. This rhetorical strategy reached a frenzied climax in 1872, when the Great Reforms were largely complete and Russians celebrated Peter's bicentennial on May 30 in one of the first true mass commemorations of Russian history. In his toast at a ceremonial banquet, one O. Bogoslavskii, deputy of the Novgorod zemstvo, reproduced the analogy between Peter I and Alexander II that was endlessly repeated in the newspapers and on the streets: "The worthy successor on the Russian throne has called out to his Truly Great Grandfather: 'Come and see!' . . . He has called out to the spirit of the Great Transformer, that it might descend into Russia from on high and bless our Tsar Liberator."[7]

In the twin capitals, in provincial seats of government and in far-flung regions, the first emperor's birthday was observed with extraordinary pomp. In St. Petersburg, the Imperial Court and chosen representatives of all military divisions dating from the Petrine era performed an elaborately choreographed religious, military, and naval ceremony involving chosen Petrine relics—his bullet-scarred helmet, sword, and so on—in the central squares of the city and on the Neva River, reportedly observed by hundreds of thousands of residents and visitors to the city.[8] In Moscow, events centered on the Polytechnic Exhibition, an industrial and scientific showcase of unmatched scale dedicated to the legacies of the great reformer, modern industry, and the achievements of empire—and which featured in a central pavilion the fabled "little boat" (botik) in which Peter first learned to sail and dreamt of his future naval conquests.

The bicentennial conjoined the Westernizers' historical vision and the political discourse of the reform era. Its aims were perhaps best expressed by Solovev in his celebrated public lectures at the Polytechnic Exhibition, which were attended by the cream of Moscow society. To be sure, Solovev, like many

7. "Vnutrennie izvestiia," *Pravitel'stvennyi vestnik* 140 (June 15, 1872), 3.

8. The festivities continued into the evening on the Tsaritsyn Meadow, where a gallery of portraits and historical paintings on Petrine themes as well as a large-scale map of the Russian Empire in Peter's era, accompanied by explanatory placards, were hung in a special pavilion. An account of Peter's life and activities, as presented in the exhibit, was printed in brochures distributed for free at the pavilion. The print run was ten thousand. For reports on the planning and execution of the celebrations, see "Vysochaishe utverzhdennye tseremonialy prazdnovaniia v S.-Peterburge 200-letiia so dnia rozhdeniia Imperatora Petra Velikogo," *Pravitel'stvennyi vestnik* 112 (May 12, 1872), 1; "Vnutrennie izvestiia," *Pravitel'stvennyi vestnik* 128 (May 31, 1872), 1; and "Vnutrennie izvestiia," *Pravitel'stvennyi vestnik* 130 (June 2, 1872), 2.

contemporary liberal thinkers, harbored profound doubts about the direction
of progressive reform and the worthiness of Russia's present ruler in comparison with Peter the Great.[9] Yet in his public lectures the historian elided these
doubts, and described Peter as a heroic leader of state-led social progress who
expressed in the purest form the essential being and great potential of the Russian people: "A great man is given only to a great people, and in comprehending the greatness of the man, we comprehend the greatness of the people. By
his activity, a great man erects a monument to his people; what people can
then refuse to erect a monument to the great man?"[10] In concluding, Solovev
called for the Petrine principle of progressive transformation to be inscribed as
a transcendent motto of Russian social life: "Let our celebration not be not
merely a reminiscence of the past; in remembering, let us fulfill the testament
of Peter: 'In the future, too, we must continue to labor and always strive to
anticipate the future, for lost time is as irreversible as death.' "[11]

Yet when we turn to representations of Russian history on stage, we find a
completely different state of affairs. This was "Ivan's kingdom." Despite the
overwhelming prominence of Peter in the Russian historical imagination, and
recognizing the dramatic and performative qualities of the bicentennial celebrations themselves, the great reformer was virtually absent from nineteenth-
century Russian theaters. A telling exception to this rule is Nikolai Polevoi's
patriotic play *The Grandfather of the Russian Fleet* (Dedushka russkogo flota,
1838), an absurd fluff piece centering on the construction of the legendary
Little Boat. The character of Peter himself appears here only in a brief "manifestation," mounted on a horse in the final seconds before the curtain as someone shouts out a paraphrase of Lomonosov "On your knees! He's not just a
tsar—he is your demigod, O Russia! Hurrah!"[12]

9. Despite the resonance of Solovev's rhetoric with the celebratory exaltation of Alexander
II as a "new Peter," in his private writings the historian expressed a rather different assessment
of the reigning emperor, indicative of a deep disappointment in reform efforts of his day and
the ensuing political crises of the 1870s and 1880s: "Historical transformations are carried out
with success by the likes of Peter the Great; but only misfortune follows when they are undertaken by a Louis XVI or an Alexander II. A reformer like Peter the Great, even on the steepest
incline, can rein in his horses with a strong hand—and the coach is secure. But reformers of the
second sort let the horses run at a gallop downhill, lacking the strength to restrain them, and
the coach is doomed to destruction" (Solov'ev, *Izbrannye trudy; Zapiski*, 346).

10. Ibid., 52.

11. Ibid., 179. Wortman's account of the Petrine bicentennial tends to view the entire
event through the lens of liberal dissatisfactions with Alexander II's leadership, concluding
that the celebration as a whole was a half-hearted affair. In my view, the celebrations were
characterized by a great divide between public and private sentiment and rhetoric, matching
the complexity both of the political stakes and of the historical discourse of the era. See
Wortman, *Scenarios of Power*, 2:120–25.

12. Polevoi, *Dramaticheskie proizvedeniia*, 43. The phrase "On your knees" may be a
reference to a legendary episode in Nicholas's biography, when during the cholera epidemic
of 1831 he confronted a maddened crowd on Moscow's Sennaia Square, commanding his
subjects to get on their knees and repent for their riotous actions. I am indebted to Ilya Vin-

Polevoi's work, which portrayed the first emperor without actually portraying him, met with the emperor's personal approval at its premiere in 1838 and became a "cult classic," perennially performed as a part of Petrine ritual on anniversaries and dedications of new monuments. Yet another example of Peter's conspicuous absence from Russian imperial stages is to be found in Modest Musorgskii's uncompleted final opera *Khovanshchina* (1880, completed in 1886 by Rimskii-Korsakov), in which the struggle between Muscovite civilization and Petrine modernization is represented—without, however, presenting Peter himself on stage.

Peter's notable absence from Russian theaters derived from a repeatedly affirmed censorial ruling, emanating from the throne itself, according to which no member of the Romanov dynasty could be portrayed on stage because of the perceived impropriety and popular nature of theatrical representation.[13] Yet this same censorial ban had the perhaps unintended effect of channeling the attention of playwrights and composers onto the history of the immediately preceding era—the Time of Troubles and the last reigns of the Rurikid grand princes and tsars—bringing to the fore Boris Godunov, the fictional peasant hero Ivan Susanin, and Ivan the Terrible. Perhaps the best-known dramatic works to focus on Ivan were the verse tragedies *The Death of Ivan the Terrible* (Smert' Ioanna Groznogo, 1866) by Aleksei K. Tolstoi and *Vasilisa Melent'eva* (1867) by Aleksandr Ostrovskii, Petr Chaikovskii's opera *The Oprichnik* (Oprichnik, 1874), and Nikolai Rimskii-Korsakov's operas *The Maid of Pskov* (Pskovitianka, 1872, rev. 1896) and *The Tsar's Bride* (Tsarskaia nevesta, 1899)—all of them important works that were performed frequently, subsequently canonized, and incorporated as a central part of the repertoire to the present day.

A great many other, now largely forgotten works also featured the Terrible Tsar, including the plays on which these prominent operas were based—Lev Mei's *The Tsar's Bride* (1849) and *The Maid of Pskov* (1860), Ivan Lazhechnikov's *The Oprichnik* (1859)—and lesser operatic transpositions of canonical literary works, including Anton Rubinstein's *The Merchant Kalashnikov* (Kupets Kalashnikov, 1880), based on Lermontov's poem, and Grigorii Kazachenko's *Prince Serebrianyi* (1892), derived from Tolstoi's novel.[14] And so, in some

itsky for this intriguing observation. On the historical event in question, see Shil'der, *Imperator Nikolai I*, 379–80; and Wortman, *Scenarios of Power*, 1:301–2.

13. Nicholas I issued a blanket decree allowing dramatic (but not operatic) representation of tsars predating the Romanov dynasty (with the exception of saints, such as Aleksandr Nevskii). Nicholas's opinion, expressed in connection with Pogodin's play on Peter, that depiction of the first emperor on stage would constitute a "blasphemy" illustrates the operations of this ruling. The ban was also applied to stage depiction of later rulers and was even extended at times into a censorial interdiction of plays representing Peter's ministers and generals. See Drizen, *Dramaticheskaia tsenzura*, 20–24, 81–82.

14. Here we may also mention earlier, celebratory theatrical works, such as Aleksandr Gruzintsov's verse tragedy *Kazan Conquered, or the Mercy of Tsar Ivan Vasilevich, Called the Terrible* (Pokorennaia Kazan', ili miloserdie tsaria Ioanna Vasil'evicha, poimenovannogo Gro-

measure simply as a consequence of decorum and censorship, whereas Peter ruled over Russian public life and professional historical discourse, Ivan came to dominate his own theatrical fiefdom.

Compounding the institutional factors that impeded stage portrayals of Peter and deemphasized Ivan's place in political rhetoric, the two figures were by their distinct positions in the course of national history ripe for exploitation in different arenas. The professionalization of Russian historical scholarship in the mid-nineteenth century was catalyzed by the liberalization of censorship and a sudden flood of new publications of historical documents, especially concerning the eighteenth century. The availability of a huge new fund of sources on the Petrine era coupled with openness to issues previously considered too sensitive for public exhumation focused historians' attention squarely on Peter.[15]

Ivan, by contrast, gained far less both in novel historical problems and in the discovery of new sources—and therefore occupied a less prominent place in historical research and debate.[16] In addition, the parties and policies of Peter's day translated easily and directly into the political landscape of nineteenth-century Russia. His reign was the founding moment of the modern era, the instant of the creation of the present itself, connected to current experience by an uninterrupted process of genealogical and institutional transmission. As "raw material," Peter was an overdetermined object of political rhetoric.[17] Ivan, in contrast, could not be viewed as connected to contemporary Russia by any continuous story of development—from the vantage point of the nineteenth century he stood on the other side of the profound historical ruptures of dynastic col-

---

znym, 1811), as well as Gavriil Derzhavin's libretto for an unrealized opera, *The Terrible Tsar, or The Conquest of Kazan* (Groznyi, ili pokorenie Kazani, 1814, published in 1868). Other minor dramatic representations devoted to the Terrible Tsar in later decades include E. Baryshev's *Third Marriage of Ivan IV* (Tretii brak Ioanna IV, 1846); Nikolai Chaev's *Terrible Tsar Ivan Vasilevich* (Groznyi tsar' Ivan Vasil'evich, 1868); Dmitrii Averkiev's *Fortress of Bondage* (Sloboda nevolia, 1867)—published but never performed as a result of censorial interdiction; an 1879 German-language treatment of Ivan's conduct of the Livonian War, intended for performance in the Baltic provinces, by a certain Bekstrom—never performed as a result of a censorial ban; and even a ballet depicting the fall of Kazan—Ivan was ultimately excised by the censor. See Drizen, *Dramaticheskaia tsenzura*, 12–18, 306, n. 349.

15. As Herzen observed in 1860: "The times of the Tatar Yoke are incomparably more familiar than is the reign of Catherine II or that of Paul" (A. I. Gertsen, review of *Zapiski* by I. V. Lopukhin, in his *Sobranie sochinenii*, 14:296–300, here 296).

16. It should be noted that, independently of policies of state secrecy, the totality of sources regarding Ivan's era is insignificant by comparison with the records left by Peter's modern bureaucracy. In this light, it is perhaps unsurprising that Solovev wrote only a single volume on the reign of Ivan the Terrible in his monumental history but devoted no fewer than six to Peter the Great and his era.

17. Finally, one may hypothesize that Peter's predominantly positive political valence impeded dramatic development of his character—as a study in personality, the first emperor devolved toward the uninteresting heroic but "pragmatic" individual, as Kavelin suggests. Ivan, in contrast, was by his nature "spectacular"—by his conflation of royal greatness and moral and political downfall perfectly suited to tragedy.

lapse and Peter's revolution. Rather than representing the historical foundations of the here and now, Ivan was significant as a mythic forebear from the
distant, epic past—an allegorically charged archetypical figure of the kind ideally suited for representation in the opera house or the poetic text.

Finally, one may note that the standard roles commonly assigned to the two
rulers in the Russian historical imagination matched their distinct cultural assignments. Already in the first half of the century, Peter was coming to appear to
Russians as an embodiment of abstract "historical" forces rather than as a human being—as we have seen in our discussion of such works as Lazhechnikov's
Last Novice and Pushkin's *Bronze Horseman*. In contrast, representations of
Ivan commonly revolved around two staple tragic plots—the tsar's unintended
murder of his own children, on one hand, and the destruction wrought by his
uncontrolled appetites and reign of terror on the romantic attachments of his
subjects, on the other. Once again, these quintessential motifs had already come
to the fore in the earlier portion of the century, as in Tolstoi's *Prince Serebriannyi*, for example. In contrast to the "abstraction" of Peter, Ivan appeared to his
audiences first and foremost as a psychologically complex individual, ruled by
emotions and libidinal attachments.

In summary, it was the combination of all the factors described above that
consigned Ivan and Peter to their very different positions in Russian social and
cultural life. Furthermore, the fundamental features of the two rulers' myths
cannot be separated from the institutional factors and pragmatic considerations
of political rhetoric that raised one onto a pedestal and the other onto the stage,
for their diverse cultural assignments reinforced their "meanings" just as much
as the latter dictated their institutional fates. The distinction between an "artistic" or "dramatic" Ivan and a "historical" or "political" Peter derived from
a complex dialectic between the incidental vagaries of institutional and political
history and the immanent features of the two figures. Ultimately, however, this
dynamic shaped their very substance as historical myths.

Bloody Fathers and Dead Children:
Tsarevich Aleksei and Tsarevich Ivan

A feuilleton published in the newspaper *Birzhevye vedomosti* on May 28,
1872, two days before the Petrine bicentennial, broke ranks with the triumphal rhetoric of the occasion. Noting sarcastically that he could predict what
would be said on the great day, the anonymous author offered a lovely parody
on the well-worn genre of eulogy to Peter's all-encompassing significance:

> The orators of Liakhta will demonstrate, to the point of exhaustion, that
> Peter's greatness lay precisely in the fact that he divined the world-historical
> meaning of Liakhta and for that reason brought it into being, for the good
> of humanity. The orators of Okhta will confirm, until they are red in the

face, that Peter clearly foresaw the great future awaiting his creation Okhta. University orators will prove that Peter, although he founded no universities, planned to do so. [. . .] Classicists will demonstrate that Peter worshipped antiquity, and realists will reveal that Peter valued above all the sciences of the real. In a word, all will be in keeping with the proverb: "Wherever you itch, that's where you scratch."

The author then gave his own deflationary account of Peter's significance, which, as he explained, lay not in the emperor's reforms, which had been largely unintended outgrowths of military or economic undertakings, but in his inauguration (also unintentional) of the characteristic Russian phenomenon of "fathers and children." According to the feuilletonist, Peter had created an "impassable abyss between the old and the new generations" and a "resultant dissent between fathers and children," bringing both positive and negative consequences for modern Russia. On one hand, the alienation of generations was a by-product of modernization and of the undoubtedly great benefits of Peter's "emancipation of Russian thought" from its "internal enslavement." On the other, the author is skeptical of the actual progressive utility of intergenerational conflict per se, which in his view leads too often not to the advance of enlightenment but to political stalemate. In any case, concludes the contrarian author, both in the past and in the present the sons' interest in innovation stems less from devotion to progress than from the simple desire to torment the fathers—an observation applied to Peter himself in the author's parting shot: "In Peter himself you may note many of the characteristic features of a 'son.' Truly, it would be a mistake to attribute a deep consciousness to Peter's actions. [. . .] Peter felt an instinctive hatred of the entire Old Russian way of life."

This last remark elegantly turns the tables on the rhetoric of the Petrine bicentennial. Since the publication in 1862 of Ivan Turgenev's *Fathers and Children* (Ottsy i deti), intergenerational conflict had been one of the most frequently deployed metaphors for the contest between reform and reaction in Russia; and in this sense, there is a certain justice in naming Peter the Great, idolized model for present reformers, as an unruly son, dragging his unenlightened fathers along the path of progress. Yet this brash application of the metaphor to Peter, especially when linked with the feuilletonist's blanket condemnation of "sons" as motivated by filial hatred, is jarring: Peter, one must recall, was the "father of the fatherland," who had raised up an infantile nation through patient instruction and strict education. Imagining the nation through the metaphor of the family, frequently projected against the family of the tsar, was a deeply ingrained reflex in the nineteenth-century Russian political imagination. As Richard Wortman has observed, the cult of the ruling family established with the reign of Nicholas I made it "a central symbol of the moral purity of autocracy—the purest form of absolute monarchy."[18] Yet as the battle

18. Wortman, *Scenarios of Power*, 1:334–35.

of metaphors above demonstrates, application of this rhetorical commonplace to Peter was complicated by his liminal inconstancies as at once rebellious son and founding father.

The family romance of Petrine history came to a head in connection with one of the most explosive topics of Russian historical scholarship in the decades leading up to the bicentennial: the scandal surrounding the death of Tsarevich Aleksei Petrovich. Here, Peter clearly appears in his role as paterfamilias. Yet the same episode reveals the violence embedded in the family romance of Petrine history, illustrating how "the reforms of Peter murdered the Muscovite order of things."[19]

Aleksei's mother was Peter's first wife, Evdokiia, whom the tsar forcibly committed to a monastery when the tsarevich was eight years old. According to the standard account of Aleksei's life, he never developed enthusiasm for Peter's policies as a result of his affections for his persecuted mother, who was herself an enemy of reform. The autocrat was consistently disappointed in his son for his weakness as a student and his incompetence in the business of governance and in military leadership. Fearing that his son's affections for "the old ways" would lead to the undoing of his own great projects, Peter compelled the now adult Aleksei to renounce his claim to the throne as soon as Tsaritsa Catherine I bore a rival heir in 1715. Yet the emperor continued to regard Aleksei as a threat and ordered that he either reform and prove his worthiness or enter a monastery. As all concerned were aware, neither option was much of a solution: the tsarevich could feign reform, reverse a renunciation of the throne, or emerge from a monastery to claim power.

Fearing his father's more decisive measures, Aleksei fled to Europe in 1716, where he and his serf concubine Efrosynia enjoyed the unenthusiastic protection of the Habsburg emperor Charles VI. He was ultimately convinced to return to Russia in 1718 with the promise of a pardon that would finally leave him in peace to marry Efrosynia and live a simple life confined to his villages and away from the court. However, it was not to be: the investigation into the tsarevich's flight eventually concluded that he was at the center of a palace conspiracy to place him on the throne and eliminate Peter. Tens of Aleksei's supporters, drinking partners, and confessors, ranging from simple members of the tsarevich's household to highly placed members of the court and the Imperial Senate, were tortured and publicly executed, their bodies left to rot on the hangman's spikes or dismembered and cast to the dogs. The tsarevich himself, condemned to the same fate, ultimately died in his cell.

From the time of the events themselves, the basic outlines of this scandalous episode were broadly known. Indeed, Peter intentionally subjected the tsarevich to a public trial in the Imperial Senate and made no effort to conceal the results of the official inquiry, promulgating an official "Investigative Case" (Rozysknoe

19. A. I. Gertsen, "Rossiia i Pol'sha; Otvety stat'iam, napechatannym v 'Przeglądie Rzeczy Polskich'; Pis'mo piatoe," in *Sobranie sochinenii*, 14:50–59, here 50.

delo) and "Announcement" (Ob'iavlenie) about the tsarevich's death in considerable print runs both in Russian and in translation into various European languages.[20] It seems clear that this open process was intended both to serve the pragmatic purpose of intimidating the tsarevich's sympathizers and to invest the affair with the formal clarity and legitimacy of the rational, impersonal law—certainly among the emperor's personal ideals.

Although the original printed versions of official announcements concerning the case were banned and destroyed during the brief reign of Peter II, Aleksei's son (1715–30, emperor from 1727), they were known to Petrine historians in translated versions during the eighteenth century and were republished in Russia with the approval of Nicholas I in 1829.[21] Yet, as might be expected, the official version of Aleksei's life was far from complete or accurate: little was known of the content of communications between Peter, Aleksei, and their agents; and the most explosive details of the affair, regarding the torture and death of the tsarevich, remained a state secret. According to the "Investigative Case," the tsarevich died of a stroke brought on when he learned of his death sentence.[22] But already at the time of the events themselves rumors circulated, hinting that Peter had ordered Aleksei's throat to be cut or for him to be suffocated or poisoned.[23] In sum, little was known by way of facts outside of the official account until the nineteenth century, and public discussion of the affair of the tsarevich was impossible before the era of Alexander II.

In 1858, Herzen's émigré press published a letter that purported to be from the pen of Captain of the Guard Aleksandr Rumiantsev, whom Peter initially sent to Europe to trace the whereabouts of the runaway tsarevich, and who played a central role in returning him to Russia and in the ensuing official investigation. This document, which is almost certainly a later forgery, offered a lurid blow-by-blow account of how Rumiantsev and three others had suffocated Aleksei in his cell at the express command of the emperor. This item perhaps served as the catalyst for the appearance in the following year of the sixth volume of Ustrialov's *History of the Reign of Peter the Great* (Istoriia tsarst-

---

20. Eidel'man, *Gertsen protiv samoderzhaviia*, 64–68.

21. On the publication history of materials relating to Aleksei, see ibid., 67–68.

22. "On being informed of his death sentence, the tsarevich collapsed into oblivion. After some time he recovered consciousness and began once again to express his repentance and to ask for his father's forgiveness before the assembled senators. Yet the prospect of such an unfortunate death had dealt such a powerful blow to his heart that he could not fully recover nor regain hope in his health, and [. . .] after accepting the final sacraments he passed away [. . .] on June 26, 1718." Cited in Eidel'man, *Gertsen protiv samoderzhaviia*, 62.

23. During the 1830s, Pushkin, in the course of research for his history of Peter the Great, gained access to significant materials from the imperial archives regarding the tsarevich, yet the poet's work was never completed. On the basis of forged diaries of James Bruce (Iakov Brius), Pushkin was convinced that the tsarevich had been poisoned. See Eidel'man, *Gertsen protiv samoderzhaviia*, 68–69; Feinberg, *Nezavershennye raboty Pushkina*, 144–50, 232–37.

vovaniia Petra Velikogo), which consisted in the publication and cautious analysis of a great many new documents, including previously unpublished official, diplomatic, and private correspondences, interrogation transcripts, and other materials. Rumiantsev's letter is the final document in the volume's appendixes, reproduced from the "many manuscript copies" in circulation, but the historian printed it merely to dismiss it as a probable fake.[24]

Ustrialov's volume served up the investigation and trial of Aleksei to the Russian educated public, evoking extensive discussion and published responses. The Moscow University historian Mikhail Pogodin answered the Petersburg historian with a public lecture that openly took up questions of the justice and legitimacy of the case against the tsarevich. Delivered first in Moscow and subsequently twice in Petersburg—once to the assembled Academy of Sciences and once in a public lecture in the fashionable concert hall of the Passazh market on Nevskii Prospekt—Pogodin's address served as the basis for a lengthy journal article that was quickly reprinted as a separate volume. Review articles on Ustrialov's volume by critically disposed voices in the thick journals—the left-leaning historians Mikhail Semevskii and Petr Pekarskii—offered alternate interpretations that derived parables of autocratic abuse and torture from the case of Aleksei. Once the initial furor had died down, the story of the tsarevich continued to occupy professional historians such as Solovev and Kostomarov, who used the episode to focus attention on the nature and implications of Peter's reign of enlightening violence.[25]

From the time of the trial itself, response and representation was shaped according to the overriding historical mythology of Peter's reign, which projected the opposition of father and son as both an archetypal familial conflict and a battle between the Imperial Russian future and the Old Russian past. Already in Peter's manifesto of February 3, 1718, in which he declared Aleksei unfit to inherit the throne and proclaimed his infant son Petr Petrovich as heir, this pattern is evident. Peter explains how he had hoped to inculcate in his son the values and skills of a modern ruler. But Aleksei "not only failed to devote himself to his education, but learned to hate it"; he "wasted his time with wicked and evil companions, of coarse and vulgar manners"; he spurned his wife, Princess Charlotte of Braunschweig-Wolfenbüttel, taking up with "a certain lazy serf girl." As a result:

> In consideration of his unworthiness and of all the aforementioned wicked deeds, We cannot in good conscience allow him to remain the heir to the Russian throne, knowing that he, by his improper conduct, will undo all the national glory and state benefit that has been achieved by God's grace and

24. Ustrialov, *Istoriia tsarstvovaniia Petra Velikogo*, 6:619–28.

25. Solov'ev, *Istoriia Rossii s drevneishikh vremen*, 9:105–91; Kostomarov, *Istoricheskie monografii*, 125–66.

our tireless efforts. For, as is known to all, we have accomplished with such great labor not only the return to our state provinces seized by enemies but also the addition of many new lands and important cities and the education of our people in all manner of useful military and civil sciences to the benefit and glory of the state.[26]

This and other public documents around the trial cast Aleksei as the "anti-Peter," who was opposed in principle and by character to social modernization and to its corollary of cultural and political contact with western Europe.

Subsequent interpreters followed Peter's cue, using Aleksei as a means to personalize the civilizational faults of the Muscovite past. As Ustrialov explained, the tsarevich had been infected in childhood by the evil predilections of his mother, "hardened in the superstitions of the past and hating everything that pleased Peter."[27] In his analysis, Solovev argues that Aleksei took after "educated men of the seventeenth century" such as his grandfather, Peter's father Aleksei Mikhailovich, and his uncle Fedor Alekseevich, who were "smart and curious [. . .] but slow to rise." Like them he was "incapable of persistent activity, of the tireless motion characteristic of his father; he was physically lazy and therefore a homebody who liked to learn about interesting things only from books and conversations."[28]

Historians dwelled on Aleksei's personal faults—his love of drink and of hazy conversations with bookish monks and priests, his impracticality and fearfulness, and his abusive relationship with his unhappy wife, who died giving birth to the future emperor Peter Alekseevich in 1715. His relationship with the domineering and ultimately traitorous serf Efrosynia appears as a symptom of his attachment to the "backwards" idiocy of the lower orders and a further illustration of his weak, effeminate character. In short, in the standard account that has persisted largely without critical examination to the present day, Aleksei has been represented as everything that Peter is not: a typical and damning example of Old Russian vice, superstition, and civilizational inferiority.[29]

---

26. *Polnoe sobranie zakonov,* 5:534–39.

27. Ustrialov, *Istoriia tsarstvovaniia Petra Velikogo,* 6:11.

28. Solov'ev, *Istoriia Rossii,* 9:109.

29. Paul Bushkovitch was the first historian to seriously question this interpretation. His work, which is based on an examination of the large body of unpublished archival materials relating to the case both in Europe and in Russia, concludes that Aleksei's worldview was actually far closer to "the piety of late Baroque Europe" than to any sort of caricature of "Old Russia." Furthermore, Bushkovitch reveals that the standard interpretation of the affair diminishes the extent to which Russian elites pinned their hopes on Aleksei as an opponent to Peter's reformist activities. Bushkovitch frames his research as an indictment of Ustrialov for an intentional falsification of history. In the interests of erasing an episode of aristocratic opposition to the throne from the national past, the St. Petersburg historian published a biased and edited selection of documents and a skewed analysis. I view Ustrial-

Perhaps the most striking feature of the debates around the case of the tsarevich during the 1850s and 1860s is their combination of fascination with the most gruesome details of seemingly illegitimate violence and a nearly unanimous exoneration of Peter's actions as historically necessary. Pogodin's work provides a stark example of this contradictory approach.[30] His preamble announces that the trial of the tsarevich is "one of the most important events in Russian history"—no less than "the border between ancient and new Russia, watered with the blood of a son, shed by a father."[31] Yet this transformation of Aleksei's ordeal into an echo of the Passion of Christ is not the only scriptural *topos* Pogodin activates:

> The judgment of contemporaries, with all their decisions and sentences, has been turned over to a higher judge—the judge of posterity, of history. The judges themselves, raised from their graves, join the ranks of those whom they once accused, awaiting with humility a new and most final earthly sentence.
>
> History's high calling! One feels an involuntary tremor in one's heart when one sees how the mightiest lord in the world, whose will never knew any limitations over his entire life and throughout the whole of his realm [. . .]; this lord, the transformer of a multitudinous nation, who with his strong arm propelled it, unwilling, along a wholly new path; this conqueror, legislator, founder; [. . .] I repeat, one feels an involuntary tremor in one's heart when one sees how, in short, Emperor Peter the Great is called to account for his deeds, how the last of his researchers may examine his deeds as they are laid bare in the most secret documents, may ask him questions that he cannot refuse to answer, may level accusations against which he can offer no justification.[32]

In intending to call the emperor to account, the historian hijacks the rhetoric of the Petrine historical documents themselves, which repeatedly emphasize humility by recognizing that earthly decisions will in turn be submitted to a higher judgment. Yet this higher instance is not posterity, but rather "the just and unerring last judgment of all-powerful God."[33]

---

ov's work less as a falsification than as the expression of his loyalty to a pre-scripted notion of the matter, derived from earlier accounts. See Bushkovitch, "Power and the Historian."

30. According to Pogodin's biographer, his lecture and monograph were virtually identical. See Barsukov, *Zhizn' i trudy M. P. Pogodina*, 17:258–63.

31. Pogodin, *Sud nad tsarevichem Alekseem Petrovichem*, 3.

32. Ibid., 1–2.

33. Peter himself admitted to being unfit to pass judgment since "it is natural to be able to see less in your own affairs than others can; just as doctors, no matter how talented they are, do not attempt to cure themselves." Therefore, "in order not to sin" he instructed the Imperial Senate to rule on the tsarevich's case, "not attending to his station but delivering justice

While Pogodin's gesture to the Passion would render Peter's sacrifice of his son an inscrutable act of the divine mover of history, his pretension to raise the dead from their graves, to call the judges to judgment, to make the last first would appear to usurp the place of the divine for the historian himself. And so at the start of his monograph, Pogodin's barrage of scriptural reference poses the question where authority ultimately lies: with the divine Peter who sacrificed his son to wash away the sins of Old Russia, or with the historian's secularized judgment day?

Pogodin proceeds to offer an account that is calculated to make inescapably clear the needlessness of Aleksei's death. In contrast to most other interpreters, Pogodin portrays the young tsarevich both as a brilliant student of military science and governance and as an adept agent of his father's will in the numerous tasks assigned to him. According to his account, Peter was grooming Aleksei for the throne until he fell afoul of a traditional stumbling block of palace politics: Catherine I produced a rival heir, and her party sought to discredit and disinherit Aleksei to cement her position in the bloodline. For Pogodin, Peter is a delusional victim of the machinations of his rivals and of his own paranoia—there is no plot, only a "seeming conspiracy"—and the tsar's demands that his son reform are self-fulfilling prophesies that render the tsarevich an enemy of the throne and unfit to rule by pronouncing him to be such. As a final touch, the historian paints a vivid picture of the barbarity of Peter's police methods, narrating such details as the vain pleas of suspected co-conspirators for final absolution as they slowly died, impaled on spikes. The violence and arbitrariness of Petrine justice is gruesomely plain:

> Wife, sisters, uncles, aunts, in-laws, friends, acquaintances, strangers, priests, confessors, those who saw, heard, might have guessed. We don't know anything! Didn't hear anything! Don't know? Didn't hear? Into the dungeon! And the unfortunates are tortured, their blood flows, they are crushed by fear and trepidation. They confess to invented crimes—their own and others'—and in consequence are subjected to more torture: three times, five times, ten times over! "Into the dungeon!" cry the merciless, savage judges. Have pity! There's not a drop of blood left in them; their eyes are sunken and extinguished; they've lost all understanding, all feeling; they no longer know what they are saying. Even the rack is fatigued, the dungeon exhausted; the axe has grown blunt, the knout dull.[34]

The historian, as it seems in passages like this, indeed claims the position of transcendent judge who can pass through the veil of time, enter the dungeon, and even plead for mercy toward the innocent victims of Peter's beastly brutality.

---

and therefore not damning your own souls, so that your consciences will be clean on the day of the last judgment" (Ustrialov, *Istoriia tsarstvovaniia Petra Velikogo*, 6:516).

34. Ibid., 79.

Yet despite the lucid conclusions held out by his narrative, Pogodin refuses to bring his argument to closure. He ends his account with a discussion of Peter's activities during the days of the tsarevich's trial, death, and burial:

> Judge for yourselves, gentlemen: what *was* this nature; how great was his strength of mind; how inexhaustible was his body; how firm was his will; how . . . inflammable was his heart—that at the same time as he was torturing his own son and tormenting innumerable others, he could devote himself as well to intellectual questions of the greatest importance, resolve legal briefs, define relations with European powers, conduct accounting affairs, measure ships, plant trees, order the collection of specimens of biological abnormality, and feast with his comrades? With such strength of spirit and body, beyond all human scale, his fear for the safety of his institutions was needless. Russia, propelled by Peter along a new path, was physically incapable of turning in any other direction.[35]

But then, in answer to the question "What sentence shall we pronounce over Peter?" Pogodin refers his listeners to the greatness of the Petrine accomplishment, to the "fateful deed that was somehow mysteriously demanded by history itself," to the "cruel suffering" that Peter must have experienced during the trial of the tsarevich, and which "his soul must be enduring even now, if he hears our deliberations." In the face of all this: "our tongues are incapable of pronouncing words of judgment. [. . .] We, Russians, can only pray for forgiveness of his sins and peace for his soul."[36] And so, after developing huge momentum toward the condemnation of Peter's actions, Pogodin hands authority back to the superhuman emperor, the unfathomable mysteries of history, and a truly divine, yet deferred, judgment.[37]

Pogodin's text outlines the peculiar mechanism that almost all voices in the debates over the fate of the tsarevich deployed in one way or another. At one and the same time they recognized the great extent of Peter's brutality, yet always returned to the blinding magnificence of his role in Russian history, setting up an opposition between the merely human matter of a bloody family confrontation and the grander exigencies of state or cosmic history. Solovev's authoritative account, published in the seventeenth volume of his history, projects this very opposition back onto the individuals in question in an exoneration of Peter even more compelling than Pogodin's. Although Solovev deemed the confrontation of father and son to be tragic, it had been a reflection of the "difficult and bloody battle that commonly marks periods of great transformation

35. Ibid., 85.
36. Ibid., 85–86.
37. One could, of course, read Pogodin's refusal to judge the first emperor as a strategy to appease the censor. However, the historian's sincere piety before the figure of Peter is well documented. The reactions of contemporaries who knew Pogodin reveal that they, at least, interpreted the historian's statements as sincere. See Barsukov, *Zhizn' i trudy M. P. Pogodina*, 17:263–71.

in the lives of nations, a battle that is not restricted to the social arena but penetrates to the sacred interior of the home, creating antagonism in the family itself." In Solovev's version, the conflict between Aleksei and Peter was not merely a clash of Russia's past and its future, projected into private life, but a struggle between the principles of private interest and the public good:

> The distinction between the father and the son consists in the fact that, on one hand, the father's house was always too small for him, even if that house was a palace—he only had enough room to breathe when he was journeying across Russia, Europe, across the wide ocean. The son, on the other hand, could not endure these journeys, these broad open spaces, and yearned for the house, for the intimate family circle where it was quiet, cozy and peaceful. [. . .] The son of the tsar, of the hero-transformer, had the humble character of a private person, concerned chiefly with fuel for the stove.[38]

For Solovev, this "private person" is moved by simple-minded, domestic desires, expressed in the purest form in Aleksei's passion for his serf concubine. He identifies the tsarevich not with any rival political direction at all but with the negation of politics, rendering his unfitness to rule axiomatic. He emerges not as a rival to the throne but as an unhappy and powerless pawn, subject to the manipulation of its enemies. Peter, in contrast, is so fully identified with the state as to be replaced by it: stepping lightly around the matter of the tsarevich's manner of death and Peter's possible involvement, Solovev successively divorces the emperor as an individual from the trial and investigation, focusing on the authority of the Senate in delivering the tsarevich's death sentence. Whereas the tsarevich was clearly an unhappy victim, he was a victim not of the tyranny of his father but of the exigencies of history and the impersonality of law. Solovev's treatment of the case demonstrated the insignificance of the merely personal, of the body and of bodily interests, before the rationality of the state and of history itself.

All these treatments of the case of Tsarevich Aleksei, ranging from Pogodin's to Solovev's and including many other voices as well, manifest the same peculiar combination of fascination with and justification of the violence of this episode. In this, they exemplify the persistent anxieties afflicting the historical mythology of Peter during the Epoch of the Great Reforms. Ironically, the effort to bury the body of the tsarevich may just as easily be viewed as a monument that marks its presence, mimicking the general structure of Petrine historical mythology, in which the blanket of heroism is continuously dislodged by the trauma—the chosen but disavowed collective trial—that it covers.

Turning back to Ustrialov, the first attempt at a historical interpretation of the affair, the ironic implications of the historian's efforts are apparent in the publication history of the work. The first three volumes of his *History of the*

---

38. Solov'ev, *Istoriia Rossii*, 9:131–32.

Reign of Peter the Great had been published in 1858, followed a year later by the sixth, containing the story of Aleksei. The fourth was to appear only in 1863, while the projected fifth and final volume was never completed. According to his own account, Ustrialov had been at work on the case of the tsarevich since the very start of his research for the *History of the Reign of Peter* in 1846, and he seems to have produced the sixth volume out of order as a sort of proleptic appendix that had to be gotten out of the way before taking care of the main events of Peter's reign—a necessary yet somehow extraneous comment that had to be ejected from the overarching narrative he sought to shape.

Rumiantsev's purported account of the grisly details of the tsarevich's death—the final item in Ustrialov's work, published only to be dismissed as inauthentic—occupies a place within the sixth volume analogous to the position of the volume itself within the *History* as a whole. Yet given the historian's failure to bring his project to completion, the lurid tale of the sixth volume and the "alien" germ of Rumiantsev's letter might also be seen as an eruption of Petrine historical trauma, rendering the clean imperatives of Russian history obscure and narrative closure ultimately impossible.[39] More than any other document, precisely because of its forged nature, the Rumiantsev letter renders in sharp relief the historical fantasy of the era. As nineteenth-century Russians debated the story of the tsarevich's death, they persistently conjured up and just as persistently disavowed a single troubling image—an image of the all-powerful, patriarchal state's horrific, ritual humiliation of private interests, of the body, and of the individual in an act of murderous rape:

> Then Tolstoi, stepping closer to him, said: "Lord tsarevich, by the judgment of the finest people of the Russian land you have been sentenced to die for your many betrayals of your royal father and your fatherland. We have come to you by the order of his royal majesty to carry out that sentence. For that reason, prepare yourself by prayer and repentance for your demise, for the time of your living is already close to its end." As soon as the tsarevich heard these words he raised a great cry and called for help, but failing to elicit any response he began to cry bitterly, saying, "Woe is me, poor me, born of the tsar's blood. Wouldn't I have been better off to have been born the lowliest subject?" Then Tolstoi, consoling the tsarevich, said, "The Lord, as your father, has forgiven you for your sins and will pray for your soul; but as Lord and Monarch, he cannot forgive your treasons and oath breaking, fearing to subject his fatherland to some evil. Therefore, leave your wails and tears, befitting only for women, accept your fate in a manner suitable for one of royal blood, and say your final prayers for forgiveness." But the tsarevich did not listen, and cried and cursed his

---

39. See Ustrialov's own commentary on the volume in his introduction: Ustrialov, *Istoriia tsarstvovaniia Petra Velikogo*, 6:6–7. Also see Eidel'man, *Gertsen protiv samoderzhaviia*, 69–72; and Bushkovitch, "Power and the Historian," 201–4.

father, calling him a filicide. And when we saw that the tsarevich would not pray, we laid hands on him and placed him on his knees, and one of us, from my fear I forget who, began to speak for him. [. . .] And then we threw the tsarevich onto his back on his bed and, taking two pillows from the head of the bed, we covered his face and held him down until his legs and arms stopped moving and his heart stopped beating, which happened quickly, given his infirmity.

—⁂—

If anything in the history of Peter's reign is suited for theatrical representation, it is his conflict with his son, which presents perfect material for tragedy with its age-old concern with fatal intergenerational conflict. Nineteenth-century Russians did not overlook the dramatic potential of Aleksei's bloody fate, but they were stymied in their efforts to exploit it. In 1831, Pogodin devoted the apologetic play *Peter I* (Petr I) to the case of the tsarevich, but it was immediately banned from theaters by the express order of Nicholas I and could not even be published until after the historical revelations of Alexander II's reign. The bicentenary year 1872 brought the publication of Dmitrii Averkiev's play on the same topic, *Peter and Aleksei* (Petr i Aleksei). Neither work was ever approved for performance in the imperial period. Yet here, one of the more startling, because completely accidental, convergences in the history of Ivan and Peter lucidly illustrates their divergent institutional fates. Peter was not the only Russian ruler to have killed an adult son. In 1581, in a fit of rage that sources explain variously, Ivan struck his heir apparent, also named Ivan, in the temple with his staff, killing him (inadvertently, it seems). The killing of Tsarevich Ivan was a standard element in historical accounts of Ivan, figuring as a climactic scene in Karamzin's history. Yet in contrast to the case of Aleksei, the death of Tsarevich Ivan offered mid-century Russian historians little by way of new evidence or argument, and for this reason it gave rise to no comparable ferment in historical scholarship. However, the episode's similar potential for dramatic representation, not subject to the automatic censorial interdiction pertaining to Peter, was fully realized, both in treatments of historical events as such and in fictional accounts that displaced Ivan's filicide onto the deaths of other, imaginary offspring of the Terrible Tsar.

The most important dramatic meditation on the death of Tsarevich Ivan was Aleksei K. Tolstoi's 1866 verse tragedy *The Death of Ivan the Terrible*, the first installment in what was to become a trilogy of historical dramas (the two subsequent plays concerned the reigns of Fedor Ivanovich and of Boris Godunov, the latter character being the linchpin of the trilogy as a whole).[40] As with

40. Some members of the Imperial Censorship Committee found that Tolstoi's representation of Ivan's despotism "calumnied" the tsar in unacceptable fashion. However, the majority of committee members reasoned that the horrors represented in the play derived from the historical specificities of the tsar's personality and of his times, presenting "no analogy with contemporary times" and that therefore the play "by no means undermines the princi-

Tolstoi's novella on Ivan, the play is based primarily on Karamzin's history.[41] Yet in distinction from Romantic historical fiction, which by focusing attention on a fictional character who witnesses great events holds history's great figures at a certain distance, historical drama typically concentrates attention directly on the experience of the great of the world. The play opens with an aged Tsar Ivan in deep depression after the accidental slaying of Tsarevich Ivan. The tsar has informed his boyars that he no longer wishes to rule and will retire to a monastery and has ordered them to select a replacement for him, since his other adult son, Fedor, is so feeble-minded as to be unfit to rule, and Dmitrii, his son by his last wife, Mariia Nagaia, is still in his infancy. Ivan's advisor, the masterful politician Boris Godunov, manipulates the boyars into rejecting the tsar's command and begging him to continue to rule, for this is in Godunov's interests. As it turns out, Ivan's desire to give up his throne has faded. Good news from the ongoing Livonian War and a provocative letter from the traitor Andrei Kurbskii have renewed Ivan's desire to rule. Ivan begins to negotiate with the English ambassadors to marry Lady Hastings, announcing his intentions to send Tsaritsa Mariia to a nunnery.

Ivan's new lustiness and desire for power is short-lived: granting an audience to the Polish envoy, the tsar expects an offer of an advantageous peace but instead learns that the war has taken a turn for the worse and that the Swedes and the Tatars are also attacking Muscovy. This blow shatters his will to rule and his health. Seeing a sign of his imminent demise in a comet, Ivan calls on magicians to predict his end. They inform him that he will die on March 18, the feast of St. Cyril. The same magicians predict to Godunov that he will one day become tsar.

Ivan, anticipating his downfall, offers a disgraceful peace to Poland and advises the "womanish" Tsarevich Fedor that when he assumes power he should follow the advice of Godunov in all things. In the final act, the day of Ivan's predicted death arrives, and Ivan feels somewhat recovered, but Godunov learns from his doctors that the tsar's condition is so fragile that any upset could cause his convulsive death. Ivan, convincing himself that he will live on, lays plans to burn the magicians alive the next day and sends Godunov to inform

---

ple of autocracy." The work was allowed with minor censorial impositions: the symbolic attributes of the tsar's power were not to be displayed on stage. Subsequently, however, as a result of a scandalous public reaction to the play in Voronezh in 1868, the play was banned for performance in the provinces by the direct order of the tsar. See Drizen, *Dramaticheskaia tsenzura*, 156, 163. On Tolstoi's dramatic conceptions, with concentration on the final play in the trilogy, see Emerson, "Pretenders to History."

41. Most of the events presented in the play are related in Karamzin's work, yet Tolstoi adds fictional characters and considerably compresses the chronology of the final years of Ivan's life. See I. G. Iampol'skii's commentaries to the play for a fuller exploration of Tolstoi's reliance on Karamzin, in A. K. Tolstoi, *Sobranie sochinenii*, 3:508–15. Emerson notes Tolstoi's close friendship with Kostomarov, which undoubtedly influenced his work on the trilogy ("Pretenders to History," 273–74).

the unfortunates of their death sentence. When he returns, however, the crafty advisor tells Ivan that the magicians claim, "their science is correct . . . St. Cyril's day is not yet over." Ivan, recognizing this as an attempt to kill him, flies into a rage:

> Not yet over?—St. Cyril's day?—You dare—
> You dare look me in the eyes—villain!—You—you—
> I see it in your gaze!—To murder me—
> You've come to murder!—Traitor!—Executioners!—
> Fedor!—Son!—Don't believe him!—He's a thief!—
> Don't believe him—Ah!
> (3:137)[42]

Ivan dies, Fedor does not hear Ivan's warning, and Godunov quickly takes advantage of his complete power over the new ruler to banish his own political enemies and to send Tsaritsa Mariia and the infant Dmitrii to Uglich.

Tolstoi's evocation of the death of Tsarevich Ivan to frame the action of his tragedy activates many of the same elements of the historical imagination present in debates over the case of Aleksei Petrovich, but it organizes these elements in a sharply contrasting configuration. In distinction from the notion of Peter's son as his rival and antitype, historical and literary mythology identified Ivan the son with Ivan the father as a similarly despotic and depraved nature. Karamzin, largely on the basis of the tsarevich's demonstrable presence during episodes of the elder Ivan's despotic brutality, considered that the son had inherited the flaws of the father—describing, for instance, how the tsarevich participated in the bloody massacres of Novgorod, "as if to deprive Russians of all hope for a better reign to come!"[43] And so, rather than the elimination of a threatening rival, as the death of Aleksei was thought to have been, the tsarevich's murder resonates with the death of Ivan the Terrible himself and acts out the downfall of the principles associated with him. The circular action of the play, which begins with the death of one Ivan and ends with the death of another, turns the murder of the tsarevich, a reflection of the tsar's brutal violence, back on himself. In this manner, Tolstoi makes Ivan responsible for his own demise—in killing the tsarevich, he kills himself.

---

42. The work is reproduced in A. K. Tolstoi, *Sobranie sochinenii*, 3:5–144. References to this edition are given in text.

43. Karamzin, *Istoriia*, 9:98. This was the characterization that Tolstoi himself popularized in his *Prince Serebrianyi*. There is little hard evidence on the character of Tsarevich Ivan, whose presence at and participation in the activities of the court of Ivan the father would have been expected as a matter of course and so cannot really be attributed to his personal volition. Solovev, a more careful reader of sources than Karamzin, offers no characterization of Tsarevich Ivan at all—perhaps in a reflection of his overall positive vision of the father Ivan, and perhaps simply because he saw little real evidence concerning the personality of the tsarevich. Imaginative treatments have tended to follow Karamzin's lead, making Tsarevich Ivan into a miniature Ivan.

The implications of these twinned deaths extend far beyond the end of Ivan's reign. As a result of the death of Tsarevich Ivan, the succession passed to the physically and intellectually weak Fedor (1557–98, tsar from 1584), who died without issue, ending the Rurikid dynasty, leading in turn to the reign of Boris Godunov (1551–1605, tsar from 1598) and finally to the ensuing interregnum known as the Time of Troubles (1605–13). In this sense, in killing his son, Ivan brings about not only his own downfall but that of the dynasty itself.

These larger implications are already fully evident in *The Death of Ivan the Terrible*, which establishes the character and intent of both Fedor and Boris with an eye toward later historical developments, and in the structure of the dramatic trilogy, which from the originative scene of Ivan's filicide unpacks the fate of Muscovite Russia in toto. Whereas Russians envisioned Aleksei's death as a sacrifice that was necessary to ensure the continuity of Petrine civilization— the death of Tsarevich Ivan appeared as the symbolic kernel of dynastic collapse and historical discontinuity.

Tolstoi does not render this historical fissure merely as a final downfall, effectively ending Ivan's reign of terror. The structure of this play, in which one death calls for another, is repeated in the trilogy as a whole, in which one tragedy calls for another. And most compellingly: one killing calls for another. Whereas the slaying of Tsarevich Ivan gives the action its initial impetus, *The Death of Ivan the Terrible* anticipates and sets the stage for the murder of his youngest brother, Tsarevich Dmitrii. In their fateful interview with Godunov, the magicians inform him that:

> Your constellation is intertwined
> With those of enthroned lords of the land,
> But three stars still outshine
> Your greatness. [. . .]
> (3:117)

Godunov's three rivals are Ivan, Fedor, and the infant Dmitrii, who all must die before he can assume power himself. It is this key revelation that, in a self-fulfilling prophecy, plants the seeds of slaughter in Godunov. He has already been revealed as gifted in governance, but he is driven to the exercise of power more out of personal vanity than any sense of idealism. This interview catalyzes his decision to speed destiny along, first through the calculating murder of Ivan and later through the murder of Dmitrii, which he orchestrates in the course of the second play in Tolstoi's trilogy, *Tsar Fedor*.[44] The murder of Tsarevich Ivan is the first in a series of unlawful deaths, echoing forward toward the mass violence of the Time of Troubles and to Godunov's ultimate pronouncement that "from evil only evil is born—it's all of a piece" (3:442).

---

44. On historical views concerning Boris Godunov's involvement in the death of Tsarevich Dmitrii, see Vernadsky, "Death of the Tsarevich Dmitry"; and Emerson, *Boris Godunov*, 48–61.

So although *The Death of Ivan the Terrible* acts out the self-destruction of bloody, autocratic violence—a story of rupture and discontinuity—this murderous cycle echoes forward into subsequent ages, threatening to reemerge again and again up through the Russian present itself in an uncontrollable continuity.

Tolstoi's tragedy mobilizes tensions between private and state interests, between individual bodily desires and the needs of the nation's collective body similar to those evoked in accounts of the death of Peter's son. Ivan's downfall is his inability to control his animal urges, his sexual desires, and his taste for violence in order to pursue the collective good. The death of the tsarevich itself is, of course, a result of Ivan's unbridled rage. Godunov's will to rule derives from his vain desire for power. Ivan's pursuit of a new marriage at his advanced age is presented as a sinful distraction from matters of state. And in Tolstoi's most compelling illustration of the destructive potential of emotion, Ivan's death is the result of his own wild anger, skillfully directed by the crafty Godunov. In this, the tragedy of Ivan and his son is a mirror image of the conflict of Peter and Aleksei, demonstrating the transcendence of state interests over merely personal or carnal needs, not as a justification for the intergenerational violence of Aleksei's execution but as a foundation for condemning the catastrophic intergenerational violence of Tsarevich Ivan's murder.

While accurate, this formula fails to capture the full significance of bodies and emotion in the historical mythology of Ivan and his children as it appeared on the stages of Russian theaters and opera houses. The complexity of the intimate emotional life of the despot is most visible in a different set of works devoted to Ivan and his offspring, which focus not on the historical material of the tsarevich's death but on a fictional case of filicidal bloodshed. Lev Mei's verse tragedy *The Maid of Pskov* was first published in 1860 and, despite some censorial interference, formed a part of the theatrical repertoire during subsequent decades.[45] Eight years later, in 1868, the ambitious young composer Nikolai Rimskii-Korsakov undertook an opera of the same name on the basis of Mei's play, producing a libretto with the help of the composer Petr Chaikovskii, the author Vsevolod Krestovskii, and the critic Vladimir Stasov. Having passed through some censorial interventions, the opera premiered in 1873 and was well received in this first redaction.[46] Later, Rimskii-Korsakov was to revise his work twice, in 1894 creating the version that has formed a part of the operatic canon since that time. Like Tolstoi's play, Mei's drama and

---

45. The play was initially approved for performance in 1861 but subsequently withdrawn by a decision of the censor: "The given drama presents a historically accurate depiction of the horrible epoch of Ivan the Terrible and a vivid representation of the *veche* of Pskov with its unruly freedoms. Such plays have always been banned." It was then reapproved for performance in 1865 with the omission of some provocative rebellious comments by the youth of Pskov. See K. K. Bukhmeier, "L. A. Mei," introduction to Mei, *Izbrannye proizvedeniia*, 39–40; and Drizen, *Dramaticheskaia tsenzura*, 160–61.

46. On the censorship's reaction to the opera *The Maid of Pskov*, see Drizen, *Dramaticheskaia tsenzura*, 161; Rimskii-Korsakov, *My Musical Life*, 125–33.

Rimskii-Korsakov's opera about the ill-fated maid of Pskov extract lessons in the dangers of unbridled passions and the tragedy of self-reflective violence from the history of Ivan's reign. Yet in contrast to Tolstoi, Mei and Rimskii-Korsakov also hold out the possibility that individual needs and bodily desires might ultimately be reconciled with state rationality and interest.

Whereas Tolstoi's account had relied on Karamzin's *History*, Mei's *Maid of Pskov* was animated in large part by Solovev's vision of Ivan IV. As Richard Taruskin has observed, Mei's Ivan himself debates the merits of the traumatic versus heroic readings of his reign—a further example of the "survey of interpretations" formula common in this era.[47] In the end, however, the tsar justifies his brutality by reference to the great imperatives of state building. The action of the drama follows suit, envisioning Ivan immediately after the bloodletting at Novgorod, which is described in a poetic redaction of the most lurid historical details of tortured, broken bodies:

> For a whole month now, from the bridge over the Volkhov
> They've thrown tormented folk into the seething waters:
> First they tie their arms with rope
> And bind their legs, then they torture them
> With a burning substance—brimstone, they call it—
> And cast them, burning, from the bridge into the waters . . .
> And if anyone floats up, they catch him
> With boathooks and stab him with a poleax
> Or slice his head off with an ax.
> Infants are bound to mothers—
> And thrown into the water, too.
> (475)[48]

Despite the horror of such gruesome violence, Mei views the slaughter at Novgorod as justified: Ivan's cruel retribution was elicited by the traditionally independent city's refusal to accept to the authority of the Moscow throne and, possibly, by the city elites' intent to betray the tsar and give allegiance to the Polish crown. Ivan himself informs Boris Godunov and Tsarevich Ivan of the basis of his historical and political vision:

> Vanya, here's the testament of your father for you:
> If God decides to call me to him
> And you will be the tsar of all Rus,
> Let the virgin intercessor keep you—lest you offend
> *One of these little ones . . .* Remember:
> Only that kingdom is strong and great,

---

47. Taruskin, "The Present in the Past," 145–46. My reading of this opera owes a particular debt to Taruskin's interpretation.

48. From L. A. Mei, "Pskovitianka," in his *Izbrannye proizvedeniia*, 423–535. References to this edition are given in text.

In which the people knows that it possesses
Only one lord, just as in one flock there can be only one pastor. . . .
   If the sheep
Get freedom by the shepherd—the whole herd perishes! . . .
And not from wolves, either: they will tear at one another
And cast their guilt off on the dogs. . . .
How I desire to achieve my aims,
And bind Russia in a law like armor,
But will God grant me reason and strength to do so?
(514)

In short, the play's view of history resonates with Solovev's teleological conception, which acknowledges that Ivan was frighteningly, excessively cruel but places this mayhem in service to the centuries-long imperative of constructing a great Russian state.

Yet the action of the play is not simply historical or even chiefly concerned with this historical plot. It is concerned with Ivan's deeds in Pskov, which escaped the fate of Novgorod by submitting to the tsar. Instead of representing overt violence between rebellious subjects and the cruel authority of the state, Mei projects the conflict between private interests and rationality onto the intimate relationships of the tsar himself. Note that the passage above ties Ivan's imagination of the great future of the state to an ultimately illusory vision of Tsarevich Ivan's future reign. In this, Mei reminds his audience that Ivan's excessive violence, even if seen as legitimate in a long historical perspective, struck down not only potentially rebellious subjects but the tsar's loved ones and the tsar himself.

Mei fully explores tragic intergenerational violence by means of the fictional main character of the play, the eponymous maid of Pskov. Olga is Ivan's illegitimate child, whom he recognizes only as he is imposing his law on the people of Pskov. Olga herself, who never learns of her parentage, is the play's chief representative of a properly patriotic love for the Russian tsar—she is moved beyond comprehension in anticipation of the tsar's arrival in Pskov. While her fellow Pskovians are infected by a sick fear at Ivan's arrival, Olga gazes at the tsar "lovingly" (507). The young girl's romantic interest is the hotheaded Mikhail Tucha. Unlike the older and wiser city leaders who submit to Ivan's authority, Tucha raises an armed resistance to the tsar's forces. In the play's final act Olga is apprehended by the tsar's men on her way to a tryst with her lover and brought to Ivan's camp in the forest. When the rebels attack, apparently with the chief purpose of freeing Olga, Tucha is killed. Olga, in despair, commits suicide.

Note the complete parallelism of Olga's illegitimate love for Tucha and Ivan's illegitimate liaison with her mother: Ivan, like Olga, is caught between his lawless intimate attachments and his devotion to the state. In the end, these warring attachments are impossible to reconcile: the tsar's just exercise of authority over the rebels leads to the death of his own beloved child. In this, Mei deploys a tragic nexus similar to that of Tolstoi's play: the circularity of despotic violence, striking back at Ivan, acts out the fatal dangers of the tsar's emotional excess, of his unbridled sexuality and his boundless violence.

Yet in contrast to Tolstoi's drama, Mei's play, despite its reference to the fate of Tsarevich Ivan, renders the bloody collision of state violence and bodily desires as Ivan's personal tragedy—for the death of Olga strikes not at the dynasty but rather at the tsar's heart. It is only at a higher level of abstraction, with far less damning implications, that Mei's tragedy projects the tsar's personal story back onto the political. In this connection, *The Maid of Pskov* consistently impedes the opposition of intimate passions and state rationality that functions so cleanly and completely in Tolstoi's play. On one hand, Olga's loving attachment for Ivan as tsar is founded on her secret filial relationship to him: as a child she was taught to pray for her "father and lord" and even saw the tsar Ivan in her dreams (530). On the other hand, the tsar's decision to spare Pskov is motivated by his recognition of Olga as she offers him a greeting gift of bread and salt. In this projection of the abstract relationship of throne to subject onto the personal ties of father and child, the play holds out a vision of a universe in which these bonds would in fact coincide—a realm that would perfectly realize the metaphor of the tsar's paternal care for his loving subjects that was so key to the political rhetoric of nineteenth-century Russia.

This unrealized potential is figured in the final scene of the play, in which Ivan witnesses Olga's death and comprehends the catastrophe that has occurred. "Showering her with kisses," Ivan is informed by his physician that "only God may raise the dead" in a cathartic scene of repentance that offers the hope for a Christian transcendence of the fateful conflict of body and state (535). Rimskii-Korsakov's operatic version of the curtain scene amplifies this range of significance even further, following a lament by Ivan with a concluding chorus that explicitly claims Olga's death as a Christian sacrifice that reconciles Pskov with the authority of Muscovy and saves the city from the tsar's bloody punishment:

> People of Pskov, Orthodox people,
> The will of God has come to pass.
> For your native Pskov, for your love
> You have given, Olga: life, beauty, and youth.
> Russian people, people of Pskov,
> Let us forget our ancient quarrels
> And pray for her soul:
> Let the Lord forgive her sins,
> God's mercy is eternal and without limit![49]

Ultimately, *The Death of Ivan the Terrible* and *The Maid of Pskov* present radically different visions of how the tragic collision of state and individual in

---

49. Rimskii-Korsakov, *Maid of Pskov*, 283–85.

Ivan's filicidal violence attaches to the longer perspectives of Russian history and to the nineteenth-century present. Tolstoi's work functions as a classical tragedy, in which the consequences of ancient sin echo ironically and uncontrollably forward in time. Mei's and Rimskii-Korsakov's dramas, in keeping with their justification of Ivan's ancient bloodshed in light of the grander imperatives of the state and its historical fate, offered up the tsar's repentance as a redemptive moment of Christian transcendence, liberating the Russian present from the traumatic shadows of the national past.

Finally, let us view this tradition of theatrical representations of Ivan and his murdered children together with the story of Peter and his son that unfolded in parallel, cordoned off in the separate realm of historiography. No intertextual references join these discursive contexts together as part of a content to be interpreted or authorial intention, either subtle or overt. Rather, these similar stories of intergenerational violence are disparate expressions of an integral cultural mechanism lying at a deeper level of the historical imaginary, which drove Russians' obsessive return to the problems of autocratic might and bloodshed in the service of progress and enlightenment. The total cultural field of these countless benevolent or despotic father-tsars and murdered or accidentally killed subject-children—Ivan, Peter, Tsarevich Ivan, Tsarevich Aleksei, Olga, Tsarevich Dmitrii, not to mention their echoes in Turgenev's *Fathers and Children* or in Pushkin's *Bronze Horseman*—is the context in which all these works individually must be interpreted. And in that context, each may be seen as a treatment of the basic political and historical dilemmas of nineteenth-century Russia: How can progress be served by autocracy? Can the violence of the regime's founding be left behind by later generations, or does its seed remain in later rulers' relationships to their subjects? Is Alexander a new Peter, or could he be a new Ivan? Yet the "disarticulation" of this cultural mechanism—in which Ivan and Peter, despotism and enlightenment, and terror and greatness seldom came together in one story, analysis, or institutional frame—was also important to its social function. For precisely this peculiar feature—the distance of Peter from Ivan—maintained a collective identity based on the celebration of greatness combined with the disavowal of terror.

. . . and Canvas: The Murdered Tsareviches in Historical Painting

The resonances between the stories of Aleksei and Tsarevich Ivan—each in its own way an expression of anxiety over the conflict of body and state, private and public, ancient suffering and modern prosperity—are all the more striking in light of their largely separate fates in the distinct cultural institutions of historiography and theater. Tracing the stories of the murdered tsareviches forward brings us to the moment in these decades when they came closest to being fully articulated together and brings us to a cultural arena that occupies

Figure 5: *Peter I Interrogates Tsarevich Aleksei Petrovich at Peterhof*, by Nikolai Ge, 1871, State
Tretiakov Gallery (Moscow, Russia). Reproduced with permission.

something of a mediating position between history and politics, on one hand,
and the stage, on the other: that of historical painting.

Nikolai Ge's *Peter I Interrogates Tsarevich Aleksei Petrovich at Peterhof*
(Petr I doprashivaet tsarevicha Alekseia Petrovicha v Petergofe, 1871, fig. 5)
was first exhibited in 1871 and 1872 at the inaugural show of the Association
of Itinerant Art Exhibitions—the first triumph in the Itinerants' effort to break
the formerly all-powerful system of imperial patronage and academic adjudica-
tion and exhibition in the visual arts.[50] Ge's painting coincided with the heightened interest in Peter occasioned by the 1872 bicentennial of his birth. By this
time, the heated historical debates of the early to mid-1860s concerning Aleksei's fate had largely subsided, but Ge's painting quickly sparked a reprise of
the scandal, provoking a new storm of controversy concerning both the interpretation of the historical events depicted and the proper interpretation of the
work of art itself. Critical responses to the painting retrace the anxieties evident in the historical debates of the previous decade but achieve a new clarity
concerning the contemporary significance of Aleksei's long-cold corpse.

50. The Association of Itinerant Art Exhibitions (1870–1923) was an influential group of
realist artists who organized group exhibitions outside the official structures and shows of
the Imperial Academy of Arts. See Valkenier, *Russian Realist Art*.

Some commentators thought the painting perfectly complemented the triumphal official rhetoric of the bicentennial. As *Peterburgskie vedomosti* reported, "our painters could not have presented a better gift for the two hundredth birthday of the great worker-tsar."[51] Yet such pious sentiments were not limited to loyalist voices. Mikhail Saltykov-Shchedrin, writing in the liberal *Otechestvennye zapiski*, saw the painting as a triumphant communication of Peter's greatness and of the grand historical logic that brought him to have his own son killed: "every viewer of these completely untheatrically presented figures must agree that he is witness to a most striking drama, that will never be erased from his memory." For Saltykov-Shchedrin, Ge's Peter is deeply human in his suffering, yet also heroic in his determination to suffer without complaint. He is cruel, but his "cruelty is rational, and is not comparable to that beastliness for the sake of beastliness that is characteristic of grandees of more recent times."[52] In short, Saltykov-Shchedrin, like Ustrialov before him, presents Peter overcoming personal interests and attachments to make a sacrifice in the name of political rationality and future prosperity.

Note here as well the critic's observation of the "untheatrical" nature of Ge's work—a reflection of the evident lack of emotion of the figures depicted that would become a leitmotif of criticism of this painting. In a separate review in *Peterburgskie vedomosti*, the influential liberal critic Vladimir Stasov expressed an opinion similar to Saltykov-Shchedrin's regarding the significance of the painting itself, but his review went on to criticize Ge for telling only one side of the story. According to him, Aleksei was not drawn sympathetically enough, and this suggested a total exculpation of Peter for an act "from which history turns her eyes in disgust." As Stasov concluded—echoing Pogodin's conflicted fascination both with Peter's unassailable right and with the cruelty of his exercise of it—this worked to oversimplify the dramatic significance of the scene: "Not only Tsarevich Aleksei but also Peter himself should be seen as deeply tragic personalities."[53]

These exculpatory readings of Ge's vision of Peter were hardly the only opinions the work elicited. The reviewer for the more stridently oppositional journal *Golos* agreed with Saltykov-Shchedrin regarding the expressive effectiveness of the painting's "untheatrical" composition but read the scene somewhat differently: "[Peter's] gaze is simply cold, but it freezes the blood in your

51. Cited in Stasov, *Nikolai Nikolaevich Ge*, 235. Stasov provides a useful collection of excerpts from reviews in various publications.

52. Cited in ibid., 233.

53. V. V. Stasov, "Peredvizhnaia vystavka," *Sankt-Peterburgskie vedomosti*, December 3 and 8, 1871 (Nos. 333 and 338); repr. in his *Sobranie sochinenii*, 2:329–42. Typical of the controversy surrounding the painting, the editors of the newspaper accompanied Stasov's article with a disclaimer: "We do not share the opinion of our respected author concerning the painting by Mr. Ge, and for our part, do not see in this painting the one-sidedness of which the critic complains."

veins. In the silence of the two figures one may hear groans of torture and the horrors of the dungeon."[54] The critic Apollon Matushinskii, perplexed by that same lack of evident drama, wrote in the conservative *Russkii vestnik* that the painting "fails to produce the impression that it ought to, given its high-tragic subject matter." The reviewer goes on to complain that "the artist did not penetrate deeply enough into his task . . . did not present the viewer the possibility to look into the inner souls of the actors . . . of the chosen drama." This led him to wonder whether Ge was clumsily attempting to express a "lack of sympathy for the tsarevich."[55]

Even more strikingly, the reviewer for the more radically disposed journal *Delo* voiced a completely different interpretation of the emotional restraint of the work: "Looking from the figure of Peter, heavily seated and with a beautiful but fat and mindless face, over to the exhausted but quite expressive visage of the tsarevich, with his high forehead and sunken cheeks, it's as if you are seeing an extraordinarily attractive, well-developed, but half-tormented prisoner, standing before a triumphant investigator or a bourgeois, with the beastly habits of a village policeman." This reviewer's general interpretation was that the work "was painted by a very talented artist, but a Slavophile artist, an inveterate enemy of the Petrine reforms and an apologist for Old Russian retrograde principles."[56]

Although these reactions by no means exhaust the range of opinion on Ge's work, I will mention only one last example. Some four years after the painting was first exhibited, the historian Nikolai Kostomarov, a friend and ally of Ge, published his lengthy article "Tsarevich Aleksei Petrovich (Concerning N. N. Ge's Painting)." Curiously, the article is a historical account of the life and death of Aleksei, echoing the historical debates occasioned by the documentary revelations of the late 1850s and early 1860s; Ge's painting is mentioned nowhere other than in the title and in one passing reference to the specific episode it portrays.[57]

From the record, it is clear both that Ge's painting was a tremendous success and that there was absolutely no consensus as to its proper interpretation. If the "coolness" of the painting was intended to dampen emotional responses to the depicted scene, projecting instead the rational necessity of Aleksei's death, it also left the painting open for a wide range of responses. On careful consideration, however, this interpretational scatter is not as complicated as it may at first appear, for the divergent views of the painting correspond in straightforward manner to the ideological positions of the voices that articulated them. These

54. See Stasov, *Nikolai Nikolaevich Ge*, 232.

55. A. M. Matushinskii, "Poslednie khudozhestvennye vystavki," *Russkii vestnik*, 1872, no. 6: 778–91, here 780–82.

56. Stasov, *Nikolai Nikolaevich Ge*, 235.

57. N. I. Kostomarov, "Tsarevich Aleksei Petrovich (Po povodu kartiny N. N. Ge)," *Drevniaia i novaia Rossiia: Ezhemesiachnyi istoricheskii illiustrirovannyi sbornik*, 1875, no. 1 and 2; repr. in Kostomarov, *Istoricheskie monografii*, 125–66.

positions recall the interpretive attitudes of the "first round" of historical debate concerning Aleksei, yet they also demonstrate the changing stakes, as the
Epoch of the Great Reforms wore on, of interpreting both the reformer Peter
and the reformer Alexander II.

Furthermore, responses to Ge's painting were far more overt than earlier
historical interpreters had been in reading Peter's confrontation with Aleksei
as an allegory for present realities—in looking through this window on the
past in order to see the present. At one end of the spectrum, loyalist reviewers
who viewed Ge's painting as a "birthday gift" to the first emperor simply assimilated the painting to the rhetoric of the bicentennial, glorifying not only
Peter and his reforms but by association Alexander II and his analogous era of
state-sponsored social transformation. Their hermeneutic certainty in reading
the painting as a dithyramb to Peter's just punishment of his son reflects their
political certainty regarding the meaning of Alexander's accomplishments—an
interpretive stance reflected, for instance, in Vice-Admiral Petr Kozakevich's
toast to the notables of Kronstadt, assembled for the official celebration on
May 30, 1872: "Our times are fortunate, for we too live in an era of great reforms, which allows us to correctly assess the deeds of Emperor Peter."[58] Interestingly, Ge records in his memoirs that he saw the painting in a celebratory
key himself but later became less sympathetic to Peter's role in the trial and
death of Aleksei.[59]

Yet whereas at the start of Alexander's reign even radical critics such as
Aleksandr Herzen were open to viewing the contemporary era and tsar as ana-
logues of Peter and his reign, by the 1870s many in Russian society had become
less convinced that the Tsar Liberator, Alexander II, should be seen in the tradition of the transforming tsar Peter. In the course of the 1860s, the public eu-
phoria of the start of Alexander II's reign had given way to recriminations over
the course of the reforms, political polarization, and the first rise of organized
terrorism in Russia. The most significant turning point was Dmitrii Karakazov's
attempted assassination of the emperor in 1866, which triggered a fast slide of
progressive state policy into the far more conservative positions in education,
censorship, and police intervention of the ensuing "white terror."

In the wake of this volte-face, the educated public was divided over whether
Russia's ruling emperor in fact deserved the mantle of her first. In some circles,
the perceived failure of Alexander's reforms could be communicated via the contrast with Peter. This is the clear implication of liberal reviews of Ge's painting—
evident, for instance, in Saltykov-Schedrin's suggestion that Peter was admirable
despite his brutality, in contrast to "grandees of more recent times." This stance
is even more apparent, although coupled with an opposed reading of the painting's intent, in *Delo*'s denunciation of Ge for presenting Peter not as a "despot-

58. "Vnutrennie izvestiia," *Pravitel'stvennyi vestnik* 132 (June 4, 1872), 2.
59. See Zograf, ed., *Nikolai Nikolaevich Ge*, 100.

reformer with a sparkle of genius and a crushing iron will in his black eyes" but rather as a "bureaucrat of the good old days, vicious in his temperament, limited in his views."[60]

Stepping away from Ge's own assessment of his intent, the mere choice of scene, pregnant with the critique of Peter's brutality that animated earlier discussions of Aleksei's fate, evokes less a purely triumphal account of the Petrine reforms and their present day equivalents than one might think appropriate at a birthday party. This suggests that the painter and his critics were expressing the need for a more nuanced meditation on the ironic mechanisms of historical progress than the rhetoric of the bicentennial otherwise occasioned, or at the very least an apology for Peter's despotism in the service of enlightenment. This was the interpretation put forward by the painting's most incisive critic, Stasov. His view of Ge's work as a portrayal of an episode "from which history turns her eyes in disgust" in the biography of a great man might be read as a retrospective critique of the shortcomings of *both* Peter's and Alexander's reforms—as a lament that in Russia, progress seems inextricably bound to coercion and violence. Ge's interpretively open treatment of one of the most controversial episodes in Peter's reign presented viewers with a handy allegorical game board by which one could broadcast a reading of the present, engaging with other viewers in "proxy wars" of disguised polemic concerning the fate of the contemporary Epoch of the Great Reforms.

—m—

Thirteen years later, a different historical painting evoked a no less contradictory range of responses: Ilia Repin's *Ivan the Terrible and His Son Ivan, 16 November 1581* (Ivan Groznyi i ego syn Ivan, 16 noiabria 1581, 1885, fig. 6). Now, Repin's painting resonates in startling manner with Ge's not only in its parallel subject matter but also in composition and interpretational potential, and I argue below that it may be read as a response to the earlier work. Yet first, I will follow the lead of all previous viewers and interpreters of Repin's painting and take it up apart from any relationship to Ge's.

Ivan the Terrible and His Son Ivan was first shown at the 1885 Itinerant exhibition, and it quickly provoked not only controversy but a full-blown scandal. The remarks of Repin's friend, the painter Ivan Kramskoi, in anticipation of the exhibition describe in an almost prescient manner the contours of the ensuing furor:

> It is still not finished, but what there is of it is so intense, so striking, that people with theories, with systems, and smart people in general are made to feel a tad uncomfortable. In my opinion, Repin has acted almost indelicately: I had just settled happily on the theory that historical subjects should be painted only when they render a canvas relevant to the

60. Cited in Stasov, *Nikolai Nikolaevich Ge*, 232.

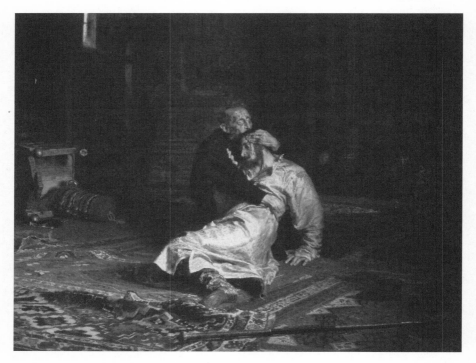

Figure 6: *Ivan the Terrible and His Son Ivan, 16 November 1581*, by Ilya Repin, 1885, State Tretiakov Gallery (Moscow, Russia). Reproduced with permission.

present—when the historical painting, one might say, touches on the vital interests of our time. And then all of a sudden: the devil knows what! No theory![61]

If the responses to Ge's painting resonate with the privileging of the historical over the theatrical, of rationality over emotion, and of the state over the body in the reception of the story of Aleksei, in the case of Repin's canvas the situation is neatly reversed—this is a canvas that overwhelms rational interpretation and causes a physical and emotional response.

When placed on exhibition, *Ivan the Terrible and His Son Ivan* caused a commotion. Kramskoi and others report visitors to the exhibition turning away, fainting, exclaiming that the painting was indecent and should not be shown: "It's regicide, after all!" (which it is not, although Repin had considered calling it "Filicide" and then abandoned this title, apparently considering it too

61. I. V. Kramskoi, letter to P. O. Kovalevskii of January 1, 1885, in *Ivan Nikolaevich Kramskoi*, ed, Stasov, 506–8, here 507–8. Kramskoi repeated similar comments in a letter to A. S. Suvorin of January 21, 1885, in ibid., 508–12.

sensational).[62] During the exhibition, the Imperial Academy of Arts, no friend to the Itinerants, invited a certain professor of anatomy Anatolii Landtsert to read a lecture demonstrating that Repin's painting depicted a number of anatomical impossibilities and, in something of a leitmotif of commentary on the painting, simply too much blood. Landsert's lecture was promptly published.[63]

Repin's allies leapt to his defense: urged on by Kramskoi, the wealthy publisher Aleksei Suvorin penned a glowing review of the painting, in which he praised its realism, expressiveness and ability to "terrify and evoke pity—the murderer terrifies us, while the victim evokes pity, touching us to the point of pain." Suvorin's review closes with the claim that the painting is a masterpiece that deserves to be hung in a separate room in a gallery, where it would "loudly proclaim with pride 'this is Russian painting, the Russian school, Russian art.' "[64] For his part, Stasov penned a refutation/parody of Landsert's lecture, which concludes with the sober reflection that anatomical rules have nothing to do with the expressive capacity of art, with its ability to "evoke terror and pity."[65]

The clamor over Repin's bloody canvas soon provoked official intervention. In a report to Emperor Alexander III of February 15, Director General of the Holy Synod Konstantin Pobedonostsev characterized the painting as straightforwardly obscene and "antihistorical":

> From various quarters it has been brought to my attention that the Itinerant Exhibition includes a painting that offends the moral sensibilities of many: Ivan the Terrible with his murdered son. I saw the painting myself today and could not look at it without revulsion. [. . .] It is difficult to comprehend what the artist is thinking, recounting such moments with such realism. What's the point of Ivan the Terrible here? [. . .] One can't call this historical painting, since this moment and the entire setting is entirely fantastical, rather than historical.[66]

Rumors concerning the impending prohibition of the painting began to circulate. Although no official action was taken during the course of the exhibition

62. For Kramskoi's report of reactions to the painting, see his letter to Suvorin of February 12, 1885, in ibid., 516–20, here 516. Also see Grabar', *Il'ia Efimovich Repin*, 1:266.

63. I have not been able to obtain the original publication of Landsert's lecture: A. Landtsert, "Po povodu kartiny Repina 'Ioann Groznyi i ego syn 16 November 1581,'" *Vestnik iziashchnykh iskusstv* 3, no. 2 (1885): 192–98; excerpts are reprinted in Voloshin, *O Repine*, 59–64.

64. Neznakomets (A. S. Suvorin), "Kartina Repina," *Novoe vremia*, no. 3218 (February 12, 1885), 1. Suvorin was the publisher of *Novoe vremia*.

65. V. V. Stasov, "Po povodu lektsii professora Landtserta o kartine Repina," *Novosti*, May 9, 1885, no. 126; repr. in Stasov, *Sobranie sochinenii*, 2:857–59. Stasov did not, in fact, approve of Repin's painting, which he did not find sufficiently "historical," yet his friendship with the artist moved him to write in his defense.

66. K. P. Pobedonostsev, letter of February 15, 1885, to Alexander III in *Tainyi pravitel' Rossii*, ed. Prokopov, 176–77.

in St. Petersburg, when it moved on to Moscow the painting was ordered removed from the show.[67] Repin's patron Pavel Tretiakov, who had already
purchased the painting before the exhibition's start, was prohibited from hang-
ing it in his public gallery. Only after months of negotiation and the interces-
sion of court insiders with the emperor himself was the prohibition lifted and
the art collector allowed to place the painting on display.

The clamor surrounding Repin's painting, like that provoked by Ge's a decade and a half earlier, was motivated as much by the contemporary resonances
of his canvas as by the scandalous nature of the scene it depicted. By the time
Repin was painting his work, the Epoch of the Great Reforms was emphatically past—consigned to history by the bomb that killed Alexander II in 1881,
inaugurating the reign of Alexander III, devoted to the preservation of the
autocratic principle by all means. And it is this crucial moment of royal bloodshed that constitutes the evident allegorical reference of Repin's work. The
artist later recalled that he began work on the painting as a reaction to the assassination and the public execution of the terrorist conspirators, at which he
was himself present.[68] The title of the work goes to awkward lengths to include the date 1581, which surely constitutes a hint at allegorical reference to
the assassination that took place precisely three centuries after the depicted
scene. The outrage of viewers concerning "regicide"—a word that in 1885 could
only evoke the assassination of Alexander II—surely demonstrates that this
reference was not lost on them. In an age awash with the tsar's blood, the brazen depiction of Tsarevich Ivan's blood was nothing short of pornographic.
Yet the allegorical content of the painting is rather puzzling: certainly, we have
two Ivans and two Alexanders, yet how can the father Alexander, murdered by
terrorists, be related to the son Ivan, struck down by his own father?

Repin's allegory links up with contemporary events with an intentional
looseness—a looseness that "revises" the present, redirecting attention from
prevalent conceptions of political violence to contrasting ones. Composed in a
moment of confrontational extremist politics following the tsaricide, the painting condemns autocratic violence and calls for a reconciliation before it is too
late. Activating motifs similar to those of Tolstoi's *Death of Ivan the Terrible*,
the overturned throne in the background broadcasts a warning that political
bloodshed may lead to dynastic collapse.

Furthermore, with his suggestive allegorical revision of the assassination of
Alexander II, Repin announces that the source of Russian political violence lies
not with rebellious sons but with despotic fathers. The root cause of the bloodshed of the present is to be found not in the rebellious conspiracies of terrorists
but in the age-old, reflexive violence of the autocracy. In a letter to Tretiakov
in April 1881, Repin wrote: "with their Turkish ideals of complete slavery,

<hr />

67. Memoranda from the Moscow authorities to Tretiakov are reproduced in Grabar',
Il'ia Efimovich Repin, 1:264–66.
    68. Ibid., 151.

merciless retribution, and arbitrary authority, such people evoke terrible opposition and shocking turns of events, such as, for instance, [the assassination of Alexander II on] March 1."[69] In a similar manner, *Ivan the Terrible and His Son Ivan* identifies the conservative reaction of the autocracy to revolutionary unrest with the despotic father of Russia's medieval past, guilty of killing its own son—Russia's aspirations for social progress. Yet following the hopeful model of Mei's and Rimskii-Korsakov's redactions of Ivan's filicidal myth, the anguished figure of Ivan also presents a model of penitence and hope. Both contemporary observers and later critics concur that Ivan's embrace of his son, his wildly pained eyes, and the bloody staff thrown to the margins of the work express the tsar's anguished remorse and repentance. As Kramskoi put it: "Just think: a huge amount of blood, but you don't even think about it, it doesn't have any effect on you, because of the painting's horrific, overbearing expression of fatherly grief."[70]

In the context of its allegorical import, this aspect of the painting's expressive work must be seen as a call to transcend violence and seek national reconciliation. In this, *Ivan the Terrible and His Son Ivan* presents a pictorial equivalent to the famous appeals of Lev Tolstoi and Vladimir Solovev to Alexander III in the immediate aftermath of the assassination of his father, urging that repentance and forgiveness, not harsh measures and executions, were the proper response of the throne to revolutionary violence.[71]

The Christian implications of this message, matching the content of Tolstoi's and Solovev's appeals, are most apparent in the religious references of Repin's canvas. Some commentators have suggested that Repin's work references two Rembrandt paintings that hang in the Hermitage, *David and Jonathan* and *The Return of the Prodigal Son* (figs. 7 and 8; 1642, 1668, resp.), to which I believe one may add another of the Hermitage's Rembrandts, *Abraham's Sacrifice* (fig. 9, 1635). Clearly, the biblical stories represented in all three of these paintings share with Repin's work a basic mythic plot concerning the sacrifice of children by fathers and the hope of forgiveness and divine redemption.[72] Yet the most obvious religious model for Repin's work, communicated

69. I. E. Repin, letter of April 8, 1881, to P. N. Tret'iakov, in Repin, *Izbrannye pis'ma*, 1:250. The individual whom Repin had in mind is the publisher M. N. Katkov.

70. Kramskoi, letter to Suvorin of January 21, 1885, in *Ivan Nikolaevich Kramskoi*, ed. Stasov, 509.

71. In a public lecture delivered on March 28, 1881, which was something of a scandal in its own right, Solovev stated that the proper response to the assassination was to pardon the assassins in the spirit of Christian forgiveness. Otherwise, the new emperor would "embark on a bloody cycle" and the Christian, Russian people would turn away from him. Lev Tolstoi made much the same point in a letter addressed to the emperor at about the same time. See V. I. Fatiushchenko and N. I. Tsimbaev, "Vladimir Solov'ev—kritik i publitsist," introductory essay in V. S. Solov'ev, *Literaturnaia kritika*, 12; and L. N. Tolstoi, letter to Aleksandr III (draft), in his *Sobranie sochinenii*, 18:879–87. The final draft of the letter is not extant.

72. See Valkenier, "Writer as Artist's Model," 207–16; van Os and Scheijen, *Ilya Repin*, 50–51.

Figure 7: *David and Jonathan* by Rembrandt van Rijn, 1642, The Hermitage (St. Petersburg, Russia). Scala/Art Resource, N.Y. Reproduced with permission.

Figure 8: *The Return of the Prodigal Son*, by Rembrandt van Rijn, 1668–69, The Hermitage (St. Petersburg, Russia). Scala/Art Resource, N.Y. Reproduced with permission.

Figure 9: *Abraham's Sacrifice*, by Rembrandt van Rijn, 1635, The Hermitage (St. Petersburg, Russia). Scala/Art Resource, N.Y. Reproduced with permission.

in the painting's figural composition, is a different instantiation of this same myth: the traditional *topos* of the Pietà (fig. 10)—a reference that renders the dead Ivan, and by extension the dead Alexander, as a figure of Christian sacrifice in the name of national unity and salvation.[73]

———

Taken separately, each of these canvases presents a rich instance of the historical mythologies surrounding Ivan and Peter. Yet this hardly exhausts their interpretive potential, for they may also be seen as voices in a dialogue—a dialogue between the cases of Aleksei and Tsarevich Ivan, greatness and terror, heroism and trauma. Neither in the reception of Repin's canvas nor in documentary materials relating to its production is there any conclusive evidence that *Ivan the Terrible and His Son Ivan* was intended or interpreted as a response to *Peter I Interrogates Tsarevich Aleksei Petrovich*. Yet a comparative reading of the two is not entirely unmotivated, either. Repin and his viewers knew Ge's canvas well. As the first Itinerant historical painting, which Repin's patron Tretiakov had acquired and hung prominently in his gallery, it was an obvious point of reference for the younger artist in his work in the historical genre, which was not thought to be his *métier*.[74]

The historical episodes in question speak to each another. Yet beyond this thematic contiguity, one must be struck by Repin's apparently systematic incorporation of details evocative of Ge's work. The chief decorative motifs of *Peter I Interrogates Tsarevich Aleksei Petrovich* are the Oriental carpet on the table and the checkerboard parquet on the floor. Repin adopted these same motifs, placing the checkerboard on the walls and the carpet on the floor. In terms of compositional elements, the use of perspective and dimensions of the room are similar. Repin's placement of the stove behind and to the left of the figure of the tsar echoes Ge's hearth in the same position. Finally, in the first known preparatory sketch for Repin's work, one may discern behind the figures of the tsar and son in the foreground a table and two high-backed chairs,

73. By including this image here, I do not mean to suggest a direct influence of Michelangelo on Repin's painting. I claim that Repin's work references the *topos* of the Pietà, rather than any one instantiation of it. One may note, however, that among the countless examples of this traditional composition that Repin probably saw during his travels in Europe in the 1870s and 1880s, he also certainly contemplated Michelangelo's when he visited St. Peter's. Repin's reactions to Michelangelo were of unrestrained admiration, although he condemned St. Peter's and Rome itself for what he viewed as its "Catholic ostentation." See Repin's letters to Stasov of June 4, 1873, March 20, 1880, and June 18, 1887, in his *Izbrannye pis'ma*, 1:64–67, 233–35, 328–29.

74. Repin recalled visiting Ge's studio while the older artist was at work on the painting. Any number of times Repin publicly expressed his admiration for Ge, whom he viewed as instrumental in the creation of the figure of public intellectual/citizen artist to which he himself aspired. Repin would have seen the painting frequently in his patron Tretiakov's gallery. On Repin's admiration for Ge and visits to the older artist's studio and later to his country home in the 1880s, see Stasov, *Nikolai Nikolaevich Ge*, 215, 228–29; and I. E. Repin, "Nikolai Nikolaevich Ge i nashi pretenzii k iskusstvu," in his *Dalekoe blizkoe*, 296–324.

Figure 10: Pietà, by Michelangelo Buonarroti, c. 1498–99, St. Peter's Basilica, The Vatican. Scala/ Art Resource, N.Y. Reproduced with permission.

arranged analogously to those of Ge's painting, yet with one of them over-turned.[75] The sight lines of the paired figures are also similar—the son looking down and into the frame while the father looks up and out in each case, although the relative positions of the figures in Ge's work are reversed in Repin's, as though seen in a distorting mirror.

Of course, in reading Repin's work against Ge's, the former cannot be reduced to a repetition of the latter. Each of the continuities in representation linking the two is charged with transformative tension, through which *Ivan the Terrible and His Son Ivan* "revises" *Peter I Interrogates the Tsarevich Aleksei Petrovich*. As critics agreed, Ge's dramatic encounter is lacking in emotion, presenting a moment of terse silence in a rational political conflict. Peter and Aleksei are ciphers, their psychological depths concealed from viewers—figures on an allegorical chessboard. The one sign of violence is the crumpled paper at Peter's feet, perhaps a copy of the tsarevich's first, incomplete confession that has been thrown aside by a pounding fist. The focal point of the canvas is the lawgiver's pen, poised to condemn Aleksei to torture or to sign a death warrant. The inclusion of the Germanic place name "Peterhof" in the title, the line of Dutch paintings on the wall, the interior and costume all stress Peter's identity as the "Westernizer" of Russia.

In response, Repin presents a stereotypically "eastern" scene, activating the rhetoric of Oriental despotism associated with Ivan. The section of carpet on the table in Ge's canvas and the discrete, crumpled sheet of paper give way in Repin's work to a profusion of crumpled carpets and cushions. The row of paintings is replaced with an icon. The overturned throne in Repin's work, with its allusion to dynastic collapse, responds to the regally enthroned Peter, who evokes the stability of the political order that he founded. Ivan's throne is itself modeled after the "eastern" seat held in the Moscow Armory, supposedly acquired during the conquest of Kazan. Most important, in place of the dispassion of Ge's painting, which asserts the rational order that legitimated the death of Aleksei, Repin's canvas presents an explosion of irrational violence that results in the failure of the line of descent. The lawgiver's pen and ink gives way to Ivan's staff, lying in a pool of blood, while at the focal point of the canvas Repin has placed human bodies in contact—the overwhelming anguish of a father losing his son. *Ivan the Terrible and His Son Ivan* palpably fills in the silences of *Peter the Great Interrogates the Tsarevich Aleksei Petrovich at Peterhof*, as though the emotionally restrained figures suspended at the margins of Ge's canvas have rushed to the center of Repin's, where they have collided and even somehow exchanged positions.

75. The sketch is reproduced in Liaskovskaia, *Il'ia Efimovich Repin*, 248. In a similar convergence of the two compositions, when Repin visited Ge's studio, he saw an earlier version of Ge's painting which featured windows in the background, rather than the Dutch paintings of the final version. One may note the window in the background of Repin's work.

As noted above, the evidence of Repin's intentional reference to Ge's painting is not conclusive, although the above suggests that both the artist and informed members of his audience could well have viewed the paintings as voices in a dialogue in the mid-1880s. Possibly, the absence of such views in the record reflects dampening effects of the obscenity of Repin's subject on critical discussion in the painting's public reception, which was dominated instead by scandalous outcry. But whether or not Repin intended his canvas as a response to Ge's, our joint reading of the two works uncovers important features of the integral cultural mechanism of anxiety concerning fathers and sons and greatness and terror that animated Russian historical imagination on a deeper level. Even more: perhaps the startling absence of interpretations of the later canvas as a response to the earlier one is the most telling feature of all—for this refusal to recognize the obvious expresses, once again, the psychic economy of chosen yet disavowed trauma characteristic of Russian thought about Ivan and Peter. So what is the content of this unrecognized dialogue?

A decade and a half after Ge's interpretively open painting asked viewers how they saw the present in the crystal ball of Petrine Russia, Repin's canvas offered an emphatic answer: modern Russia is not the heir of Peter's epoch of westernization at all but rather the offspring of Ivan and the Orient. Or perhaps: when Russia strives most strenuously to become western, as under Peter I and Alexander II, its eastern nature becomes most apparent. Seen as a response to the earlier painting, Repin's canvas "builds out" Ge's historical allegory to grasp not only the Petrine greatness of the reform era but also the terror of the decade that followed, announcing that the hard, impenetrable surface of Ge's depiction of raison d'état in fact belied depths of despotic violence. For the reforms that were intended to shore up the autocracy and advance the cause of enlightenment—thereby recalling and even reenacting Peter's founding of modern Russia—instead concluded in bloodshed, executions, and the looming threat of dynastic catastrophe.

In sum, *Ivan the Terrible and His Son Ivan* reveals that those who had hailed Ge's work as an appropriate "birthday present" for Peter could not have known how right they were, for Ge's portrayal of Peter tells a story of greatness based on the refusal to recognize terror. In this dialogue of allegories, Alexander is shown to have followed Peter's precedent not only as a benevolent father granting progress to his childlike subjects but also as a murderous one who put his most rebellious subject—his son—to death in order to protect his state. That Repin's audience has for over a hundred years refrained from articulating the allegorical interweaving of these two canvases, which still hang in adjoining rooms in the Tretiakov Gallery, merely illustrates the basic mechanisms of Russian collective identity, based on chosen yet disavowed trauma.

Comparative reading of the two paintings pays off on a number of additional levels. In light of Repin's use of religious iconography, the resonance of *Peter the Great Interrogates the Tsarevich Aleksei Petrovich at Peterhof* with religious imagery snaps into focus. Subjects involving both righteous and in-

Figure 11: *Christ Interrogated by Pilate* (panel from the back of the *Maesta altarpiece*), by Duccio di Buoninsegna, c. 1308–11), Museo dell'Opera Metropolitana (Siena, Italy). Scala/Art Resource, N.Y. Reproduced with permission.

iquitous judgment (King Solomon, Orthodox saints martyred at the hands of unjust rulers) commonly present supplicants or accused standing with downcast eyes facing enthroned judges. Yet the most suggestive religious iconographic resonance of Ge's work is that of Christ before Pilate (fig. 11).[76] Significantly, the painting's composition has little in common with images of the Last Judgment— either from the western Renaissance canon or in the formulaic structure of Orthodox icons. So, although this element of Ge's work recalls the scriptural *topoi* that had been applied to the story of Aleksei by historians like Pogodin, the implications here are more lucid and damning for the emperor—reference to the Passion's judgment scene renders the tsarevich a Christ figure and pointedly dismisses Peter's authority over him. By this reading, Peter and all those who pursue progress through violent means are complicit in the illegitimate

76. Interestingly, Ge was later to paint a significant rendition of the scene of Pilate's judgment, *What Is Truth?* (Chto est' istina, 1890). Although this work is remote in both style and composition from *Peter I Interrogates Aleksei Petrovich*, one may speculate as to how the two paintings and their divergent treatment of the Pilate *topos* reflect the development of the painter's views.

hubris of secular power, which must ultimately cede before a higher spiritual power.

Here, too, Ge's painting finds an answer in Repin's—either an intentional yet unnoticed reply or an efflorescence of the disavowed content of the Petrine historical myth, and hence the "response" of Russian historical myth itself. When seen from the perspective of Repin's canvas, Ge's evocation of Pilate in Peter represents the psychosocial nightmare of the state as a murderous father, whereas Repin's rendition of Ivan as Mary holds out the hope of reconciliation in the name of an all-pardoning God.

Finally, comparison of the two canvases draws attention to the manner in which each responds to the cultural contexts through which the Russian public had come to know their subjects. Ge's painting staked a position in a historiographic debate, and its mode of representation reflects the terms of historical discourse—offering a dispassionate, scholastic depiction that renders Peter and Aleksei the representatives of abstract historical forces and conceals their humanity. In contrast, the overtly "operatic" quality of Repin's canvas resonates with stage representations of Ivan as a filicide. The gestural vocabulary of the work is stylized to the point of melodrama—from the wild motions communicated in the staff, throne, and carpet to the overdrawn emotional expressiveness of faces and hands. One may note as well that Repin's "theatrical" image of Ivan resonates with a well-established tradition of dialogue between artistic and stage representations of that tsar. In the 1872 production of Rimskii-Korsakov's *The Maid of Pskov*, Osip Petrov created a sensation when he used Antokolskii's celebrated 1871 sculpture *Ivan the Terrible* as the overt model for his representation of the tsar.[77] Performing Rubinstein's opera *The Merchant Kalashnikov* in 1880, Fedor Stravinskii (father of the composer) followed Petrov's precedent and modeled his own version of Ivan on Antokolskii's as well (figs. 12 and 13).[78] So what shall we make of the affiliations of these two canvases with historiography and theater?[79]

Rather than treat these contexts as historical circumstance, irrelevant to the meaning of these images of Ivan and Peter, let us take them as a further level of

77. On Petrov's use of Antokolskii's image, see V. V. Stasov's comments in his much later article "Kurinaia slepota," *Birzhevye vedomosti*, April 13, 1898, 5.

78. Press accounts attest that the reference was not lost on the audience. See the review from *Golos* reproduced in *F. Stravinskii*, ed. Kutateladze, 185. Also see A Raskin, "Mnogogrannost' talanta (O risunkakh F. I. Stravinskogo)," in ibid., 67.

79. It is intriguing to speculate concerning a possible operatic reference for Repin's *Ivan the Terrible and His Son Ivan* in the final scene of *The Maid of Pskov*. There is good reason to suppose that a Pietà arrangement figured in the opera's original version—stage directions call for Ivan to cover Olga's body in kisses; and given that the tsar does not sing in this final, choral finale, it would seem natural for him to cradle his daughter's body in his arms. However, it is difficult to ascertain the exact staging of this scene in the original 1872 production of *The Maid of Pskov*. In later productions of the opera in its final revision, Fedor Chaliapin based his interpretation quite consciously on Repin's canvas.

Figure 12: *Ivan the Terrible*, by Mark Antokolskii, 1871, State Tretiakov Gallery (Moscow, Russia). Scala/Art Resource, N.Y. Reproduced with permission.

Figure 13: Fedor Stravinskii in the role of Ivan the Terrible, for the Mariinskii Theater production of Anton Rubinstein's *The Merchant Kalashnikov*, 1889. Sankt-Peterburgskii gosudarstvennyi muzei teatral'nogo i muzykal'nogo iskusstva (St. Petersburg, Russia). Reproduced with permission.

meaning to be interpreted—as Kavelin or Aksakov might have done. For the two paintings represent not only alternative views of Russia's past and present but correspondingly alternative modes of seeing those realities. By the time Ge and Repin were at work on their paintings, the filicidal historical myths of Peter and Ivan had become parts of the standard repertoire of separate institutions engaged in the representation of Russia's past—of the historical discipline, on one hand, and of the dramatic and operatic stage, on the other.

In the two paintings, these institutional affiliations are as much a component of the significance of these figures as is any other dimension of their cultural mythology—historical, geographical, or iconographic. Ge's painting concealed the flow of blood in history to allow Peter and Aleksei to appear as abstract historical forces. Repin forced viewers to face blood—a figure for the collective life tying generations, classes, and political opponents together. Ge's painting and the historical debate it participated in presented a rational analysis of history, of development and cost, charted out on the neat political accounting ledger of Peter's own westernized political culture, rendering the suppression of bodies and their pain axiomatic. Repin's Ivan represents the rejection of theory, calculation, and politics in favor of the transformative power of the "nonwestern" motifs of affect, repentance, and religious transcendence.

Finally, the two works map these contrasting pairs—Peter/Ivan, west/east, state/body, rational/affective, Pilate/Mary—onto a symbolic tension between history and politics, on one hand, and artistic expression, on the other. Ge's explicitly "historical" work crystallized the intelligentsia's fading hope in a political rebirth of Russia along the lines of western societies, valorizing the Petrine rational historical processes that were to enable this transformation. Repin's operatic canvas instructed viewers that Russia's salvation lay not in the fallen western category of the political but rather in the transformative power of the sensuous and the aesthetic, which the artist associates with true Russian identity. In this, Repin's work might be seen as a rephrasing of Dostoevskii's famous dictum that "beauty will save the world." One may add that in Repin's view, and in Dostoevskii's as well, salvation by means of the aesthetic was a peculiarly Russian idea.

In the first half of the nineteenth century, representations of Ivan the Terrible and Peter the Great uncovered their range of possible historical significances, revealing the rich and variable potential of these liminal figures, as well as the intractable complexities they presented for attempts to "settle" historical meaning in any one form. Their usefulness in civic life was based on the submersion of certain interpretive potentials as a disavowed but potent significance: the myth of Peter the Great was the cornerstone for a collective identity based on failure to recognize the violence of the imperial state; Ivan's reign of terror served as a chosen trauma, cementing together a community of victims who nevertheless closed their eyes to the tradition linking Ivan to his successors.

During the latter portion of the century, this set of interrelated interpretive positions functioned as an established cultural and political mechanism, exerting its influence over representations of these autocrats. Of course, the representation of history is always dependent on a history of prior representations, yet the integral mechanism of Russian thought about Ivan and Peter endowed this state of contingency with a unique intensity. Each of the works examined in this chapter, which strove to offer up a novel historical explanation or allegorical revision of present Russian experience, had to contend with the "afterimages" of prior representations. At times, later redeployments of Ivan and Peter ran up against subterranean flows of irony: in claiming Peter as his predecessor, did Alexander II recognize that he might be casting himself as heir to a tyrant?

As works like Mei's *Maid of Pskov* and Repin's *Ivan the Terrible and His Son Ivan* reveal, however, engagement with these accreted layers of significance could yield its own form of interpretational richness—enabling a self-conscious interrogation of prior visions of the past that lays bare how uneasily greatness is balanced on trauma and how insistently the past reasserts itself even in the midst of revolutionary transformations. In just this manner, Repin's work gains purchase not only on earlier representations of Ivan but on Ge's painting and, through it, on the tradition of representation of Peter as well—on the entire psychic and symbolic system of heroism intertwined with trauma and of progress linked with coercion and violence. Here, then, is an object lesson in the insight that signs (Repin's canvas) refer not to referents (the historical actor Ivan) but to other signs (Mei's and Rimskii-Korsakov's *The Maid of Pskov* or Ge's painting of Peter).

The embedding of history in its own history grows in complexity over time as layers of use and significance accumulate—as the chain of signifiers becomes ever more involuted and distant from the historical referent and as the use of the past becomes ever more laden with political and psychic significance—a process that at times may become a central focus of interpretive attention in its own right.

As we have seen, an intriguing twist in this metahistory is the story of how just such a fraught series of revisions ultimately attached Ivan the Terrible and Peter the Great, and in particular their filicidal episodes, to the discrete cultural contexts of theatrical representation, on one hand, and historical and political discourse, on the other. As a result of a slowly unfolding dialectic between deployment and meaning, the tsar and the emperor each came to carry an additional "sheen" of historicity or theatricality, respectively, in any medium; Ge's and Repin's paintings are a case in point—paintings in which Peter appears as a historical character and Ivan as an operatic one.

This more specific case of the feedback loop between the representation of history and the history of representation reveals how later images of the past may inherit not only the "content" of earlier images but also their "form." In their self-conscious thematization of these aspects of the two tsars—of Peter's cultural assignment to his monument and Ivan's to his stage—Ge's vision of Peter and Repin's treatment of Ivan grant these seemingly contingent institutional attachments historical significance in their own right. In *Peter the Great*

Interrogates Aleksei Petrovich and *Ivan the Terrible and His Son Ivan*, the historical Peter and the aesthetic Ivan become emblematic of a conflict of national fates—between the positive example of Peter's rational, western politics of modernization and the negative lesson of Ivan's remorse, which points back to the Russian national principles of spiritual unity, blood kinship, and aesthetic transfiguration.

In conclusion, one might ask where is the truth of history—of Ivan's and Peter's history—in all this? To temper the skepticism of my dismissal of the fundamental truth claims of the works discussed here, let me turn to other implications of my approach. If each novel representation of Ivan or Peter bears the traces of many prior ones, then it is in a sense also a synecdoche for its own situatedness—a device by which one can read off a position in the strata of meanings accumulated over the generations around the bones of historical facts. Or perhaps we should see it as an archive of historical representation. When looking to representations of history for an original referent—a fundamental truth—what we find instead is the chain of signifiers leading back into the past. Yet rather than despair and throw up our hands, we could instead realize that each of our stories projects around itself an archive that refers to the twisted path that historical representation has taken in its journey through culture. What we discover in representations of the past is not the "truth" of history—a reality somehow anterior to the representation. Neither is it "just" the artificial coherence of a story or the relationship between story and a discrete historical and ideological context. Instead, we discover the structure of human time, which is the time of repetition, folded and refolded again.

CHAPTER FOUR

Prognostication

A living feeling of kinship and a shared idea link us to Peter. In him we see ourselves, and in ourselves, we see him.

—Pavel Miliukov, "Peter the Great and His Reforms," 1925

I, myself, am fire. Rebellion is in my nature,
But fire needs the chain and blade.
It's not the first time, that, dreaming of freedom,
We're building a new prison.
Yes, beyond Moscow—beyond our stifled flesh,
Beyond bronze Peter's will—
There is no path for us: leading us into the swamp
Are the fires of a devilish game. [. . .]
In the quiet of night, starry and frozen,
Like a fierce black widow,
Moscow wove, in the days of the dark and terrible tsars
Her tight, unending circle.

—Maksimilian Voloshin, "Kitezh," 1919

What direction will you gallop, proud steed,
And where will you set down your hooves?
O, you potent lord of fate
Did you not, just so, over the abyss
Upon the heights, with an iron bit,
Raise up Russia on her haunches?

—Aleksandr Pushkin, *The Bronze Horseman*, 1833

History as Myth

By the dawn of the twentieth century, the overall landscape of Russian public life had become so vast, in comparison to the intimate public world of a century earlier, that it may seem difficult to imagine any unifying logic informing the range of representations of Russia's first tsar and first emperor. The accelerating professionalization of historical scholarship and literary life, the spread of literacy to new classes of readers, and the differentiation of diverse realms of social activity—all contributed to a dizzying growth of new sites of representation of Russian history. Among these, one may mention the works of Lev Zhdanov, who created a cottage industry of patriotic historical fiction and drama, devoting several works to Ivan and Peter; and the burgeoning genre of *lubok*—popular commercial literature—that disseminated in mass editions now traditional images of Peter as heroic modernizer and founder of empire and Ivan as cruel despot.[1] The court and the growing state bureaucracy continued their elevation of key historical figures, and especially of Peter the Great, in mass holidays and public ritual—1903, in this vein, saw the public celebration of the founding of St. Petersburg on a scale that rivaled the pomp and circumstance of the Petrine bicentennial some thirty years before.[2] Finally, the rapid development of education brought a growing stream of textbooks and other educational materials.

In this variegated landscape of representations of history, the extent to which professional historiography, on one hand, and cultural and artistic life, on the other, had diverged with regard to fundamental questions regarding the very nature of history is particularly striking. In 1872, an age when historiography, literature, art, and even opera reflected a broadly shared consensus on the primacy of a realist representation of social experience, the historian Nikolai Kostomarov, exiting a performance of Musorgskii's *Boris Godunov*, could exclaim with satisfaction "Now there's a page of history!"[3]

It is hard to imagine such an expression of solidarity between scholarly and artistic endeavors at the start of the next century. Historians of the late nineteenth century had increasingly adopted sociological and materialist positions in which the role of individual actors such as Peter and Ivan was minimized.[4] To consider one prominent example, Vasilii Kliuchevskii, Solovev's successor as the leading light of Russian historiography, held that "the Terrible Tsar fantasized more than he ever accomplished and acted less on the state order than he did on the imaginations and nerves of his contemporaries—without Ivan, the life of the Muscovite state would have developed before and after him just the same as it did with him, except that this development would have taken place more evenly and easily."[5] Similarly, Kliuchevskii radically overturned traditional explanations of Peter the Great. He was no longer to be seen as the prime mover of national history but merely as its willing (and glorious) instrument: "the reforms of Peter the Great arose on their own out of the fundamental needs of the state and the people, which were instinctively understood by a man of power with a sharp mind, a strong character, and many

---

1. On representations of Ivan and Peter in popular commercial literature, see Brooks, *When Russia Learned to Read*, 193, 219, 255; Brooks, "From Folklore to Popular Literature"; and Raikova, *Petr I*.

2. For discussion of the 1903 celebration, see Wortman, *Scenarios of Power*, 2:378.

3. Cited and translated in Taruskin, "Present in the Past," 123.

4. See Riasanovsky, *Image of Peter the Great*, 166–215; Emmons, "Kliuchevskii's Pupils"; and Manchester, "Contradictions at the Heart of Russian Liberalism."

5. Taken from Lecture 30 in his *Course of Russian History* (Kurs russkoi istorii) in Kliuchevskii, *Sochineniia*, 2:198. The *Course* was in fact published only in the form cited in 1904–11, but it represents a synthesis of the author's work in his university lectures, delivered from the 1870s onward.

talents."[6] In marked contrast to such depersonalized views of history, the dominant tendencies in the cultural life of the fin de siècle, in step with a widespread rejection of realism, materialism and positivism and reflecting a turn instead toward mystical and antirationalist views, elevated emblematic figures such as Peter and Ivan as mythic emanations of the collective being.

Nevertheless, despite this differentiation of historiography from cultural life more generally, one may observe certain overarching trends. The most important feature of the era's historical consciousness, common to a great many Russians who came of age in the last decade of the nineteenth century and first decade of the twentieth, was a sense of the present as the final stage in the history of an empire that was rushing toward a social cataclysm. Russian society—at least in the cities and among the educated classes—was divided between those actively working to bring about revolutionary transformation and those expectantly awaiting the upheaval with dread or delight. The mass disorders of the 1905 revolution and the halting reforms in its wake only heightened this shared sense of a looming threat of resurgent violence that would plunge the empire into uncharted waters. Now, despite the accuracy with which, it seems, an entire generation foresaw the coming revolution, one should neither make too much of Russians' prognostic powers nor dismiss as insignificant the prerevolutionary era's "theurgic atmosphere." Prognostication was in the air, and years later many Russians felt with some sense of vindication that their predictions of catastrophe had come to pass in 1917. As we shall see, in the popular pastime of divining Russia's future, Ivan, and especially Peter, proved useful tarot cards. As Russia's long history was rethought from the perspective of its "terminus," the reigns of the two liminal tsars seemed to model the present and prefigure the ever more ominous future.

Characteristic of Russian culture's engagement with the figures of Ivan and Peter at the fin de siècle was a broadly shared sensitivity to their ironic amalgamation of terror and greatness, as well as a heightened awareness of the legacy of canonical, nineteenth-century representations of the two tsars. Both of these typical features were in evidence on January 13, 1913, when a young man named Abram Balashov, armed with a dagger and unhinged by psychosis, committed an act of violence that set the Russian public reeling. The object of Balashov's mad attack was not a person. Instead, he plunged his dagger three times into the center of Repin's painting *Ivan the Terrible and His Son Ivan*. Some saw this act as a fulfillment of Futurist demand to "Throw Pushkin, Dostoevskii, Tolstoi, etc., etc. overboard from the ship of modernity," and certain voices even suggested that Balashov had carried out a "contract killing" of the

---

6. From Lecture 68 in the *Course*, in Kliuchevskii, *Sochinenii*, 4:220. For additional discussion of Kliuchevskii's views of Peter I, see Riasanovsky, *Image of Peter the Great*, 166–76; and Byrnes, *V. O. Kliuchevskii*, 198–202.

canvas.[7] Others saw Balashov's act as symptomatic of the infection of modern Russian society by the archaic violence depicted in the painting itself.

Yet this violent attack was not the only notable resurfacing of Repin's painting in these years. As we have seen, that work strongly resonates with mid-nineteenth-century operatic and dramatic representations of Ivan. This dialogue between the painting and the stage continued in subsequent decades. In 1894, Rimskii-Korsakov composed a revised, final redaction of *The Maid of Pskov*, which was staged by Saava Mamontov's Private Russian Opera Company in 1896. The young Fedor Chaliapin appeared as Ivan—a breakout role to which he would return many times. In his memoirs, Chaliapin notes that he created the role of Ivan by studying artistic representations of the Terrible Tsar, including, of course, Repin's famous canvas. As numerous photographs and souvenir postcards illustrate, Chaliapin composed an explicit homage to Repin's work in staging the opera's curtain scene, which, like the painting, explored the psychological impact of Ivan's filicide and the necessity of Christian repentance and humility (see fig. 14).[8] Some years later, Chaliapin recreated his *tableau vivant* of Repin's painting, but for an even broader audience, in the silent film *Ivan the Terrible* (1915, see fig. 15).

These episodes in the "reception" of Repin's painting demonstrate the complexity of the era's stance toward the Russian past. On one hand, many educated Russians shared a desire to renounce the principles of Russian social life symbolized by the great despots of the past and their paler, present-day heirs. For some, this rejection of history was catalyzed by a Nietzschean call for the "transvaluation of values," for others by a more pragmatic revolutionary drive. From this vantage point, what an Ivan or a Peter had wrought the present must undo, symmetrically reversing the transformational eras of the past with a new revolutionary era.

Yet this same intuition of the commonality of the present, seen as the last days, and the deep past, seen as a historical origin, could also play out in a heightened perception of the current moment as an inadvertent echo or intentional restaging of earlier historical scenes. From this angle of vision, some saw evidence of that vulgarized Nietzschean commonplace—time as eternal recurrence. Others perceived the dialectic movement of class conflict across the ages. The present, therefore, was either a new turn in the cycle of Russian historical experience or its final stage. As in these examples involving Repin's painting, the motif of repetition was frequently projected through the prism of prior

7. Cited from D. D. Burliuk, A. E. Kruchenykh, V. V. Maiakovskii and V. V. Khlebnikov's infamous 1912 manifesto "A Slap in the Face of Public Taste," translated in *Russian Futurism through Its Manifestoes*, ed. Lawton, 51–52.

8. See Chaliapin's memoirs, where he reports studying both Repin's and Antokolskii's representations of Ivan (Shaliapin, *Stranitsy iz moei zhizni*, 218–19, 527–28, n. 75). In attributing the restaging of Repin's painting to Chaliapin, one should keep in mind that during the period in question performers carried the responsibility for creative decisions concerning costuming, makeup, and even staging.

Figure 14: Fedor Chaliapin, cir. 1900, in the role of Ivan the Terrible, for a production of Rimskii-Korsakov's *The Maid of Pskov* (1896). Sankt-Peterburgskii gosudarstvennyi muzei teatral'nogo i muzykal'nogo iskusstva (St. Petersburg, Russia). Reproduced with permission.

Figure 15: Fedor Chaliapin, in the role of Ivan the Terrible, for a silent film based on *The Maid of Pskov*, 1915. Courtesy, Gosfilmofond (Moscow, Russia).

artistic or literary representations, borrowing their allegorical momentum as a proof of the essential patterns of Russian history: as in the deep past (Ivan), then again in Alexander II's day (Repin), so too in ours (Balashov, Chaliapin). These examples, however, also suggest how renunciation of history's origins was enmeshed in a troubling embrace of repetition. Ultimately, did Balashov renounce Ivan's violence, or repeat it? Likewise, did Chaliapin's multiple re-stagings of Repin's painting, which originally delivered a call to transcend the bloodshed and confrontation of past eras, heal the wounds of Russian history or demonstrate that they still festered?

Prominent representatives of more sober-minded professions, including professional historians, held related views concerning the ironic complexity and enduring significance of the Russian past. I examine below one prominent example of such a stance in historiography—Pavel Miliukov's influential *Outlines of Russian Cultural History* (Ocherki po istorii russkoi kul'tury, 1896–1903), which recast Russian history as a series of false starts and misaligned forces. Such views were especially potent for the artists and writers of the period—from the Decadents of the 1890s to the Symbolists of the first decades of the twentieth century to huge proliferation of other modernist movements that followed in their wake. As Boris Gasparov has observed, the dominant temporal intuition of modernists in Russia was in essence "mythical"—a perception of superhistorical, repeating patterns tending toward their explosive final iteration in the present day. In Russian cultural life of the decades around the turn of the twentieth century, temporality as myth, which is to some extent proper to any allegorical vision of history, including many of the literary and artistic works I have examined above, overwhelmed the idea of history itself as an unfolding of events in sequence. As Gasparov puts it: "Modernist culture did not view itself as the most recent historical 'stage,' but rather as an eschatological and messianic 'phenomenon' which was conferring new (and perhaps ultimate) meaning over the entire course of 'history' and on all of history's preceding development. [. . .] Historical succession gave way to mythological simultaneity."[9]

Gasparov's observations are geared specifically toward his analysis of the Pushkin myth in Russian modernism—the tendency of artists and writers to interpret present events and experience as a repetition or reflection of the life and times of Russia's national poet. Yet his comments are therefore doubly pertinent to one of the central obsessions of the modernist reception of Pushkin: the poet's own mythic reception of Peter the Great, in particular as expressed in *The Bronze Horseman*. In a period cast by many as the end of the Imperial Russian order, this heightened concern with its founder as he was represented by its most celebrated poet is hardly surprising. Refracted through the age's fixation on the "centennial return" of Pushkin's age, the poet's meditation in his last epic poem on the paradoxical persistence of Petrine elements in the Russian historical experience—from the triumphal to the traumatic—figured as a prior

---

9. Gasparov, "Golden Age," 2.

instance of the modernist access to this same intuition. The Petrine origin was, in this manner, refracted through Pushkin's era into the present—projecting three hypostases of an essential, superhistorical plane of existence. The central feature of this modernist redaction of Pushkin's Petrine myth was the widely shared certainty that the seeds of an impending collapse were inherent in the very founding of the imperial order. Pushkin's ironic vision of the Petrine era and legacy—as a despotic imposition of enlightenment and the creation of a civilization buttressed by continued traumatic violence—translated for modernists into a projection of ends onto beginnings, fashioning the mythic parallelism of past and present as an apocalyptic return to the origin that foretold an inevitable downfall.

The number of modernist literary and artistic returns to the figure of Peter the Great via a contemplation of Pushkin's poetic masterpiece is astonishing. As Aleksandr Ospovat and Roman Timenchik have shown, almost every poet of the age offered one or many meditations on *The Bronze Horseman*. Innokentii Annenskii, Aleksandr Blok, Valerii Briusov, Zinaida Gippius, Viacheslav Ivanov, Vladimir Maiakovskii, in lyric poetry; Aleksandr Benois, in a variety of visual art media; Andrei Belyi, in his masterful novel *Petersburg* (Peterburg, 1913); and many other artists and writers in all manner of media worked and reworked this vein. Their creations formed a network of mutual reference and self-reference that cemented Pushkin's representation of Peter into the historical consciousness of the early twentieth century.[10] The concluding stanzas to a lyric poem by Ivanov that lifted its very title from Pushkin, "The Bronze Horseman" (Mednyi vsadnik, 1905–7), illustrate the mystical energy that radiated from Pushkin's rendition of Petrine history. Addressing his muse, the poet intones:

> At night, you appear to me as a Sybil . . .
> What are you muttering, aged one?
> Are you threatening me with the grave?
> Or foretelling the death of the world?

> You put a silencing finger
> To your lips—and I, through the whisper,
> Hear the clatter of bronze hooves,
> Their muted, heavy stamp. . . .

> Freezing in place, with a pale shriek,
> I call out, "I'm afraid, o Virgin,
> In this triumphant gloom
> Of bronze-galloping Fury. . . ."

> Sybil's reply: "Hear how dully
> The bronze hits the pavement . . .

10. Ospovat and Timenchik, *Pechal'nu povest' sokhranit'*, 110–93.

And then on corpses, corpses, corpses
The hooves stumble."[11]

For Ivanov and his contemporaries, Pushkin was an oracle, a prophet who had read the violence of Peter the Great's age as a mythic precursor of the revolutionary fin de siècle.

The modernist author who heard the clatter of bronze hooves most clearly was undoubtedly Andrei Belyi. His *Petersburg* presents a novel-length meditation on antistate terrorist violence, projected onto the rebellion of a son against a father and passed through the metaphorical prism of the ominous recurrence of the revolt of Pushkin's Evgenii against the monumental Peter.[12] In this novel's climactic, hallucinogenic dream sequence, Peter abandons his pedestal and thunders across the city to ascend to the Dostoevskian gables where the terrorist Aleksandr Ivanovich Dudkin lives. The bronze emperor grotesquely, horribly, confronts Evgenii's heir, the modern-day revolutionary:

His dull metallic cape hung heavily from the brightly reflective shoulders and the scales of his armor; his lip, cast in bronze, melted and trembled equivocally, for the fate of Evgenii was now being repeated once more, just as the past century was being repeated—now, in the very moment when beyond the threshold of this meager entryway the walls of the old building were crumbling into the corroded expanses; just precisely as the past of Aleksandr Ivanovich was yawning open. He exclaimed, "I remembered, I was waiting for you . . ."

The bronze-headed giant had run through the epochs up to this moment, bringing a forged circle to closure; the century's quarters had passed by; and Nicholas had taken the throne; and the Alexanders had taken the throne. Aleksandr Ivanovich, a shade, had tirelessly traced that same circle, the same epochs, running through the days, the years, the minutes, along the raw Petersburg prospects, running while sleeping, waking . . . to the point of exhaustion. And chasing behind him, behind all, was metal striking like thunder, shattering life; metal striking like thunder, in the wastelands and countryside; striking in the cities; striking in the entryways, on the landings, on the steps of midnight stairwells.

The epochs struck like thunder; I have heard that thunder.
Have you heard it?[13]

The scene appears to be driving toward a repetition of Pushkin's concluding passage, in which the monumental horseman will crush the momentary revolt of the powerless individual. However, capitalizing on the ironic ambivalences of Pushkin's text, Belyi's horseman turns in a different direction:

11. Ivanov, *Cor Ardens*, 1:50–51.
12. On the historical and philosophical underpinnings of Bely's *Petersburg*, see Maguire and Malmstad, "Petersburg," esp. 125–35.
13. Belyi, *Peterburg*, 376.

Everything, everything had now been illuminated, when, ten decades later, the Bronze Guest had himself arrived and pronounced hollowly, "Greetings, my boy!" [. . .]

Aleksandr Ivanovich, Evgenii, for the first time at this point understood that he had been running for a century in vain, that metal had struck thunderously behind him with no rage—in the villages, cities, entryways, stairwells. He had been always, already been forgiven, and all that was, together with all that was to be, was only an overstated, embroidered passage through torments in preparation for the horn of the archangels.

He fell at the feet of the Guest. "My teacher!"[14]

Here, Pushkin's expression of the incoherence of the liminal historical figure emerges as the key mechanism in the modernist interpretation of the prerevolutionary moment. Peter, embodying both the crushing weight of the autocracy and the revolutionary rejection of the past, serves as an all-encompassing but overdetermined sign of the present, in which terrorists and representatives of the state compete in authority and brutality—all of them equally heirs of Russia's intertwined tradition of greatness and terror. At the conclusion of Belyi's nightmarish scene, "in utter delirium, Aleksandr Ivanovich trembled in a thousand-pound embrace: the Bronze Horseman, as molten metal, poured into his veins."[15] For Belyi, the incoherence of the conflict of state and individual, of the story of heroic greatness welded to the terror of Russia's originative trauma, presaged an inevitable, apocalyptic collapse, a second coming, or a new world order.

Belyi's revisitation of Pushkin's *The Bronze Horseman* and Chaliapin's restaging of Repin's *Ivan the Terrible and His Son Ivan* illustrate the characteristic features of the age's engagement with Russia's history. Heirs to the great works of nineteenth-century culture that had revealed both the profound traumas of the deep past—Peter's founding of Petersburg on a bed of corpses—and the persistence of violence in subsequent reigns—the pounding of hooves through the decades—many Russians saw the present as a final, convulsive repetition of historical patterns that reached back to the two liminal tsars. In his masterful 1909 lyric "Petersburg," Annenskii captured this sense of history's oppressive presence, refracted through Dostoevskii's yellow fog and the imagery of Pushkin's *Bronze Horseman*:

---

14. Ibid., 377. The epithet "Guest" is a reference to another of Pushkin's reanimating statues, the monument of the Commodore in Pushkin's rendition of the Don Juan tale, *The Stone Guest*. Belyi's conflation of the two images into one mythic image illustrates his acute sensitivity to Pushkin's poetics, anticipating the insights of Roman Jakobson's seminal study *Pushkin and His Sculptural Myth*.

15. Belyi, *Peterburg*, 378.

Yellow fog of Petersburg winter,
Yellow snow, stuck to sidewalks . . .
I don't know: where are you and where we?
I just know we are welded together as one.

Were we composed by decree of the tsar?
Did the Swedes forget to drown us?
In place of a fairy tale, our past contains
Only stones and accounts of horror.

The magician gave us only stones,
And the stormy-yellow toned Neva,
And wastelands of mute squares,
Where executions were held before dawn.[16]

As we have seen, in Pushkin's day the disavowal of the violence of Russian history and political experience was a key mechanism in Russian articulations of collective identity. In that era, the amalgamation of terror and greatness in the historical myths of Ivan and Peter had the character of an "open secret"—deeply significant but seldom acknowledged. By the fin de siècle, however, an obsessive fixation on the ambivalence and irresolution of these liminal figures had become dominant in the Russian historical imagination. For Annenskii, the ironic duality of Russia's history of terror and greatness was itself formative of collective identity.

In this attentiveness to the complex irresolution of the myths of Ivan and Peter, the fin-de-siècle constituted a watershed moment—a high point of self-consciousness regarding the problems that form the central concerns of this book. Yet the history of this era also illustrates the resilience of the vision of selfhood and political life communicated in Russian historical myth. For the age's sophisticated insight into the ironies of Russian history did not lead to critical engagement or transcendence of that tradition. Instead, Russians resolved their intuitions about the incoherence of Russian political life in a manner rather wanting in irony. For Belyi, as for many of his contemporaries, Russian history's tendency to reduce toward flux and incoherence was the most compelling proof of a looming apocalyptic dissolution, "an overstated, embroidered passage through torments in preparation for the horn of the archangels." In this manner, Belyi squared irony's circle, deriving utopian and apocalyptic visions rather lacking in irony from his sophisticated comprehension of Russia's history of terror and greatness. As we shall see below, such a leap from insight into blindness—for all its obvious, superordinate irony—was also typical of the age.

---

16. Annenskii, *Izbrannoe*, 156.

Divination: Dmitrii Merezhkovskii's *Antichrist (Peter and Aleksei)*

In 1910, Dmitrii Merezhkovskii—a leading poet, theorist, and novelist of the
first generation of Russian Symbolists—published a meditation that derived its
impetus from two basic references: first, the legendary prophecy attributed to
Peter's first wife, whom he had forcibly committed to a nunnery, that "Petersburg will be empty"; and second, the key lines from Pushkin's *Bronze Horseman*
taken as an epigraph for this chapter. Merezhkovskii plays off the homonymic
relationship of "dyby," haunches, to "dyba," an early modern Russian torture
device akin to the rack, in order to glimpse in Pushkin's poem a prediction of
Russia's headlong rush toward its final crisis:

> *The Bronze Horseman* [. . .] is the most revolutionary of all of Pushkin's
> works. [. . .] Here, under the guise of humble praise, a brazen question is
> posed about the entire "Petersburg period of Russian history: ". . . by whose
> fateful will / Was a city founded here at the edge of the sea." The word
> "dyba" designates a torture instrument, a rack on which people were beaten
> with the knout. Peter's son, Aleksei, was raised up on the "dyba" in the
> dungeon two days before his death, "given twenty-five blows" and "asked
> about all his affairs." [. . .] "He said that his teacher, Viazemskii, had said
> to him [. . .]: 'Stepan Beliaev sings with his chorus in your father's [Peter's]
> presence, that God, whenever he so wills, may overturn the order of the
> elements; and they all sing that in flattery to your father; and that is pleasing
> to your father, that they equate him with God.' " [. . .] Petersburg is just
> such a miracle. Here, the "order of the elements" has been overturned by a
> "wonderworking builder," not by a man, but by a "god." Feofan Prokopo-
> cich called him a "Christ," that is, one who has been anointed, and the Old
> Believers called him "Antichrist." Is Petersburg—the eternal rack, on which
> torture is inflicted—a Christ or an Antichrist? Dostoevskii understood that
> in Petersburg Russia had come to some sort of "final point" and hangs
> "suspended over an abyss." [. . .] But it can't stand, rearing up like that
> forever. The horror is inherent in the implication that "to set down its
> hooves" means to plunge into the abyss. And here, the brazen question gives
> way to a brazen answer, to a mad challenge: "All right, wonderworking
> builder, / [. . .] You just watch out! . . ." This is the final point of our
> madness, our delirium, our horror: Petersburg will be empty![17]

The subject matter of Merezhkovskii's essay, the research that went into it,
and the apocalyptic conclusions would all have been familiar to readers from

---

17. D. S. Merezhkovskii, "Zimnie radugi," in his *Akropol'*, 220–27, here 225–26. The
several unattributed citations in the passage are from Pushkin's *Bronze Horseman*. The quotation from Dostoevskii is drawn from an open letter to the students of Moscow University
of 1881, in his *Polnoe sobranie sochinenii*, 30:21–26, here 23.

the author's novel, published several years earlier, *Antichrist (Peter and Aleksei)* (Antikhrist [Petr I Aleksei], 1904). Although the essay's link between historical "facts" and exalted conclusions is rather obtuse, a reading of this novel allows us to chart out not only the Symbolist author's mystical logic but also the precise relationship between an ironic comprehension of the historical myth of Peter and the prophetic visions of the modernist age in general.

Antichrist (Peter and Aleksei) was the final installment in a trilogy of historical novels entitled *Christ and Antichrist* (Khrist i Antikhrist, 1895–1904)—a key work of the fin de siècle and Merezhkovskii's most successful foray into historical fiction. The first novel in this trilogy treated the reign of Julian the Apostate, the last pagan Roman emperor (331–63, emperor from 360), while the second represented the biography of Leonardo da Vinci (1452–1519). The third work, *Antichrist (Peter and Aleksei)*, covers the era of Peter the Great, focusing on the conflict between the emperor and his son. The trilogy as a whole is informed by a Nietzschean and eschatological scheme of history as the scene of recurring cycles of mythical conflict, tending toward an ultimate apocalyptic resolution. Merezhkovskii's key terms, the "Christ" and "Antichrist" of the trilogy's title, are superhistorical, transcendent principles, available to human experience only through the mediation of symbols—as bodied forth in artistic works, elements of religious systems, and culture in general.[18] "Christ," for Merezhkovskii, is identified loosely with Christian teachings, which the poet considered as bearing the "truth of the sky"—a core of beliefs and values including the drive to self-abnegation, communitarian selflessness, and universal love yet also marked by a certain lack of vitality and dynamism. As he began work on the trilogy, Merezhkovskii imagined "Antichrist" as a fundamentally opposed but equally compelling "truth of the earth" affiliated with Hellenic paganism and the values of artistic beauty, heroic individualism, and uncontainable life force. While working on *Antichrist* the author moderated his views and his terms radically—embracing a mystical version of Christianity and renouncing Hellenism, with important implications for the reading of the novel. As a result, the trilogy presents not so much periods linked by a historical or causal logic as three scenes of the unfolding conflict between these principles.[19]

The plot of *Antichrist* is less a dramatically coherent narrative than a chronology of the last few years of Tsarevich Aleksei's life: his deteriorating relationship with Peter, flight to Europe, return to Russia, trial, and eventual death. This constrained historical plot is punctuated by reminiscences of earlier periods in the tsarevich's biography. Merezhkovskii interweaves historical and

---

18. The "symbol," in the thought of Russian Symbolists, was a nebulous and contested concept. As Marina Tsvetaeva once remarked, "in the life of a Symbolist, everything is a symbol." On Belyi's theories of symbolism, see Cassedy, "Bely's Theory of Symbolism."

19. For an examination of Merezhkovskii's trilogy as a whole in the context of his life and thought, see Bedford, *The Seeker*, 60–90. For a treatment of the trilogy as a statement on history, see Christensen, "*Christ and Antichrist* as Historical Novel."

fictional materials, the latter infused with intertextual references to the canonical Petrine and Petersburg texts of Pushkin, Dostoevskii, and others. An intricate overlay of mythic and scriptural reference transforms the "historical scene" into a verbal analogue of a much revered and reworked Orthodox icon, set in an ornate frame of precious metals and gems. Merezhkovskii communicates his cyclic, mythic vision of history through continuities and analogies with the early novels in the trilogy but also through analogies in Russian history—including Ivan the Terrible's killing of his son. Yet the several mentions of that earlier episode of filicide are but a minor example of Merezhkovskii's self-conscious reception of earlier traditions of historical interpretation.[20]

The major conflict of the novel is between Peter and Aleksei, and it is based in the familiar antinomies of the Petrine epoch: Peter represents technological, social, and military advances; Aleksei represents Old Russian civilization and peaceful inactivity. Peter is identified with St. Petersburg; Aleksei is drawn to Moscow and the provincial scene of the countryside. Peter is pictured in "European" costume—as a Dutch sea captain or a European lord; Aleksei, when not dressed for occasions of state, appears in stylized Russian national dress. Peter is associated with secular knowledge and with religious institutional reform, inspired by the Protestant and Catholic west; Aleksei is shown in the company of traditionalist clerics and the mystically inclined oppositional figures centered around his mother Evdokiia, in her monastic exile. In particular, Merezhkovskii closely echoes Solovev's explanation of the distinction between Peter, brilliant man of action and deeds, and Aleksei—intelligent, bookish, and given to reflection but slow-moving and weak. Also familiar from Solovev's history, the comparison to another Aleksei, Tsar Aleksei Mikhailovich the "Most Quiet" (*tishaishii*), forms a leitmotif in Merezhkovskii's description of the tsarevich: "The grandson fulfilled the testament of the grandfather: hold the clergy higher than yourself" (2:483–84).[21]

All these historically based but mythically exaggerated oppositions align with Merezhkovskii's fundamental tension between Christ and Antichrist, between the Old Russian humility and weakness of Aleksei and the almost pagan individualism and vitality of Peter, who appears as a Nietzschean superman, existing beyond the moral code and regarding all around him as mere raw material or historical detritus.[22] Merezhkovskii's identification of historical actors with transcendent principles is underwritten by the belief common among Old Believers that Peter was literally the Antichrist, a legend that figures large in

20. For the repeated mention of Ivan the Terrible's murder of his son in the novel, see Merezhkovskii, *Sobranie sochinenii*, 2:388, 504, 524.

21. Ibid. References to this edition are given in text. For other instances of the comparison of Tsarevich Aleksei with Tsar Aleksei Mikhailovich, see ibid., 2:324, 403. Note that Merezhkovskii's identification of Aleksei Mikhailovich with the principle of subordination of state to church is historically inaccurate. See Crummey, "Eastern Orthodoxy," 302–24.

22. For discussion of Merezhkovskii's engagement with Nietzsche's thought, see Rosenthal, "Stages of Nietzscheanism," 69–93.

the novel. The novel's first words are uttered by one Larion Dokukin, a folk religious thinker, who explains to the tsarevich that: "The Antichrist wants to come into being. He himself, the final demon, has not yet arrived, but his whelps have already multiplied" (2:319). Later, the "schismatic elder and prophet of self-immolation" Kornilii, pronounces:

> Attend, Orthodox people, who now rules as tsar, who has taken possession of you since the year 1666, the number of the Beast. First, Tsar Aleksei Mikhailovich and Patriarch Nikon turned away from the faith, precursors of the Beast. After them, Tsar Peter uprooted piety entirely, abolished the patriarchate and stole for himself all divine and churchly authority, rising up against our lord, Jesus Christ. [. . .] According to prophecy—in the name of Simon, of Peter, there will rise in Rome the proud prince of the world, the Antichrist—thus in Russia, that is, in the Third Rome, Peter has appeared, the son of ruin, heretic and enemy of God: the Antichrist. (2:356, 362–63).

At the novel's melodramatic climax, Aleksei himself rises before Peter and the Imperial Senate, assembled to sentence him, howling at his father: "villain, murderer, beast, Antichrist! Be damned! Damned! Damned!" (2:707).[23]

Symmetrically, Merezhkovskii deploys a related cycle of folk myth that assimilated Aleksei to legends about the arrival of a saintly "true tsar" who would set all to rights in Russia—a belief that figured historically in the mythic identities of any number of pretenders and peasant rebels, usually projected around a former tsar, rumored to be still living, or a dead heir to the throne such as Tsarevich Dmitrii.[24] So, at a moment when Peter lies ill and seemingly near death, one of Aleksei's flatterers tells him that he is destined to become "the pious, religious lord Aleksei Petrovich, autocrat of all the Russias [. . .], at once tsar and patriarch!" (2:481).[25]

Merezhkovskii's conceptual categories of "Antichrist" and "Christ" are distinct from the legendary imagination of Russia's religious dissenters, whom Merezhkovskii both values as repositories of folk wisdom and denigrates as wild-eyed fanatics led by opportunistic fakes (the ranting, chain-wearing elder Kornilii, for instance, organizes mass self-immolations from which he himself emerges unscathed). Yet the author makes use of folk legend as a support for

23. For other discussions of Peter as Antichrist, see Merezhkovskii, *Sobranie sochinenii*, 2:319–22, 355–67, 369–71, 390–91, 474, 657–60, 712–13.

24. For accounts of the pretender myth, see Chistov, *Russkie narodnye sotsial'noutopicheskie legendy*, 24–220, esp. 112–24; Uspenskii, "Tsar and Pretender"; Emerson, *Boris Godunov*, 17–19.

25. Later, when Aleksei is in hiding in Italy, he himself imagines his future reign in similar terms: "I'll labor for the peasants, for the weak and downtrodden, for Christ's little ones. I'll gather an assembly of the land and the church, the representatives of the whole people: let all speak truth to the tsar, without fear, with the freest voice, in order to repair the kingdom and the church with common council and with the advent of the Holy Spirit for all ages" (Merezhkovskii, *Sobranie sochinenii*, 2:556).

his own mystical vision, allowing a historically based yet stylized religious delirium to occupy the level of distant cultural echo of the author's "true" transcendent values. Likewise, Peter and Aleksei themselves are not to be taken as Antichrist and Christ in any straightforward sense but rather as the unwitting historical representatives of Merezhkovskii's grand ideals.

Yet the relationship between these characters is more dynamic than one of simple conflict. Neither father nor son, nor the transcendent realities that they represent, are completely static or absolutely locked in opposition to each other; for Merezhkovskii makes use of Peter's liminal capacity to imagine both him and his son as mediating the semiotic borders not only between traditional and modern Russia but also between the author's own opposed "truths" of the earth and of the heavens. Strikingly, Aleksei, in moments of anger or of intense struggle with his father, eerily comes to resemble him. Early in the novel, a meeting where Peter demands and receives Aleksei's renunciation of the succession ends in a wordless standoff, both men realizing how hollow any such oath must be in practice: "Aleksei was silent, casting his gaze downwards. His face appeared now as a deadened mask, just like Peter's. Mask against mask—and between the two a sudden, strange, somehow ghostly resemblance—a similarity between extremes" (2:499). At another moment, the normally meek and yielding Aleksei beats and rapes his peasant lover, Efrosynia, who comments that he is "just like his daddy," her ardor perversely excited by his attack.[26]

Peter, for his part, frequently appears not as a well-defined representative of enlightened ideals but instead as an incomprehensible composite of irreconcilables. In Aleksei's experience, Peter alternates between loving, tender father and cruel tyrant and torturer. His earliest memories are of spiritual union with his father, "a merry, quick eyed boy with curly hair," who carries him carefully and lovingly aloft in the triumphal parade following the victorious Azov campaign of 1695–96: "and it seemed to him that all his father's movements were his own; that all of his father's strength, was his own; and that he and his father were one" (2:508). In these moments of intimate contact Peter acquires nonmasculine, motherly characteristics: a "grandmotherly" dimple on his chin and a "feminine" curve to his smiling lips (2:333, 512, 521).[27] Yet in a later reminiscence, the eight-year-old Aleksei runs away from his tutors and becomes witness to a different aspect of his father: the horrific sight of Peter's mass torture and execution of the *Streltsy* rebels:

> People were being roasted on the fire, raised up on the rack and ripped
> apart, so that their joints cracked; their ribs were being broken with red-hot

26. Ibid., 2:583; for other examples of convergence of Peter and Aleksei, see 2:485, 622, 701. Efrosynia herself reflects Aleksei's duality—at times his attraction to her reflects the purity of a selfless, folk Christianity, and at other times she appears as a figure for unbounded, delirious pagan sensual ideals—a double of Venera.

27. For a description of Peter's fear of insects as being like that of a "cowardly woman," see ibid., 2:418.

clamps; "nails were being cleaned"—scorching needles were being thrust up
under them. Among the hangmen was the tsar. His face was so fearsome
that Aleksei didn't recognize his own father: it was him, but not him—as if
it were his twin or a werewolf. He was personally torturing one of the rebel
leaders, who was bearing it all in silence. The rebel's body was already like
a bloody piece of meat, from which the butchers had ripped all of the skin.
But he said nothing through it all, looking right into the tsar's eyes, as if he
were laughing at him. Suddenly, as he died, he lifted his head and spat right
into the tsar's eyes: "take that, son of a bitch, Antichrist!" The tsar seized
his dagger from its sheath and plunged it into his throat. Blood spattered
into the tsar's face. (2:513)

For those around Peter, the impossible irresolution of his character is axiomatic. As Aleksei's wife's lady-in-waiting writes of Peter in her diary: "Sometimes
it seems that the contradictions of the two elements dear to him, fire and water, have been fused in him in one being, strange and alien. I don't know if he
is good or evil, divine or devilish—but he is certainly not human" (2:414). Peter's unpredictable duality, his alternation between love and cruelty, identity and
alienation, man and woman, fire and water—continues throughout the novel, so
that even in the final chapters, which concern the tsarevich's trial for treason
after his return from Europe, Peter combines loving concern and pity for his
son with personal participation in the torture of his own child.

These mitigations of categorical opposition illustrate Merezhkovskii's inheritance from Pushkin's *Bronze Horseman*: an ironic conception of history
founded on the liminal inconsistencies of the first emperor. For Merezhkovskii,
as for Pushkin, Peter the Great's historical incoherence rises out of his concatenation of the high goal of social progress for the common good with the cruel
means of its imposition on subjects who cannot or would not achieve those social goods in any other way. Merezhkovskii lays plain to his readers the vicious
trap of progress through coercion, for the reforms themselves, despite their
beneficent intent, cannot but sink back into the quicksand of archaic, autocratic
habits. As the tsarevich intuits while he lingers in exile in Naples: "That Europe, which Tsar Peter was introducing to Russia—mathematics, navigation,
fortification—was not all of Europe and not even its most important element.
[. . .] The true Europe possesses a higher truth, of which the tsar was ignorant.
And without this truth, despite all the scientific innovations, the old Muscovite
barbarity would be replaced only by a new Petersburg idiocy" (2: 548).

As in the historiographical treatments of the death of the tsarevich, in *Antichrist* the historical irony of progressive reform effected through archaic means
plays out in family romance: "Aleksei's father beat him many times, both casu-
ally, with fists, and ceremoniously, with the staff. The tsar did everything in a
new manner, but he beat his son the old-fashioned way, according to the
Household Rules [Domostroi] of Father Silvestr, advisor to Ivan the Terrible, the
filicide" (2:524). Yet in a departure from the historical accounts, Merezhkovskii

sees Aleksei as no mere repository of mindless conservatism or merely private, bodily interests. The tsarevich represents a different and no less compelling set of social and political priorities: those of a truly humane love of others. At one point he even clumsily attempts to plead with Peter on behalf of the suffering common people, yet this only convinces the emperor of Aleksei's unfitness to rule (2:523).

For his part, Peter experiences his relationship to his son as a microcosm of his general political situation, seeing his alienation from Aleksei as an extreme instance of his unutterable solitude amid a people whom he cannot trust to carry out his projects except out of fear and servility (2:608). Yet despite the laudatory nature of Aleksei's social ideals, he, too, is subject to the same ironic concatenation of progress and reaction that afflicts Peter. In Merezhkovskii's rendering, pre-Petrine Russian society is in obvious need of reform, trapped in a stifling obscurantism and in the swamp of petty corruption which like a congenital disease infects the traditionalist clerics who support Aleksei. Ultimately, resistance to his father's plans in the name of higher Christian values transforms uncontrollably into Aleksei's grandiose, drunken dreams of his own autocratic power and thirst for his father's blood.

For Merezhkovskii, the implications of this ironic vision, which reduces the fundamental notion of progressive reform in Peter's reign to self-defeating absurdity, are far reaching. Through such means as a recurring image of St. Petersburg fog, in which all solid categories melt away, or an extended episode concerning the 1715 flood of the Neva, the novel persistently references the nineteenth-century Petersburg tradition of works concerning the Russian mating of autocracy and humanism. In one instance, the tsarevich's reflections, as he listens to the scientific conversations of Peter's advisors, borrow the conceptual plot of Pushkin's epic poem: "In this discussion the same thing was happening with ideas as occurred with snow in a Petersburg thaw: everything was melting, thawing, decaying, transforming into slush and mud, washed over by a putrid western wind. Doubt in everything, negation of all, without a backward glance, without restraint, rising like the waters of the Neva, blocked by the wind and threatening to overflow" (2:468).[28]

Here, as in the passage of Belyi's *Petersburg* cited above, the reference to Pushkin's poem projects the historical legacies of Peter's mating of greatness and terror into the centuries to come. With more literal specificity, prophesies of doom form a continuous refrain, echoing forward to the twentieth-century reader with a rumble of imminent disaster. To the historically attested prophecy of Aleksei's mother that "Petersburg will be empty," Merezhkovskii adds Aleksei's own fictional prophetic curse, analogous to the critical content of Repin's *Ivan the Terrible and His Son Ivan*: "'You will be the first to shed the blood of a son, the blood of the Russian tsars, on the executioners block!' The tsarevich spoke again, and it seemed to him that he was no longer speaking for

---

28. For metaphorically charged uses of fog, see ibid., 2:401–2.

himself; his words sounded like a prophecy. 'And this blood will fall from one head to the next, down to the last Russian tsar, and all of our line will perish in blood. God will punish Russia for your deeds!' " (2:341).[29] From the instability of its historical base in the Petrine reforms, Merezhkovskii derives the downfall of Russian imperial civilization.

However, on a higher level of abstraction, that of his grand symbolical system and the eschatological vision of history that it supports, the author points the novel's motif of convergence of opposites in a different direction—toward an impending utopian moment in which opposed categories will dissolve into one another in a moment of redemptive spiritual union. The vehicle of this more hopeful derivation is Tikhon Zapolskii, the main character of a nearly wholly independent secondary plot. The orphan son of an executed *Strelets* mutineer, Tikhon is a questing spirit, an epileptic who experiences his fits as an apocalyptic presentiment, a "sense of the end" or "horror of the end" recalling Dostoevskii's epileptic character, the Christlike Prince Myshkin, with his utopian intuitions of timelessness.[30] Precisely the same age as the tsarevich, Tikhon is a double of Aleksei, ultimately arriving at the same point by a different route.[31] From his adoptive childhood home in Moscow, where he is exposed to the mystical imagination of Russia's religious dissenters, Tikhon's path runs to the opposite Petrine extreme; he receives a technical education in science and mathematics and by virtue of his evident talents is selected for further education abroad, in Europe. Yet his first sight of St. Petersburg, from where he is to debark for the west, shocks him into running away with the Old Believer elder Kornilii.

In a distant schismatic camp, Tikhon willingly joins in a mass self-immolation as an act of resistance to the encroaching soldiers of the imperial "Antichrist," recalling the final scene of Musorgskii's *Khovanshchina*. Tikhon is "miraculously" saved when the duplicitous Kornilii drags him from the flames via a secret escape passage. Abandoning Kornilii, he subsequently joins an underground Khlysty sect in Moscow given to orgiastic group worship—an episode that ends in a scene of narrowly averted human sacrifice. Saved by his former teachers from punishment, Tikhon becomes for a time the librarian to Peter's powerful religious advisor Feofan Prokopovich before running away again, landing in a remote hermitage on an island in Lake Ladoga.

Through Tikhon's oscillations between east and west, between secular rationalism and the wild extremes of mystical experience, Merezhkovskii charts a path toward a nonironic meeting of the novel's opposed symbolic clusters. Early in the work, Tikhon overhears a conversation among Peter's advisers

29. The prophecy is first uttered by Dokukin as Peter is torturing him. Peter later remembers and repeats the prophecy (ibid., 2:643, 722).

30. For some reason, several western critics have incorrectly labeled Tikhon as a peasant—he is in fact a member of the service gentry. For discussions of Tikhon's epileptic attacks, see ibid., 2:371, 372.

31. Tikhon's name, which evokes the epithet of Tsar Aleksei Mikhailovich, "Most Quiet" (tishaishii from "tishina," quiet), also ties him to the tsarevich.

concerning the possibility of mating faith with reason, which eventually turns to Newton's "Commentaries on the Apocalypse":

> At that very time when Newton was composing his commentaries, at the other end of the world—that is to say, here in Muscovy—the wild heretics whom they call schismatics were composing their own commentaries to the Apocalypse. And they came to almost precisely the same conclusions as Newton did. Anticipating the end of the world and the second coming at any time, some of them lay down in coffins and sang the psalms, while others set themselves on fire. [. . .] In this apocalyptic delirium, the extreme west and the extreme east, the greatest enlightenment and the greatest ignorance, all converge, which in truth might suggest that the end of the world is nigh and that we will all soon go to the devil! (2:376–77)

This intuition of these men of western science concerning the mystical identity of east and west is matched by Tikhon's complementary discovery of the unity of opposites in the depths of folk religious culture. Searching for a realization of the Christian ideal of communitarian self-sacrifice and love, Tikhon instead discovers a resurgence of pagan rites of ecstatic orgy, blood sacrifice and earth worship. The leaders of Russia's folk religious movements, no Christian meek ones, exhibit as extreme a Nietzschean will to power as does Peter the Great himself. In terms of Merezhkovskii's master categories, looking for Christ, Tikhon finds Antichrist instead.

Yet Tikhon's ethnographic journey through the byways of Russian religious culture is only a prelude to the last, revelatory scenes of the novel. In his final days, Tsarevich Aleksei is graced by a vision of a saintly old man, "John, son of Thunder"—St. John the Apostle—who administers to him a mystical last communion, filling him with certainty that "there is neither sadness, nor fear, nor pain, nor death, but there is only eternal life, the eternal sun—Christ" (2:713). In the work's final pages, Tikhon, too, has a vision of St. John, but a far more extensive one. John instructs him that:

> I will soon gather you all into the new church of the Lord to Come. There was the ancient church of Peter, the standing rock, and there will be the new church of John, the flying thunderbolt. Lightening will strike in the rock, and the living water will flow. The first testament was the Old—the Kingdom of the Father—the second testament was the New—the Kingdom of the Son— and the third testament is the Final—the kingdom of the Holy Spirit. One are as Three and Three are as One. He who is and was and is to come, the Lord is true to his promises!

Subsequently, Tikhon has an ecstatic vision of Christ himself and is stuck dumb forever, fated to "walk, in his eternal silence, until he has trodden all the paths of the earth, and finally come into the church of John" (2:757–59). Complementing the prophesies of doom that Merezhkovskii derives from his notion of the Petrine project's ironic incoherence, Tikhon and Aleksei's visions offer a complementary prophesy of redemption in a postapocalyptic transcendence of symbolic antinomies, a union of the truths of the earth and of the sky.

There is much conceptual slippage in Tikhon's final vision, in which the Old Testament "Church of the Father" takes the place of the pagan, "Anti-Christian" principle—a slippage that corresponds to Merezhkovskii's own spiritual trajectory as he progressed from a fashionable infatuation with Nietzscheanism and Hellenism to a Christian rebirth (although never in the terms of formal religious institutions—his was a peculiarly personal, apocalyptic Christianity, corresponding to Tikhon's church of John).[32] As he explained this trajectory himself some years later:

> When I began the trilogy *Christ and Antichrist*, it seemed to me that two truths existed—Christianity, the truth of heaven, and paganism, the truth of the earth—and that the absolute religious truth lay in the future union of these two truths. But as I was finishing it, I already knew that the union of Christ and Antichrist was a blasphemous lie; I knew that both truths, of heaven and earth, had already been united in Jesus Christ. [. . .] But I now also know that I had to follow this lie to its end, in order to see the truth. From divarication to synthesis; such is my path.[33]

Based in ecstatic revelation, there is precious little discursive or historical logic to Merezhkovskii's view of temporality: ultimately, history is present in *Antichrist* only to demonstrate its own incoherence, to presage its own dissolution.[34] The choice of Petrine history as the site for this demonstration was dictated by Russian cultural history, in which Peter's concatenation of heroism and trauma was the cornerstone of collective identity and therefore constituted the wellspring of the fundamental ironies afflicting Russian social life. Merezhkovskii's vision of history is shaped as a dialectic, but this is a mystical dialectic that leads forward into a synthesis available only through the author's theurgic vision. In the face of this new, postapocalyptic truth, Peter and the imperial era he founded were to crumble in ruin.

Dialectic: Pavel Miliukov's *The Outlines of Russian Cultural History*

Merezhkovskii's comments on his work on *Christ and Antichrist* point toward the basic congruence of the figure of irony and the analytic mechanism of the

---

32. On Merezhkovskii's "Religion of the Third Testament," see Bedford, *The Seeker*, 91–112; and Matich, "Merezhkovskys' Third Testament," 158–71.

33. D. S. Merezhkovskii, "Ot avtora," in his *Polnoe sobranie sochinenii*, 1:iii, quoted and translated in Bedford, *Seeker*, 91.

34. For discussion of Merezhkovskii's conclusion as a form of historical thinking, see Christensen, "*Christ and Antichrist* as Historical Novel," 75–76.

dialectic when it comes to visions of history. The dialectic is predicated on a comprehension of the equivocality of the historical process, projecting a vision of the past characterized by fundamental forces locked in a conflict that appears to be insoluble and contradictory: this is the historical object as an ironic sign, pointing equivocally in many directions at once. Dialectic schemes of historical becoming are not always ironic: often enough—as in the schematic political rhetoric so familiar from Soviet public discourse—they describe the lucid conflict of the good guys versus the bad guys, the oppressed classes versus oppressors, for control over society's productive forces. Yet the greatest and most influential practitioners of dialectical critique—Hegel in the *Philosophy of History*, Marx in *The Eighteenth Brumaire of Louis Bonaparte,* or Marx and Engels in the *Communist Manifesto*—were deeply invested in a notion of historical process in which each age appears as an ironic riddle, in which the true outlines of historical conflict are hidden from most or all of history's actors and interpreters, who often enough in their pursuit of self-interested or reactionary aims are in fact furthering the basic, progressive causes of world history: "Men make their own history, but they do not make it just as they please."[35]

It should also be noted that irony is not necessarily dialectical. Certainly, as a rhetorical figure the baffling or stylish ironic turn is often a prelude to a plain-talking decoding that dispenses with all equivocation, often through a synthetic step. Yet ironic views of history also have the potential to abandon interpretation high and dry in unresolved and truly unresolvable crisis—the stuff of tragedy—and the stuff of *The Bronze Horseman*.

For a dialectical but nonironic rendition of Russian history, and of the distant centuries at issue in this book, one need look no further than Kavelin or Solovev, whose dialectic of Russian history traced out the state's self-evidently glorious struggle to perfect Russian society. An ironic dialectic of Russian history would be articulated only decades later, at the turn of the century, by a historian and political figure who owed much to those earlier scholars, Pavel Miliukov. Miliukov's historical writings, although very distant from a Symbolist worldview, complement Merezhkovskii's in their basic architecture, underwriting a prophecy of the imminent demise of the Russian social order. There are other ironies afoot here as well. Similar to the political practice of revolutionary movements and presaging the development of Soviet public culture in later decades, Miliukov raised the standard of the materialistic rejection of the role of "historical individuals" such as Peter or Ivan, only to return via a circuitous route to the principle of transformative historical change effected by human will. Like Merezhkovskii's, Miliukov's prognoses were destined to be confirmed, although not in the manner he imagined.

---

35. Karl Marx, "The Eighteenth Brumaire of Louis Bonaparte," in *Marx–Engels Reader,* ed. Tucker, 595. On the relationship of irony to dialectical thought, see Burke, *On Symbols and Society,* 247–60.

In December 1900, the students of the St. Petersburg Mining Institute invited Miliukov to address an illicit meeting in memory of one of the leading theoreticians of the People's Will revolutionary movement, Pavel Lavrov. Miliukov, both in his historical writing and later in his political practice as a leading light of the Constitutional Democratic Party, consistently sought a liberal path toward social progress in Russia.[36] Yet during this earlier portion of his career, at a moment when oppositional Russian political movements were vaguely defined and minimally differentiated, Miliukov was affiliated with Marxist intellectual circles and radical and revolutionary youth movements. He later recalled how on that evening in 1900 he explained to a packed room how police repression had transformed the initially "idyllic" reformist movements of the 1870s into conspiratorial terrorist organizations, leading him to conclude that violence was the logical outcome of any unsuccessful revolutionary activity. When listeners asked him to elucidate Russia's present political situation in light of this conclusion, Miliukov responded with a "historical explanation" from which his auditors drew a "practical conclusion." Among those auditors was a police informer, as a result of which Miliukov was soon sitting in a prison cell. Yet another was the radical student Boris Savinkov, who years later recalled that evening to Miliukov, remarking that "in fact, I am your student."[37] Immediately subsequent to the historian's lecture, Savinkov's career led him through revolutionary activity, arrest, exile, and escape abroad to a position of leadership in the Socialist Revolutionary Party, and ultimately to participation in the assassinations of Minister of Internal Affairs Viacheslav von Plehve in 1904 and Grand Duke Sergei Aleksandrovich in 1905.

I offer this peculiar genealogy linking Miliukov's activities as a public intellectual with far more radical and violent modes of political action not to impugn his credentials as a liberal. Rather, I want to suggest that the Russian experience of political polarization in the prerevolutionary years made it difficult to disentangle liberal views of history from extremist "conclusions" in the present, and that although Miliukov always strove to effect an admirably moderate political program, his intellectual and practical positions were also symptomatic of the broader currents that culminated in the October revolution and the bloodshed that followed it. For ultimately, Miliukov's historical writings, which he hoped would reveal to Russians a mode of comprehending the past that would enable them to transcend it, contributed instead to the reenactment of scenes from history in Russia's present.

36. In the years after the revolution of 1905, Miliukov participated in the founding and leadership of the Constitutional Democratic Party. In 1917, he assumed the position of minister of foreign affairs in the Provisional Government, becoming a symbol of revolutionary moderation and bourgeois values, hated or beloved depending on the observer's political orientation.

37. Miliukov had met Lavrov in Paris some years earlier and had penned an obituary earlier in 1900. For Miliukov's account of the lecture and his later exchange with Savinkov, see Miliukov, *Vospominaniia*, 1:208–9. Also see Riha, *Russian European*, 38–39.

Miliukov's training, under the direction of Kliuchevskii, had prepared him for a brilliant academic career. During the late 1890s and the first years of the new century, however, as a result of the young scholar's conflicts with his adviser, his growing political engagement, and the resulting punitive measures of the state, he was confined to marginal academic positions in provincial exile or abroad in Bulgaria and the United States. Increasingly he found himself in the center of oppositional public life.[38] Whereas his 1892 dissertation was a thoroughly academic study of the extent of Peter I's actual involvement in the reform process, based on extensive original archival research, Miliukov's magnum opus, published in three volumes from 1896 to 1903 and reissued with enormous popular success in many revised editions up to the revolution and beyond, was a broad synthetic work aimed at both professional historians and educated Russians in general: *The Outlines of Russian Cultural History.*[39] As Miliukov later recalled, this work, a thematically articulated study of the entire sweep of Russian history, was intended to foster the political maturity of society, combating the "antihistorical and dangerous" policies of the state, which were "consciously aimed at the retardation of enlightenment among the Russian people."[40]

In 1896, in the first volume of the *Outlines,* covering "population and economic, state, and estate structure," Miliukov made plain precisely what form of political activity he hoped to catalyze with his writings. The introduction to the volume offers a meditation on the role of the individual in history, initially seeming to reject entirely the possibility of goal-oriented political action by individuals. According to Miliukov, whereas in the past historiography had been concerned with individual biographies and events, current scientific approaches must focus on the life of society as a whole. All historical phenomena are governed at base by general sociological processes and regularities, conditioned by local geography and the specificities of neighboring societies. According to this view, even the actions of individuals, in essence, reflect these more fundamental factors.[41]

38. For Miliukov's relationship with Kliuchevskii, see Stockdale, *Paul Miliukov,* 23–26, 101–2; and Emmons, "Kliuchevskii's Pupils."

39. The term "cultural history" should not be confused with contemporary usages. As Miliukov explains in the introduction to the first edition of this work, he uses the term "cultural history" not to indicate any restriction of his object of study to culture, high or otherwise, but in reference to his innovative method, in which equal weight is given to economic, cultural, and institutional history (the objects of the three volumes of the work), which he considers as separate spheres of experience that are causally interlinked in a complex dialectic. See Miliukov, *Ocherki,* pt. 1, 4th ed., 3–4. On Miliukov's historical method, see Stockdale, *Paul Miliukov,* 53–80.

40. Miliukov, *Vospominaniia,* 1:173–79. Miliukov describes the *Outlines* as a continuation of other sorts of "enlightening" activity that he undertook in the 1890s: publication of self-education pamphlets, public lecture series in the provinces, etc. On the reception of the *Outlines* in general, see Stockdale, *Paul Miliukov,* 74; and Laurie Manchester, "Contradictions at the Heart of Russian Liberalism."

41. Miliukov, *Ocherki,* pt. 3, 1st ed., 1:14.

Yet the historian was not willing to discount completely the place of the individual in history, especially with regard to political aspirations. To resolve the tension between a historical science that denied the role of personality and a politics of reform that depended on individual initiative, Miliukov turned to a rhetorical formula that is familiar from Marxist theory of this period, and that would become a staple of public discourse in subsequent decades: the dichotomy between "spontaneity" (*stikhiinost'*) and "consciousness" (*soznatel'nost'*). As the historian explained, while *most* actions of men and women in history are "spontaneous," that is, blinded by a lack of insight and hence governed entirely by unrecognized causal factors, "conscious" actions, in which goals are clearly envisioned and in accord with social historical processes, may influence the course of events.[42] Surprisingly, given Miliukov's initial gestures of dismissal toward the "great men" of history, at the conclusion of his introduction Miliukov cites Thomas Carlyle's writings on "The Heroic in History":

> "All things that we see standing accomplished in the world are properly the outer material result, the practical realization and embodiment, of Thoughts that dwelt in the Great Men sent into the world: the soul of the whole world's history, it may justly be considered, were the history of these." In this view only one thing is correct. Given the lack of consciousness and the spontaneity with which social evolution has everywhere and always been carried out, it has truly been only the official or moral leaders of the masses who have accomplished socially purposeful deeds. But even then, these isolated actions of individuals have run up against the idiocy of the masses, and these individual purposeful deeds have not brought in their wake firm, socially decisive results. Yet to suppose that this has been and always will be the case would be to give in to excessive, or at any rate premature, pessimism. We cannot deny the possibility of the dissemination of social consciousness among the people, and therefore we cannot predict any limit to the development of the socially conscious behavior of the masses. [. . .] Only one path can lead to the replacement of a spontaneous historical process by a conscious one: the gradual transition from the socially purposeful actions of individual personalities to the socially purposeful action of the masses.[43]

Immediately after these remarks, Miliukov explains that "all this has been intended to open to the reader the general point of view from which we propose to interpret the cultural history of Russia." Clearly, the *Outlines* were meant to foster precisely the sort of enlightenment necessary so that socially "conscious"

---

42. On the terms "consciousness" and "spontaneity," alternately and more precisely translated as "elementality," see Wolfe, *Revolution and Reality*, 135–58; Clark, *The Soviet Novel*; and Platt, *History in a Grotesque Key*, 126–30.

43. Miliukov, *Ocherki*, pt. 1, 4th ed., 17–18. The quotation is from Carlyle, *On Heroes*, 1.

masses might seize the reins of history formerly guarded, and of necessity inef-
fectually exploited, by "official or moral leaders."

Earlier in the introduction, Miliukov dismisses all "philosophies of history"
as attempts to impose a teleological "sense" on history, to apply an a priori
yardstick to human experience, but the paragraph cited above reveals Miliukov's own normative theory of history: a vision of social progress toward
democratic forms of government in which human communities, informed by a
sure knowledge of social laws, will be able collectively to govern their own
fates. And if it appeared at the start of the introduction that Miliukov's express
goal was to dispense with an unscientific concentration on great men, by the
end it is clear that his work will offer a normative critique of great men as incapable of effecting a "correct" social progress, despite their best efforts. The
traditional primary figures of history remain near the center of Miliukov's attention, but the historian's task is now to demonstrate the extent to which
these leading actors were playing roles in a grander drama, the contours of
which were hidden from them—at the mercy of historical forces and dynamics
that from the undertakings of the world's great ones wrought unintended results, antithetical to their intentions. It will come as no surprise that Miliukov
accords disproportionate attention to Ivan the Terrible and, especially, to Peter the Great, who epitomize both grand social transformation by the leader's
will and the irony of reforms that, *volens nolens*, reinstate the evils they set
out to eradicate. As Miliukov puts it, both Ivan and Peter faced "large-scale
historical battles," and "were forced to stride toward the goal across the dead
and to drown the pangs of rebellious conscience in blood and wine."[44]

The chief lever of Miliukov's explanation of Russian history as a whole and
of the reigns of Ivan and Peter in particular is the historian's perception of the
cardinal distinction between Russian and western European historical development. In Miliukov's view, the distinctiveness of Russian historical processes
arose out of its enormous expanses and the perpetual threat of hostile neigh-
bors, which brought a hypertrophied and accelerated development of military
and administrative institutions. In western Europe social institutions formed
"from within, organically, from the lower floors to the higher ones," beginning
with the local organizations of the lower orders and progressing through stages
of economic and cultural advance and progressive articulation of centralized
institutions of state. Yet in Russia, as a result of the need to create strong central
institutions to avoid perishing as a society:

> In fact, historical processes went in the reverse order—from the top down.
> [. . .] Here, state power secures the landowners beneath itself; then the
> landowners secure the peasants beneath themselves. This manner of
> articulation preserved for a considerable period the leading role of the
> heights of Russian society and of state power in the processes of historical

44. Miliukov, *Ocherki*, pt. 3, 1st ed., 1:132.

construction. The Russian state not only did not have to struggle with the rights and privileges of individuals and social groups; on the contrary, it undertook to call these groups into being and activity, to make use of this activity for its own ends. Only in the most recent period have Russian social groups begun to show signs of an internal life and to demonstrate a tendency to independence and at the same time to lose the trust of the central power.[45]

The debt here to the State School of historians, Kavelin and Solovev, with their exaltation of the state as the chief motive force in modern Russian history, is clear.[46] Even so, Miliukov's vision of social construction from above is by no means as straightforward or triumphant as that of those earlier historians. As the rhetoric of the above citations indicates, and despite his frequent gestures of dispassion, the historian views the state-initiated character of Russian development as "backwards" and unnatural. The consequence of this backwardness is the artificiality of progressive innovations in the Russian historical experience: from the growth of cities, to the formation of political ideologies, to the introduction of industry and capitalist exchange, and so on.[47] The perversity of Russian institutions derives from their artificial genesis. Time and again in Miliukov's analysis, institutions that have been "called into being by the state" must struggle to free themselves from the heavy hand of administrative power and realize their own natural or innate ends. The most telling example of this dynamic, as is evident from the above, is the story of society as a whole and the "critical" consciousness that gives rise to aspirations for self-governance.

A first watershed in this story of national becoming through ironic, unintended consequences is the reign of Ivan the Terrible, which Miliukov, following the statist historians, sees as the culmination of Russia's centuries-long process of administrative centralization. Like Solovev and Kavelin, Miliukov imputes a high degree of historical rationality to Ivan's administrative and political reforms and to the bloody measures that effected them. As he explains in part 1 of the *Outlines*, the consolidation of the state in the interests of self-defense called first for the subordination of the formerly independent appanage princes

45. Miliukov, *Ocherki*, pt. 1, 4th ed., 124–26.

46. In essence, Miliukov's view of Russian history presents an immanent, historical, and causal grounding of the Hegel-inspired idealist vision of the leading role of the state. Miliukov had gained a reputation as a critic of the State School of historians, which led to some confusion and critical crossfire over the apparent influence of their thought in the *Outlines*. For Miliukov's statement on the State School, see his "Iuridicheskaia shkola v russkoi istoriografii (Solov'ev, Kavelin, Chicherin, Sergeevich), *Russkaia mysl'* 1886, no. 6, 80–92; repr. in his *Ocherki istorii istoricheskoi nauki*, 401–12. For discussion of Miliukov and the State School, see Manchester, "Contradictions at the Heart of Russian Liberalism"; Stockdale, *Paul Miliukov*, 18, 296; and Hamburg, "Inventing the 'State School,'" 102–3.

47. On the artificiality of Russian industry, international trade, administrative organization, and creation of cities, respectively, see Miliukov, *Ocherki*, pt. 1, 4th ed., 84–85, 107, 162–63, 192–94.

to the Muscovite throne, and then for their replacement in the power structure by the more dependable and strategically important middle service (military) class. This process began in the late fifteenth century and came to its completion in the era of Ivan:

> The monarchical power, in the person of Ivan the Terrible, initiated a systematic battle with a social element inimical to itself, a battle that was conducted with merciless diligence and finished quickly. [. . .] As the final step in this political effort, the tsar began to "butcher" the leading families—to butcher them not by personal whim or antagonism but as a result of this same political initiative, killing not individual representatives of one or another family, but rather, insofar as was possible, all representatives of every family: "clanwide" in Kurbskii's expression.[48]

Here, "the person of Ivan the Terrible" carries out the bidding of a historical principle, so much so that the moral or human implications of his "butchery" are reduced to a political principle void of any "personal antagonism."

Yet the relationship between the actions of individuals or even classes and the outcomes to which they lead is no mere blind, mechanical transmission of historical force. In the third volume, devoted to the study of "nationalism and public opinion," Miliukov explains in detail the sixteenth-century ideological formations that drove this political "butchery," and that carried forward as the foundation of later Russian political life. Miliukov sees the late fifteenth and sixteenth centuries as the moment in which two fundamental political traditions took root in Russia: the "nationalist" tradition, a fundamentally conservative and static sense of group identity, on one hand, and the "oppositional" or "critical" tradition, which Miliukov identifies with progressive historical aspirations, on the other.

Initially, both these formations were rooted in non-Russian influences, adapted to Russian circumstances. The national idea, deriving from western conceptions of monarchy and religious community, served as the basis for the aggrandizement of the Muscovite prince as autocrat and defender of Orthodox Christendom, culminating in the crowning of Ivan IV as tsar. Oppositional thought, rising out of South Slavic mystical and fundamentalist religious dissent, provided the intellectual foundation for all manner of nonconformist aspirations to political autonomy, which by the mid-sixteenth century came to underpin the political views of boyar grandees in their aristocratic resistance to the tsar's accumulating power.

In Miliukov's account, these basic political currents never fall completely into alignment with individual actors, movements, or social groupings. In Ivan's era, the ideological formations of the "boyar-constitutionalists" and of the tsar and his "autocratic camp" were each to some extent progressive: they were equally innovative political programs geared to the fundamentally new conditions of a

48. Ibid., 181–82.

unified Muscovy and working in turns toward social improvement and cultural advance. In ideological coloration, however, both power centers appealed to a certain conservatism, seeking legitimating ground in an imagined immemorial past: the boyars projecting an ancient right to council and limit the prince, and the autocrat tracing his lineage and a tradition of supreme secular and religious authority to the Byzantine throne.

Finally, practically speaking, Ivan's triumph was clinched by his "democratic" policies that coopted the objectively oppositional underpinnings of the boyar program, in particular his promotion of the militarily necessary middle service class, and his populist appeal to the interests of the people as a whole. Ultimately, then, Miliukov presents Ivan's reign as an object lesson in the ironic dynamics of Russian history in toto—as a moment when conservative nationalist ideology served progressive reforms; and when the acute concentration of unlimited state power was cast as an expression of mass sovereignty.

These misalignments of ideology and practice were not without their historical consequences:

Taking under its protection with such decisiveness the interests of one class (one must add: and not of the class that was currently dominant but whose power would shortly be revealed as unstable, that is, of the boyars,—but of the class to whom the future belonged, that is, of the lesser gentry [dvoriane]) the Moscow regime by this very token prepared for itself a new opposition. This new opposition was both less ideological and more dangerous, even when it was acting passively, rather than actively. This was a fundamentally social opposition—that of the peasants and serfs [kholopy].

Here, in syntax that acts out the convolution of Miliukov's ironic dialectic of history, the historian credits Ivan (or the historical principle that he serves) with equal measures of historical foresight and blindness. The brilliant and prescient turn to precisely the social group "to whom the future belongs," nevertheless creates an even more dangerous opponent where there was none before. For the alliance of state and people is unstable, based on the ideological fiction of the commonality of autocratic and popular interests, which may yield progressive results in one moment and tragic bloodshed in the next.

At the conclusion of his account of the era of Ivan, Miliukov turns to folk songs about how "Once upon a time, a beauteous sun rose up, / The Terrible Tsar was enthroned over us," recounting how Ivan "boasted" about his assumption of autocratic power and his triumph over internal "traitors."

Here, it seems, have been preserved fresh impressions of how the living, not legendary tsar Ivan Vasilevich, truly "boasted" before his people, standing on the Place of Skulls [Lobnoe mesto], casting all blame for disorders in the realm on the boyars and promising to set all to rights himself; or how that very same Ivan the Terrible a decade and a half later publicly pronounced the disfavor of the upper echelons of society and his indulgence of

the lower orders, asking of the latter extraordinary powers to exact vengeance on their enemies and on his own—in order to "root out treason."
However, as we have seen, the internal political program of the Terrible
Tsar and his supporters was nowhere near as democratic as it might appear
at first glance. The "beautiful sun" of the Muscovite tsar was soon to be
revealed as the bloody blaze of a social conflagration.[49]

A half a century after Kavelin and Solovev first elected Ivan as a hero of progressive Russian state building, a liminal figure governing the passage from the
medieval past to the modern future, Miliukov in many ways followed their
lead, describing the era of the Terrible Tsar as a first apotheosis of the social
and political patterns of modern Russian history. Yet whereas the earlier statist historians had seen the self-defeating violence of Ivan's reign as a reflection
of the prematurity of the Terrible Tsar's undertakings, in Miliukov's account
the ironic imbrication of despotic measures and progressive results, of rational
ideological conflict and mindless mayhem, becomes emblematic of the modern
Russian experience per se—all of which is a long twilight of transition from
the state domination inscribed in its base to an ultimate emancipation of Russian society, in which the state serves as unwitting midwife.

The next major phase in Miliukov's dialectic of Russian enlightenment is
the era of Peter the Great, whose activities enunciate these same patterns at a
greater depth of ironic involution. Despite the objectively "oppositional" features of Ivan's political program, Miliukov casts that era as the triumph of the
"nationalist" ideological principle. During the seventeenth century, in the historian's view, the opposed "nationalist" and "critical" traditions were consoli-
dated in a sort of gestation phase, awaiting rebirth in a new period of conflict
and civilizational advance. This new outbreak of ideological combustion came
in the form of the Petrine reforms, which enacted a complementary victory of
the critical over the nationalist principle:

> We have seen how, beginning at the end of the fifteenth century and
> continuing to the end of the seventeenth, to an ever greater extent, critical
> elements, borrowed from the life of the European nations, penetrated into
> the Russian national existence. We have also seen that the first, proximate
> consequence of this influence of critical elements was by no means the
> reform of the national life but, in contrast, the more or less conscious
> formulation of its local specificities, which were gradually composed into a
> national ideal, not subject to any reform whatsoever. The subsequent stage
> in this influence [. . .] was the triumph of the critical elements over the
> national ideal that had just taken shape, a triumph that was expressed in a
> complete reform of social life. At first, however, this victory turned out to
> be superficial and formal, since it was achieved by means of the violent
> measures of the state, and not by any internal evolution of the national life.

49. Miliukov, *Ocherki*, pt. 3, 1st ed., 1:73–74.

This is which we have named this victory, characteristic of the second period of the struggle between Russian nationalism and the critical tradition, by the term "official."[50]

In explaining the "violent" and "official" character of the Petrine reforms Miliukov restages his discussion of Russian development as a whole: seventeenth-century Russian society was so institutionally and intellectually weak that it could neither carry out social reforms nor resist them. Nevertheless, "it had already become completely clear that reform was unavoidable, and an extreme, rather than a moderate reform, at that—not an ideological reform, prepared with books and literature, but an unmediated reform, spontaneous, flowing directly out of the demands of life."[51]

Miliukov sees Peter, like Ivan, as the instrument of historical necessity, whose policies derive from military and economic exigencies. In contrast to his impersonal treatment of Ivan, however, Miliukov's portrait of Peter obsessively returns to the question of the "personal" character of the reforms, which Miliukov both allows and seeks to circumscribe by a grander historical logic:

> The Petrine reforms were forced and violent—those who implemented them doubted this as little as those who resisted. They were forced not only in those aspects that were accidental and arbitrary but also in those that were essential and necessary. Furthermore, the forced nature of the reforms gave an accidental and arbitrary character even to their essential and necessary aspects—that is, it endowed the essential with accidental form. For this reason, recognition of the forced, personal nature of the reforms by no means is equivalent to a denial of their historical necessity; and in complementary fashion, a demonstration of the necessity of the reforms is by no means a denial of their forced character. The historian's task in the given situation is to show why reforms that were in essence necessary *had to be*, could not avoid being, clothed in the form of the personal arbitrariness of one person over the masses, and why such an imposition of arbitrary will was *possible* at all.[52]

Miliukov's subsequent explanation unpacks these seemingly paradoxical formulations. Although the reforms everywhere bear the marks of Peter's personality, they are by no means the products of his conscious planning. In a repetition of the dynamic whereby the weakness of Russian society forces a strong state to prosecute necessary reforms, the weakness of the leading actors in Russian elite society necessitated that a single, strong individual would provide the chief impetus for reform by imposition of his personal will. For this very reason, the reforms could never achieve a fully "conscious" or rational character: a more

50. Ibid., 1:130–31.
51. Ibid., 1:139.
52. Ibid.

thoughtful and politically inclusive approach to reform would have sunk in Russia's political and institutional disorganization; only a despotic leader, who "began with deeds, and proposed to think later," could effect transformative change.[53]

So, even though history itself called Peter to step into the breach to effect a completely necessary transformation of Russian life, the resulting reforms are crippled by their self-defeating derivation of progressive, "critical" reform from archaic, despotic authority. Miliukov describes the devolution of power upward toward the tyrannical will of the autocrat as a sickness, a vicious cycle, leading to tragic results:

> Of course, Peter did not lack for advice or counselors: with each passing day there were more of them. But this did not prevent him from feeling, with each passing day, more and more alone, which, of course, increased the mark of personality that he imprinted on his reforms—often to their undoubted detriment. With his distrust of people, the tsar fell into a vicious cycle. Valuing above all loyalty to himself, he had a very limited choice of people and was unable to place a truly capable person in any position of power. [. . .] This, however, only rendered the necessity for Peter to manage everything himself more acute, as a result of which the reforms, despite the involvement of specialists, gained an accidental, fragmentary, and amateurish character, reflecting the temperament and level of knowledge of the tsar-reformer himself.

In corresponding fashion, Peter's loyal if ham-fisted appointees could have little interest in or enthusiasm for reforms carried out by command rather than inspiration, apart from the personal interest exemplified, for instance, in Menshikov's grotesque enrichment.

Such concatenations of dull-wittedness and petty self-interest among the Petrine elite only reinforced the tsar's distrust of his advisers, explaining why "so many brilliant careers, begun in Peter's day by men of the hour, ended with the scaffold or exile."[54] Yet this tragic disconnect was not only theirs but Peter's as well:

> Toward the end of his reign this dissonance between a newly created routine and the unmitigated nihilism of the tsar, who retained in new

---

53. Ibid., 1:134. To illustrate the impossibility of politically legitimated reform "from below," Miliukov compares Peter's reforms to the limited reforms of Prince Vasilii Golitsyn, Sophia Alekseevna's favorite early in her regency (1682–89). According to Miliukov, Golitsyn's tendency to compromise and his efforts to secure broad political support drowned his undertakings in Russian society's political immaturity. In a reversal of the ironies of Peter's reforms, in which despotism served progressive ends, Golitsyn's progressive attempt to found policy on a broad political base led to a collapse toward conservative positions (ibid., 1:134–37).

54. Ibid., 1:145–46.

circumstances all his old habits [. . .], became more and more sensitive and difficult for all involved. With his demand for complete freedom of movement and emptiness around him he became more and more of an anachronism amid the web of new daily ceremonial that he himself had woven; those who surrounded him became exhausted by the need to be forever on guard and made efforts to hide something away for a rainy day. Peter [. . .] wavered between the desire to destroy everything, to strike out in all directions with fearsome blows, and the consciousness of the impossibility of doing everything all over again, from the ground up. The single remaining exit from this tragic situation was death.[55]

Although the social and cultural content of the reforms was, in Miliukov's view, an undeniably beneficial historical advance toward technological innovation, enlightened cultural values, and a meritocratic and efficient state bureaucracy, the successful prosecution of the reforms rendered the emperor himself more and more archaic.

Yet the dissonance between reformist aspirations and despotic agency left its mark not only on Peter's personal tragedy but also on the substance of the reforms. Miliukov's Peter, man of action and pawn of historical exigencies, ultimately had not the slightest inkling of the grand civilizational ideals that should have informed his efforts. How could he, when his chief personal contribution to the reforms, without which they could not have taken place, was the exercise of overweening yet unthinking will? For this reason, Peter's efforts to transform his subjects, to make "beasts into men," were aimed at purely technical and superficial effects: Russians would dress and act like Europeans, study western technology, language, and institutional structure. Whether they would be able think or create like Europeans never entered the emperor's mind.

> He had will in abundance. Consequently, he had only to subject Russians to his will—forcing them to learn what he had learned in the German Quarter. Did it even enter Peter's mind that this was far from all that might be learned from the west; that it was impossible to teach so simply the most valuable content of European culture, for it had to be gained by experience and fostered in the self—in a completely different manner from the one in which the emperor was "educating" his contemporaries? If he even thought about such matters, as a pragmatic he would not have paused over that which was not in his powers to accomplish. Probably, however, he did not even suspect in the slightest that true culture, with its conventional and necessary forms of everyday interaction, with its respect for the individual as such, would have rendered his own methods of inculcation of "culture" completely inapplicable and impossible.[56]

55. Ibid., 1:146–47.
56. Ibid., 1:153.

And so, as a result of the hypertrophied, personal, despotic basis of the reforms, they were necessarily superficial, mechanical, violent, and wasteful. Uninformed and incapable of being everywhere in his enormous empire, Peter imposed hit or miss policies that were lacking in comprehensive planning and generated no end of pain, bloodshed, and mayhem. Whereas other historians, such as Solovev, had seen Peter's great personal involvement in the reforms as evidence of the emperor's grand historical vision, Miliukov drives the argument in precisely the reverse direction: Peter's ceaseless imposition of autocratic will is the base cause of the violent character of the reforms and an illustration of the emperor's lack of foresight and inability to understand his own historical role.

Miliukov's analysis by no means simply dismisses the Petrine reforms as a failure, however. For in a further turn of the screw of historical irony, the historian also pronounces that the key to the reforms' success lay precisely in these same perverse features:

> This endless repetition and accumulation of experiments, this ceaseless cycle of destruction and creation, and in its midst some kind of inexhaustible life force, which no sacrifice, no loss or failure could interrupt or halt—all these features recall the wastefulness of the natural world in its blind, elemental creation, rather than the political art of a man of the state. Drawing this conclusion, we should not forget another feature, visible in all of the preceding. For it is precisely in this form that the reform stops seeming to be a miracle and sinks to the level of surrounding reality. It had to be such, in order to correspond to that reality: the reform's accidental character, arbitrariness, personal nature, and violence are its necessary features; and despite its sharply antinational superficial appearance, it was wholly rooted in the conditions of the national life. The nation received the reform of which it was capable.[57]

The great achievements of the reforms, as well as their ironic consequences, are visible in all subsequent Russian history. Although the Petrine transformation of Russian life was intended to serve only narrow, practical goals, its forceful destruction of the Old Russian way of life cleared the way for truly novel social forces to rise up and fill the "empty" forms of the new reality with true, lived contents. These contents, as Miliukov explains, are the progressive aspirations of educated Russians who in the course of the two centuries that followed would begin to comprehend the real significance of the cultural innovations rooted in Peter's arbitrariness. In Miliukov's view, then, the fulfillment of the "critical" promise of the Petrine reforms, as well as the negation of their despotic and autocratic form, still lay in Russia's future.

In concluding his treatment of Peter's reign, Miliukov reiterates his view that the goals of the era's transformative policies were at base military and economic, geared to strengthen the state and expand the empire, not to effect progress, adding, "undoubtedly, in the Petrine reforms the critical elements constituted only the means, while the goals were completely nationalist in nature."[58] In this formula, Peter's era articulates the same fundamental historical ironies evident in Miliukov's account of Ivan's reign, only in inverted form. Whereas Ivan's era was a nationalist consolidation of power that effected unintended progressive change, Peter's was a critical revolution in the service of nationalist programs. In Miliukov's account, Ivan's era and Peter's represent the twinned apotheoses of Russia's opposed political tendencies, each of which illustrates the unresolved dialectical tension between illusory, ideologically inflected intentions and hidden historical processes—a tension that demands future resolution. In this ironic disjunction of historical intent and consequences, the tsars are revealed as blind, would-be visionaries serving ends other than those they imagine. Like a Greek god, history fools these great men into doing its bidding. For, serving the interests of the state, these periods of ideological conflict gave rise to the very social forces and critical consciousness that would one day lead to the state's downfall, when a truly progressive transformation will transfer power to the ascendant, politically inspired people.

Although Miliukov's basic intuitions concerning historical processes were far from comparable to the mystical worldview of Symbolists like Merezhkovskii, the basic commonality of their ironic visions of Russian history and its liminal figures led them to similar, prophetic ends. Just as Merezhkovskii's perception of the Petrine era's self-defeating concatenation of creation and destruction led him to project an end to Petersburg civilization that would redeploy these same opposed forces in an apocalyptic confrontation, Miliukov saw the characteristic Russian dialectical tension between opposed political traditions leading to a final moment of transcendence. Like many modernist authors, the historian maintained that Russians at the turn of the twentieth century could see themselves reflected in the reforms of Peter.[59] Although he imagined a "gradual" development of inclusive, mass political life, in keeping with the law-governed process of transition to parliamentary government, the first volume of the *Outlines* ends by projecting a rather different resolution to the dialectical unfolding of Russian history. Following a discussion of Russia's need to choose between nostalgia for an archaic past and forward-looking political traditions, Miliukov writes:

> One may, depending on one's tastes, envy the solidity of the pre-Petrine way of life or hate its insipidity. But no matter how one views it, with sympathy or antagonism, one cannot either desire or fear that it might be restored in our times in those of its aspects that already disappeared long ago, nor preserved in those aspects that persist as ruins. The life that brought it into being led

58. Ibid., 1:179.

59. See Manchester, "Contradictions at the Heart of Russian Liberalism." Manchester cites and translates Miliukov's remark on contemporary Russia's "kinship" with Peter from a 1925 essay, written for the bicentennial of Peter's death, P. N. Miliukov, "Petr Velikii i ego reforma," *Na chuzhoi storone*, 1925, no. 10, 21.

inexorably to its destruction—earlier, even, than education and reform could have accomplished consciously. It is, then, completely understandable that our own conscious activity must be directed not at the preservation of this archeological trace of a distant past but at the creation of a new Russian cultural tradition in correspondence with our contemporary social ideals:

The old is crumbling down—the times are changing—
And from the ruins blooms a fairer life.

Here, the present appears as the final chapter of Imperial Russian society, in which the seeds of destruction sown with the founding of that order will bear fruit. Miliukov's final citation, from Act IV, Scene II of Schiller's antityrannical drama *William Tell*, completes the picture with a gesture toward revolutionary violence that flies in the face of the gradualist pretensions of his introduction—a gesture fully congruent with Merezhkovskii's vision of the present as prelude to a transformative moment of revolutionary redemption.

Irony's Reprise: Ilia Repin's *Ivan the Terrible and His Son Ivan*

Before considering how Miliukov's and Merezhkovskii's prognostic revolutionary visions look in the light of the revolutions that actually came to pass, I want to return to the attack on Repin's *Ivan and Terrible and His Son Ivan* in 1913. As with *Antichrist (Peter and Aleksei)* and *The Outlines of Russian Cultural History*, this episode epitomizes the concatenation of repetition and renunciation characteristic of the period's reception of Ivan and Peter. Yet rather than illustrating how the ironic incoherence of these borderline figures could be leveraged into a prophecy of the imminent collapse of the social order they represented, the attack on Repin's canvas and the response to it demonstrate the difficulty of controlling the ironic potential of Russian history. By the time the psychotic Balashov attacked *Ivan the Terrible and His Son Ivan* in 1913, the furor surrounding the painting that led in the 1880s to a temporary ban on its exhibition had long since given way to a celebration of Repin as an artist of the first water and of this canvas in particular as a masterpiece.

Nevertheless, the painting's combustive coupling of graphic violence with the image of the autocrat that had offended the public in 1885 was undoubtedly also the cause of the madman's assault almost thirty years later. According to newspaper accounts, Balashov, the son of an icon painter and an Old Believer, visited the Tretiakov Gallery a number of times in the weeks before the attack and obsessively contemplated both Repin's work and another less explicit representation of a violent episode from the Russian past.[60] Finally, he

---

60. This was Vasilii Surikov's *Boiarynia Morozova* (1887). See "Izudorovannaia kartina Repina," *Russkie vedomosti*, no. 14 (January 17, 1913), 4; "V Tret'iakovskoi galeree," *Russkie vedomosti*, no. 15 (January 18, 1913), 4; "Kartina Repina," *Russkie vedomosti*, no. 16 (January 19, 1913), 3; and "V Moskve," *Pravitel'stvennyi vestnik*, no. 14 (January 17, 1913), 2.

drew his weapon and threw himself at the painting. As he did so, he cried out, "Blood! Why the blood? Down with blood!"—a peculiar echo of the "anatomical critics" who had complained of the painting's unnatural abundance of blood in 1885.[61] Even more curious, Balashov's attack immediately elicited a torrent of editorial outrage that projected the work's subject matter—the murder of a child—onto present events, offering sympathy to Repin for the injury of his "offspring." Ilia Ostroukhov, the director of the Tretiakov Gallery, retired in disgrace, to be replaced by the young artist and critic Igor Grabar. Experts in art preservation and restoration from the State Hermitage Museum in St. Petersburg were brought in to repair the physical damage, and Repin himself traveled to Moscow from his retreat in Kuokalla, Finland, to repaint the obliterated portions of the work.

Yet Balashov's attack was not the only act of violence perpetrated on Repin's painting in early 1913. Three days later the artist, poet, and critic Maksimilian Voloshin published a short essay "On the Significance of the Catastrophe That Befell Repin's Painting."[62] In brief, this essay argued that the madman's attack had been instigated by the painting itself, which, with its gory representation of violence, had shocked and tormented viewers for decades before finally pushing poor Balashov over the edge. Although the essay did not create much of a sensation, about a month later Voloshin elaborated on his view of the incident in a public lecture and debate at the Moscow Polytechnic Museum, itself an overdetermined site of Russian national history, sponsored by members of the Futurist group "Jack of Diamonds." Among the other participants in the debate was the Futurist artist David Burliuk, and seated in the audience was none other than Repin himself. Like the original essay, Voloshin's lecture was an act of avant-garde épatage calculated to offend the sensibilities of the staid and the bourgeois. Repeating his argument that the work was an irresponsible application of the techniques of illusionistic naturalism to evoke the viewer's horror, Voloshin argued that "in the figure of Balashov we are dealing not with a criminal, but with a victim of Repin's painting."[63] The critic ended with the somewhat sardonic conclusion that *Ivan the Terrible and His Son Ivan* was a dangerous work of art that caters to a mass taste for sensationalism and cheap thrills, and that it:

> has no place in the National Gallery, which forms the artistic tastes of the young. Its real place is in some grand European Panoptikon like the Musée Grévin. There it would be a magnificent example of its genre. There, it would deceive no one, for everyone who goes to such a place knows what he is after. But since this is impossible, the curators of the Tretiakov Gallery

61. "Izurodovannaia kartina Repina."
62. The essay is reprinted in Voloshin, *O Repine*, 5–10. Concerning the episode, see also Iablonskii, "Pokushenie na 'Ioanna Groznogo,'"; Valkenier, "Politics in Russian Art," 23–24; and Parker and Parker, *Russia on Canvas*, 127, 142.
63. Voloshin, *O Repine*, 31–32.

must certainly, at the very least, place this painting in a separate room marked with the sign "entrance for adults only."[64]

Following Voloshin's outrageous lecture, Repin himself ascended to the podium and offered a rather disjointed but clearly enraged response. Other participants in the debate, apparently as shocked as everyone else, offered their own awkward comments. Wild clapping, booing, and foot stamping punctuated the entire evening.

Voloshin's lecture and the public discussion that followed it rivaled Balashov's attack itself in the frenzy of press accounts and outraged essays that ensued. Many of these voices—including Repin's own in his response following the lecture—compared Voloshin's intentionally appalling words to Balashov's dagger as analogous acts of criminal aggression. According to Voloshin, Repin dismissed the critic's major arguments as "rubbish" and "tendentiousness," steadily losing self-control and working himself up to conclude: "And now they are saying that the painting should be sold abroad. They will never commit such an absurdity. Some Russians want to finish what Balashov started. . . . Balashov is a fool. . . . A fool like that is easy to pay off."[65] This final remark, as Voloshin pointed out in the published version of his lecture, lines up with a series of other comments that Repin made regarding Balashov's attack, suggesting that it was a reflection of the modernist rejection of past art and culture.[66]

Critical voices in the press echoed this view, pronouncing Voloshin's lecture a continuation of Balashov's violence: "Repin arrived to hear people defaming his painting and his talent, demanding that the work be donated to a carnival, and exhorting the painting's attacker Balashov to 'Finish it off!' "[67] Yet others who equated the madman and the critic saw more hopeful implications in the events of 1913. A letter from sixteen prominent members of the Union of Russian Artists to Repin announced that "two events of no real significance—the act of a lunatic and the tactless pronouncements of a few individuals—gave rise to an occurrence of huge public import and lucid spiritual beauty. This occurrence—is an expression of the blood ties linking the artist and the nation."[68]

Ultimately, this exchange of attacks and counterattacks, accusations and counteraccusations, is founded on a paradoxical divergence of opinion concerning the source of the episode's violence. On one hand, Voloshin links Balashov's assault to the aesthetic violence of the painting itself: Balashov "did to the painting precisely what the painting has done to the souls of visitors of the Tretiakov Gallery for thirty years."[69] On the other hand, Repin and his sup-

---

64. Ibid., 33. The Musée Grévin is a famous wax museum in Paris.
65. Ibid., 40.
66. For an independent confirmation that Repin indeed expressed such a theory publicly, see "V Tret'iakovskoi galeree."
67. Sergei Iablonskii, in *Russkoe slovo*, cited in Voloshin, *O Repine*, 48.
68. Cited in Iablonskii, "Pokushenie na 'Ioanna groznogo,'" 334.
69. Voloshin, *O Repine*, 10.

porters and defenders identify Balashov's assault with the attacks of Voloshin and "unbridled" avant-garde artists in general, ready to destroy the masterpieces and values of past generations. One newspaper response explicitly invoked the scandalous formula of the best-known Futurist manifesto by way of explanation: "A slap in the face of public taste! The Burliuks announce, shamelessly: 'The past is too small for us. The Academy and Pushkin are incomprehensible hieroglyphs. And therefore, throw overboard from the steamship of modernity Pushkin, Dostoevskii, Tolstoi, and so on and so forth.'"[70]

So how are we to sort out this bout of finger pointing and blame? That is, what was the real source of the violence of 1913, and how are we to interpret it? For an answer to this question, one must observe, above all, how these later actors appeared to be responding to the script laid out by the painting's original significance and subject matter. It was this basic allegorical content that lay like a hidden variable in the gush of public statements and press accounts that poured out of Repin's slashed canvas. As we have seen, *Ivan the Terrible and His Son Ivan* was composed as a response to the violence, political polarization, and threat of continued confrontation that followed the assassination of Alexander II in 1881. The work points to the ancient, historical brutality of the autocracy, evident in the traumas of the reign of Ivan the Terrible, as the true source of the violence of late Imperial Russia—the violence of the regime and of the revolutionaries alike. Through its dramatic representation of Ivan's fatherly anguish as well as through its religious iconography, Repin's painting calls for a redemptive moment of Christian repentance and national unity between "fathers" and "sons," which might offer an avenue to transcend violence in Russian society and political life.

Voloshin's critique aptly captures a peculiar dimension of Repin's painting: its paradoxical tendency to use violence to overcome violence. Whereas the painting was intended as a call to overcome violence, its lesson is inculcated by means of shock. The bloody scene of the tsarevich's gushing blood and the tsar's anguished remorse, which reportedly caused some viewers to faint away in alarm and amazement, hits viewers at a visceral level to force them to confront in a new way the bloodshed of their own epoch. The moral lesson of the painting—concerning the need to transcend violence and confrontation—demonstrates that great leaps of repentance and growth may be attained precisely by great acts of brutality. Repin's violence is brutality of an aesthetic sort, but it is brutality nonetheless, and the history of the work illustrates as well that impassioned condemnations of violence are capable of evoking quite physically violent reactions. As Voloshin points out, Balashov's attack, accompanied by his shriek ("Down with blood!") is entirely analogous to the main expressive significance of the painting: each rejects violence with an act of

---

70. *Moskovskii listok*, cited in Voloshin, *O Repine*, 53. The manifesto in question is "A Slap in the Face of Public Taste." See Lawton, ed., *Russian Futurism through Its Manifestoes*, 51–52.

violence.[71] In this regard, both follow the pattern of the acts of political violence to which Repin's aesthetic statement originally responded: the terrorist
bomb that killed Alexander II. Voloshin aptly points out that all these events
were supposed to make possible a transcendence of historical violence. Instead, they seem to have had the result of perpetuating it.

Yet we cannot be too quick to side with Voloshin against Repin, for the
ironic interpretational space around this painting may be exited through a
number of different fissures. Repin and his supporters were absolutely right in
pointing out that Balashov's attack and Voloshin's scandalous lecture were in
many ways analogous acts of aggression. Of course, the attacker was not
"paid off" by the avant-garde; and one suspects that, bearing in mind Merezhkovskii's conflation of his own exalted apocalypticism with traditional folk
varieties, Balashov's attack had more to do with the anarchical tendencies and
hatred of imperial authority characteristic of Russia's sectarian population
than with any aesthetic program.[72] Truly, Voloshin's brutal critique of the
painting in the name of a condemnation of Repin's aesthetic violence is analogous to Balashov's attack on the painting in the name of a condemnation of the
violence of Russian history.

Other representatives of the avant-garde recognized that Balashov's attack
on the painting was a splendid metaphor for their own iconoclastic rejection of
past aesthetic and political life. As though confirming the suspicions of the
critics who had invoked the Futurist manifesto "A Slap in the Face" to accuse
the modernists of complicity with the madman, another avant-garde manifesto
shortly thereafter proudly claimed Balashov as a kindred spirit.[73]

So both sides of the debate occupied defensible positions. What neither
seems to have recognized, however, is that the interpretational space of the
painting placed all of them together in a common position. Voloshin, despite
his incisive critique of Repin's sensationalistic work, failed to recognize that
the "shock therapy" his lecture directed at its staid, bourgeois listeners, including Repin, was analogous to the cruelty and violence he saw in Repin's canvas.
Repin, for his part, failed to recognize how much Voloshin was his cultural
heir. At the time of the first exhibition of the *Ivan the Terrible and His Son*

---

71. Voloshin, *O Repine*, 10.

72. In this connection, recall that the other focus of Balashov's obsessive gaze in the Tretiakov Gallery, Surikov's *Boiarynia Morozova,* is a representation of the state persecution of
Old Believers. The attack on Ivan, whose name has often been linked to arbitrary violence
and demonic forces, might therefore be a rejection of "unholy" state violence. However, it
should also be noted that Ivan, whose reign ended nearly a century before the Schism, was
not generally a target of vilification by Old Believers. On Ivan's place in the folk mythology
of autocrats as antichrists, see Beliakova and Chertoritskaia, "Krug chteniia staroobriadtsa-
spasovtsa," 306–12. For discussion of Old Believer views of Ivan, see Platt, "Antichrist
Enthroned."

73. See the manifesto "The Trumpet of the Martians," in *Russian Futurism Through Its
Manifestoes,* ed. Lawton, 103–5.

Ivan, Repin and his Itinerant colleagues constituted the avant-garde of the Russian art world. His intentional provocation of his original audience foreshadowed Voloshin's own *épatage* and served a similar purpose—to call for a reevaluation of the Russian past and a transcendence of its violence.

In fact, all the figures involved in this bizarre episode share in the irony of a violent rejection of violence—Repin, Balashov, Voloshin, the members of the People's Will who threw the bomb at Alexander II in 1881, and Repin's later defenders, with their hope that Balashov's and Voloshin's "bloody" acts of violence against the painter's "child" would ultimately foster a national unity and realization of "the blood ties linking the artist and the nation." Yet others in Repin's camp had different hopes for the affair's final outcome. As one supporter of the painter ominously ended his commentary: "A congress of governors will shortly take place in Petersburg to consider the matter of the battle with people of a certain sort. All power to the administration. One can only look ahead with hope to a time when there will no longer be elements in Russian society capable of insulting Repin. And that time is near."[74]

So what does this episode reveal about the significance of Ivan the Terrible and Peter the Great in the decades before the Russian revolution? Like the other examples I have analyzed in this chapter, Voloshin's response to the attack on Repin's painting, like that painting itself, was animated by an awareness of the ironic potential of the Russian tradition of historical myth—a tradition that constitutes the self through acts of self-abnegation, founding the triumphant celebration of the collective being on the disavowal of terror and trauma. Voloshin's solution was to reject this Russian heritage—acting on a premonition that Russian history and society would soon collapse under the weight of its accumulation of historical irony and hastening the end with a little aesthetic push. Yet the superordinate irony of the Balashov affair is certainly the extent to which all participants, including Voloshin, fell back into the script provided by these same historical myths, which Repin's allegorical painting had so brilliantly diagnosed in the first place. Here, then, is a demonstration of the uncontrollable ironic potency of the liminal historical figure, which presents a convenient allegory for any historical eventuality. Repin rejects Ivan's violence but with such violence that he becomes conflated with the bloodshed he rejects, becoming a target for Balashov's and Voloshin's attacks. Voloshin rejects Repin's violence with such cruel brutality that he reenacts, in the eyes of Repin and his defenders, the trauma that he seeks to overcome. Who is Ivan and who his son in these restagings of Repin's allegory? Note, too, that this aesthetic and discursive cycle mimics the tragic story of political violence that the painting set out to diagnose. Belyi makes the connection most precisely in *Petersburg*: the revolutionary rejects the violence of the state but does so with such murderous zeal that he merely rehearses the trauma inscribed at the state's foundation. In just this manner, when the revolutionary

---

74. N. V. Glob in *Golos Moskvy*, cited in Voloshin, *O Repine*, 55.

conflagration foreseen by Belyi, Ivanov, Miliukov, Merezhkovskii, and many others did actually come to pass, it took the paradoxical form of a transcendence of Russian history that was at the same time its resurgence.

—⁓—

Years after the Balashov affair—after the death of Repin himself—Grabar, the art historian who was appointed director of the Tretiakov Gallery in the scandal's aftermath, published an addendum to the story of the attack on Repin's painting. According to this account, Repin arrived to repaint the canvas when Grabar was away from the gallery on other business. Returning later that day, Grabar learned that Repin had completed his repairs and departed. On inspecting the canvas, the director found to his horror that the aged artist had not only restored the areas damaged by Balashov's knife but had repainted the faces of the tsar and tsarevich "in unpleasant lilac tones," completely transforming his masterpiece—and not for the better. The director took decisive measures to save the day. He wiped the still wet paint from the canvas and restored the original composition himself. According to Grabar's reminiscences, on Repin's next visit he studied the work in puzzlement before apparently deciding that the repairs were his own and that memory was playing tricks on him.[75] This account once again demonstrates the peculiar ironic narrative logic surrounding this celebrated representation of the Russian past. Grabar's story reveals yet another act of violence against Repin's canvas, a secret obliteration of the original. Yet this destruction of the work of art simultaneously reinscribed the original image, accomplishing a peculiar reversal of categories. Grabar, with his iconoclastic modernist sympathies, became more classic than his realist predecessor—just as the revolutionary renunciation of the past ended by repeating it.

In 1913, Voloshin was apparently oblivious to the concatenation of renunciation and repetition in his encounter with Russian historical myth. Yet in an interesting turn of events, his was soon to become one of the most prominent voices articulating the analogy of present-day revolutionary violence with Russia's ancient legacy of despotism—a view he expounded in a number of poems of the immediate postrevolutionary years.[76] Although it is not clear whether the poet's experience in the Balashov affair played any role in his new stance toward Russian historical myth, Voloshin's new vision clearly owed a debt to Symbolists like Ivanov, Belyi, and Merezhkovskii, who had seen the threat of social conflagration in the autocratic violence of the deep past. Yet whereas those authors had foretold Russia's history of terror and greatness reaching a catastrophic terminus, now Voloshin perceived the superordinate irony of the revolution's rein-

---

75. To be entirely fair, Grabar also justifies his decision to "overrule" Repin's own restoration on the basis of art-restoration considerations—Repin's use of new oil paint over old would have resulted in mismatched colors after drying. Grabar', *Il'ia Efimovich Repin*, 1:271.

76. In addition to "Kitezh" (1919), cited in the second epigraph to this chapter, see also his epic poem "Russia" (Rossiia, 1924) in Voloshin, *Stikhotvoreniia i poemy*, 1:235–37, 339–51.

scription of those same historical principles. In his postrevolutionary poetry the drive toward a violent renunciation that only rebuilds what it set out to destroy rises as a demonic fate inherited by Russians in their marrow, in their spirit. As he pronounced in his 1920 lyric "Northeast" (Severovostok):

Demons have broken into dance, have gone wild
From one end of Russia to the other—
Snowy curtains tear and twist
The frozen northeast.
[. . .]
The crushing weight of leaden ages is in this wind:
The Rus of Maliuta, Ivan, and Godunov;
Of predators, *oprichniki*, *Streltsy*;
Of those who flay still-living meat;
Of deviltry, whirlwind, and satanic cavorting;
The past of the tsars and the reality of the Bolsheviks.
What has changed? The symbols and leadership?
The very same hurricane is on all paths:
The idiocy of autocracy is in the commissars,
The explosions of revolution were in the tsars.
[. . .]
Today—long ago—it's all the same:
Wolves' snouts, masks, and evil faces,
The stifling atmosphere, the barbarous mind,
The Secret Chancellery's investigations and kitchens,
The drunken cries of demonic creatures,
The burning whistle of whips and lashes,
The wild dream of military colonies
Phalansteries, parades, and leveling,
Of Pauls, Arakcheevs, and Peters,
Of horrible Gatchinas and fearsome Petersburgs,
The schemes of raging surgeons
And the abandon of broad-shouldered craftsmen.[77]

A few years later, Voloshin published the epic poem *Russia* (Rossiia, 1924), a grand account of Petrine history as the fountainhead of the bloody present that offered a concise formula of the ironic turn of revolutionary history: "Peter the Great was the first Bolshevik."[78]

Voloshin was not alone in noting the archaic quality of Bolshevik violence, nor in communicating his observation through analogy with Ivan and Peter. It is important to note, however, that already in this early Soviet period some authors, rather than view the present through the apocalyptic lens modernists

77. Voloshin, *Stikhotvoreniia i poemy*, 1:310–12.
78. Ibid., 1:45, cited in Tucker, *Stalin in Power*, 61.

had prepared before the revolution, were able to ride out the ironic potential of Russia's great despots in quite different directions. Osip Mandelstam's Pindaric poem of 1923, "The Horseshoe Finder" (Nashedshii podkovu), casts Peter as an ambivalent precursor to present-day revolutionaries at a moment when the revolution, in the poet's view, was a grand, yet unfinished project.[79] Others referred to Peter more straightforwardly in order to reclaim the triumphal energy of past Russian revolutions for the present. This tendency, in an echo of imperial political rhetoric, focused on Peter, rehabilitating a grand image of the tsar reformer for contemporary public life—Ivan, for the time being, remained outside the range of positive historical models. In this manner, the politically adept Valerii Briusov could in 1920 address a poem "To Russia" (Rossii) with genuine patriotism:

> Was it not you, who with a glance like hot steel,
> Responded to the commands of power
> In the days of Peter's revolution?
> And once again, in an hour of worldwide reckoning,
> Breathing across the mouths of cannons,
> Your breast has tasted the fire—
> Ahead of all, o leader nation,
> You have raised a torch above the gloom
> Showing all other peoples the way![80]

In a further demonstration of just how undecided the allegory of Petrine history was in the 1920s, Briusov's masterful "Variations on a Theme from *The Bronze Horseman*" (Variatsii, na temu *Mednogo vsadnika*, 1923) recapitulated prerevolutionary Symbolist readings of Pushkin's masterpiece in a mode of retrospective resolution, casting the revolutionary present as the era when the contradictions of state and individual, coercion and progress, had finally been resolved.[81] Clearly, the utility of the national past, and of Peter in particular, was not exhausted with the end of the political order that he had forged.[82] What Briusov missed, however, was the extent to which his disavowal of the costs of revolutionary progress was itself a legacy of prerevolutionary Russian conceptions of history. By declaring the end of Russia's history of terror and greatness, his "Variations" were symptomatic of its continuation.

I return, for now, to historical ruminations more critically inclined toward the revolution, which complete my account of the fate of modernist visions of the horrible persistence of Russian greatness and terror. In European exile,

---

79. Cavanagh, *Osip Mandelstam*, 167–68; Broyde, *Osip Mandel'shtam*, 181.

80. Briusov, *Sobranie sochinenii*, 3:47–48.

81. Ibid., 3:188–89. Anatolii Lunacharskii characterized the poem as an expression of Briusov's faith in revolutionary society in his obituary of the poet "Konchina V. Ia. Briusov," *Pravda*, no. 233 (October 12, 1924), 3.

82. For an overview of various uses of Peter's day as a historical analogy for the present in the 1920s, see A. N. Lur'e, "Poema A. S. Pushkina 'Mednyi vsadnik,'" 42–81.

Merezhkovskii published an energetic stream of anti-Bolshevik essays that read as a continuation of his earlier thought on Russia's historical fate. In 1920, for example, he asked:

> Who are the men of strong will in Russia? The Pugachevs, the Razins, the Lenins, and the Trotskiis. In the greatest illustration of Russian willpower, in Peter, will is not balanced with intellect and conscience. Is it not the case that the entirety of Petrine Russia is now falling in ruins because her foundation, the essence of Peter himself, was itself fractured, precisely in the division of mind and conscience from will? I will not insult the memory of the great; I will not say that Peter was "a Bolshevik." But one must speak the truth all the same: a blood tie unites Peter and the Bolsheviks, and to break this tie, the whole of Russia must now be drenched in blood. Truly, our curse consists in the fact that Russian willpower is given over to evil, to sin, and to madness, and Russian saintliness and wisdom to passivity.[83]

In short, Merezhkovskii viewed the cataclysms of 1917 as a confirmation of his notion that Russia was doomed to act out the script provided by Peter's era. Years later, Miliukov made similar claims concerning the prophetic accuracy of his prerevolutionary writings. In the introduction to the "Jubilee Edition" of *Outlines of Russian Cultural History*, published in the course of the 1930s with the financial support of the Russian émigré community as a tribute to the aging historian and statesman, Miliukov remarked that his analysis of the dynamics of Russian culture had been largely proved correct by the first two decades of the Soviet era:

> In the course of forty years [since the initial publication of the *Outlines*— K.M.F.P.] two generations have passed, and a third has already come on the scene. In these years Russia has survived two revolutions. My work has faced a double test: of changing political doctrines and of extraordinarily significant lived experience. It appears fair to say that the *Outlines* have withstood this test. In composing the introduction to the sixth edition of the first volume (1909), I considered myself justified to say that: "the most recent events (the revolution of 1905) have not only not overturned or altered the basic structure of the *Outlines*, but on the contrary, they have served as a confirmation and further development of the author's conclusions." At present, publishing the "Jubilee" edition of the *Outlines* at a moment when Russia is enduring profound transformations, unprecedented in her entire history, I may reconfirm this statement.[84]

One must give both men their due, for their premonitions of the imminent collapse of Petrine civilization indeed anticipated the social upheavals to come.

---

83. From the article "Savinkov," first published in *Poslednie novosti* on December 16, 1920, repr. in Merezhkovskii, *Tsarstvo Antikhrista*, 134–41, here 138.
84. Miliukov, *Ocherki*, Jubilee ed., 1:1–2.

Yet we should not be too amazed at the predictive capacity of meditations based on the tradition of historical thought centered on Ivan the Terrible and Peter the Great. In truth, no matter what course history had taken, the prognostications of Merezhkovskii, Miliukov, and the many others who pinned their understanding of the present on the mythic resonance of the Petrine or the Ivanian past—on the wild ride of the Bronze Horseman—would have been proved correct. For the extraordinary predictive powers of these historical allegories were of a piece with their uncontrollable ironic potential.

Decades earlier, in the 1890s, Lev Tolstoi invited Miliukov to pay him a visit to explain "the general meaning of history." At the end of an interview in which the aging author and spiritual leader listened attentively to all that the young historian had to say, the two retired to drink tea in the sitting room, where Tolstoi pointed to a cake on the table and gave his response to the historian's lecture, "So that's science for you! If I want, I can slice it this way, or I can slice it that way—just like that!"[85] Miliukov records being a bit put out by at the writer's incomprehension of rigorous historiographic analysis. But Tolstoi's comment hits close to the mark regarding the predictive powers not only of Miliukov's thought but of Merezhkovskii's as well. Standing on the shoulders of the nineteenth-century tradition of historical interpretation, the modernist era's characteristic ironic vision of Ivan and Peter referenced all the variant readings of the Russian past: from the traumatic to the heroic, from the foundational to the revolutionary, from visions of these figures as symbols of history's perpetual advance to a conception of them as architects of Russia's downfall. It was precisely this overdetermined quality that rendered Peter and Ivan failsafe bellwethers for prognostication, for one could be certain that the encrustation of historical myth enveloping these figures was capacious enough to account for any historical eventuality. This is the basic semiotic function of myth: to provide an ordering principle that can encompass any angle on a disordered world. Seen through these liminal figures, the mythical analogy of past and present was tautological, in that any course of events could be read in retrospect as a confirmation of some version of historical myth: whether the state triumphed over the revolutionary or the revolutionary over the state, the significance of Pushkin's equivocal Horseman and the many Symbolists who read the future out of it would be reconfirmed.

Ultimately, Merezhkovskii's and Miliukov's writings proved prophetic in ways that they did not predict and never, in fact, recognized. For the superordinate irony that afflicted Briusov's triumphal Petrine allegory applied equally well to their quite different visions. Prognostications of an end to Russia's history of greatness and terror, in retrospect the writings of each folded neatly back into a story of that history's repetition. Merezhkovskii, who imagined himself as the prophet of a final, synthetic redemption that would resolve the Petrine witches' brew of coercive political will and enlightenment, instead wit-

85. Miliukov, *Vospominaniia*, 1:172.

nessed a cataclysmic rejection of the Petrine inheritance that reiterated the imbrication of humanism and cruelty that he had analyzed so well. Miliukov, who had dreamed of a dialectical transformation of Russian social life in which the masses would finally acquire the political maturity needed to wrest control of history from the state, instead saw the rise to power of men who felt that they had been called to impose necessary social progress on a people that was too weak, disorganized, and unenlightened to achieve it in any other way—in short, an illustration of the same historical dynamic that he had described in his brilliant analysis of the Petrine age. In this light, nothing could be more apt than to apply Miliukov's aphoristic formula concerning the Petrine reforms to the Bolshevik revolution: "Russia received the revolution of which it was capable."

CHAPTER FIVE

Rehabilitation

While the birth of the revolution in Germany is taking place only slowly, our task here is: to study the state capitalism of the Germans, to adopt it *by all means*, not stopping at *dictatorial* methods in order to speed this adoption along rapidly—even more rapidly than Peter rushed the adoption of westernism by a barbaric Old Russia, himself not stopping at barbarous means in the battle with barbarism.

—Vladimir Lenin, "Left-Wing Childishness
and the Petty Bourgeois Mentality," 1918

After his return from abroad, Peter I promulgated a similar law, but many people did not obey it. Peter's son and wife were against that law. The son he executed, and the wife he locked up in a monastery. Peter did many things for the state—the fleet, shipbuilding wharves, factories, and plants. The Soviet Constitution is being constructed in the same way. I'm not against laws, but they ought to introduce an amendment regarding kolkhoz workers and daily wages lower than 20–30 kopecks.

—Spoken opinions of a certain Vorontsov, machinist in Electroequipment
artel, as reported in an NKVD intelligence report, 1936

Ivan the Terrible's wisdom consisted in an insistence on national principles and on barring foreigners from his country, protecting the country from the penetration of foreign influence. [. . .] Peter I was also a great sovereign, but he was too liberal in his relationship to foreigners. He opened up the gates too much and allowed foreign influences into the country, making possible a Germanification of Russia. [. . .] Ivan the Terrible was very cruel. It is fine to show that he was cruel. But what is needed is to show why it is necessary to be cruel. One of the mistakes of Ivan the Terrible was that he didn't completely rub out five of the larger feudal families. If he had destroyed those five boyar families then there would have been no Time of Troubles at all. Ivan the Terrible would execute someone and then go and repent and pray for a long while. God got in his way in these matters. . . . It was necessary to be more decisive.

—Joseph Stalin, during an interview with Sergei Eisenstein
and Nikolai Cherkasov, 1947

Stalinist Revisionism

Shortly after the Nazi invasion of the USSR in 1941, in a surge of patriotic fervor, the Soviet leadership announced a competition to write the lyrics for a new state anthem to replace the time-worn leftist hymn, "The Internationale," which had served in this capacity since the revolution. The decision alone reflects a profound ideological shift, which had been gathering momentum for over a decade and was now magnified by the practical realities of war—a shift from the original, transnational principles of the revolution to far more particularist ideals. Many who lived through this epoch, as well as many of the historians who have treated it, have viewed this ideological transformation as an unremarkable and historically comprehensible outcome. I would propose, however, that a renewed sense of surprise can serve as a point of departure toward different explanations of this era in Soviet history than have been offered previously. Consider, for instance, the historical imagery of a certain Ia. Kuvshinov's entry in the anthem competition, which was deemed worthy enough to be passed to the Politburo and Stalin for consideration:

> Since the Terrible Tsar, our state has been glorious.
> It bears the potent might of Peter.
> The glory of Suvorov shines behind us
> And the winds of Kutuzov's glory blow.
> As our forebears loved the Russian land,
> So we, too, love the Soviet land.[1]

Although the Soviet leadership ultimately declined to make Ivan the Terrible the lead figure of the Soviet anthem, even serious consideration of such a step demonstrates the strangeness of the Stalin era's encounter with the Russian past—and with the figures at the focus of this book in particular. In a fantastical turn of events, a regime founded on the corpses of the last Russian tsars had come to celebrate certain distant predecessors of those tsars as symbols of national and political greatness and as heroic antecedents of Stalin himself. Kuvshinov's proposed hymn illustrates the newfound prominence not only of historical figures that had once been celebrated as symbols of Imperial Russian identity, such as Peter the Great, but of a heroic vision of Ivan the Terrible that surpassed the celebratory tone of his most ardent prerevolutionary apologists. Furthermore, in both Kuvshinov's hymn and in historical thought on this

---

1. "Dokladnaia zapiska sekretaria TsK VKP(b) A. S. Shcherbakova i zam. predsedatelia SNK SSSR K. E. Voroshilova o khode raboty po sozdaniiu gimna SSSR," RGASPI, f. 17, op. 125, d. 218, ll. 86–87. The anthem competition took place in 1942 and 1943. Among other analogous entries in the competition, S. Sikorskii's "Crowned with grief and glory" (Venchannaia skorb'iu i slavoi), includes the xenophobic stanza:

"You, oh golden state, / Were tormented under the yoke by Tatars; / The Lithuanian hordes tore at you, / And the French and Polacks torched you— / But they reeled away in fear / At your countenance, calm and proud. / Let your sword be blessed, o Russia, / Crowned with grief and glory!" This and other examples were included in the general report of the Committee on Artistic Affairs to the Central Committee on the competition, dated May 1943, "Proekt postanovleniia Politbiuro TsK VKP(b), pis'ma i spravki Komiteta po delam iskusstv i Instituta Marksa-Engel'sa-Lenina o sozdanii novogo gimna Soiuza SSR . . . ," RGASPI, f. 17, op. 125, d. 217, ll. 82, 169.

moment as a whole, the mutual illumination of the triumphs of Stalin's era with those of Ivan's and Peter's was shadowed, beyond the limits of public representation, by the complementary mirroring of the state-sponsored violence of the present and past. Just two decades after Russian public life had achieved a lucid recognition of the ironic concatenation of terror and greatness in these figures, a new generation had transformed them into symbols of unalloyed heroism. How did this seemingly unlikely scenario come to pass?[2]

Scholarship has offered a variety of analyses of the rehabilitation of figures from the tsarist past in Stalinist historical thought, ranging from contextualization of this phenomenon as a part of the era's overall ideological "great retreat," to the conclusion that it was an aspect of the neotraditionalism common to many modernizing states, to its dismissal as simply anomalous.[3] Certainly, the rise of Peter and Ivan should be seen in the context of larger trends that have been well studied. As many have observed, from the late 1920s onward heroic individuals of all sorts gained increasing prominence in Soviet public life.[4] The most heroic individuals of all were Lenin and Stalin, whose political "cults" became firmly established in these years. Undoubtedly, many viewed Ivan and Peter as historical protoimages of these present charismatic leaders.[5] A second important context for the historical revisionism of the era was the evolution of Soviet policy from internationalism tempered with respect for non-Russian independence movements toward a naturalization of nationality, including Russian nationality, as a component of Soviet collective identity. In the process, Ivan the Terrible and Peter the Great somehow came to be seen as "national in form, socialist in content."[6]

2. The current chapter relies on my coauthored accounts of the rehabilitation of Ivan IV in Platt and Brandenberger, "Terribly Romantic"; and David Brandenberger and Kevin M. F. Platt, "Terribly Pragmatic": Rewriting the History of Ivan IV's Reign," in *Epic Revisionism*, ed. Platt and Brandenberger, 157–78.

3. For a representative set of stances toward Stalinist revisionist historiography, see Timasheff, *Great Retreat*, 167–81; Sheila Fitzpatrick, *Cultural Front*, 8–11; Jeffrey Brooks, *Thank You, Comrade Stalin*, 118; and Hoffmann, *Stalinist Values*, 164–66. For a debate touching on the issue, see the forum on Timasheff's "Great Retreat" thesis in *Kritika* 5, no. 4 (2004).

4. On the revival of individual actors in Soviet ideology, see Yaresh, "Role of the Individual"; on Socialist Realist heroes, see Clark, *Soviet Novel*, 8–10, 34–35, 72, 119, 136–55, 148, 8–10; and Dobrenko, *Making of the State Reader*, esp. chap. 3.

5. On Soviet heroes, see McCannon, *Red Arctic*; on the Lenin cult, see Tumarkin, *Lenin Lives!*; and Corney, *Telling October*, 175–99.

6. In early formulations of Soviet nationalities policy pride in Russian national identity had no place, because it was not seen as serving the politically progressive end of independence from imperial domination. In distinction from the national pride of non-Russian groups within the former Russian Empire, "Great Russian chauvinism" was historically compromised by its service to imperialism. In later formulations, Russian national identity was once again legitimated in a reflection of the neoimperialist hegemony of Stalin's USSR (Suny, *Revenge of the Past*, 84–126; Martin, *Affirmative Action Empire*, esp. 1–27, 394–431; Slezkine, "USSR as a Communal Apartment").

Additionally, certain quite deliberate shifts in Soviet policy made possible the rehabilitation of Ivan and Peter. David Brandenberger, Aleksandr Dubrovskii, and I have recently argued that the rehabilitation of Russian national sentiment and tsarist historical figures reflected the adoption of political values of "Russocentric etatism" among party elites, including Stalin, and their pragmatic decision that mobilization and political unity demanded the valorization of the Russian state and ethnicity as core ideals of "Soviet patriotism."[7] Our research over the past decade has helped to unearth archival traces of the party-led renovation of the Russian past, beginning in the early 1930s with efforts to revise Soviet school curricula and leading by the end of the decade to mass campaigns rehabilitating heroic figures of tsarist history in scholarship, propaganda, and cultural life. Catalyzing the rehabilitation and celebration of Ivan and Peter in particular were elements of their historical myths that rendered them especially useful as mobilizational tools, especially in the late 1930s: their military conflicts with European powers in the Baltic region, their policies of social and political transformation, their larger-than-life mythic personalities.[8] Perhaps most important, in a resurgence of the dynamics of nineteenth-century historical mythology, their liminal qualities—as symbols of Russian national identity who cherished cosmopolitan aspirations and oversaw imperial expansions, as representatives of the prestige and power of the state who pursued "revolutionary" programs in the face of "reactionary" resistance—allowed them to symbolize both the national and the supernational, the patriotic and the revolutionary, features of Soviet collective identity.

Much recent scholarship on Stalinist historical revisionism has been focused on questions of what party elites intended to accomplish with these initiatives, how political control over public discourse was enforced, and how possibly dissenting voices—most notably that of Sergei Eisenstein in his film project on Ivan the Terrible—subverted this officially articulated and imposed vision of the past.[9] Clearly, questions of "what Stalin's regime did with Ivan the Terrible and Peter the Great" and "the resistance of a few individuals" are of no little importance in explaining the historical mythology of this period. Stalinist modernization was an attempt, largely driven by the initiative of party elites, not only to mold all aspects of society—from the economy to the newspapers—according to centralized plans but to deliberately shape the very subjectivity of Soviet citizens and to create an ideologically orthodox "new Soviet person." The history projects of the era were part of this overall, party-led effort.

7. Brandenberger, *National Bolshevism*; David Brandenberger and Kevin M. F. Platt, "Introduction," in *Epic Revisionism*, ed. Platt and Brandenberger, 3–14, 157–78; Dubrovskii, *Istorik i vlast'*.

8. Lane, *Rites of Rulers*, 181; Werth, *Russia at War*; Uhlenbruch, "Annexation of History"; Perrie, "Nationalism and History," esp. 12.

9. An exception to this focus on elites and their intentions is David Brandenberger, "The Popular Reception of S. M. Eisenstein's *Aleksandr Nevskii*," in *Epic Revisionism*, ed. Platt and Brandenberger, 233–52.

Although I, too, am interested in the party's administration of Soviet public discourse and in gauging the level of discoordination, contingency, and resistance that met the Stalinist attempt to remint tsarist history, my analyses are aimed instead primarily at hermeneutic problems that, I suggest, are of equal or even greater weight in questions of historical revisionism and ideological discourse. Carrying forward the trajectory of previous chapters, I investigate how the system of historical thought that the Soviets inherited from Imperial Russia imposed specific constraints and possibilities on historiographical innovation. The Stalin-era rehabilitation of tsarist heroes is indeed comparable to the "invention of traditions" common to many modernizing societies, yet the specific conditions of a revolutionary regime, ostensibly founded on the repudiation of prior traditions and invested in exaggerated notions of the present as a culminating epoch in history, imparted unique features to these historical imaginings. Furthermore, although the public celebration of tsars, princes, and generals was fueled by the pragmatic decisions of party elites, such decisions were themselves driven in significant part by an inherited context of historical interpretation that persisted quite independent of deliberations in the Kremlin, at Stalin's dacha or in "dissenting circles." For the ability of both representatives of the state and of dissenting voices to dictate the meaning of history was ultimately restricted by the resistances of the prior tradition, which imposed limits on their agency at least as significant as those relating to institutional complexity or political competition. In short, beyond the story of what Stalin or Eisenstein did with Ivan the Terrible and Peter the Great, I seek to tell what Ivan and Peter did with them.

To gain some purchase on the fundamental riddle of the celebration of tsars by commissars, I begin with a discussion of Russian historical mythology during the 1920s. I focus on the works of the dean of early Soviet historiography, Mikhail Pokrovskii, and on the contrasting writings of Nikolai V. Ustrialov, the theoretician of the Change-of-Landmarks movement. Close consideration of these examples of the historical thought of the 1920s can show how the Stalinist vision of history was in fact somewhat less of a revolutionary departure than it was announced to be and has subsequently been described. As I show, Stalinist views of the past combined elements drawn from Pokrovskii's officially endorsed views together with other early Soviet tendencies, visible in Ustrialov's works, that were operative outside of state discourse and sanction— both of these being, in contrasting manner, derived from prerevolutionary traditions in Russian historical thought. The radical character of Stalinist revisionism consisted less in its interpretative innovations per se than in its alchemical combination of seemingly antithetical interpretive positions, coupled with its perverse drive to obliterate or conceal through an enforced forgetfulness these profound and contradictory debts to earlier traditions.

Ultimately, however, this cooptation of earlier traditions in Russian historical myth enacted a more profound repetition of their basic mechanisms than any party commissar could have intended. In the second half of this chapter,

I demonstrate this thesis through a reading of the Stalinist official line on the Russian national past, as it is represented in the most authoritative history textbook of the era, Andrei Shestakov's "instant classic," *The Short Course in the History of the USSR* (*Kratkii kurs istorii SSSR*, 1937). In the Stalin age the dynamic imbrication of trauma and heroism in Russian historical myth reached its apogee, matching the concatenation of triumph and terror in Stalinist political culture as a whole. The Stalinist establishment articulated revised myths of Ivan and Peter that minimized and naturalized the violence and excess of their reigns as essential aspects of any period of social transformation in the service of human progress and enlightenment.

Through the heroization of Ivan and Peter the regime sought to supersede and even obliterate histories—such as those of the prerevolutionary generation of Miliukov and Merezhkovskii—that cast the bloodshed of their eras as the natural corollary of their tyranny or the futility of their projects. However, in practice the cults of Ivan and Peter reiterated in exponentially magnified form many of the functions that the cult of Peter had played in Imperial Russia. The result was a model of Soviet collective identity predicated on the disavowal and memorialization of trauma and the acceptance and internalization of the state's cruel discipline. For although Stalinist historical myth was supposed to articulate a final, corrected version of historical knowledge, in practice it revolved through continuous and repeated modifications that enacted over and over again its fundamental mechanisms of disciplinary forgetting. Under Stalin, historical myth, like social and political life in general, projected a divided consciousness—a façade of triumphant, noisy celebration and a morass of terror beneath—committed to silence but never in fact forgotten. For this reason, an archeology of Stalinist historical myth, ostensibly committed to covering its own tracks in history, presents a wealth of opportunities to trace history's footprints in time.

The 1920s: History without Actors, Historiography without the State

The Bolshevik historian Mikhail Pokrovskii, who enjoyed the support of Lenin himself and institutional preeminence throughout the 1920s, formulated his views in *Russian History from the Earliest Times* (Russkaia istoriia s drevneishikh vremen, 1910–13) and his popular *Russian History in Most Concise Form* (Russkaia istoriia v samom szhatom ocherke, 1920). In these works, Pokrovskii adopted what must have seemed the obvious approach for a dedicated Marxist and a pupil of Kliuchevskii. He extended the development of Russian historiography toward the minimization of the role of individuals in historical processes. Scoffing time and again at the "personalized method, that traces all historical transformations to the actions of individuals," Pokrovskii sought to "leave the personalities in peace" and examine the social and economic factors that he held to lie truly at the base of historical phenomena.[10] Yet this radical depersonalization of history did not prevent him from "getting personal" with the traditional characters of the Russian past—corrupt and oppressive members of the exploiting classes, who required a proper revolutionary dethroning. Turning to Ivan and Peter, he revealed not only that they had been the insignificant pawns of historical forces, but also that they were simply despicable: Ivan was a "hysterical despot" and Peter, "called 'the Great' by obsequious historians," was a cruel, egotistical, syphilitic tyrant.[11] Such views enjoyed great prominence in Soviet public discourse throughout the 1920s. After the historian's death in 1932, though, they were condemned as out of step with the rehabilitation of the "great men" of history. Violently rejected as emblematic of the historiographic sins of the 1920s, the former paragon of Soviet historiography served as a bugbear, exemplifying how history should *not* be viewed, until the end of the Stalin era. "Pokrovskyism's" two cardinal sins—endlessly denounced in newspaper articles, scholarly volumes, and "self-criticism" gatherings—were its depersonalized "vulgar sociological" method and its denigration of all past social elites according to the "false slogan" that "history is politics projected into the past."[12]

As was so often the case in the Soviet era, however, this loud proclamation of a total break with the errors of the past masked a great deal of continuity. Despite the vilification of Pokrovskii in the 1930s, the fundamental outlines of his conception of Russian history remained in Stalinist revisionism with little modification. Furthermore, these same, persistent elements of Pokrovskii's account of the national past owe significant debts to preceding traditions of Russian historiography even beyond materialist circles. Although Pokrovskii denigrated both Ivan and Peter as individual actors, he saw the social and economic transformations of their eras as the most significant progressive advances in precapitalist Russian history and reasoned that the accompanying violence was a necessary and normal symptom of radical social change. So, even granting that Ivan's policies reflected his basically vicious nature, the hallmark features of his bloody rule—the *oprichnina*, the wars and executions—in actuality served the cause of the lesser service nobility, allied with the townspeople,

---

10. The examples are drawn from Pokrovskii, *Russkaia istoriia s drevneishikh vremen*, 4 vols. (1933–34), 1:121. References to this edition are given in text. Subsequent references to this work are to this edition, except where otherwise noted.

11. The first quotation is from Pokrovskii, *Russkaia istoriia*, 1:162; the second is from M. N. Pokrovskii, "Russkaia istoriia v samom szhatom ocherke," in his *Izbrannye proizvedeniia*, 3:112–13.

12. See, for example, two lead newspaper articles in the public denunciation of Pokrovskii's "school," "Za vysokoe kachestvo sovetskoi shkoly," *Pravda*, May 16, 1934, 1; and "O prepodavanii grazhdanskoi istorii v shkolakh SSSR," *Pravda*, May 16, 1934, 1. Also see the two-volume collection of critiques edited by Boris Grekov, *Protiv istoricheskoi kontseptsii*. On Pokrovskii and his rise and fall more generally, see Mazour, *Writing of History*; Enteen, *Soviet Scholar-Bureaucrat*; and David-Fox, *Revolution of the Mind*.

in their struggle against the boyars: "the path of 'battle' led across the corpse of old Muscovite feudalism, and that renders this 'battle' progressive independent of its immediate motivations" (1:204). Ivan's "revolution"—a word Pokrovskii repeats several times—marked "the establishment of a new class regime" (1:212). Moreover, he argues: "there can, of course, be no doubt that the regime of the service landholders was a terrorist one. In such circumstances, in the face of powerful 'traitors' as well as external enemies, gaining in strength with each passing hour, [. . .] even in more cultured eras, revolutionary governments have ruled with the help of terror" (1:213). Passages such as these transparently cast Ivan's era as comparable to other revolutionary periods, including that of the early twentieth century, according to a schematic conception of progressive history.[13]

Pokrovskii's interpretation of Peter's era extends this scheme. Here the historian offers an explicit comparison with the era of Ivan, noting that just as the "enormous carnage" of Ivan's era had been the expression of the transfer of power from the boyars to the service gentry, the "revolutionary and catastrophic character of the Petrine transformation" consisted in its transfer of power from the gentry to the ascendant bourgeois interests of merchant capitalism (2:214).[14] Even Peter's wars of conquest served the new economic model that overran Russia from the west: when Peter "lay siege to Riga, he was, in essence, the liberator of Baltic merchant capital, which had been held captive by Swedish violence" (2:192). Yet as in the case of Ivan, Pokrovskii left his readers no doubt that Peter himself, as an individual, was as despicable and practically insignificant in the course of history as any other tsar. For progress took its inevitable course quite independent of the initiatives of the emperor and his ministers:

> The opinion that political conditions forced the development of Russian capitalism in the seventeenth and eighteenth centuries is completely false; rather, the political carapace of the service gentry government actually inhibited the development of capitalism. Peter's autocracy, here, as in other areas, could create nothing—but it could destroy much. (2:207)

In Pokrovskii's account, Peter's involvement in craft and industry is a myth, his rule most often took the form of blind outbursts of violence, and whatever innate abilities he had for thought or work were dulled by endless drunkenness and grandiose carousing.

---

13. The historian's initial intent in the cited passage concerning revolutionary terror could only have been intended to refer to the French revolution—for the passage was written prior to 1917. Yet in postrevolutionary editions, in which this passage was reprinted without modification, readers could not but connect the typological dots with their own revolutionary era. For the identical passage in a prerevolutionary edition: M. N. Pokrovskii, *Russkaia istoriia s drevneishikh vremen*, 5 vols. (1913–14), 2:123.

14. In another passage Pokrovskii notes that Peter's initiation of the Northern War "resurrected the operational line of the Terrible Tsar" (*Russkaia istoriia*, 2:192).

In sum, Pokrovskii's divorce of individuals from historical processes allowed him to combine *ad hominem* attacks on Ivan and Peter with an emphatically positive assessment of the historical achievements of their eras, which he linked together in the time-honored tradition of prior teleological accounts of the Russian past: "Whether or not Ivan Vasilevich was the initiator or not (most likely, not), his *oprichnina* was an attempt some 150 years before Peter to lay the foundations of Petrine personal autocracy."[15]

Pokrovskii's work represents an innovative combination of the materialist views of Kliuchevskii and Miliukov, who championed deindividualized sociological and economic approaches to the past, with strong reminiscences of the teleological views of Russian historical development originally offered by State School historians such as Kavelin and Solovev. A finely nuanced interpretive position, the Soviet historian's assessment of Russian history allowed him to steal the thunder of revolutionary transformations, tied in other accounts to the names of Ivan and Peter, recasting the ancient momentum of progressive history itself as the force that eventually would lead to the downfall of the tsars and the triumph of the oppressed masses in 1917.[16]

Furthermore, the few recorded remarks of the Soviet leadership during the decade following the revolution regarding premodern Russian history—for a particularly forceful one, see the first epigraph to this chapter—cleave closely to this approach, in which Ivan and Peter, themselves worthy of no more adulation than any other Russian tsar, nevertheless were thought to have reigned over epochs of revolutionary transformation that marked the inevitable path of development toward the Soviet future.[17]

15. In a marked echo of Kavelin's formulation of the connection of Ivan and Peter, Pokrovskii goes on to note: "This attempt was too far ahead of its time, and its failure was unavoidable: but those who undertook it stood, without a doubt, higher than their contemporaries" (*Russkaia istoriia*, 1:204–5).

16. Pokrovskii's rationalization not only of the violence of Peter's era but also of the most infamous aspects of Ivan's as coherent elements of progressive social and political transformations participated in a broad scholarly consensus with the views of non-Marxist historians—in particular with the works of the leading historian of early modern Russia, S. F. Platonov. See Hellie, "In Search of Ivan the Terrible," xviii–xix; and Platonov, *Ivan Groznyi*.

17. Stalin offered relevant remarks several times in the 1920s. In 1926, in a speech concerning industrialization policy, the leader referred to the reigns of both Ivan and Peter as previous epochs of economic transformation, although his point was that neither figure was a true industrializer. Similarly, in 1928, Stalin described Peter's era as comparable to the present in terms of the age-old problem of Russian competition with western powers: "When Peter the Great, in dealing with the more developed countries of the west, feverishly constructed mills and factories for the supply of the army and the strengthening of the country's defense, he was making an original attempt to break free from the state of backwardness." Stalin qualified his remarks with the claim that the Petrine era did not, ultimately, achieve economic parity with the west—only the present regime could eliminate Russian backwardness once and for all ("O khoziastvennom polozhenii Sovetskogo Soiuza i politike partii," in Stalin, *Sochineniia*, 8:116–48, esp. 121; and "Ob industrializatsii strany i o pravom uklone v VKP(b)," *Sochineniia*, 11:245–90, here 248–49). For the Lenin quotation

In light of this reconsideration of Pokrovskii's work—the closest thing to an "official" view of Russian history during the Soviet 1920s—both the conservative and the innovative features of Stalinist revisionist historiography come into sharper focus. In 1931, as Pokrovskii's conceptions of historical process were waning fast, the German biographer Emil Ludwig interviewed Stalin, asking him how it was possible to reconcile Marxist views with the celebration of the historical achievements of individuals. Stalin's response recalls nothing so much as Hegel's conception of the "historic individual": "Every generation is met with certain conditions that already exist in their present form as that generation comes into the world. Great people are only worth something insofar as they are able to correctly understand these conditions and what is necessary to alter them. . . . Marxism has never denied the role of heroes. To the contrary, it gives them a significant role, albeit in line with the conditions which I have just described."[18]

Some six years later, on November 7, 1937, at a private gathering of party leaders on the twentieth anniversary of the revolution, Stalin delivered a toast articulating with startling clarity his perspective on prerevolutionary Russian history: "The Russian tsars did much that was bad. They robbed and enslaved the people. They led wars and seized territory in the interests of the landowners. But they did do one good thing—they put together an enormous Great Power [stretching] out to Kamchatka. We inherited this Great Power."[19]

Pronouncements such as these, which formed a steady crescendo in the historiography and public discourse of the 1930s, signaled the two fundamental innovations in the historical vision of the era: the reinstatement of heroic leaders as the chief agents of history and the valorization of state building as their paramount accomplishment. Yet one must recognize that neither the return of the hero to the helm of the ship of history nor the ship's identification with the state fundamentally changed the Soviet leadership's views about its course. Far from rejecting Pokrovskii's views in toto, the revisionists of the 1930s poured prerevolutionary heroes like Ivan and Peter, along with the Russian state that they were thought to have constructed, back into the teleological mold of history's revolutionary cycles, which Pokrovskii had himself borrowed from his nineteenth-century predecessors.

—◊—

This perspective on the relative continuity of "progressive" views of history from the prerevolutionary period forward to Stalin's day somewhat demystifies the general contours of revisionist history. Still, it is one thing to recognize

---

taken as an epigraph, see V. I. Lenin, "O 'levom' rebiachestve i o melkoburzhuaznosti," in his *Polnoe sobranie sochinenii*, 36:301.

18. I. V. Stalin, "Beseda s nemetskim pisatelem Emilem Ludvigom," *Sochineniia*, 13:104–23, here 106.

19. The toast is described in Dimitrov, *Diary*, 65. For additional discussion of this toast, see Brandenberger, *National Bolshevism*, 55.

the movement of progressive history in Ivan's and Peter's reigns but quite another to proclaim those eras to be heroic, mythic precedents for the events and leaders of the Soviet period. How, in short, did Ivan and Peter come to serve as condensation points of Soviet collective identity? As with the genealogy of the Stalinist narrative of Russian history, light can be cast on these questions of allegory and affect by consideration of the experience of the 1920s, but in this case I turn to unofficial voices of the first Soviet decade.

As we have seen, quite apart from the views of Pokrovskii or the Soviet leadership, the mythic identification of the revolutionary age with the era of Peter the Great, and secondarily with that of Ivan the Terrible, was a commonplace during the 1920s. Certainly, it is hardly surprising that Russians, who had for decades imagined and called for a revolution by projecting into the present Ivan's and Peter's renovations of Russia, continued in this mode once the revolution had come to pass. That being said, in the wild profusion of early Soviet nonofficial writing, no specific formulation of the interconnection of the Soviet present with the Russian past achieved anything like common acceptance. Instead, Russian thought in the key of historical allegory ranged from the extremes of Voloshin's and Merezhkovskii's critiques of the archaic nature of the revolution to Briusov's celebration of the historical roots of the Russian people's progressive energy.

This diversity of historical vision was made possible not only by the relatively unrestrictive conditions for public expression of the 1920s but also by the surprising lack of interest in such mythically minded historical thinking on the part of official representatives of Soviet power. In this, the postrevolutionary decade constitutes a unique moment in modern Russian history—perhaps the only period during which political life offered no authoritative center to which the historical myths of Ivan and Peter were interpretatively anchored. Political institutions had surrendered their command over Ivan and Peter, as it were, opening them up for exploitation by "private interests." The reception of the writings of Nikolai V. Ustrialov, one of the most influential émigré publicists of the early 1920s, provides an instructive example. Ustrialov was perhaps the most important ideologue of the Change-of-Landmarks movement, which promoted among disaffected former imperial elites a transfer of loyalties to the new regime, and which enjoyed for a time the equivocal tolerance of the Bolshevik leadership. In 1925, as this tolerance was fading, the author collected a number of his previously published articles in the volume *Under the Sign of Revolution* (Pod znakom revoliutsii)—a work that quickly attracted the attention of the Bolshevik leadership for its politically volatile arguments that Soviet policy and ideology in the New Economic Policy (NEP) period were evolving inexorably toward the recreation of the mighty empire of the tsars in a new and better form as a bourgeois, capitalist, Russian state.[20]

20. For a recent survey of Ustrialov's biography and thought, see Bystriantseva, "Mirovozzrenie"; for a more focused account of his theoretical statements, see Kraus [Krausz], *Sovetskii termidor*.

Ustrialov's essays are rich with historical analogies. Without a doubt, the most important of these is the ideologically charged analogy of the October revolution and subsequent events with the history of the French revolution of 1789—a commonplace comparison that elicited heated political debate in the first decade of Soviet power.[21] Yet Ustrialov also refers not infrequently to the Russian national past, as in the following passage, one of his most pungent:

> This is how it comes out: the people, crushed by oppression and dreaming of being saved by a foreign intervention, during these same decades of "tyrannical rule" with all its horrors, brought into being the great Muscovite state, surpassing the glories of Ivan Kalita. . . . And, strange enough, the people then glorified in countless legends the tyrant, from under whom they had ached to be released, even at the cost of a foreign invasion. [. . .] Ivan the Terrible, Peter the Great, our days—there is a deep, intimate continuity here. [. . .] Inexhaustible potential for psychological and historical parallels. [. . .] Ivan the Terrible and Peter the Great were the bearers of a "new world," which they realized by "revolutionary" means. The same can be said of our epoch. The people hated Ivan's *oprichnina* and Peter's administration no less than they hate the Cheka today. They did not understand the meaning of the demolition. But later, they understood by its fruits that it had been necessary and granted legitimacy to the completed revolution. They will grant the same legitimacy in our day, despite all the horrors and crimes of the revolutionary powers.[22]

Ustrialov's perverse conception of history as a scene of lamentable yet historically necessary slaughter is part and parcel of his provocative central thesis that the Bolshevik overthrow of the tsars should be seen as a predestined Russian national drama, rather than as a stage in world revolution. In just this vein, Ustrialov's epitaph to Lenin explores French revolutionary analogies for the Bolshevik mastermind ranging from Robespierre to Napoleon, then ends with the corrective that, all the same: "He was, undoubtedly, Russian from head to toe. [. . .] Personal enmity will pass, and then will come 'the onset of history.' Then, once and for all, everyone will comprehend that Lenin was ours—that Lenin was a true son of Russia—her national hero—together with Dmitrii Donskoi, Peter the Great, Pushkin, and Tolstoi."[23]

---

21. Kraus [Krausz], *Sovetskii termidor*.

22. Ustrialov, *Pod znakom revoliutsii*, 346–47. Similarly, in an essay devoted to Bolshevik terror, Ustrialov meditates on the reigns of Ivan the Terrible and Peter the Great: "In time, the horrible heroes of the Cheka will likely come before the judgment of history together with the *oprichniki* of Ivan the Terrible—who showed no mercy to the representatives of Old Russia [. . .] in service to the glory of the new—and along with the awful cohorts of Peter the Great, who rebuilt Russia on the bones of the fine people of old and on the blood of the meek tsarevich Aleksei" (ibid., 80).

23. Ibid., 75.

Deemed a serious enough ideological challenge to form a topic of discussions in the Politburo, *Under the Sign of Revolution* elicited two extensive critical essays by ranking Bolsheviks Grigorii Zinovev and Nikolai Bukharin in *Pravda*, the latter of which was republished as a separate pamphlet.[24] As Tamás Krausz has argued, Ustrialov's combination of enthusiasm for Soviet power and for his conception of the "real" implications of the NEP with disdain for the core ideological tenets of communism made his writings politically volatile in the context of intraparty fractional struggle in the middle 1920s.[25] Both articles offered extensive arguments against Ustrialov's deployment of the analogy of October with the French revolution. Yet remarkably, the single reference to Ustrialov's Russian historical analogies in either article is a dismissive sniff at the "miraculous transformation of Lenin into Dmitrii Donskoi."[26]

As this episode reveals, while some Russians—perhaps many—continued to see the present in the shadow of the liminal figures and epochs of the past, the Soviet leadership was fundamentally unconcerned with the allegorical potential of the stock figures of Russian history. While it is impossible to fully explain this lack of concern, one may suggest that the Bolsheviks, still cleaving to a vision of the revolution as radically innovative and international in significance, simply did not take such thinking seriously. This is to say, the French revolution, the *locus classicus* for discussions both of the theory and practice of revolution in general, occupied a firm position in the Bolshevik historical cosmos. The archetypal figures of Russian national history did not.

The outcome of this *laissez faire* policy toward national historical myth was not only great variation in interpretation but outright confusion concerning Russian history's liminal figures, as a brief consideration of another intriguing episode concerning "unofficial" historical discourse of the 1920s may illustrate. In 1922, Robert Vipper, better known as a historian of classical antiquity and western religion, published his monograph *Ivan the Terrible*.[27] Vipper's book was unabashedly apologetic. Whereas Pokrovskii's work concealed its debt to Ivan's nineteenth-century supporters Kavelin and Solovev, Vipper's monograph openly adopted and racheted up the views of these statist historians. It de-

24. Ustrialov's book appears as an item for discussion in the agenda of the Politburo of the Party Central Committee for November 28, 1925. Adibekov, Anderson, and Rogovaia, eds., *Politbiuro TsK RKP(b)-VKP(b)*, 1:416. The official responses relating to these discussions included G. E. Zinov'ev, "Filosofiia epokha," *Pravda*, September 19, 1925, 2–3; and September 20, 1925, 2–3; and N. I. Bukharin, "Tsezarism pod maskoi revoliutsii," *Pravda*, November 13, 1925, 2–4; November 14, 1925, 2–4; and November 15, 1925, 2–3; republ. as Bukharin, *Tsezarism*.

25. Kraus [Krausz], *Sovetskii termidor*, 115–40.

26. Bukharin, *Tsezarism*, 40. Zinovev brushes off Russian historical parallels in a similar manner ("Filosofiia epokha," September 19, 1925, 2).

27. Regarding Vipper's career and works, see Safronov, *Istoricheskoe mirovozzrenie*; Graham, "R. Iu. Vipper"; Perrie, *Cult of Ivan the Terrible*, 12–19, 92–99; and Dubrovskii, *Istorik i vlast'*, 763–70.

picted Ivan as a subtle diplomat, military superman, and populist leader who served the interests of the common people, carrying out brilliant and historically necessary social and political reforms in order to create a glorious and durable state. The key features of Ivan's triumph were "the growth of the Muscovite state, its great tasks of conquest, Ivan's broad conceptions, his military innovations, and his diplomatic genius."[28]

In an interesting twist of fate, some two decades later, this book was to become the cornerstone of the Stalinist rehabilitation of Ivan, a celebratory treatment of the Terrible Tsar's battle with external and internal enemies in service to the great Russian state, with transparent allegorical significance for the events and leaders of the late 1930s and ensuing war years. In the 1920s, though, the mythic import of the book was anything but transparent. Some interpreters, such as the religious thinker Georgii Fedotov, read Vipper's elevation of Ivan as an expression of nostalgia for the autocracy—as an enraged reaction against the weak tsars and liberal reformers who had paved the way for Russia's revolutionary downfall.[29] Certain commentators from the opposite end of the political spectrum concurred, such as the historian Militsa Nechkina, a student of Pokrovskii, who in a historiographic digression appended to her 1933 article on Ivan IV for the *Great Soviet Encyclopedia* (Bol'shaia sovetskaia entsiklopediia) inventively explained that Ivan had been the darling of many prerevolutionary historians for his cruel antirevolutionary élan, and that Vipper's views continued in this tradition. Vipper, in Nechkina's view, had set Ivan up as "a counterrevolutionary apotheosis of [. . .] the autocratic dictator, concealing in the 'historicity' of his topic a direct call to struggle against Bolshevism."[30]

Yet in a curious anticipation of the Stalinist cooptation of Vipper's work, the historian Ivan Polosin could write in the introduction to his 1925 translation of Heinrich Von Staden's account of Muscovy during Ivan's reign that Vipper, like many others who had been drawn to study the "social revolution" of the sixteenth century by virtue of its resonance with the present epoch, had authored a "brilliant sketch" charged with the "stirring atmosphere of the last decade." For Polosin, Vipper's "general assessments of the military-autocratic communism of the Muscovite tsar reflects the mighty influence of contemporary reality."[31] In short, although Vipper's book could not have been clearer in its apologetic intent and cried out to be interpreted as a projection of present

28. Vipper, "Ivan Groznyi," in his *Ivan Groznyi*, ed. Volodikhin, 101–211, here 206.

29. Fedotov wrote: "Vipper in his patriotic anguish sought a tyrant, consoling himself retrospectively by taking refuge from the Moscow of 1917 in that of the Terrible Tsar" (*Sviatoi Filipp*, 106–7). For other reviews and responses to the first edition of Vipper's *Ivan the Terrible*, see Platonov, *Ivan Groznyi*, 24; and Iu. V. Got'e, review of *Ivan Groznyi* by R. Iu. Vipper, *Russkii istoricheskii zhurnal*, 1922, no. 8, 295–97.

30. M. V. Nechkina, "Ivan IV," in *Bol'shaia sovetskaia entsiklopediia*, 65 vols. (1926–47): 27:326–29, here 329.

31. Polosin, "Zapadnaia Evropa i Moskoviia," 10.

historical experience into the myth of the past, the valence of such interpretations was radically undetermined, reflecting the hermeneutic "open season" on
Russian national historical myth of the Soviet 1920s.

—ᴍ—

In June 1931, at the peak of the first Five-Year Plan and very early in, if not
prior to, the Stalinist reinvention of history, Boris Pasternak described in private correspondence the scale and tempo of industrial construction in Chelia-
binsk, remarking: "Although it has been said a hundred times, the comparison with Peter's construction is impossible to avoid."[32] Statements such as
this—and there are many other examples—lay plain something of the context
of Stalinist revisionism. For the Bolshevik leadership did not invent the mythic
resonance of Ivan and Peter with their revolution; they merely adapted it to
suit their own purposes.

Given the reemergence of great men and great states as central conceptual
categories in official history and public life in the 1930s, as well as the growing
investment in particularist "Soviet patriotism," historians, political elites, and
cultural managers faced a choice concerning Ivan and Peter. Yet this was not a
choice whether or not to take the two as mythic touchstones, but rather how
this already given resonance was to be managed or resisted, amplified, or di-
minished. Should these figures be treated as positive allegories for present experience, to be celebrated as crowned revolutionaries, or as negative ones, to be
suppressed and counteracted by an energetic character assassination of them as
tsarist antiheroes? The myths of Peter, and of Ivan as well, had been articulated
"a hundred times." For this reason, a simple refusal to engage was not really
possible. Russians had already mapped national history onto the present. The
question was, how was an officially engineered mass culture to respond?

I do not wish to suggest that the rehabilitations of Peter and Ivan were necessary or predictable, for party elites faced a true quandary. On one hand,
what Marxist revolutionary would desire to be compared to the tsars, especially with ones of such a despotic, bloody nature? On the other hand, as Pasternak put it, such comparisons were "impossible to avoid"—both in terms of
the legendary achievements of Ivan and Peter and in terms of their equally
legendary brutality. Pasternak's poem of 1931, "A century and then some . . ."
(Stoletie s lishnim . . .), in which the poet restages lines from Pushkin's *Stanzas*
of 1826, which compared Nicholas to Peter, may be seen as a meditation on
the polyvalence of the myth of Peter at this juncture:

> A century and then some—it's not just yesterday,
> But the same old force is in the temptation,
> In hopes of glory and of bliss,
> To look at things without fear.[33]

32. Ibid., 10.
33. Pasternak, *Sobranie sochinenii*, 1:421.

Here Pasternak relives Pushkin's sense of the openness and indeterminacy of the Petrine myth. If Stalin was a new Peter, did his revolution represent a truly glorious new Petrine beginning, or a collapse into despotism à la Nicholas I?[34]

At about the same time as Pasternak was musing on the ubiquity and the indeterminacy of the comparison of the Soviet present to Peter's day—and on the hope, temptation, and fear folded into the shadow Peter cast on the present— Ludwig confronted Stalin with the same historical analogy in his 1931 interview, and the latter's response is revealing. Asked point-blank if he recognized a parallel between himself and Peter the Great, the Soviet leader shot back the unequivocal "not by any means." Yet he immediately began to backtrack: of course, it was true that Peter had "done a great deal" within the context of the eighteenth century and deserved recognition. However, Stalin considered it absurd to take the tsar as a model for twentieth-century leadership: "I am a pupil of Lenin. [. . .] Peter the Great [. . .] is a drop in the ocean, whereas Lenin is the ocean itself."[35]

Echoes of such equivocation would persist throughout the heyday of Stalinist revisionism, which even at the height of celebration of tsarist heroes shied away from straightforward equations of past and present. Nevertheless, by allowing that Peter was a drop in the "Sea of Lenin," a position consistent with Pokrovskii's account of Russian history and with the established views of many Soviet elites, Stalin had already opened the door to Peter's eventual elevation. In the course of a drawn-out process of contestation, equivocation, and debate during the 1930s, Soviet public life arrived at successively more triumphal endorsements of Russia's first emperor as a herald of revolutionary progress—no Lenin or Stalin, to be sure, but their historical protoimage.[36] Nevertheless, throughout this process and even at the height of the Stalinist celebration of Peter, the contradictory ideological implications and interpretive potentials of the first emperor's historical mythology continued to haunt the scene, ensuring that, beyond all management and calculation, the significance of the first emperor would exceed the intentions of the party elites.

34. On Pasternak's "A century and then some . . . ," see Fleishman, *Boris Pasternak v dvadtsatye gody*, 249–52; Fleishman, *Boris Pasternak i literaturnaia zhizn' 1930-kh godov*, 59–60, 130; and E. B. Pasternak, *Boris Pasternak: biografiia*, 457–60. A number of other literary works of the late 1920s and early 1930s offer meditations on the political indeterminacy, or incoherence, of the historical myth of Peter the Great, including Andrei Platonov's "Epiphany Locks" (Epifanskie shliuzy, 1927) and Iurii Tynianov's "Waxen Effigy" (Voskovaia persona, 1930). I comment more extensively on these works in Platt, "Antichrist Enthroned," 115–18. On the historical poetics of Tynianov's work in particular, see Kujundžic, *The Returns of History*, 135–80.

35. Stalin "Beseda," 13:105.

36. The comments of the machinist Vorontsov, cited in the second epigraph to this chapter, suggest how widely disseminated this view of Peter became by the mid-1930s (Ts-GAIPD, f. 24, op. 2v, d. 1846, l. 45). I am indebted to David Brandenberger for sharing this citation.

The elevation of Ivan as a Soviet hero proceeded in analogous fashion in the wake of Peter's rehabilitation. As early as 1934, the father of Socialist Realism, Maksim Gorkii, reflected aloud at the first congress of the Union of Soviet Writers that a "people's" history of Ivan the Terrible, based in folklore, might temper tsarist historiography's negative portrayals of him. The next year Aleksei N. Tolstoi began to plan a work on Ivan as a natural outgrowth of his increasingly celebratory treatments of Peter.[37] Nevertheless, scattered evidence indicates that the denunciation of Stalin and his supporters as a "new Ivan the Terrible" with his "new *oprichniks*" was a not infrequent mode of anti-Soviet abuse in the early 1930s.[38] As late as 1937, the People's Commissariat of Internal Affairs (NKVD) was interrogating the writer Iurii Iurkun about his criminal comparison of Stalin to the Terrible Tsar—an incendiary, anti-Soviet conception, indeed![39]

The interpretive conundrum of Ivan, then, remained unsettled long after Peter had been inducted into the Stalinist Hall of Fame. Here, too, Soviet elites faced a difficult choice: between suppressing criticisms like Iurkun's while continuing to hold Ivan in contempt as a bloodthirsty despot or, alternately, pursuing Gorkii's suggestion to rehabilitate the first tsar as a weapon in the Soviet agitational arsenal. As with Peter before him, these options were weighed in an incremental process of politically complex infighting in the mid- to late 1930s that led eventually to the adoption of the latter strategy.

37. Despite his dismissal of tsarist historiography, Gorkii's observation that representations of Ivan IV in Russian folk epics were more positive than contemporary and historiographic assessments revived a commonplace dating to Karamzin. See Karamzin, *Istoriia*, 9:278–80; and *Pervyi vsesoiuznyi s'ezd*, 10. Regarding Aleksei N. Tolstoi's work on Ivan, Vladimir Bonch-Bruevich wrote to Maksim Gorkii in January 1935 that Tolstoi "is devoting much time to the history of Ivan the Terrible, collecting material and portrayals. He says that in his opinion Peter has his source in Ivan the Terrible and that Ivan the Terrible is even more interesting than Peter—more colorful and varied. He wants to write about him" (cited in Shcherbina, *A. N. Tolstoi*, 471).

38. For examples of denunciatory comparisons of Stalin and Ivan, see Deutscher, *Stalin: A Political Biography*, 349; and Perrie, *Cult of Ivan the Terrible*, 77–78.

39. Shneiderman, "Benedikt Livshits: arest, sledstvie, rasstrel," 84. Rising out of the indeterminate climate for interpretation of Ivan the Terrible of the mid-1930s, Mikhail Bulgakov's theatrical farce *Ivan Vasilevich* (about the accidental time travel of Ivan the Terrible to present-day Moscow and that of an Ivan look-alike—a "tyrannical" house manager—to sixteenth-century Moscow) was, strikingly, not intended to map the convergences of two "revolutionary epochs," whether of a denunciatory or a celebratory nature. The banning of the play in March 1936 seems to have been symptomatic of the increased anxiety over representation of the Russian national past in general. As has happened with many other equivocal allegories of Russia's liminal rulers, the play was later incorrectly interpreted as a critical satire on the Stalinist cult of Ivan. For attempts to read *Ivan Vasilevich* as a satirical critique of the Stalinist present, see Lur'e, "Ivan Groznyi i drevnerusskaia literatura"; Doyle, "Bulgakov's *Ivan Vasil'evich*"; and Nikitin, "O pol'ze al'ternativnykh vzgliadov," 3–6. For the most informed assessment of the play and its fate, see Perrie, "Terrible Tsar as Comic Hero."

So in the course of the 1930s and 1940s, a drawn-out negotiation among party elites, cultural managers, writers, historians, and Soviet society as a whole—for which the equation of past and present had long been both obvious and politically equivocal—strove to master the Russian national past for the purposes of the present. Yet the farther official pronouncements and public discourse pursued such mastery, the more visible became the pertinacious complexity of liminal figures such as Ivan and Peter and the more self-evident the impossibility of attempts at the official "management" of historical knowledge. How, indeed, could Stalinist mythmakers both take advantage of the mechanisms of significance inherited from previous generations and at the same time emphasize the radical, revolutionary novelty of this new vision of the past? How were figures defined at base by their multivalent significance to be pinned down once and for all to fixed interpretational clarity? And how was this stability of meaning to be achieved in an age when orthodox interpretation itself was progressing at a remarkably rapid pace from one position to the next?

Finally, in this maximally heroic version of the great reigns of the past, matching in its high pitch the tones of Soviet celebration of the revolutionary present, what was to be the valence and function of the traumatic scars of liminal epochs past and present? While party leaders and cultural figures may indeed have imagined that the bloody stains were to be finally, completely washed out of Ivan's and Peter's robes, their narrow understanding of a consciously tailored "usable past" failed to comprehend the unintended, excessive functionality of these historical myths in Russian culture. For even granting that the representatives of the state sought to erase or transcend, once and for all, historical visions of Ivan and Peter as cruel despots, ultimately their whitewashing of ancient violence functioned in Stalinist society in an entirely different manner.

At issue here was not the actual erasure of other visions of the past (an impossible goal anyway) but the public enactment of such an erasure. For just as in the case of the myth of Peter the Great in the age of Nicholas I, the Stalinist naturalization and legitimization of both Ivan's and Peter's patently despotic mayhem articulated a model of collective identity predicated on acceptance of (and complicity with) state-sponsored violence—toward persons, toward knowledge, and toward the self. In the end, this unintended functionality of the myths of Ivan and Peter—that of chosen yet disavowed trauma—sustained and defined the dynamic of historical knowledge of the Stalin years no less than did the intentionally deployed "usable" elements of those myths. In these years, Soviet men and women lived in two planes simultaneously: on one hand, the ecstatic public celebration of the justice of the state, and on the other, the sure knowledge, never given public voice, of massive persecutions and iniquities. Historical knowledge functioned as an analogue and training ground in these quintessential Soviet habits of mind, for in the end it carried out not the erasure of the collective trauma of Ivan's and Peter's reigns but its disavowal. And so, in Stalin's day, in an apotheosis of the cultural tendencies evident in previous epochs, these primordial scenes of violence served as touchstones of collective identity and myths of leadership in which greatness was predicated on a submerged base of terror.

Last Words: Andrei Shestakov's *Short Course* in the History of the USSR

The Short Course in the History of the USSR, edited by Andrei Shestakov and first published in 1937, was the Stalinist "last word" on history. More than any other single text, this multiauthor work, resulting from years of juried competitions, internal debates, and editorial work directed by Andrei Zhdanov and other party leaders, including the active involvement of Stalin himself, established a standard interpretation of Russian national history for the Stalinist era. Although the work was intended as an elementary-school textbook, it quickly assumed a central position in Soviet educational and propaganda efforts at all levels, extending from classrooms full of fresh-faced schoolchildren up through secondary schools, to party courses, military training sessions, and agitational reading circles. In the following decades, the work was reprinted in multiple mass editions and translated into all languages of the Soviet Union, as well as major languages of Asia and the west, remaining the fundamental statement on the prehistory of the Soviet lands until Stalin's death opened a new era in historical and educational practice in the middle 1950s.[40]

Among the many startling innovations of this text, the most fundamental was its radical reconfiguration of the relationship between the Russian national past and the Soviet present. In Pokrovskii's now discredited account, the history of Russia per se had figured as a necessary precondition for the revolutionary transformations of Russia in the twentieth century, but as nothing more—history was a battlefield of social forces and actors who were alien to the classes and political institutions of the Soviet present. Although at times, the Russian state appeared in Pokrovskii's account as an engine of social progress in the abstract, there could be no question of attaching the Soviet state or the identity of its citizens to any element of Russian history, apart from the revolutionary working class and its leaders, who were forged in the maelstrom of the past. Russian history was, in effect, a history of the "other," culminating in the emergence of the proletariat and its apotheosis in the revolutionary overthrow of the tsars.

The Shestakov text, in marked contrast, was founded on a principle of political and social genealogy linking the Russian past and the Soviet present, and it exhorted readers to realize an affective continuity with the progressive actors of Russian history, whose accomplishments blurred together in a coherent, grand

---

40. Brandenberger provides a fascinating and detailed account of the history of this work, its production, and its application in his *National Bolshevism*, 43–62, 251–60.

march toward Soviet reality. In effect, the Russian state and people, as well as certain of their champions, were now staged not as representatives of the vanquished other but as prior instantiations of the self, worthy of celebration and emulation. As the introduction of the new textbook informed readers: "We love our motherland, and we must know her remarkable history well. He who knows history can better understand life today and will better fight with the enemies of our country and strengthen socialism."[41] Here and in the book as a whole, a timeless "motherland," with roots reaching into the deep past, appears as continuous with "our country" in the present—the Russia of the tsars and Soviet Russia became, in effect, one entity—differentiated across time, to be sure, but whole. Present-day social and political identity had been firmly installed on the base of this newly rediscovered, "remarkable" history of the self.

However, if on the macrohistorical level the eternal persistence of "the motherland" was axiomatic, *The Short Course in the History of the USSR* certainly could not claim all aspects of Russian political and social history as bases for the legitimacy and collective identity of a revolutionary state. First, the villains of Marxist history and recent revolutionary experience—landowners, capitalists, the final Russian tsars, and all rivals to Bolshevik power—could not but remain despised enemies. Second, in elevating the history of the Russian state and people as the prehistory of the Soviet state and people, the story of Russia's brutal domination of ethnic minorities and colonies required careful management to allow non-Russian Soviet citizens their own foothold in a shared political identity. The key to resolution of both these problems was a simplified, two-tiered scheme of history in which premodern and modern periods and actors were given sharply differing treatments.

As Brandenberger has noted, the Shestakov textbook is almost completely lacking in any analytical discussion of historical stages of social or political development. Nevertheless, the work acts out an unannounced strong theory of history, aligning an evaluative leap from adulation of tsars to adulation of revolutionaries with the hinge between the premodern and modern periods. Premodernity figures as an era of nation building and state building, both of which are cast as progressive ends. Heroic leaders familiar from "old-fashioned" Russian national history—Aleksandr Nevskii, victor over "Swedes and Germans" in the thirteenth century; Ivan Kalita, "gatherer of lands" in the next; Dmitrii Donskoi, vanquisher of the Tatars, and so on—are treated uncritically as the champions of these noble causes, assigned by history itself. Almost as a formality, some minimal account is given of the sufferings of the common people, blamed on anonymous "boyars and princes" rather than on any of Russia's great heroes. In the proleptic absence of the leadership and organization of the working class, peasant uprisings are cast as futile affairs. The sufferings of conquered non-Russian peoples are given similarly short shrift.

---

41. Shestakov, ed., *Kratkii kurs istorii SSSR*, 4. References to this edition are given in text.

Yet with the onset of modern Russian history, the Shestakov text abruptly changes its strategy, turning from this emphasis on state and nation to focus on Russian imperialism and on revolution—beginning, of course, with the French revolution. The tsars and their loyal servants are uniformly cast as corrupt despots, directly responsible for the exploitation and oppression of their subjects, for harsh colonial policies, for willful intervention in republican and revolutionary movements in Europe, and for cruel suppression of rebels and revolutionaries at home. Out of the ruling elites, only revolutionaries (the "martyrs" of the failed 1825 Decembrist coup; the renegade publicist Aleksandr Herzen, etc.), cultural and scientific figures (Lomonosov, Aleksandr Radishchev, and Pushkin), and military heroes (Suvorov) are treated as worthy representatives of the greatness of Russian civilization.

With the vilification of the modern imperial state, the text is now licensed to cast anticolonial resistance movements and leaders, such as the Caucasian rebel Shamil (1798–1871), as heroic freedom fighters.[42] Yet the true heroes of history are now the leaders of the international and Russian revolutionary movement—Marx, Engels, Plekhanov, Lenin, Stalin, and other Bolshevik leaders—and finally the working class itself. A simple inspection of chapter titles reveals the work's narrative strategy: typical early titles like that of chapter 2, "The Kievan State," or of chapter 4, "The Creation of the Russian National State" give way to headings like those of chapter 7, "Russia under the Tsars—Gendarme of Europe" and chapter 9, "The Growth of Capitalism in Tsarist Russia."

The transitional moment in this macrohistorical structure reflects a tradition in historical interpretation extending back through Pokrovskii, Platonov, and Miliukov to nineteenth-century statist historians such as Solovev and Kavelin. This narrative hinge encompasses a period beginning with the late sixteenth century, the reign of Ivan the Terrible, and reaching through the seventeenth century, the era of the first Romanov tsars and the earliest rulers subject to the textbook's harsh critique, up to the early eighteenth century, the era of Peter the Great, who is the last tsar to be treated as a heroic leader in the Stalinist version of the Russian national past.

The central place in the Shestakov textbook of Peter as the instigator and genius of eighteenth-century modernization participated in a reinvention of the first emperor that had begun in Aleksei N. Tolstoi's works and that was further hammered home in Soviet mass public discourse by the two-part film, *Peter I* (Petr I, 1937 and 1939). Based on the same author's screenplay and directed by Vladimir Petrov, the first part of this highly successful epic historical film hit screens across the USSR simultaneously with the publication of *The Short Course in the History of the USSR*.

---

42. The case of Shamil is particularly interesting. Originally cast as a "national leader," in later editions of the textbook he was presented in a negative light, reflecting the rise of an apologetic stance regarding Russian imperialism. See Brandenberger, *National Bolshevism*, 121–22; and Dubrovskii, *Istorik i vlast'*, 287, 591–94.

The reinvention of Ivan the Terrible unfolded in a markedly different manner, however. A number of researchers have dated the official endorsement of a heroic image of Ivan to later years—to the appearance of literary works such as Valentin Kostylev's lowbrow trilogy of historical novels, Aleksei N. Tolstoi's plays, and Eisenstein's film project. Attentive reading of *The Short Course in the History of the USSR* demands qualification of such accounts.[43] Not only did the work's treatment of Ivan unequivocally establish the foundation for later projects in its apologetic tone and interpretive strategy, but the positioning of the tsar in the narrative of Russian history as a whole established the historical logic underlining his importance. Ivan's significance is evident from the scale of the textbook's treatment alone. In fact, the only Russian leader of any era up to the revolution who is discussed at the same length as Ivan is Peter. Out of a total of seventy-four pages covering all history up to the end of the eighteenth century, six pages (an entire short chapter) are devoted to Ivan and seven to Peter. By contrast, such important figures as Ivan Kalita and Aleksandr Nevskii receive at most a few short paragraphs. It may be more accurate, then, to distinguish between wholesale promulgation in cultural and propagandistic works and rehabilitation as a progressive actor in authoritative works of history. Whereas in Peter's case the former process preceded the latter, in Ivan's case historiographical rehabilitation predated by several years his mass popularization.

Each of the textbook's rehabilitative accounts of the two liminal tsars is shaped as a chronology of accomplishments attributed directly to the initiative of the ruler, punctuated by concise, synthetic—yet qualified—statements of his progressive significance as the key figure in an epoch of transformative change. After initial mention of Ivan's persecution as an orphaned youth at the hands of "arrogant" boyars, who "fostered his bad qualities," the textbook embarks on a celebratory account of Ivan as an enlightener, consolidator of state power, and military leader. We learn that he was responsible for assumption of the title and unfettered power of an autocrat and the introduction of printing into Russia. The *oprichnina* is described as a tool in the political struggle to centralize power: Ivan "completed in a fashion the gathering of the scattered appanage principalities into a single strong state that was begun by Ivan Kalita" (40–41). As a result of the tsar's conquests of Kazan and other new territories to the east, many non-Russians began to enter into his service, and "Russia began to be transformed from a national into a multinational state" (39). Turning to the west, the Livonian War is billed as an effort to combat Swedes and Germans who were intentionally impeding Russian contact with western European nations. These military undertakings, along with the conquest of Siberia, support

43. For later datings of the official rehabilitation of Ivan, see Ia. S. Lur'e, "Perepiska Ivana Groznogo s Kurbskim v obshchestvennoi mysli drevnei Rusi," in *Perepiska Ivana Groznogo*, ed. Ia. S. Lur'e and Iu. D. Rykov, 214–49, here 216–17; Uhlenbruch, "Annexation of History," 269–70; Kozlov, "Artist and the Shadow of Ivan," 112; Perrie, "Nationalism and History," 112–13; and Perrie, *Cult of Ivan the Terrible*, 78.

the chapter's general conclusion: "Under Ivan IV the domains of Russia were increased many times over. His realm became one of the largest states in the world" (42).

In similar fashion, discussion of Peter begins by characterizing him as a "smart and effective young tsar" who "began to introduce a new order of things" (60). Convinced early on of the need "to reconfigure the entire life of his country and to adopt military and maritime technology of the Europeans," he embarks on his diplomatic mission to western Europe, where he: "worked in the shipyards with an axe in his hands. Peter spent almost two years abroad, and he learned much there" (61). The next few pages cover the emperor's wars in the north and the south, the founding of Petersburg, and the conquest of new territories, leading to the triumphant conclusion: "Peter I achieved his goals. The shores of the Baltic Sea were in the hands of Russia. Russia had become closer to Europe. Peter waged a tireless struggle with the backwardness of Russia and remade the order of things in a European fashion" (64). The final segment on Peter's reign describes his domestic reforms, concentrating on administrative and tax reforms, the development of manufacturing, education and enlightenment, calendar reform, and the introduction of European culture and fashion.

The Shestakov textbook credits Ivan and Peter with the completion of the great work of premodern Russian history—state consolidation, imperial expansion, and lastly, modernization and enlightenment—and hence with the very creation of that integral entity, the motherland, to which Soviet collective identity and affective energies were to be attached. Yet despite its celebratory tone, the work's approach to the bloodshed and violence of their reigns was not one of simple minimization. Certainly, its account can only be termed "sanitized" when compared with works that view these eras as scenes of either completely senseless mayhem or of state-sponsored brutality so excessive that it annihilated the legitimacy of the autocrats and their policies. But the text was also perfectly frank both about Ivan's and Peter's bloody methods of rule. During Ivan's reign, "the condition of the peasants considerably worsened," and many "fled from the center of the Russian tsardom from the looting and violence of the landowners and *oprichniki*" (41). Discussion of Peter's reign includes accounts of popular uprisings and of the state's response with merciless mass executions and the physical destruction of rebellious villages. Yet these classic portraits of class domination, reminding readers that Peter and Ivan were ultimately the champions of oppressive regimes, are somewhat perfunctory, and are interlarded with discussions of other instances of state violence that are ennobled by the progressive causes that they served. So: "After his initial defeats in the [Livonian] War, Ivan discovered the treason of larger-scale boyar estate holders. [. . .] Tsar Ivan hated the boyars, who sat on their estates like little miniature tsars and attempted to limit his autocratic power. [. . .] Ivan IV and his *oprichniki* destroyed many boyars" (40–41). In similar fashion, Peter "personally led the executions of the rebel *Streltsy*, who were pulling Russia backwards," for their uprising was "a reactionary mutiny" of those "dissatisfied with Peter's innovations and demanding a return to the old ways" (61).[44] The work's concluding statement on Peter exemplifies this combination of celebration of the emperor's contribution to progress with matter-of-fact acknowledgment of his despotism: "Under Peter I Russia moved forward considerably but remained a land where all depended on the oppression of the serfs and the arbitrary rule of the tsar. The strengthening of the Russian Empire under Peter I was achieved at a cost of hundreds of thousands of deaths of the laboring masses, at the cost of the ruination of the people" (66).

Though the *Short Course* can by no means be described as a whitewash of the brutality of Ivan's and Peter's reigns, it presented an ambivalent assessment of state-sponsored violence. On one hand was violence ennobled by progressive ends, on the other sheer brutality toward the common people. Yet this distinction is never rendered explicit, allowing these categories to blur together. On balance, the textbook's celebration of the triumphs of the two tsars' progressive projects suggested that their "cost" in human lives had been justified.

As recent investigations into archival materials relating to the textbook competition and editorial process that led to the publication of *The Short Course in the History of the USSR* demonstrate, the highest levels of the party leadership played a strikingly active part in its production—at times usurping the authorial role itself.[45] These interventions from above had no little significance for representations of Ivan and, secondarily, of Peter. In early 1937, for example, Zhdanov and the Central Committee member Iakov Iakovlev compiled a memorandum reporting jury deliberations back to the brigade of historians working on the text. Their directives included not only the general call to "to strengthen throughout elements of Soviet patriotism and love for the socialist motherland" but also more specific instructions with direct significance for work on the two liminal rulers: "give something on the progressive significance of centralized state power"; "explain the reactionary nature of the *Streltsy* rebellion."[46]

At about the same time, Stalin himself initiated revisions of the draft textbook with even greater specific significance for Ivan and Peter. In one of the earliest drafts showing the general secretary's markup, he excised Repin's painting *Ivan the Terrible and His Son Ivan*, likely objecting to its gory depiction of despotic violence, perhaps with an eye toward sheltering young readers from such a bloody scene (the draft textbook's caption for the painting had incorrectly and tendentiously renamed it *Ivan the Terrible's Murder of His Son* [Ubiistvo Ivanom Groznym svoego syna]).[47]

---

44. This account is something of a distortion, given that Peter had introduced few if any earth-shattering innovations by this point in his reign.

45. Platt and Brandenberger, "Terribly Romantic"; Brandenberger, *National Bolshevism*, 52–62, 251–60; Dubrovskii, *Istorik i vlast'*, 269–304.

46. This document is cited from Dubrovskii, *Istorik i vlast'*, 276–78. Also see Brandenberger, *National Bolshevism*, 51.

47. RGASPI, f. 558, op. 3, d. 374, ll. 108–9.

In a later prepublication version of the textbook, either Zhdanov or Stalin eliminated key passages impugning the tsar's character, such as a sentence relating how as a youth, "Ivan would ride through Moscow on horseback, scaring and running down peaceful residents for amusement." A description of the frightening "uniform" of the *oprichniki* was also cut from this draft: "The *oprichnik*, clad in black from head to toe, rode on a black horse with a black harness." Similarly, Stalin himself struck out a phrase announcing that Ivan had ordered the massacre of the population of Kazan following its sack and, most significantly, composed and inserted the sentence cited above crediting Ivan with completion of Ivan Kalita's "gathering" of the Russian lands into a "strong state."[48] In a less extensive if still significant revision of the treatment of Peter, the Soviet leader interpolated the textbook's characterization of the *Streltsy* rebellion as "reactionary" and based in antireformist demands. As Dubrovskii, who has pursued the archival record of the Shestakov textbook's production farthest, concludes, Stalin was personally responsible for a "lucidly formulated evaluation of the accomplishments of Ivan the Terrible" as a "personification of the idea of the strong centralized state," and he had an equal part in the "state idealization of Peter."[49]

In the narrative that resulted from this "authoritative" editing process, Ivan and Peter came to act out collective history on the stage of distant eras, bridging the deep past of national becoming and the recent past of revolutionary struggle. By completing the great work of premodern history, the two liminal rulers partake in the larger-than-life heroism of the mythical events and actors

---

48. In earlier publications on the Stalinist rehabilitation of Ivan, Brandenberger and I attributed all the revisions mentioned here to Zhdanov, based on copies of the textbook held in Zhdanov's personal *fond* in the former party archives. See Platt and Brandenberger, "Terribly Romantic"; and Brandenberger and Platt, "Terribly Pragmatic," where we cite RGASPI, f. 558, op. 3, d. 374; f. 77, op. 1, d. 854. Since that research was performed, additional materials in Stalin's *fond* have been declassified and described by Dubrovskii, showing that many of these changes originated with the general secretary himself. See Dubrovskii, *Istorik i vlast'*, 284–85. Dubrovskii refers to Stalin's copy of the draft textbook held at RGASPI, f. 558, op. 3, d. 1584. In connection with the editorial process, it should be noted that many of these changes correspond to comments submitted by the professional historians involved with the final stages of preparation of the textbook. So, for instance, the elimination of the description of the black clothing of the *oprichniki* likely originated in the historian Sergei Bakhrushin's observation in his review that "the costume of the *oprichniki*, as it is described in the text, has no basis in fact. All that is known is that a [dog's] head and broom were attached to the saddles of the *oprichniki*." Bakhrushin's more general critique, that the "meaning of the *oprichnina* in the process of the formation of a strong state is not reflected," among similar comments offered by other members of the jury, may have provided an impetus for Stalin's interpolated synthetic conclusion concerning the "gathering of the principalities." See Bakhrushin's review at RGASPI, f. 17, op. 120, d. 365, ll. 53–87, here ll. 62 and 81. The views of the party hierarchy, it appears, developed in a dialogue with the interpretations of professional historians engaged in the project. For additional discussion of the interplay of various readers of the draft textbook, see Dubrovskii, *Istorik i vlast'*, 278–81.

49. Ibid., 285, 287.

of the deep past, like them, offering condensation points for collective identity and patriotic pride. Yet Ivan and Peter also set the stage for the work's treatment of subsequent ages, moving the narrative focus to the modern problems of class struggle and revolution. One must be struck in reading these accounts of Ivan and Peter by the many echoes in vocabulary and plot of contemporary Soviet events and political experience—from the stress in each on conflict with Germans in the Baltic to the progressive need for violent elimination of reactionaries, traitors, and antireformists and the struggle with "backwardness." Such convergences might be read as an effort to produce instructive allegorical doubles for Soviet experience and leaders. Yet I think that, in the case of this text in particular and of Soviet historiography as a whole, it would be a mistake to conclude that such effects reflected a bald attempt to create some sort of crude, coded message about the present. Rather, these suggestive correspondences derived from the text's more fundamental allegorical drive, residing in its projection of the essential wholeness of the motherland and of the homogeneity of its experience over time.

The Short Course in the History of the USSR established a coherent "theory" of historical becoming, in which commonalities of present and past eras of radical social transformation were motivated by the transhistorical givens of Russian and Soviet progress, dictating that liminal moments, past and present, followed similar patterns of development and encountered analogous pitfalls, for each constituted a step forward in the long-term unfolding of the unchanging core of identity of the polity.[50] In this sense, the Shestakov textbook rendered Peter and Ivan not as allegorical figures for present leaders but rather as their comrades-in-arms and predecessors in the ancient struggle to drag Russia into the future through scenes of inevitable blood and gore—a struggle that was undergoing its final stage in the Soviet present. Indeed, it is in precisely this spirit of present-oriented teleology that the Shestakov textbook was conceived—as a lucid, settled, and unquestionable "last word" on history, a glimpse into the profound truth of the past, made possible by the conclusive perspective offered from history's endpoint in Soviet revolutionary reality. In effect, with the publication of *The Short Course in the History of the USSR*, the Stalinist end of history had brought with it the end of historical interpretation, after which essential modification of the view back over time was to become inconceivable, leaving historians with only the details to worry about.

—⁓—

Yet it was not to be. Perhaps the most striking feature of *The Short Course in the History of the USSR* is the cut-and-dried manner with which it established the Russia of princes, tsars, and emperors as a prefiguration of the Soviet Union. The work could well afford its tone of certainty in delivering the received truth, for it derived authority from the greatest possible official

50. For further discussion of Soviet historiography and allegorical thinking, see Platt and Brandenberger, "Terribly Romantic."

sanction, as publicly evidenced in the extensive campaign of laudatory reviews in all manner of journals and newspapers, loudly and unanimously judging the textbook a "Victory on the Historical Front."[51] Nevertheless, despite both the calm certainty broadcast by the Shestakov textbook and the authority of the state and its leaders that backed it up, Russian national history was never a simple or comprehensible matter in the Stalinist period, either before or after *The Short Course in the History of the USSR* made its appearance. Even at the end of history, historical interpretation, as it turned out, proved difficult to bring to a halt.

For example, records from the competition and editing process dating from 1935–37 demonstrate the striking variety of competing historical interpretations in play until just months before the publication of the textbook's final version. Certain of these cast both Ivan and Peter in a far more negative light, as important figures in historical development who self-consciously served the interests of their class, with unintended consequences for general social progress. Consider the textbook manuscript for more advanced elementary-school students and classes written by Pokrovskii's student Nechkina. Drafted in 1935 and considered by juries in 1936, Nechkina's work was not judged successful enough for publication. Although Nechkina concurs with the Shestakov textbook in assessment of the political significance of Ivan's elimination of the boyars as effecting a transfer of power to the new ruling elite of the service gentry, she characterizes both of these social groups as despotic oppressors. Recalling the distant precedent of Karamzin's account, Nechkina describes Ivan himself as "extraordinarily cruel," a "fearsome tsar" whose reign brought mass executions, massacres, "orgies," and so on. Nechkina characterizes Ivan's military campaigns as motivated solely by greed for more territory, adapting a formula usually reserved for characterization of the oppressive colonial policies of the later Russian Empire: "Muscovy—prison of peoples."[52]

Peter's era comes off no better. In Nechkina's view, Peter's diplomatic mission abroad was a self-glorifying adventure in the service of imperial expansion, and one that bled the treasury and therefore cost the Russian peasant dearly. In fact, all the reforms and victories of the Petrine era served the well-being of the ruling classes at the expense of the peasants, whose suffering increased proportionally. In her final paragraphs on Peter, Nechkina concludes:

---

51. The citation is the title of an unsigned editorial review, "Pobeda na istoricheskom fronte," *Literaturnaia gazeta*, August 27, 1937, 1. For other reviews of the textbook, see I. Sosonkin, "Istoriia velikoi sem'i narodov," *Literaturnaia gazeta*, August 30, 1937, 2; K. Malakhov, "Istoriia i literatura," *Literaturnaia gazeta*, August 30, 1937, 2; and S. Nisel'son, Iu. Zisman, and F. Furmonova, "Nachinaetsia uchebnyi god," *Izvestiia*, September 1, 1937, 3. For discussion of the reception of the textbook, see also Brandenberger, *National Bolshevism*, 54–55, 259–60; and Dubrovskii, *Istorik i vlast'*, 292–93.

52. M. V. Nechkina, "Rukopis' uchebnika 'Istorii SSSR,'" RGASPI, f. 17, op. 120, d. 357. Ivan's reign is discussed on ll. 181–205; I cite the text at ll. 194, 202, 203.

Celebrating the formation of the new empire, the serf owners, naturally, concealed their true intentions under a facade of false phrases. They assured all that the creation of the empire was, primarily, a path of glory for the people as a whole, a path leading Russia into the ranks of the great European powers. [. . .] The central concern of the administration of Peter I was the intensification of the oppression of serfdom. Without this, it would have been impossible to build the empire. Without this, it would have been impossible to shore up the gentry.[53]

In short, although she conformed to the mandated return of great personalities and key events to Russian history, Nechkina retained significant elements of her mentor Pokrovskii's anti-tsarist vision. In marked distinction from the Shestakov textbook, Nechkina's draft told the story of an oppressor state ruled by class enemies. Several other competition entries—such as one coauthored by Nikolai Vanag, Boris Grekov, Anna Pankratova, and Sergei Piontkovskii—shared this view of history, which broke with Pokrovskii's views in form but not in substance.[54]

Yet another approach to Soviet history that circulated, unrealized, in the textbook competition reveals the extent to which historical interpretation was truly in flux in the mid-1930s. This was an "internationalist," or perhaps "multinationalist" account of the Soviet Union's past, which deemphasized the role of Russia and presented an integrated history of all the national and ethnic groups of the USSR. At an earlier stage in the effort to retool the past this approach had enjoyed high-level support in the scholarly and political establishment. Stalin's, Kirov's, and Zhdanov's influential *Pravda* article of 1936, which singled out one early textbook proposal for extensive critique, called its authors to task above all for their narrow focus on the Russian national past: "The group [. . .] has composed an outline of Russian history, rather than of the history of the USSR—that is, a history of Rus without the history of the nations [*narody*] who compose the USSR."[55] Although the highest party leaders came

53. Ibid., l. 346.
54. For the detailed outline of this competing project, see "Prospekt uchebnika 'Istorii SSSR,' sostavlennyi avtorskim kollektivom v sostave N. Vanaga, B. D. Grekova, A. M. Pankratovoi i Piontkovskogo," RGASPI, f. 17, op. 120, d. 356, ll. 14–16, 23–25.
55. I. V. Stalin, S. M. Kirov, and A. A. Zhdanov, "Zamechanie o konspekte uchebnika 'Novoi istorii,'" *Pravda*, January 27, 1936, 3. This document was one of the few public pronouncements regarding history education bearing the name of Stalin. As a result, it became something of a touchstone, to which all referred in subsequent years to claim legitimacy for new history texts. In practice, however, the shifting nature of official priorities rendered the status of the article's pronouncements problematic. The situation was not helped by the odd publication history of the piece. Written in 1934, it was published only in 1936 as part of the campaign against Pokrovskii and his followers. This delay meant that some of the article's recommendations (such as its endorsement of the formula "tsarism, prison house of nations") were already outdated by the time the text became public. See Brandenberger, *National Bolshevism*, 47–49; and Dubrovskii, *Istorik i vlast'*, 231–50.

later to embrace precisely the sort of "history of Rus" they had excoriated in this article, anxiety about an increasingly Russocentric tendency in historiography and calls for a different vision of the past continued up to the very publication of *The Short Course in the History of the USSR*. In early 1937, the party veteran Fedor Kretov, who held important posts in the press and the Academy of Sciences, completed a review commissioned by the ranking Bolshevik Karl Bauman, head of the Science Section of the party's Central Committee, of the remaining candidates for publication in the textbook competition (including the draft Shestakov textbook, a draft by a collective including Nechkina and a separate project by the group including Vanag). Kretov lambasted all these authorial brigades for their Russocentrism. Observing a fine line, reflecting the sensitivity of this topic, in the first pages of his review he observes: "The authors have offered a history of Great Russia, as they should, from start to finish, in a proper reflection of the remarkable role that the Russian nation played in history and continues to play now, of the fact that the Russian nation is the first, leading nation. But the authors do not understand and do not want to understand that the Russian nation is first among equal—let us stress, *equal*—nations of the USSR."[56]

For the authors of the draft textbooks: "no nations exist apart from the Russian nation, that alone moves history, alone generates progress, alone creates new technical, economic, and cultural advances, alone leads the struggle for social and national emancipation, while other nations, one might say 'are in attendance.'"[57] Complaining that non-Russians appear in the textbooks only when they perform some function in the history of Russia and so are left effectively "without history," Kretov called instead for "a history of all the nations, so every nation might find in it their own history."[58] Although by 1937 Kretov's views were those of a minority, this minority had powerful supporters: Bauman and Vladimir Zatonskii, the Ukrainian commissar of education, continued to call for a "multinational" account of the prehistory of the Soviet Union up to the eve of the publication of the Shestakov textbook. As Zatonskii grumbled in his own prepublication review of the work in mid-1937: "it hasn't turned out to be a history of the USSR at all so far. Basically, it's a history of the Russian state."[59]

The confusion and dissent prior to the promulgation of the authoritative conception of the Russian past in *The Short Course in the History of the USSR* may well reflect the political complexity of the moment. However, the confusion and behind-the-scenes bickering that followed the textbook's publication

---

56. F. D. Kretov, "Sem' konkursnykh uchebnikov po istorii SSSR," RGASPI, f. 17, op. 120, d. 367, l. 10. Kretov was at this time deputy director of the Academy of Sciences Institute of History and head of the Central Committee Science Sector, among other things.

57. Ibid., ll. 16–17.

58. Ibid., l. 10.

59. Cited in Brandenberger, *National Bolshevism*, 52.

illustrate how difficult it proved to diffuse this complex diversity of views. Though the most divisive episodes of infighting over tsarist history concerned representations of heroic figures in mass culture, professional historians generated no small amount of interpretational friction. In early 1939, for example, the veteran theater critic Vladimir Blium—who had apparently been stewing for some time about the direction of Soviet historical literature, theater, and film—began to raise a hue and cry in semipublic professional meetings.[60] The critic's complaints that the representations of the past of recent years—including among others the first part of the film *Peter the Great*—had, at base, revived tsarist nationalist rhetoric soon elicited a slew of newspaper articles, including one by Shestakov himself, refuting Blium's "pernicious thesis" that such works "would have received the eager endorsement of Shvartz, the most reactionary of Nicholas II's ministers of education."[61] Ultimately, the feisty critic, convinced that logic and ideology were on his side, addressed a letter to Stalin himself, complaining that contemporary treatments of the Russian past were "beginning to display all the characteristics of racial nationalism." He fell silent only when, in response to his missive, party authorities including Zhdanov forced him into retirement.[62]

Throughout the late 1930s and the war years, sparring between proponents of critical anti-tsarist positions and the dominant line continued in newspaper and journal reviews of educational texts, artistic works, and new monographs.[63] In particular, almost all the most prominent popularizing treatments of Ivan the Terrible—including Kostylev's novels, Tolstoi's plays, and Eisenstein's films—were subjected to energetic public and private attacks. In

60. On the Blium affair, see David Brandenberger, "An Internationalist's Complaint to Stalin," in *Epic Revisionism*, ed. Platt and Brandenberger, 315–23.

61. "Snova Blium . . . ," *Literaturnaia gazeta*, January 26, 1939, 5. Also see A. Shestakov, "Propaganda vrednogo tezisa," *Literaturnaia gazeta*, January 10, 1939, 5; and A. Shin, "Na sobranii dramaturgov Moskvy," *Vecherniaia Moskva*, January 20, 1939, 2.

62. The critic's letter is published in Brandenberger and Petrone, " 'Vse cherty rasovogo natsionalizma . . .'; in translation, it is published in Brandenberger, "An Internationalist's Complaint to Stalin."

63. See, for instance, Nechkina's review critiquing Sergei Bakhrushin's treatment of tsars, including Ivan and Peter, in the first volume of a multiauthor university-level history textbook released in 1939. Although Bakhrushin largely cleaved to the interpretive line established by the Shestakov textbook, Nechkina claimed that his celebration of the tsars was more reminiscent of bourgeois historiography. See Lebed'ev, Grekov, and Bakhrushin, eds., *Istoriia SSSR*; M. V. Nechkina, "*Istoriia SSSR*," *Pravda*, December 2, 1940, 4. For an extensive treatment of this textbook and its reception, see Dubrovskii, *Istorik i vlast'*, 331–67; and for a somewhat differing assessment of this episode, see Perrie, *Cult of Ivan the Terrible*, 79–80. Yet another case of infighting, in a different manner, is evidenced in Iu. V. Gote's review of a 1939 monograph by B. G. Verkhoven on the reign of Ivan the Terrible. See Verkhoven', *Rossiia v tsarstvovanii Ivana Groznogo*; and Iu. V. Got'e, "Plokhaia kniga," *Kniga i proletarskaia revoliutsiia*, 1939, no. 11, 92–95. For my own more extensive consideration of these materials with David Brandenberger, see Brandenberger and Platt, "Terribly Pragmatic," 159–60; and for a different reading, see Perrie, *Cult of Ivan the Terrible*, 81–82.

some instances these attacks came from ardent promoters of the patriotic line in the party's cultural management bureaucracy, who were often dissatisfied with insufficiently triumphal representations, and in other cases from historians, both those concerned simply to maintain a modicum of historical accuracy and those outraged by extremes of patriotic ferment.[64]

In this last connection, the prominent but frequently embattled historian Anna Pankratova, unconcerned by the heightened demand for patriotic historical propaganda of the war years—or perhaps it would be more accurate to say, outraged by it—was moved to address letters to the Central Committee in 1944.[65] She argued that the Soviet historical profession had arrived at an ideologically suspect idealization of certain tsars, prominently mentioning the cases of Ivan IV and Peter I, and that increasingly forgiving and even celebratory Soviet treatments of tsarist colonial expansion were nothing but an anti-Marxist nationalist excursion. Pankratova's complaints led the party to convene a series of meetings of historians in mid-1944, at which the warring camps engaged in extensive debates.[66] Zhdanov, entrusted with the task of generating a Central Committee directive on historiography, composed a number of lengthy drafts in which he attempted to mark out a middle course in interpretation of the heroes of the tsarist past, promoting the stripped-down dialectical formula "progressive for their time" as a central analytic mechanism.[67] Yet no final directive was ever published, leaving the process of making sense out of the Russian national past suspended in an uneasy standoff of competing visions that subsided only gradually in the postwar and then post-Stalin years.

Returning to *The Short Course in the History of the USSR*, one may conclude that its most characteristic feature, reflecting the overarching dynamics of Stalinist history making in general, was the tension between its calm projection of unflappable and settled authority and the interpretive irresolution that it papered over—both the widespread lack of faith in its positions and the innate inconsistencies of its arguments and subject matter. How, in the end, could Peter the Great or Ivan the Terrible, who under other circumstances would be excellent candidates for "best illustration of the inherent violence of tsarist autocracy," be elevated by a communist state as positive heroes for the descendants of men and women whose lives had passed in abject servitude to them?

64. These are discussed, some at length, in Platt and Brandenberger, "Terribly Romantic"; and Brandenberger and Platt, "Terribly Pragmatic," 157–78. Also see Perrie, *Cult of Ivan the Terrible*.

65. On this episode, see Burdei, *Istorik i voina*, 150–58; Perrie, *Cult of Ivan the Terrible*, 99–102; Brandenberger, *National Bolshevism*, 123–30; Dubrovskii, *Istorik i vlast'*, 424–89; and Zelnik, *Perils of Pankratova*, 43–48.

66. A stenogram transcript of these meetings is published in Amiantov, ed., "Stenogramma soveshchanii po voprosam istorii SSSR." Also see Pankratova, "Pis'ma"; and "Novye dokumenty o soveshchanii istorikov."

67. The text is analyzed in detail in Dubrovskii and Brandenberger, "Itogovyi partiinyi dokument"; and Dubrovskii, *Istorik i vlast'*, 470–89.

How could non-Russians, whose ancestors perished in wars of expansion, be expected to celebrate these Russian national heroes? Only by means of the mechanisms of chosen trauma, strategically disavowed in a ritual of collective identity formation that was, as we have seen, as affectively effective as it was rhetorically unstable.

It is hardly surprising that the effort to rehabilitate and popularize these figures elicited no end of squabbles, infighting, and scandal over fundamentally insoluble political and historiographical divisions, coupled with repeated, doomed attempts to settle history "once and for all." For ultimately, perhaps the one thing that united the vast majority of party-line historians like Shestakov, orthodox Marxists like Blium and Pankratova, party bureaucrats like Zhdanov, and insider dissenters like Kretov was the continuing faith that there was a single, correct interpretation of the Russian past to be had. It was this axiomatic unity of vision across disciplines, professional castes, and generations that perpetually haunted the Stalinist history project, driving it forward toward a chimerical final synthesis that would resolve all interpretational inconsistencies. Ultimately, this very drive for unity and clarity of historical vision landed the project in an inevitable collapse into disparate shards of historical narratives that could not be reconciled.

CHAPTER SIX

Repetition

Ivan IV [. . .] was determined in his assaults on Livonia; their conscious aim was to give Russia access to the Baltic Sea and to open up paths for exchange with Europe. This is why Peter was so enthralled with him.
—Karl Marx, "Survey of the History of Scandinavia and Russia," 1882

Russians [. . .] in the course of fifteen years, having been reborn primarily through an act of will, have created a gigantic heavy industry and a mighty defense for the country. They have eliminated illiteracy and, in plain view before the rest of the world, they are leaping thousands of years ahead, building socialism. In the Petrine epoch, although on a different scale, with different goals, and with a different leading class, [. . .] something comparable took place. [. . .] In this one may see the dialogue of epochs.
—Aleksei N. Tolstoi, "Concerning How One Deals with Ideas," 1933

However appalling the Terrible Tsar's methods and means and his numerous excesses and executions may seem to us and our contemporaries, Ivan's role was progressive, as he administered a blow to feudal reaction, facilitated the acceleration of the historical process, and transformed Russia into a strong, centralized "Great Power." [. . .] Some of our historians apparently do not understand that there is a principal difference between recognizing the progressiveness of one or another historical phenomenon and endorsing it, as such.
—Andrei Zhdanov, from a draft Central Committee resolution on Russian history, 1944

Analogy and Allegory

When the theater critic Vladimir Blium wrote to Stalin in 1939, after having become embroiled in public debates over revisionist celebrations of tsarist heroes, he complained that Soviet patriotism had become "distorted" and was "sometimes beginning to display all the characteristics of racial nationalism."[1] According to Blium, Soviet cultural life was consumed by an antihistorical "search for 'our' heroes of bygone ages, a hasty, blind search for historical 'analogies,'" and was churning out anti-Polish and anti-German pablum that was all but indistin-

---

1. This and subsequent quotes from Blium in this paragraph are from his "Letter to Stalin," in *Epic Revisionism*, ed. Platt and Brandenberger, 317–19. A. I. Guchkov (1862–1936) led the prerevolutionary monarchist Octobrist Party; P. A. Stolypin (1862–1911) served as prime minister.

guishable from the mobilizational propaganda of the prerevolutionary era—from "the bourgeois patriotism of the Guchkovs, Stolypins, and Miliukovs."

Blium's missive also includes comments of a far more personal nature: "This contradiction torments me, tearing me apart with doubt, and I am sure that I am not the only one who feels this way." These remarks illustrate something of the cognitive implications of Stalinist historical revisionism—this doubly folded relationship to the past that worked in public to give birth to a new version of history for the postrevolutionary world but carried in its belly the inheritance of past generations of mythmaking. This professed effort to dictate the "final" significance of the past with scientific certainty instead served to mark historical knowledge as malleable, radically unstable, and uncertain. These contradictory implications demanded of Soviet men and women the discipline of a self-imposed forgetfulness—a discipline that in Blium's case proved impossible. In many ways, Blium's "hermeneutic anxiety" is symptomatic of the incoherence of Stalinist history in general, which ultimately landed many of the age's most ambitious rehabilitation projects in the mire of interpretational discord and scandal.

Blium's objections related primarily to historical revisionism in the Soviet cultural arena, and it was there that the contradictory implications of a Soviet Peter or Ivan were most apparent. The mainstream of professional historians preserved a fundamental conception of history as a long-term process, even as they worked to bring the Russian past into line with present needs. Stalinist filmmakers and other cultural actors were far less preoccupied with history as such. Instead, they sought to give form to superhistorical myths, in which present-day figures appeared as hypostases of recurrent, unchanging patterns manifest in the heroes of the past, offering object lessons in the proper relation of ruler to ruled and the patriotic fervor to which Soviet citizens should aspire. Aleksei N. Tolstoi's "dialogue of epochs" represented precisely the "blind search for historical 'analogies'" that Blium descried as characteristic of the era.[2]

In the case of Peter the Great, this overtly mythic approach to representation occurred largely on the initiative of authors and other cultural figures (notably Aleksei N. Tolstoi), without any centrally coordinated "campaign," though with the approval of the state's watchdogs. In contrast, Stalin-era depictions of Ivan the Terrible represent an extreme example of state management of cultural life. Following the publication of the Shestakov textbook, several popularizing accounts of Ivan's reign either skirted such topics as the *oprichnina* terror and the tsar's personal taste for cruelty or treated them in a derogatory manner (one went so far as to describe Ivan as a "psychologically unbalanced person" and blamed the *oprichnina* for "ravaging the peasantry").[3]

2. A. N. Tolstoi, "O tom, kak nuzhno obrashchat'sia s ideiami," in his *Sobranie sochinenii*, 10:204–6, here 206.
3. Verkhoven', *Rossiia v tsarstvovanie Ivana Groznogo*, 43, 45.

Either out of dissatisfaction with these insufficiently inspiring treatments or in response to the growing topicality of the history of Ivan's Livonian War, the Central Committee in 1940 resolved to commission high-profile celebratory works on the Terrible Tsar for the stage and screen.[4] In the wake of war's outbreak the following year, the campaign to rehabilitate Ivan took on an overtly mobilizational character. At the same time, Vipper's 1922 apologetic history was republished; and the aged historian, himself recently "reclaimed" from Latvia with the Soviet occupation of the Baltic, was made a member of the Academy of Sciences and set to work on a revised edition of his book and articles for the mass press. The gray-bearded muse of the Ivan revival, Vipper provided source material and inspiration for many key works in the cultural sphere. In contrast to more sober historians, he was unafraid baldly to announce that Heinrich Staden's plan for the conquest of Russia, presented to the Habsburg emperor Rudolph II in 1578, was no less than a "prophecy and a plan for the future" which would later inspire Nazi Germany to conquer and enslave the Slavs.[5] In a 1943 lecture in the Moscow Kremlin that was broadcast to a mass audience, he explained that Ivan's Muscovy had been "the prototype of the great multinational state of the USSR."[6]

Among the works focused on the figure of Ivan the Terrible produced in the early 1940s were a trilogy of novels by Valentin Kostylev, plays by Vladimir A. Solovev, Ilia Selvinskii, and Aleksei N. Tolstoi, plans for an opera (unrealized), and Eisenstein's uncompleted film trilogy.[7] During the war years these works were lauded as masterpieces, printed and reprinted in mass press runs, performed in leading theaters throughout the USSR, and awarded the state's highest honor, the Stalin Prize.

Although a record of the initial Central Committee directive on Ivan has yet to be discovered, an internal memorandum of 1942–43 from the party's ideology chief, Andrei Shcherbakov, gives a clear idea of the direction of the party elite's thinking at the height of the rehabilitation campaign.[8] Referring to the earlier Central Committee resolution, Shcherbakov states: "the task of reestablishing the historical truth about Ivan IV and rehabilitating him as a political

4. Uhlenbruch, "Annexation of History," 269; Perrie, "Nationalism and History," 112; Brandenberger and Platt, "Terribly Pragmatic," in *Epic Revisionism*, ed. Platt and Brandenberger, 157–78.

5. The remark appears in the new, Stalinist edition of the Ivan book: Vipper, *Ivan Groznyi* (1944), 159. The same claim appears in Vipper, "Ivan Groznyi," *Prepodavanie istorii v shkole*, 29.

6. Vipper, *Stenogramma publichnoi lektsii akademika Vipper*, 8–9.

7. Kostylev's novels, it should be said, appear to have been undertaken in anticipation of the Central Committee resolution on Ivan. For a more complete account of the commissioning of these works, see Brandenberger and Platt, "Terribly Pragmatic," 157–78.

8. The memorandum, which was composed as a critique of an early version of Tolstoi's plays on Ivan, is published as "Memorandum to Stalin concerning A. N. Tolstoi's Play 'Ivan the Terrible'" in *Epic Revisionism*, ed. Platt and Brandenberger, 179–98.

figure has long been a priority and remains so to the present day." He describes Ivan as "an outstanding political figure of sixteenth-century Russia" and goes on to list the tsar's accomplishments as a diplomatic genius, fearless military strategist, and progressive reformer:

> There is literally not a single aspect of domestic policy, beginning with finance and ending with the army, which did not undergo revision or reorganization during this period ([e.g.] court reforms, rural church reforms, the restructuring of the central administration, the creation of a new army, the introduction of new forms of weaponry, etc.). Ivan IV himself was one of the most educated men of the day and a champion of the broad dissemination of knowledge. He passionately supported such progressive endeavors as the introduction of the printing press in Russia.

Shcherbakov goes on to offer one of the most brazen and pat justifications of Ivan's cruel methods of governance ever penned: "these reforms met with vigorous resistance on the part of representatives of the feudal order—entrenched patrimonial estate holders, tenaciously insisting on the preservation of the feudal order. Ivan the Terrible was forced to resort to harsh measures to strike at the feudal, patrimonial privileges of the boyars." Bleeding forcefully through the entirety of Shcherbakov's memorandum is the obvious allegorical relationship between Ivan and contemporary leaders, between Ivan's reforms and wars and those of the twentieth century, between the traitors and counterrevolutionaries of the past and those of the present.

Yet even in the context of this blatant attempt to manufacture and manage historical myth—far exceeding the immoderation of the works that had alarmed Blium in 1939—one must note that, despite the dissemination of a mythic approach to tsarist history across a broad spectrum of public discursive and cultural contexts, the straightforward equation of, say, Stalin to Peter was never an acceptable move. At work here is the distinction between baldly announced historical analogies, as in Vipper's pronouncements, and historical allegory, which when deployed with subtlety may draw a mythic pattern across time without explicitly announcing it. More often than not, Stalinist revisionism required the latter, rather than the former. The Shcherbakov memorandum, for example, despite its nature as an internal party communication and the extraordinary inflation of its apologetic rhetoric, offers not a single overt comparison of Ivan or any aspect of his epoch to contemporary equivalents. Such reticence, which was the rule rather than the exception, reflected the complex historical consciousness (perhaps we should say queasiness) preserved in all but the most extreme moments of propagandistic élan during these years.

Perhaps the sticking point was the lurking and potentially damning irony of comparing the "most progressive figure of world history" and the society he ruled over to any precedent, no matter how magnificent. Or perhaps we should formulate the problem in a more abstract manner: even if Russian rulers of the past served in novels, plays, and films as convenient and instructive doubles for contemporary actors, a one-to-one mapping of leading figures of the present onto those of the past flew in the face of Stalinism's overriding emphasis on the present as the exceptional, culminating moment of history. The skillful critic Mikhail Koltsov sought to negotiate these conflicting hermeneutical imperatives when he wrote that the Socialist Realist method in historical film meant "communicating the fundamental, inner truth of the events," a truth that "has not grown old in over seven centuries" and "remains fresh and new—as if it took shape only yesterday." Nevertheless, it was only in the exceptional conditions of the present, a moment when "people's sense of sight and sound has grown more acute, and our consciousness has been raised" that this "inner truth" uniting present and past could be sensed.[9]

The involuted logic of this temporal knot is laid bare in one of Eisenstein's several mass-press articles on Ivan the Terrible. Like Koltsov, the director preserves a delicate balance between the allegorical unity of past and present, on one hand, and a distanced and more properly historical approach, respecting the unprecedented achievements of Stalinist era, on the other. He begins by historicizing the tsar's bloody elimination of his political enemies as typical of sixteenth-century Europe (a commonplace move in treatments of Ivan), comparing this to episodes of mayhem attributed to Ivan's western contemporaries:

> Historians of a certain sort and writers of a certain tendency branded him a maniac of pointless cruelty. Few would now believe that it was in fact Ivan the Terrible who [. . .] rebuked his contemporary Catherine de Medici for the pointless cruelty of St. Bartholomew's night. [. . .] One must approach different stages of history in differing manner: what was progressive in the epoch of the Russian Renaissance of the sixteenth century may be profoundly reactionary at the end of the nineteenth century or the start of the twentieth.[10]

At base, this is a straightforward example of Zhdanov's dialectical principle of historical interpretation, by which figures like Ivan and Peter were "progressive for their times."[11] As the director continues his discussion, however, we sense Ivan's superhistorical, mythic significance: he is "Ivan—the builder; Ivan—the

---

9. Mikhail Kol'tsov, "Narod-bogatyr'," *Pravda*, November 7, 1938, 2. The article is a review of Eisenstein's *Aleksandr Nevskii*. I cite the translation published in Platt and Brandenberger, eds., *Epic Revisionism*, 253–58, here 255, 257.

10. S. M. Eisenstein [Eizenshtein], "Ivan Groznyi," *Literatura i iskusstvo*, no. 27 (July 4, 1942): 3. St. Bartholomew's night refers to the 1572 massacre of French Huguenots by Catholic mobs, rumored to have been instigated by Catherine de Medici, mother of King Charles IX. Despite the fact that Eisenstein rebukes the historians of the nineteenth century for their lack of dialectical, hermeneutic sensitivity toward the past, this strategy in apologetics reaches back to that period.

11. The citation is drawn from a draft Central Committee resolution on Russian historiography held at RGASPI, f. 17, op. 125, d. 222, ll. 39–40, 44.

creator; Ivan—one of the founding fathers of the united, multinational Russian state." Eisenstein continues:

> The audience of today—English, American, or Russian—cannot fail to understand the decisive action and necessary cruelty of the man to whom history entrusted the mission of creating one of the mightiest and grandest states in the world. For now, in the days of the Great Patriotic War, as never before, all understand that he who betrays his fatherland is worthy of death; that he who goes over to the side of enemies of his motherland is worthy of severe retribution; and that one must show no mercy toward those who open the borders of their native land to the enemy.

Yet Eisenstein steps no further into outright identification of the leaders or the traitors of today with those of the sixteenth century—after all, such equations, precisely in view of the dialectical formula offered earlier, might carry the incendiary implication that Stalinist methods were reactionary holdovers, more proper to the premodern era than to the present. Here, it would seem, the essay has run up against the conceptual limits of Stalinist historical myth. Yet the problem could be ramped up and resolved on a higher level of abstraction, as Eisenstein demonstrates in his masterfully subtle conclusion.

Just as the linkage of the personalities and feats of the past to those of the present must always recognize the preeminence of the latter over the former, so the engineers of Stalinist historical myth could never forget that the Soviet present in general occupied a place in history fundamentally distinct from that of any past era. For the very principle that legitimated Ivan's rehabilitation in the first place, "progressive for his times," was itself an interpretive mechanism of a limited sort—necessary for comprehension of the past, but inapplicable to the Soviet era. Unlike the "progressive" features of the past, the achievements of the present were progressive for all time:

> To show the great tradition of patriotism and love for the motherland, the mercilessness of our struggle with enemies, wherever they are found and whomever they are—these are the goals of our film. They rest on certain premises. For it is only from the peak of social development that our country has achieved that we can, with full objectivity, look back into our own past, not fearing the truth in all its aspects and with no other goal than using this truth of the past in the service of the just cause of the contemporary moment. In the historic days of the Great Patriotic War, one may with special acuity and inspiration sense this unbreakable link between the past and the present.

Even though an "unbreakable link" bound the "historic" present to the historical past, bygone eras could be seen only as distant echoes of present experience, and their true meaning could be recovered only now by the exceptional, objective vantage opened out from the heights of present Soviet accomplishments. The past's mythic significance grew in the soil of the historical dialectic, but the myth of Soviet transcendence of the dialectic would always trump the myths of history.

In general, then, Stalinist representations of Russian history steered clear of any open proclamation that the events and heroes of the past were earlier incarnations of present-day experience and leaders. Instead, the allegorical equivalence and mythic import of figures and scenes from the past remained implicit, hovering as a commonly understood but seldom articulated relationship. As a fine last example here of the irregular and oblique surfacing of historical allegory, let us consider a photograph that Nikolai Cherkasov gave to Zhdanov in 1944 (fig. 16). It shows the actor in the role of Ivan the Terrible and is inscribed with the final line of Eisenstein's screenplay, "we are standing at the edge of the sea, and will continue to stand here"—words that Ivan pronounces on the Baltic seashore at the peak of success in the Livonian War.

There is something of an inside joke in the inscription's studied understatement. It offers Ivan as a figure for Zhdanov, who in addition to his prominent role in the Stalinist history project was party boss of Leningrad, which had withstood years of Nazi blockade. Moreover, at the moment in question he was responsible for the integration of the recaptured Baltic states into the Soviet Union. To fully comprehend the allegorical drive of the actor's inscription, however, one must recall that Ivan eventually lost all Baltic conquests in the disastrous unfolding of the Livonian War. In this light, Zhdanov is not Ivan's double but rather the realization of his historical fate. Like an Old Testament prophecy that may be rightly understood only in light of its New Testament fulfillment, Ivan's ancient words (as Eisenstein has them) are comprehensible only in the Stalinist present, when the fragile progressive accomplishments of each moment of the past have been realized by the conclusive progressive achievements of the present.

In sum, Stalinist historical revisionism carried an enormous burden of submerged interpretive complexity, of implications to be forgotten or overlooked in this moment of maximal and objective celebration and remembrance of things past. First, there were inconvenient historical facts that could not be reconciled with the "objective" historical knowledge available in the Soviet present— Nevskii's religiosity, Ivan's many military gaffes, or Peter's documented indifference to the suffering of the common people. Then there was the inheritance of a long tradition of historical interpretation—from Kavelin and Solovev to Pokrovskii—and of a rich prehistory of historical myth—Blium's "Guchkovs, Stolypins, and Miliukovs." Beyond this was the delicate balancing act between mythic allegory and historical progress in works that might point toward the identity of present and past but could seldom close this circle in explicit historical analogies. Finally, in the course of the Stalinist period itself, officially endorsed positions on history changed with disconcerting rapidity, necessitating the forgetting of each of these more recent pasts. For Blium, as for many others engaged in Stalinist history projects, these interpretational challenges presented grave difficulties.

Figure 16: Nikolai Cherkasov in the role of Ivan the Terrible. The photograph was presented by the actor to Andrei Zhdanov in May 1944. The inscription—"We are standing at the edge of the sea and will continue to stand here"—is drawn from the unfinished third part of Eisenstein's film trilogy. RGASPI (Moscow, Russia), f. 77, op. 2, d. 105. Reproduced with permission.

Yet such challenges were not only a source of political conflict, interpretational collapse, and individual crisis of faith. Perhaps surprisingly, given common views of the Stalin years as an era of total domination of society and culture by the state, the contradictory historical consciousness of the 1930s and 1940s presented opportunities for strategic intervention to those who were equipped to capitalize on them, opportunities that could be negotiated with brilliance and a refined moral sensibility. All those involved in the rehabilitation of tsarist historical figures were to some extent aware of the struggle they were waging to wrest control over history not only from one another but also from the prior tradition itself. Yet in practice, the wiggle room left for innovation in writing and rewriting the Russian past in the Stalin era yielded most readily not to exploitation by party commissars but to cultural actors like Eisenstein. For it was they who were most attuned to the growing complexity of the relationship between present visions of Russian history and previous generations of historical myth, raising ever more ironic and subtle possibilities in the representation of history.

To explore more fully the openings for creative intervention in the historical incoherence of Stalinist revisionism, I turn first to the case of Aleksei N. Tolstoi and his many works on Peter the Great. This body of work exemplifies the extent to which even of some of the most orthodox contributions to Stalinist historical mythmaking depended on sensitivity to the ironic undertow of history's own history of use and reuse. Finally, I turn to Eisenstein's second film in his uncompleted trilogy of works on Ivan the Terrible. I read this film not as an exercise in "Aesopean" critique via historical allegory, as it is most commonly seen, but rather as a stunning achievement in metahistorical analysis. I argue that Eisenstein's film should ultimately be seen not as a willful "send up" of Stalin in the guise of Ivan but as a higher order of subversion—a meditation on and critique of Stalinist historical practices as such.

Afterimages: Aleksei N. Tolstoi's Many Returns to Peter the Great

In a 1933 essay, Tolstoi remarked that "in every historical phenomenon we must take what is necessary for us, discard what is archaic, and extract that which resonates with our age."[12] Such views brought the former fellow-traveler author to the pinnacle of success in Soviet public life by the time of his death in 1945. From the earliest stages of the Stalinist revision of the Russian past, Tolstoi was the enthusiastic and undisputed leader of efforts to raise the new historiographic standards "on the cultural front," and he was from the start animated by the frankly acknowledged drive toward historical analogy signaled in such pronouncements. In 1939, he was inducted into the Soviet Academy of Sciences precisely for his historical fiction and other historiographic projects

12. A. N. Tolstoi, "Pisatel' i teatr," in his *Sobranie sochinenii*, 10:222–24, here 222.

(particularly the publication of Russian folklore, literary histories, and histories of non-Russian Soviet nationalities). In 1941, he received a Stalin Prize for his multivolume historical novel *Peter I*—certainly the most significant and enduring achievement of Stalinist historical fiction, which Tolstoi had begun some twelve years earlier. Following in the wake of his successful work on the first emperor, which he repeatedly described as "an entrance into history via the present, understood in a Marxist fashion," Tolstoi led the charge in belletristic rehabilitation of the first crowned tsar.[13] As noted above, having already conceived works on Ivan as early as 1935, the politically acute author did not actually complete any until he was expressly commissioned to do so by the Central Committee in late 1940 or early 1941.[14] And although the resulting pair of plays on Ivan, or "dramatic novella in two parts," was an object of ongoing controversy, these works eventually garnered for Tolstoi an additional, posthumous Stalin Prize. In recognition of Tolstoi's prominent role in the Stalinist reshaping of Russia's past, and in particular of the figures of Ivan the Terrible and Peter the Great, we must grant the "Red Count" the additional title "dean of Stalinist historical writing."

Nevertheless, in distinction from works like *The Short Course in the History of the USSR*, which aimed to articulate a final and correct version of Russia's past, Tolstoi's *oeuvre*, and in particular his works on Peter I, seem to have been calculated from the start to capitalize on the variability of Soviet views of history. Even as officially sanctioned Stalinist historiography charged toward a fixed vision of the past, the continual modification of historical orthodoxy worked to counter the intentions of Soviet cultural managers. Tolstoi's Petrine works, despite their canonization as the greatest accomplishments of Soviet historical fiction, are best seen as a subtle mechanism for the management of this dynamic of authority and instability, and hence as monuments to history's indeterminacy rather than to any last and best historical truth.

In the course of his career, Tolstoi wrote obsessively about the person of Russia's first emperor, producing several stories, three staged versions of a play, the screenplay for a two-part film, a children's novel, endless occasional writing, and, most important, the monumental, unfinished historical novel. Strikingly, almost all these works, particularly those written after 1929, bear a single title, *Peter I*, suggesting that Tolstoi viewed them as part of a single "work in progress." The integral unity of Tolstoi's "Peter project" indicates that it is best

13. A. N. Tolstoi, "Marksizm obogatil iskusstvo," in his *Sobranie sochinenii*, 10:201–3, here 202.

14. Shcherbakov's memorandum refers to the Committee for Artistic Affairs as having commissioned Tolstoi and others to develop works on Ivan IV. See "Memorandum to Stalin concerning A. N. Tolstoi's Play 'Ivan the Terrible'" in *Epic Revisionism*, ed. Platt and Brandenberger, 179–98, here 182. In an April 7, 1939, diary entry, Elena Bulgakova noted earlier operatic projects on Ivan involving Tolstoi and Shostakovich that apparently came to nothing—see Losev and Ianovskaia, eds., *Dnevnik Eleny Bulgakovoi*, 252.

approached in its entirety as it developed over the long term amid the authoritarian instability of Soviet historiography and public discourse.

Let us first consider the "raw data" of Tolstoi's texts. To throw the successive transformations of Tolstoi's vision of Peter into high relief, I offer here a series of comparable moments from disparate works: depictions of Peter eating and drinking with his entourage. The passages are of some length, since I return to them several times. First, at the very inception of the author's work on the tsar, in the story "Peter's Day" of 1917 or 1918, Peter appears as a brutal, cruel and drunken despot:

> [Peter's] red face, with its fat, round cheeks, wasn't gaining anything in lucidity. He had already pushed away his dish and, resting his elbows on the table, was gnawing on the amber stem of his pipe. As before, the tsar's bulging eyes were glassy, unseeing. And fear began to overcome the guests. Had a courier arrived with bad news from Warsaw? Or was there unrest in Moscow again? Or had someone seated here committed some offense?
>
> Peter pulled the pipe from his mouth, spat under the table, and spoke, grimacing from a belch stuck in his throat: "Come 'ere, Archdeacon. [. . .] I'm not joking with you [. . .]. You're trying too hard, somehow. You've been trying too hard, too hard, that's what! I'm afraid of what they might start saying about you and me. They might say, 'the tsar's fool . . .' "
>
> As often happened, he didn't finish his thought and clenched his teeth, grated them, restraining a grimace.
>
> [. . .] "I'm afraid that by your efforts—yes, yes—your excessive efforts, they might, in an instant, put your cap on my head . . . With its horns . . . They're getting ready to . . . I know . . . They've been talking, talking, you've probably heard . . . A cap with horns might be more suitable for me than a crown . . ."
>
> And again he turned his head to the left, to the right, staring intensely. His incoherent, drunken words with their obscure meaning deepened the sense of fear among the guests.[15]

In contrast to this grotesque image, the first volumes of Tolstoi's novel cast Peter as a complex figure whose progressive aspirations are weighed down by the burden of tradition and the impossibility of controlling the historical process. In a passage from volume one of the novels, dating to 1929, Tolstoi wrote:

> At lunch [Peter's] spirits again seemed to rise. Some noticed a new habit in him—a dark, steady gaze. In the middle of discussion or jokes he would suddenly fall silent and begin to stare at someone—impenetrably,

---

15. A. N. Tolstoi, "Den' Petra," in his *Sobranie sochinenii*, 3:99. "Peter's Day" was first published in the Petrograd literary almanac *Tablet* (Skrizhal') in early 1918 and was republished several times during the author's lifetime.

inquisitively—with an inhuman gaze. . . . Then he would flare his nostrils, and once again he would chuckle, drink, laugh woodenly. . . .

Foreigners—soldiers, sailors, engineers—sat merrily and breathed freely. But for Russians this lunch was a difficult one. Music was playing, and they were waiting for the ladies to arrive for the dances. Aleksashka Menshikov was looking at Peter's hands lying on the table—they were clenching and unclenching. [. . .] Suddenly, shrieking at high pitch with his neck extended like a rooster's, Peter jumped up, madly leaning across the table to Shein: "Thief, thief!"

Flinging away his chair, he ran out.[16]

This vision is displaced by yet another image that comes to the fore in the films of 1937 and 1939, and even more so in the unfinished third volume of the novel dating to 1943–45. Here Peter appears as a fearless leader, working tirelessly to increase the military, cultural, and political prestige of Russia. In the third volume of the novel, for instance, we read:

Having eaten, Peter Alekseevich rested his large-wristed hands on the table, their veins swollen after the bath. He spoke little, listened attentively. His bulging eyes were stern, almost frightening, but when he lowered them—filling his pipe or for some other reason—his round-cheeked face with its small, smiling mouth appeared genial. Go ahead, approach him, clink glasses with him: "Your health, Sir Bombardier!" And he, depending on the individual, of course, would either refrain from answering or would toss his head, throwing back his thin, dark, curly hair. "In the name of Bacchus," he would intone with his bass voice, and he would drink. [. . .]

Peter Alekseevich was feeling satisfied today that [. . .] all his people were here sitting around the table and arguing and carrying on about the great matter at hand [the construction of St. Petersburg—K.M.F.P.], not giving a thought to how dangerous it was or whether it would be crowned with success. In particular, his heart was gladdened that here, where all his distant thoughts and difficult undertakings came together, everything that he noted down randomly for memory in the fat little writing book that lay in his pocket with the gnawed end of a pencil, his pipe and his tobacco pouch—all of this had been realized in fact. The wind tore at the flag on the tower of the fortress, pilings rose out of the muddy riverbanks, everywhere people were moving to and fro, consumed by their work and cares, and the

16. A. N. Tolstoi, "Petr I: Kniga pervaia," in his *Sobranie sochinenii*, 7:358. The first volume of *Peter I* first appeared in serial form in *Novyi mir* from July 1929 through July 1930. The second appeared in the same journal from February 1933 through April 1934. The first two volumes also appeared in very successful separate editions during the 1930s. The passage I have cited is drawn from chapter 7 and represents the original text of the novel as it appeared in *Novyi mir*.

city already stood as a city—still not a large one, but already in all of its everyday life.

Peter Alekseevich, chewing on the amber of his pipe, listened and did not listen.[17]

As the above renders fully apparent, in the course of his long literary career Tolstoi's conception of Peter ascended steadily, from a nadir of ugly and violent despotism to a zenith of inspired, charismatic leadership.

Let us dig a little deeper into the diverse implications of these passages. The first presents a revolting caricature of Peter as a despot with neither political will nor historical foresight: his eyes are "unseeing," and his speech is frighteningly incoherent. "Peter's Day" was published in the immediate aftermath of the October revolution, and its representation of Peter is an outgrowth of prerevolutionary materialist views of Russian history, such as those of Kliuchevskii or Miliukov. As in the works of those historians, the shock of Tolstoi's representation lies in brazen denial of the prescient, almost divine historical vision that prior political hagiography had attributed to Peter, the founder of modern Russian civilization and creator of the empire. Instead, Tolstoi's Peter, like Miliukov's, is a product of his times—and a brutal, haphazard and disorganized one at that, whose ruthless methods undercut the beneficial effects of his reforms.[18] In keeping with this historical vision, Tolstoi's narrator muses on Peter's lack of control over the historical process in an unmistakable reminiscence of the self-defeating reversal of the ruler's will that animated Miliukov's ironic conception of Petrine history.[19] Tolstoi's narrator ends the story with the pathetic summary statement: "And the burden of this day, and of all days past and future, lay like a leaden weight on the shoulders of the individual who had assumed a burden beyond the strength of any man: one for all."[20]

The political resonance of Tolstoy's satire is uncertain. On one hand, its outright vilification of Peter's despotism capitalizes on new possibilities for denigration of Russian imperial rulers inaugurated by the revolution (far surpassing anything to be found in Kliuchevskii or Miliukov), and participates in a prominent current in *belles lettres* of the 1920s that satirized Peter as a representative of the Imperial Russian state.[21] Yet such was the allegorical indeterminacy of Russia's liminal historical figures during the postrevolutionary

---

17. A. N. Tolstoi, "Petr I: Kniga tret'ia," in his *Sobranie sochinenii*, 7:701–2. This final volume of *Peter I* was serialized in *Novyi mir* from March 1944 through January 1945, when Tolstoi's death brought the work to a premature conclusion. Since then, it has been republished many times. The first part of the film premiered on September 1, 1937; the second on March 7, 1939.

18. In the 1930s, Tolstoi had harsh words for Miliukov's historical works on Peter—see his "O tom, kak nuzhno obrashchat'sia s ideiami," in his *Sobranie sochinenii*, 10:206.

19. Tolstoi, "Den' Petra," 84.

20. Ibid., 103.

21. Radically negative postrevolutionary representations of Peter I, in particular Tolstoi's "Peter's Day" and Boris Pilniak's "His Majesty Kneeb Piter Komondor" (Ego velichestvo

decade that Tolstoi's satire on the impossibility of effecting revolutionary reforms "from above" may just as easily have been seen as an indictment of the
Bolsheviks' own attempts at social transformation.[22]

In the second passage cited above, written about a decade later in 1929, Peter appears in a far more positive light. His undertakings are now the object of
the reader's sympathy, and his motivation is comprehensible (his anger in this
passage stems from Shein's mishandling of the *Streltsy* rebellion). Yet if Peter
has gained the reader's respect, he retains something of the unruliness and lack
of both majesty and control that appear in the earlier passage in so exaggerated
a form. While he is capable of decisive action, such as the punishment of rebels
and the shaving of his boyars, his outburst at the banquet table and his demonic
stares demonstrate a certain impotence and even childishness. While Peter is
serving progressive ends in this iteration of Tolstoi's creative vision, it often appears that the tsar is the unwitting tool of impersonal historical mechanisms—
that history moves though the actions, and the suffering, of the lower classes,
rather than at the ruler's initiative. As previous commentators have noted, one
may recognize here the traces of Pokrovskii's interpretation of Russian history:
the privileging of Peter's era as a significant moment of social progress, qualified
by a depersonalization of history that assigns agency to abstract social forces.[23]
In keeping with such views, Peter himself appears to be a product of new institutions rather than their inventor; rather than being the unique mastermind of
historical progress, he is a symptomatic expression of it.

Reflecting this redistribution of historical agency, Tolstoi begins his novel
far from his nominal subject and from the seat of power: in the hut of the im-
poverished peasant family of Ivan Artemich Brovkin and his many children—
whose stories will cross and recross with those of the tsar and his retinue in a
remote echo of the structure of historical fiction after Scott. Yet in distinction
from the erotic objectives that typically drive Scott's "young men of good family" through the stuff of history to an inevitable happy marriage, Tolstoi's plot
follows his peasant characters as they realize their political and economic ambitions in the heat of social transformation. Ultimately, the Brovkins land in

---

Kneeb Piter Komondor, 1919), so outraged the eminent historian Sergei Platonov that he
responded with an explicit refutation in the mid-1920s. See Platonov, *Petr Velikii*, 5–12.

22. In an interview in 1933 with the journal *Smena*, Tolstoi stated: "The *povest'* was written at the very start of the February revolution. I don't recall what motivated me to write it.
Undoubtedly, it was written under Merezhkovskii's influence. It's a weak piece." See "Stenogramma besedy s kollektivom redaktsii zhurnala 'Smena,'" in A. N. Tolstoi, *Sobranie sochinenii*, 10:207. Tolstoi's connection of this work with the February revolution was probably intended to mask the actual relevance of the work to the October revolution, after
which it was in fact published. Tolstoi's nod toward Merezhkovskii, although not a complete
misrepresentation of the grotesque features of "Peter's Day," works to divert attention from
Tolstoi's conception of Peter's significance. It seems likely that Tolstoi's remarks were calculated to camouflage the story's original anti-Bolshevik resonance.

23. Tucker, *Stalin in Power*, 117–18.

Moscow, where Ivan achieves enormous success as Peter's most important merchant ally, his many enterprises serving the needs of military and economic development. His children participate in the creation of the new era as soldiers, sailors, army officers, translators, and navigators.[24]

Even as the sweat, ambition, and rags-to-riches success of the Brovkins represent the true and necessary engine of historical progress, however, Tolstoi does not let readers forget that the Petrine reforms also resulted in a great deal of suffering and bloodshed. Thus, he ends the first book of his novel with a deadpan description of Peter's mass tortures and executions of the *Streltsy*: "All winter there were tortures and executions. In response, rebellions flared up in Arkhangelsk, in Astrakhan, on the Don River, and in Azov. The dungeons filled up, and thousands of new corpses were rocked by the blizzards on the Moscow city walls. The old was backed into dark corners. Byzantine Rus had ended. In the March wind, on the Baltic coasts the outlines of merchant ships appeared."[25]

The novel's second book ends in a similar fashion, with a depiction of the miserable working conditions of the oppressed peasant and convict laborers in Brovkin's dungeon-like new cloth factories: "it was worse than prison both for the convicts and for the free laborer. All around was a high fence; at the gates were guards, fiercer than dogs. In dark cells, hunched at pounding machine stations, you can't even sing a song—the foreign foreman's cane will come down burning across your back."[26] Such pointedly compromising episodes serve to remind readers of the traumatic base of "necessary" historical processes. Yet the antipathy to Peter as representative of a hated regime, so evident in "Peter's Day," has now faded: the eponymous hero of the first volumes of *Peter I* is clearly a sympathetic character.

In the third passage quoted earlier, we see yet another stage in Tolstoi's vision of Peter. Here, the wise and calm emperor muses about grand affairs of

24. For a summary of the successes of the Brovkins at the conclusion of volume 2, see Tolstoi, *Sobranie sochinenii*, 7:656–59. Riasanovsky notes the influence of Pokrovskian historiography on the role and character of Brovkin Senior (*The Image of Peter the Great*, 280–82). Besides instructing readers in early Soviet historical dogma, the Brovkins' stories were calculated to kindle the imagination with visions of a rags-to-riches leap from the social depths into the heights of material comfort. Subplots such as that of Brovkin's daughter Aleksandra—a pure-hearted peasant girl who marries a boyar and removes with him to Paris and the Hague, where she learns to dance, play the harp, and chat about fashion in French—offer a historical transposition of the transformation in well-being that the "construction of socialism" aimed to secure in the Soviet present.

25. A. N. Tolstoi, *Sobranie sochinenii*, 7:364. Robert Tucker sees the novel's first volume as unambiguously "optimistic," reading the suppression of the *Streltsy* as an expression of Peter's sympathies for the working people. In my view, the novel communicates Peter's affinity for the merchant class, in keeping with then ascendant Pokrovskian views of history. The brutal pursuit of "progressive" aims in volume 1 recalls Lenin's remark that Peter used "barbarous means in the battle with barbarism." See Tucker, *Stalin in Power*, 117–18.

26. A. N. Tolstoi, *Sobranie sochinenii*, 7:662–63.

state: the creation of Petersburg and the ongoing war with envious European enemies. Advisers of a similarly lofty character surround him. Finally, Peter appears fully in control of both himself and historical events—listening attentively but without excess passion, thinking with satisfaction about the city and society he has constructed. This last vision of Peter lucidly reflects his high Stalinist cult and may be read as a straightforward literary illustration of the vision of history established with the *Short Course in the History of the USSR*. Just as that text had announced, Tolstoi here shows us how "Peter I achieved his goals," how the Baltic was "in the hands of Russia," and how Peter "remade the order of things in a European fashion." The emperor's "fat little writing book," filled with ideas and conceptions that through his leadership have gained shape and substance, projects the commonplace Stalinist obsession with "plans"—five-year plans, party directives, and so on—and their fulfillment "in fact," rendering Peter a historical hero in the terms that Stalin had explained to Ludwig at the start of the 1930s: "Great people are worth something only insofar as they are able to understand correctly these conditions and what is necessary to alter them."

As *Pravda* announced in 1941, the Soviet people and their leaders were "the lawful heirs of the Russian people's great and honorable past."[27] Tolstoi's last version of Peter adds flesh to this genealogy of the present, presenting a eulogistic allegory of Stalin and his transcendent leadership qualities. Here nearly every detail of the greatest leader of Russian national history appears to mirror the public image of the great leader of the Soviet present, from his ability to inspire action and respect in those around him to his patriarchal presence, his little pipe and "authoritative jollity." Most important of all, certainly, is Tolstoi's emphasis in this last volume on Peter's military genius—corresponding to the centrality of this feature in the depiction of Stalin in Soviet wartime propaganda.

—⁂—

Now, how does one account for the development of Tolstoi's representations of Peter? The most common explanation is that the author's vision changed in step with dominant Soviet views of the first emperor in a transparent illustration of craven eagerness to cater to the Stalinist regime. Typical of views of Tolstoi as a toady to Soviet officialdom is the article in the *Handbook of Russian Literature*, which begins: "Tolstoi, Aleksei Nikolaevich (1883–1945), a nobleman by birth, has been described as a man 'who towards the end of his life became the most authoritative apologist for the Stalin regime.'"[28] Nicholas Riasanovsky has written that the author's views on Peter evolved "as a parody of the rise and fall

---

27. Emel'ian Iaroslavskii, "Bol'sheviki—prodolzhateli luchshikh patrioticheskikh traditsii russkogo naroda," *Pravda*, December 27, 1941, 3.

28. Leon I. Twarog, "Tolstoi, Aleksei Nikolaevich," in Terras, ed., *Handbook of Russian Literature*, 475.

of Pokrovskii."[29] Robert Tucker describes Tolstoi's work on Peter simply as the fulfillment of Stalin's own literary designs.[30]

Of course, there is some merit to this view, for clearly the author was responsive to the needs of the Soviet establishment. Lev Kogan reports that Tolstoi remarked in the early 1930s, "I don't understand why people are afraid of the word 'commission' even in its more literal meaning."[31] Moreover, the evolution of Tolstoi's conception of Peter in the late 1920s appears to correspond to Stalin's own view (expressed through an intermediary) after a preview of the 1929 Moscow Art Theater production of the first version of the author's play about Peter, *On the Rack* (Na dybe): "A splendid play. Only it's a pity that Peter wasn't depicted heroically enough."[32] Tolstoi tended to test the political waters by whatever means he could, and he did not hesitate to consult with Gorkii and more powerful establishment figures, including Stalin himself, whenever the opportunity arose.[33] So, for example, in an interview regarding part 1 of the film *Peter I* Tolstoi proudly reports that "Iosif Vissarionovich went over our plans very attentively, approved them, and gave us directions, which became the foundation for our work."[34]

Granting that the overall development of the Petrine theme reflects Tolstoi's conscious efforts at accommodation, however, does not really lay to rest the matter of how this development took place. The most glaring shortcoming of such an explanation is the simplistic presupposition that public life during the early Soviet and Stalinist eras was sufficiently monolithic that one could identify a "party line" and conform to it or receive and act on a clear directive "from above." To the contrary, as I argue above, historical interpretation of Peter during the late 1920s and into the early 1930s was volatile—politically loaded yet utterly lacking in authoritative direction—and in any case never crystallized around a well-defined official view until the publication of the Shestakov textbook in 1937. During this period, Tolstoi suffered at the hands of the Russian Association for Proletarian Writers (RAPP) for his overly apologetic depiction of Peter in the early versions of the play and in his novel's first two volumes. So, for example, the RAPP critic Ilia Bachelis assailed the second

29. Riasanovsky, *Image of Peter the Great*, 281. Also see Nivat, "Alexis Tolstoi."

30. Tucker, *Stalin in Power*, 114.

31. Lev Kogan, no title, in *Vospominaniia ob A. N. Tolstom*, ed. Nikitina and Tolstaia, 203–29, here 205.

32. Ivanov-Razumnik, *Pisatel'skie sud'by*, 39–43; also see A. N. Tolstoi, "Kratkaia biografiia," in his *Polnoe sobranie sochinenii*, 1:87.

33. On Tolstoi's contacts with Gorkii and on other aspects of his political maneuvering in the Soviet establishment, see Petelin, *Sud'ba khudozhnika*, 364–82. Tucker cites anecdotal evidence that Tolstoi consulted frequently with Stalin regarding Peter and even became a "friend" of the Soviet ruler in his *Stalin in Power*, 116–18.

34. A. Danat, "U Alekseia Tolstogo," *Skorokhodovskii rabochii*, September 15, 1937, 2–3; the interview was reprinted as "Beseda s rabochimi fabriki 'Skorokhod,'" in A. N. Tolstoi, *Polnoe sobranie sochinenii*, 13:534–36. I cite the original newspaper publication.

version of Tolstoi's play *Peter I* in a 1930 review: "This play by Aleksei Niko-laevich Tolstoi—a former count, in past years a bard of the bankrupt aristoc-racy, and currently numbering among the petty bourgeois 'fellow travelers'—is the malicious, maddened sortie of a class enemy, covered over with the artful mask of 'historicity.'"[35] In a striking illustration of just how dramatically So-viet historical consciousness was changing in these years, Bachelis saw the cen-tral mechanism of Tolstoi's "camouflaged counterrevolutionary attack" as his muted evocation of a historical analogy between the Petrine and Soviet epochs—precisely the rhetorical device that would come to govern Stalinist historical discourse by the end of the decade. The degree to which attacks like this af-fected Tolstoi may be judged by the vehemence with which he would publicly attack RAPP in later years.[36]

Even in the 1930s, as the significance of Russian history in Soviet public life shifted rapidly and as the Politburo denounced Pokrovskii's "vulgar sociologi-cal" historiography, the representation of Peter remained a risky business.[37] Tolstoi faced particularly sharp criticism as he worked on the two-part film *Peter I.* The screenplay was significantly reworked before it finally went into production and continued to be revised during shooting. Some characters, such as Feofan Prokopovich, who delivers the triumphant final speech of the original screenplay, were nearly written out of the final version. The project's ideologi-cal underpinnings shifted dramatically: the Pokrovskian tenor of early drafts was supplanted by the post-Pokrovskian tone of the finished film.[38] Tolstoi's March 1937 press release regarding the final work on part 1 of the film illus-trates the author's embattled working conditions:

A pack of various staff "film theoreticians" descended on us with a mass of contradictory demands. The wobbly, hysterical Peter that they were pushing on us did not correspond at all to our conceptions. They demanded

35. I. Bachelis, "Dlia kogo sie," *Komsomol'skaia pravda*, March 2, 1930, 4. This review, which explicitly calls for a press campaign against Tolstoi modeled on the 1929 campaign against Pilniak, is the most negative public response to the play. Articles in *Pravda* and *Iz-vestiia* panned the play, calling it "distant from the Soviet audience," a pernicious resurgence of "Merezhkovskyism" and a failure, but refrained from hyperbolic accusations against its author. See N. Volkov, "Petr I," *Izvestiia*, March 9, 1930, 4; and L. Cherniavskii, "Restavrat-siia merezhkovshchiny (*Petr I* v MKhAT)," *Pravda*, March 11, 1930, 6.

36. See, in particular, Tolstoi's statement of 1937, "Prodolzhim i uglubim samokritiku," in his *Sobranie sochinenii*, 10:365–67. Here, Tolstoi "confesses" that he and the Soviet liter-ary establishment as a whole are guilty of insufficiently eradicating RAPPist errors, turning "self-criticism" into an offensive weapon.

37. Pokrovskii's investment in historical materialism and anonymous social forces, as well as his "unpatriotic" criticism of Peter the Great, tsarist imperialism, and Russian chau-vinism, were officially denounced in January 1936. See Mazour, *Writing of History*, 17–23. In 1936, Tolstoi wrote a broadside against Pokrovskii for *Pravda* that remained unpub-lished. See Kriukov, *A. N. Tolstoi*, 201.

38. Compare a March 1935 version of the screenplay at RGALI, f. 631, op. 3, d. 207, with A. Tolstoi and V. Petrov, "Petr I," in *Izbrannye stsenarii*, 4:5–94.

that we show the ultimate futility and defeat of all of Peter's transformational activity. These demands would have nullified our attempts to show
the progressive significance of the Petrine epoch for the subsequent development of Russian history. [. . .] The central idea of our film was and
remains our intention to show the power of the great Russian nation, the
indomitable nature of its transformational spirit.[39]

Scattered evidence regarding the reception of this first film indicates the extent
to which it failed to correspond to any well-established interpretive line, instead confusing its audiences. Its outright celebration of Peter so disturbed
some viewers that they asked Shestakov about the film's political correctness
in public lectures, while in Magnitogorsk at least one audience member in-
ferred from the film's treatment of Peter that it had been made abroad.[40] The
second part of the film was the target of ominous political intrigue. In May
1937, Aleksei Angarov, the deputy director of the Central Committee's Department of Cultural and Educational Work, denounced those at work on the
film for criminally negligent budgetary overruns, chiefly resulting from the
continuous rewriting during shooting. Not mentioning Tolstoi by name, Angarov explained that the "gross historical distortions" of the original screenplay made such rewrites necessary. He ends with a recommendation to halt
production and to bring those responsible to justice.[41] Perhaps only Angarov's
own arrest that summer saved Tolstoi from scandal and ruin.

Given both the fluidity of Soviet visions of Peter and the political infighting
that surrounded Tolstoi during the 1930s, it is difficult to support the view
that his changing interpretive stance reflected mechanical catering to the "party
line" on history. In contrast, one must conclude that Tolstoi's rehabilitation
of Peter extended far ahead of the general curve of Soviet historical revisionism—in short, that the author was engaging in a high-stakes political gamble
that he repeatedly won. Tolstoi's aggressive position with regard to Peter exposed him to considerable risk, but he was clever enough (or lucky enough) to
outlast his critics in the stormy cultural politics of the era. In sparring with
RAPP over his play, he was saved by Stalin's favor and his enemies' eventual
fall from grace. In later battles, Tolstoi's critics were swept away by repression
before they could effectively undermine party authorities' confidence in the "Red
Count." Rather than being a toady to official interpretive positions proclaimed
from on high, Tolstoi was a skilled politician who chose allies well and took
risks that paid off. In 1943, at a conference on historical themes in wartime
writing, Aleksandr Fadeev noted:

39. A. N. Tolstoi, "Petr I v kino," in his Sobranie sochinenii, 10:349–50.

40. Brandenberger provides a good summary of viewers' responses to the film in his National Bolshevism, 56, 87–88; see also the letters to the editor printed in Skorokhodovskii
rabochii, September 15, 1937, 3.

41. RGASPI, f. 17, op. 120, d. 256, l. 103.

It is to the greatest credit of our historical novelists that many of them understood these problems [of the importance of historical knowledge in Soviet public life] and posed them in their works when they were still poorly comprehended in broader circles of the intelligentsia. And many of these authors, having created their works, met considerable social resistance and were slapped down. *Peter I*, from my point of view, by now constitutes a classical historical work. But *Peter I* initially provoked an almost physical violence. [. . .] Now, however, it is clear why [. . .] it was necessary to raise the novel *Peter I* up and to place it in the position of honor that it deserves.[42]

Tolstoi's aggressive stance had borne fruit. He enjoyed prominence in the 1940s not only by virtue of his undoubted accomplishments in historical *belles lettres* but because of the stunning timing of these accomplishments, which anticipated with near prescience the rise of tsarist history to the forefront of Soviet public life.[43]

— ⁂ —

This retelling of Tolstoi's trajectory leads to a further line of inquiry. If the political field was contested, leading us to recast the process of accommodation into one of skilled negotiation of a mobile landscape, then what strategies did Tolstoi employ in this negotiation? Many Soviet authors adapted their works to the changing political environment by simply rewriting them. Tolstoi was remarkable for the modest degree to which he resorted to this practice. He did revise his play several times, modifying Peter's image as he went. Yet surprisingly, despite multiple new editions of the early volumes of the historical novel, he never made significant changes.[44] So how did Tolstoi engineer the long-term success of his own, mobile vision of Peter? How was it that in 1941 a Stalin Prize could be awarded to a novel that was founded on Pokrovskii's by then thoroughly discredited views? In search of answers, let us return to the three passages cited at the start of this section. Whereas my initial reading

42. RGALI, f. 631, op. 15, d. 635, l. 13.

43. See a similar recognition of Tolstoi's achievement in adapting his works on Peter to a changing political environment in a December 1945 memorandum to G. M. Malenkov from the critic O. S. Reznik, in *Literaturnyi front*, ed. Babichenko, 179.

44. Tolstoi made no significant changes in prewar editions of the novel. While writing the work's third volume during the war, the author undertook more involved rewrites of the earlier parts, reaching only chapter 5 of volume 1 before his death. Although some of these corrections were plot adjustments in the interests of consistency, others realign Peter's image in keeping with Tolstoi's later, more heroic vision—eliminating a scene where the young Peter cries from fear during the *Streltsy* rebellion, for example. Yet these changes were in general so minor as to leave original historical-interpretive implications intact. Given Tolstoi's political position and the looser political climate of the war years, one must conclude that these late corrections not reflect not political pressure but rather aesthetic considerations. Regarding Tolstoi's corrections, see also A. V. Alpatova's commentary in A. N. Tolstoi, *Sobranie sochinenii*, 7:850–51.

stressed the distinctions among those successive representations of Peter, consider now some of the intriguing continuities.

Most notably, the shared imagery, running like an undercurrent through these passages, is striking: the image of Peter's hands resting on the table, hinting at his interior state, which occurs in all three citations; the image of his well-chewed pipe stem, which unites the first with the last; his bulging eyes and penetrating gaze, and so on. These poetic linkages are matched by continuities in architectonics: Peter is characterized by separateness, impenetrability, and an unnerving tendency to take abrupt action. Note that the scene from the novel's third volume, the only one of the citations that does not end in conflict, subsequently comes into alignment with the other two in this regard as well. After leaving the gathering at Menshikov's, Peter visits the laborers' barracks and is so outraged at their rotten provisions (shades of Eisenstein's *Battleship Potemkin*) that he returns to the ongoing banquet with a piece of moldy bread and forces the comically apologetic Menshikov to eat it as punishment.[45]

Despite radical changes in the historical-interpretive implications of Tolstoi's image of Peter, then, some features remain constant. These peculiar structural constants are striking enough to suggest that Tolstoi was, in some manner, reworking the same elements in his creative conception of Peter but spinning their historical potential in different directions. In the initial fragment Peter's isolation reads as distance from servants and advisers—indeed, from reality; in the second it communicates impatience with a historical process that he cannot rush along fast enough; and in the final scene it projects Peter's divine ability to direct events from a superhistorical vantage. Similarly, the atmosphere of fear around Peter at first reflects the dread inspired by random and incomprehensible beatings directed indiscriminately at all members of Russian society. This is replaced first by the terror of those who are unable to fulfill impossible commands, horrified by the excessive bloodshed of radical social change, and then by the loving awe inspired by an all-knowing leader and fear of his just reprisals, which are now cast as a defense of the common people against the depredations of those who, like Menshikov, abuse their high station.

These reflections are relevant to a broad range of material that is repeatedly deployed in Tolstoi's Petrine works, with successive, ideologically significant modifications, including, for example, scenes of Peter in battle and of his interactions with common Russians.[46] One such recurrent theme, bearing signal importance for Tolstoi's own creative mythology, is that of interrogation and torture. As the author explained in several published discussions, he first grasped the essence of early eighteenth-century linguistic norms by studying original interrogation transcripts of that era: "Suddenly [. . .] I saw, felt, comprehended—the

---

45. Ibid., 7:708.

46. On the successive modifications of Tolstoi's representations of Peter in battle, see Kevin M. F. Platt, "Rehabilitation and Afterimage: Aleksei Tolstoi's Many Returns to Peter the Great," in *Epic Revisionism*, ed. Platt and Brandenberger, 47–68, esp. 60–61.

Russian language. The scribes and copyists of Muscovite Russia artfully recorded interrogations; their task was constrained and precise: to communicate the stories of those under torture, preserving all the peculiarities of their speech—a literary task, in a way."[47]

Considering this view of interrogation as a means to discover linguistic truths, it is curious how malleable the presentation of interrogation would become in Tolstoi's works. "Peter's Day" depicts in detail the emperor as he oversees the torture of the mystic Varlaam, who has publicly repeated the prophesy that "Petersburg will be empty":

> Varlaam had already been hanging on the rack for forty minutes. His arms, twisted up behind him, were bound above his head to the crossbar. His head hung down, and the tangled locks of his hair concealed his face and intertwined with his long beard. His dirty, naked body was suspended below, with ribs protruding, smeared with soot, and with coagulating blood dripping from his side. Vaarlam had just received thirty-five strokes with the knout, while he was being burned in front with a torch. His dirty feet, toes clenched in spasm, were locked in shackles that were bound below to a log. A well-built fellow in a sheepskin coat—the hangman—stood on the log, stretching out Varlaam's body. [. . .] Peter got up at last, approached the suspended man, and stood before him for a long time, as if in thought.
>
> "Varlaam!" he said, and all present shuddered. [. . .]
>
> "Varlaam!" repeated Peter.
>
> The suspended man did not move. The tsar placed a hand on his chest, next to his heart.
>
> "Take him down," he said. "Relocate his shoulders. For tomorrow, prepare the hot irons."[48]

In the first two volumes of Tolstoi's novel, the depictions of Peter's role in interrogations are less prejudicial. He interrogates political enemies (first, supporters of the Tsaritsa Sophia; later, the *Streltsy* rebels) and betrays his discomfort with the barbarity of torture by his overt distress and efforts to conceal this cruelty from foreign emissaries.[49] In the second part of the film (1939), Tolstoi shows Peter's complicity in the torture and murder of Tsarevich Aleksei but also the great pain Peter himself experiences in sacrificing "the flesh of his flesh" to social progress and to the defense of Russia against European enemies. Tolstoi included a similar treatment of this historical episode in the final version of the play, and he likely intended to depict this episode in the novel's third volume, as well.

47. A. N. Tolstoi, "Kak my pishem," in his *Sobranie sochinenii*, 10:141–42. Also see "Stenogramma besedy s kollektivom redaktsii zhurnala *Smena*," in ibid., 10:211–12.

48. Ibid., 3:95–96.

49. Ibid., 7:192–97, 360–64.

At the start of Tolstoi's career, then, torture figured as something of a key to historical truth, constituting the basic reality of the Petrine past. Given the ambiguous allegorical resonance of "Peter's Day" with the revolutionary events of 1917 and 1918, Tolstoi's view cannot but recall the tradition extending back through Miliukov, Merezhkovskii, Repin, and others to Pushkin's *Bronze Horseman*, in which the Petrine era is a foundational moment of traumatic violence that erupts uncontrollably in future eras. Yet as representation of this originative scene was transformed over Tolstoi's career, we witness the gradual exoneration of Peter's bloody methods, as Tolstoi minimized, humanized, and finally legitimated them in the name of grand historical imperatives. The result was a conception of the past that evoked Kavelin, Solovev, and the Shestakov textbook in its willingness to approve any price in human suffering to ensure the ideal of historical progress. In this respect, Tolstoi's personal history of writing and overwriting the motif of torture articulated the mechanism of Russian collective memory as the memorialization of a chosen but disavowed trauma. Yet the Red Count's variations on the theme of torture also give witness, once again, to the remarkable conservative streak that time and again drew him back to the same basic elements in the Petrine mythology—even those that carried the most risk in the context of the Stalinist celebration of the emperor. In short, Tolstoi's oeuvre not only participated in the disavowal of chosen trauma; it also demonstratively acted out and *revealed* this disavowal.

Beyond Tolstoi's reliance on recurrent themes and images, one may note other curious patterns of repetition in his Petrine works. He returned many times to a specific set of fictional characters: the families of the boyar Buinosov and the peasant Brovkin, who surface in various works and genres. Finally, there remains the overriding peculiarity of Tolstoi's stubborn application of a single title, *Peter I*, to all his treatments of Peter from the late 1920s on. The insistence of these elements within Tolstoi's poetical project would seem to fly in the face of the fluidity we have noted in his historical-interpretive project. If the author were striving simply to recast his vision of Peter in keeping with (or in anticipation of) the changing political line, a more obvious approach would have been to strive for distance from all aspects of the earlier Petrine works in the creation of later, more politically acceptable ones.

In this light, I suggest that Tolstoi did not, in fact, aspire to replace his earlier conceptions so much as he worked to preserve the integrity of his poetical imagination—in particular to preserve his magnum opus, the historical novel. Rather than rewrite the novel, erasing his own accomplishments in service to the Soviet erasure of outworn historical visions, Tolstoi revised his novel in a highly original way. The release of new works in other genres and media on the same topic, using the same characters and bearing the same title, acted to cast a new interpretive net over material already in print. Those who viewed the film, for example, certainly returned to the novel with a very different sense of Peter and his reign than that communicated by the printed text alone.[50] The addition of new episodes to the novel, both in these other media and through the appearance of later volumes, afforded the author an opportunity to recast the implications of old episodes, nudging readers' perceptions toward a different understanding of earlier installments.

The most obvious evidence that the author's compositions of the 1930s reflect an intentional strategy in this regard may be the never-ending task he set for himself in the first place and nursed for two decades: that of writing the historical novel itself. In effect, the novel was an open-ended bildungsroman—and a bildungsroman isn't over until it's over. By never actually bringing his work to a close, he left it open for constructive reconfigurations as new material affected the immanent implications of the old.

Tolstoi's strategy here might be formulated as one of harnessing interpretive flexibility to outmaneuver a restrictive ideological environment. This flexibility maintained the political validity of compositions that changing circumstances would otherwise have rendered obsolete, ensuring the author's safety by leaving him able to spin on a dime and recast his tale as the need arose. Undoubtedly, Tolstoi's aim at each stage of his work on the carpenter-tsar was to realize what he viewed as a "correct" image. Yet his strategy of "overwriting" rather than simply "rewriting" his text had unintended consequences. After all, the result of Tolstoi's successive tinkering is not a consistent, authoritative vision of Peter and his day but rather a multiple and shifting one. Taken as a whole, the novel betrays traces of a range of interpretive options, stacked up like geological strata. Ultimately, the syncretic character of Tolstoi's novel—and of the "hypertext" of his many Petrine works taken together—may actually have undermined the Soviet rehabilitation of Peter that the author was ostensibly serving.

Perhaps Tolstoi's own sense of the lingering afterimages of his earlier historical conceptions motivated his 1944 decision to correct the text of the first two volumes of the by then canonical novel. Yet these minor changes did nothing to alter the work's complex interpretive structure, leaving the image of Peter and his deeds blurred. He is part hangman, part hero; both young Turk and transcendent leader; protagonist of a story of glory interlaced with trauma; the face of Russian greatness, uncannily reminiscent of the face of terror. Only one thing, ultimately, is certain: Peter's era is the focal point for the affective energies of collective identity, pride, self-sacrifice, and ritual becoming.

The best metaphor for Tolstoi's syncretic works on Peter is that of the palimpsest, where a number of old images and new ones, interpretations and reinterpretations, are accumulated one on top of another, gaining in emotional force by virtue of their overinscribed character and foiling any attempt to retreat to a single interpretive position. Backing away from close consideration of Tolstoi's works, I suggest that this characterization may be applied to the Stalinist process of historical rehabilitation as a whole. Although the overt intent of Soviet elites in the 1930s was undoubtedly to establish a final corrected

---

50. A similar point is made in Dobrenko, *Stalinist Cinema*, 33.

and "usable" version of the past, political and historiographical complexities undermined this goal at every turn, substituting a secondary but perhaps more important interpretive horizon and social function. Rather than simply replacing past conceptions with fresh ones, the imperfect process of Stalinist historical revisionism left traces of outworn ideas in plain view for those who wished to see them and signaled an interpretative openness directly contradicting the authority of any single, politically correct version of history. On the highest level of abstraction, one might say that the very mechanism of revision worked against the project of erasure, for each text, calculated to replace another, in fact commemorated what it was intended to conceal.

And it is here, for both Tolstoi and Stalinist historiography, that the overt intent and actual function of historical rehabilitation in Soviet social life and public discourse part ways. In Tolstoi's accumulative revisions, as in Soviet revisionism as a whole, the perpetual urge to revise and amplify the hero's transcendence feeds off the obverse image that it both conceals and recalls. Each effort to bury the past announces and undoes itself, making necessary additional efforts at burial. For Tolstoi, this unending revisionist imperative provided room to maneuver, the possibility to mask yet preserve his own political biography and his literary achievements—the writer's own intimate store of chosen but disavowed trauma. For the historical revisionist project as a whole, the same dynamic disciplined Soviet subjects via its self-defeating circulation and disavowal of historical knowledge.

In sum, *Peter I* and Stalinist historical revisionism each demanded of audiences not only noisy celebration of the last, best truth but also complicity in a string of misrecognitions, leading inexorably from the heroic surface to the traumatic foundation beneath. As in the pages of the novel, so in Stalinist public life, beneath even the most transcendent image of Petrine greatness there lurked a vision of terror. Each reader, each Soviet subject, was compelled to take part in the cover-up. Ultimately, beneath both heroism and despotism lay the most profound and troubling questions—questions to be studiously avoided: Could a regime that could not expunge trauma from its past ever hope to do so in its present? Could an order founded on historical materialism ever hope to succeed when history itself kept slipping away?

Allegory of Historiography: Sergei Eisenstein's *Ivan the Terrible*

The occasion for the most widely discussed scandal of the Stalinist rehabilitation of the tsarist past, Sergei Eisenstein's masterful, uncompleted film trilogy *Ivan the Terrible,* is a fitting case with which to close our investigation. Tolstoi's Petrine project capitalized on the ambivalences of the new Stalinist historiography, which at once replaced and repeated the old narratives. Eisenstein's work represents a self-conscious investigation and critique of these same ambivalences. As we have seen, a fundamental stumbling block of Stalinist revisionism was its vacillation between an insistence on the exceptional status of the present as the culminating point of history and the drive to found the greatness of the present on a mythic national past. In practice, this problem was usually solved by the selective emphasis inherent to the poetics of repetition: some aspects of the past were to be remembered, while others were to be disavowed. Some implications of historical allegory (the grandeur of Russia's historical mission, past and present) were to be celebrated, while others were to be passed over in silence (the resurgence of terror and historical trauma). Yet there was nothing, ultimately, new in this configuration of memory and social identity. As I have suggested, more than a century of cultural history and social practice had grounded the affective foundations of greatness in the disavowal of terror. Eisenstein's achievement lies in his creation of a work that brings this relationship to light, showing the interdependence of the interpretational options and psychic mechanisms of triumph and trauma in Soviet historical myth and political life.

Film was the master genre of Soviet public life and of Stalinist historical revisionism: the medium that reached the broadest audience and was technically most capable of fulfilling the project's allegorical demands. More than any other medium, film could render the past seemingly present while sidestepping the overt articulation of problematic analogies. The fundamental principle of film is that when you move still pictures fast enough you create the illusion of motion. Historical films of the Stalinist era operated according to the reverse principle: if you project enough moving pictures on similar subjects, you can create the illusion of motionlessness.

To achieve and reinforce a view of the past in which myth superseded, while not explicitly contradicting, historical change and progress, Soviet filmmakers resorted to any number of different modes of repetition. Their favorite tactic was the implicit allegorical repetition of the past in the present: of Ivan in Zhdanov or Stalin, the Teutonic Knights of *Aleksandr Nevskii* in the Nazis, and so on. But other kinds of repetition were at work, too. The films themselves were formulaic: commonly, they take as their subject a heroic figure from the tsarist past, who is linked in some manner to the common people and to folk wisdom and engages in a struggle with foreign powers who are stand-ins for fascist Germany: Peter the Great against the Swedes; Aleksandr Nevskii versus the Teutonic Knights; Minin and Pozharskii against the Poles; Ivan the Terrible versus the Poles; Kutuzov versus Napoleon, and so on.

Furthermore, the same actors and directors worked on these various films over and over again, becoming "experts" at dealing with the "historical theme" but also giving the past an immediately recognizable and unchanging face. To take just the example of Cherkasov, his roles included: Tsarevich Aleksei (in Petrov's *Peter I*), Peter the Great (in Aleksei N. Tolstoi's play), Aleksandr Nevskii and Ivan the Terrible (in Eisenstein's films), and Ivan the Terrible (in Aleksei N. Tolstoi's plays). The films (and other works of the era) cross-reference one another, instructing the viewers of *Peter I*, for example, that Peter's struggle against the Swedes was contiguous with the struggle of Minin and Pozharskii against the Poles. Similarly, the viewers of Glinka's opera *A Life for the Tsar* (Zhizn' za tsaria, 1836), revamped as *Ivan Susanin* in 1939, learn that the seventeenth-century struggle against Polish invaders depicted in the opera was equivalent to Nevskii's battle with the Teutonic Knights.[51] Of special relevance to our concerns here was the formula "Ivan, who anticipated Peter's triumphant accomplishments," which became a mantra in discussion of revisionist cultural projects like Tolstoi's plays and Eisenstein's films.[52] For Soviet audiences, the mythic scene of Russians following a prescient leader, in conflict with European aggressors, must have seemed to rise up out of time as an eternal fate.

The poetics of repetition were not without their complications, however. While the self-evident rhythm of the series—Nevskii, Ivan, Peter . . . Stalin—was in general key to revisionist film, certain kinds of repetition were more problematic. As Blium's complaints to Stalin make plain, the impression that Soviet historical myth was merely a reissue of late imperial models held troubling ironic implications: if Peter had once served as a double of Nicholas I, then of Alexander II (and of every subsequent tsar), did the allegorical representation of present-day leaders bring Stalin, through the figure of Peter, into some sort of uneasy equivalence with Russia's vilified last Romanov rulers? Perhaps the most common way of dealing with this problem was through agitational bravura and a stubborn insistence on the Soviets' right to their appropriation of Russian history. In the director Vladimir Petrov's account, when the creators of the film *Peter I* balked in 1937 at the selection of Nikolai Simonov for the title role, claiming that he failed to resemble any of the "twenty-five known representations of Peter the Great," Tolstoi is supposed to have responded: "If Simonov plays Peter, then it will be he who will be remembered—this will be the twenty-sixth, most famous portrayal of the great reformer."[53] Based on their own, peculiar form of contemporaneousness with the first em-

51. Susan Beam Eggers, "Reinventing the Enemy: The Villains of Glinka's Opera *Ivan Susanin* on the Soviet Stage," in *Epic Revisionism*, ed. Platt and Brandenberger, 261–75, esp. 266–67.

52. This formula, familiar from nineteenth-century historiography, could be conveniently backed up by one of Marx's few references to either tsar. See the first epigraph to this chapter, drawn from Karl Marx, "Obzor istorii Skandinavii i Rossii," in Marks [Marx] and Engel's [Engels], *Arkhiv Marksa i Engel'sa*, 8:165. This source is not, in fact, a finished work by Marx, but rather reading notes drawn from his notebooks. Nevertheless, because they represent one of the few instances when he actually recorded his thoughts on Russian history, they became an important resource in Stalinist work on the topic. For examples of this application, see S. M. Eisenstein [Eizenshtein], "Ivan Groznyi," *Literatura i iskusstvo*, no. 27 (July 4, 1942): 3; Ia. S. Lur'e, "Voprosy vneshnei i vnutrennei politiki v poslaniiakh Ivana Groznogo," in *Poslaniia Ivana Groznogo*, ed. Adrianova-Peretts, 468–519, esp. 488; and I. I. Smirnov, A. M. Sakharov, and I. A. Korotkov, "Ivan IV Vasil'evich," in *Bol'shaia sovetskaia entsiklopediia* (1950–58), 17:266–69, esp. 268.

53. Quoted in Kuznetsova, "Petr Pervyi," 173.

peror, Soviet filmmakers could author their own no less accurate but entirely original portrayal.

Like so much else in the public pronouncements of the 1930s, however, one must treat such aspirations to an absolute, Soviet originality with care. In a culminating scene of *Peter I*, part 2 of 1939, Petrov worked with an Old Master's attention to detail not to create his own new version of Peter but to reproduce precisely the scene of Nikolai Ge's historical painting *Peter I Interrogates Tsarevich Aleksei Petrovich at Peterhof* (figs. 5 and 17). The resulting *tableau vivant* is breathtaking in its accuracy and rather complicates matters with regard to the declared goal of originality.

Still, the film's appropriation of this image did not imply a wholesale adoption of the implications of Ge's painting. The painter had offered a problematically open allegorical window onto the past, which in its lack of clear signals had allowed viewers to project their sympathy toward Peter or Aleksei according to their own views on the events of the national past and their present-day significance. Petrov and Tolstoi's film, in sharp contrast, presents Aleksei's execution as necessary for the future welfare of state and people—the

Figure 17: Nikolai Simonov and Nikolai Cherkasov as Peter I and Tsarevich Aleksei, respectively, in Vladimir Petrov's film *Peter I*, part 2, 1939. Courtesy, Gosfilmofond (Moscow, Russia).

tsarevich, a conspiring and fundamentally pernicious character, simply gets what he deserves.

Petrov and Tolstoi's redeployment of Ge's image evokes nothing so much as the Soviet repositioning of tsarist monuments—for example, the relocation of Ivan Martos's 1818 monument to Minin and Pozharskii from the center to the margins of Red Square in 1930 and, later, the relocation of Aleksandr Opekushin's 1880 monument to Pushkin from one side of Pushkin Square to the other. Such interventions acted to revise, correct, and sanitize nineteenth-century Russia's historical mythology, rendering it "new" for Soviet men and women, yet in fact simply burying contrary interpretive positions as a disavowed content. In so doing, the regime not only reclaimed but redoubled the affective power of these images for the purposes of the Soviet present. Tolstoi's statement aside, the actual project of the film and of many other works of Soviet historical film and fiction was to create representations that inherited all of the emotional potency of previous portrayals but worked concertedly to conceal this cultural debt.[54]

Despite the runaway success of Petrov and Tolstoi's *Peter I*, Eisenstein was not overly impressed by the films. As Yuri Tsivian has reported, Eisenstein jotted down a note to the effect that "acting in Petrov's film is a *succession* of *poses*. Equally, there is no montage but merely a succession of easel-painting shots. And the scenario is not an organism, but a checklist of *traits*."[55] Doubtless there were many reasons for Eisenstein's professional distaste for *Peter I*, and there are certainly many ways in which his historical films compete with Petrov's. Yet I suspect that Eisenstein may have objected in particular to Petrov's articulation of his relationship to prior traditions in the representation of history, in particular to the "posed," "easel-painting" *tableau vivant* of Ge's painting. This aspect of Ge's film was remarked on and criticized in print, in sources that Eisenstein would have been familiar with and by authors who were among his close interlocutors.[56] And, most important, Eisenstein himself would

54. In his account of Soviet historical film, Evgeny Dobrenko offers an interesting discussion of Tolstoi's comment about the "twenty-sixth portrait of Peter," concluding that the chief significance of the Stalinist version of Peter I is that, lacking in likeness to any historical referent, the image maximally corresponded to the ideological needs of the times: "The twenty-sixth portrait of Peter was primarily an ideological construct: despite his superficial lack of resemblance, he was ideally tailored according to the ideological patterns of the second half of the 1930s" (*Stalinist Cinema*, 31). Such an analysis greatly simplifies the dynamics of Stalinist historical reference, taking Tolstoi's statement too much at face value. In corresponding to the needs of the moment, the Stalinist version of Peter covered its historical tracks through a disingenuous denial of resemblance, not to Peter, but to prior representations of him.

55. Tsivian, *Ivan the Terrible*, 36. Italics and underlining in original.

56. In a 1939 collection of articles on Soviet historical film, L. Gutman published an essay on historical painting and film in which he discussed Petrov's debts to nineteenth-century artistic works, and in particular to Ge's painting, concluding that the restaging of the painting was too literal, in that it referred viewers to the artwork rather than making use of the lingering associations of the painting for the benefit of the film's affective force ("Istoricheskii

reuse past representations, and nineteenth-century painting in particular, in the *Ivan the Terrible* films, though in a manner very different from Petrov's.

In turning now to Eisenstein's final project, I focus on a discrete set of images from part 2 of the film trilogy, which offer important insights into interpretation of the whole. Much of the critical discussion of *Ivan the Terrible* has worked to elevate Eisenstein, on the basis of the banned second installment in the project in particular, as an example of willful subversion or noble resistance to the tyranny of Stalinism.[57] Yet such interpretations have found little hard evidence to support them, either in the films themselves or in the ever more thoroughly mined archival record. My own reading seeks to redirect discussion from the likely dead end of "proving" the films' critique of Stalinism to a more fertile discussion of them as a critique of Stalinist historical revisionism. In my view, Eisenstein's films present a meditation on the instability of historical discourse when it is burdened with the task of rendering comprehensible periods that have been seen as ruptures in collective identity and political formation—liminal epochs such as Ivan's and the Stalinist era of revolution and war.

In the climactic episode of part 2 of *Ivan the Terrible*, Ivan's rival and relative Efrosiniia Staritskaia, a representative of the reactionary interests of boyar grandees and church prelates who has plotted to assassinate Ivan and place her dull-witted son Vladimir on the throne, meets her own tragic downfall. Learning at his banquet of Efrosiniia's treasonous plot, the prescient Ivan arrays his would-be successor in the royal robes and crown, making the boy the target of the assassination that ensues. Immediately after the murderer has done his deed, Efrosiniia rushes in triumphantly to proclaim Ivan's death. When the living and wrathful Ivan emerges from the crowd of loyal *oprichniki*, she examines the corpse lying before her and discovers that she has engineered the murder of her own child. There follows a striking shot, thirty seconds in duration, portraying Efrosiniia keening a lullaby as she cradles Vladimir's dead body in her arms (fig. 18).

On the basis of both the scene's climactic place in Eisenstein's plot and the composition of the shot—so much like a classic *tableau vivant* in its peculiar static poses—it seems clear that one should read it as an overt reference to Repin's canvas *Ivan the Terrible and His Son Ivan* (see fig. 6), as well as to the larger tradition of representations portraying Ivan as an filicidal father. Like Repin's canvas and the final scenes of both Mei's and Rimskii-Korsakov's

zhanr v zhivopisi i kino," in *Sovetskii istoricheskii fil'm*, ed. Markovin, 84–100, esp. 95–96). Eisenstein contributed to this collection himself and was undoubtedly familiar with it. The critic and author of screenplays Viktor Shklovskii, who numbered among Eisenstein's interlocutors, noted in his review of part 1 of the film (which does not even include the *tableau vivant*) that the film's creators "interpret Aleksei according to Ge's painting," adducing this as part of a critique of the "static" qualities of the film ("*Petr Pervyi* na ekrane," in his *Za 60 let*, 219–23, esp. 220).

57. See, for instance, Kozlov, "Artist and the Shadow of Ivan"; and Neuberger, *Ivan the Terrible*.

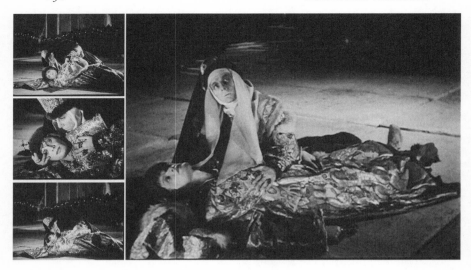

Figure 18: Serafima Birman and Pavel Kadochnikov as Efrosynia Staritskaia and Vladimir Staritskii in Sergei Eisenstein's film *Ivan the Terrible*, part 2, 1944.

versions of *The Maid of Pskov*, Eisenstein's shot sums up a tragic story of intergenerational violence among members of the ruling family, in which a parent is inadvertently responsible for the death of a child. Of course, those earlier scenes represent Ivan himself as a murderous father, whereas here Efrosiniia occupies this role. Yet certainly Ivan is metaphorically present, mediated not only through the tsar's double, Vladimir, but also through Efrosiniia, who is motivated by her hunger to seize the tsar's power for herself. Eisenstein's shot, then, holds up a distorting mirror to the earlier tradition in representation. Viewed in a broader perspective, the intriguing resemblances of these scenes underscore Eisenstein's debt to the nineteenth-century dramatic tradition surrounding the Terrible Tsar. However, Eisenstein's films do not merely repeat the earlier tradition—they speak back to it.

Like those nineteenth-century works, Eisenstein's Ivan films study the relationship between individual human desires and transcendent categories of collective experience—the state, the divine, and history itself. Certainly, Eisenstein shows Ivan's grand project of perfecting the Russian state in conflict with external enemies to the east and west—the Kazan Khanate, conquered in part 1, and Polish antagonists, shown briefly in part 2—as well as with internal enemies such as Efrosiniia and her co-conspirators. Yet, in the manner of classical tragedy, the central scene of conflict is Ivan's inner experience. The dramatic plot of each of the films (including the uncompleted third film) revolves around Ivan's excruciating, painful loss of the human contacts he holds dear. At the start of the first film, Ivan's coronation cuts directly to scenes of his wedding feast with Anastasiia. Emphatically desirable, Anastasiia ideally unites a wife's love with the love of a patriot, pronouncing her loyalty to the "Muscovite tsar and his great cause." Yet this harmony of personal and state bonds, recalling a similar alignment in Mei's and Rimskii-Korsakov's *Maid of Pskov*, is lost to Ivan when Anastasiia is poisoned at the end of part 1. Unlike the earlier works, which held out the hope of a convergence of individual, familial love with political, collective bonds in a Christian community, Eisenstein's films, which were to end with Ivan alone on the shore of the Baltic Sea, consistently trace the need to sacrifice all individual affections and even moral principles to the greater cause.

After Anastasiia's death, this pattern of progressive isolation and loss is expressed in the successive transformation of Kurbskii, Filipp, and later Aleksei Basmanov, each originally among Ivan's closest friends and allies, into opponents and enemies as a result of their inability to see past their own petty desires and hunger for power. The portrayal of Ivan himself, illustrating Eisenstein's theory of the filmic image as a "unity of opposites," strikingly alternates between planes of existence—that of the abject, prostrate figure, subject to the passions and afflictions of all mortals, and that of the erect, inspired leader, focusing his vision on a point above and beyond the confines of the dialogue, the set, and even the frame.[58] In part 1 this alternation is visible in the moment of coronation, when suddenly Ivan's gaze is drawn off to a distant horizon as he proclaims his grand designs. In part 2 a corresponding moment occurs when Ivan at first seems to mourn over the bodies of executed political opponents, but then suddenly stands erect with the words "too few!"

In short, these films instruct viewers in the need for personal sacrifice, in the unavoidable bloodshed of history, and in the necessity to "look past" trauma toward prospects of collective greatness. Yet perhaps the greatest achievement of Eisenstein's film is that, in facing more and more squarely the diremption between individual affections and superhuman imperatives, it never yields to the temptation to render these imperatives themselves completely comprehensible. At one point, Efrosiniia states that "a sovereign should not stray from the path of righteousness if he can help it but must be prepared to tread the path of evil if necessary." In a poetic twist characteristic of Eisenstein's studied maintenance of evaluative ambivalence, this sentiment unites Ivan with his enemies in the dissolution of all simple moral distinctions in the face of historical principles that will always exceed our limited, human ability to grasp them.

---

58. See Iurenev, *Sergei Eizenshtein*, 2:211. Ivan's dual nature harks back not only to the nineteenth-century tradition of representation but to a central concern animating sixteenth-century disputes concerning absolute autocracy: the dual nature of the tsar, who is "in body like to other men, but in the power of his station like unto God." On this formulation in relation to representation of Ivan, see my "Antichrist Enthroned." For the relevant premodern political theory, see Ihor Ševčenko, "A Neglected Byzantine Source of Muscovite Political Ideology," in *Structure of Russian History*, ed. Cherniavsky, 80–107; Raeff, "Early Theorist of Absolutism"; and Kantorowicz, *King's Two Bodies*.

The climactic shot of Efrosiniia cradling her dead son presents a key to grasping the films' relation to the earlier tradition in the representation of Ivan and to understanding their treatment of the disjuncture between individual experience and transcendent imperatives. Before further investigation of what this key unlocks in interpretation of the films, however, I briefly turn to consideration of the director's knowledge of the earlier works in question and of his thinking as he set to work on his Ivan project, to substantiate my suggestion that this shot not only resembles but actually refers to that prior tradition.

It hardly needs to be argued that Eisenstein was familiar with both Repin's painting and with Rimskii-Korsakov's *The Maid of Pskov*—these were canonical works that any educated member of the creative intelligentsia would have known. As is well documented, in preparation for his historical projects Eisenstein devoted an enormous amount of energy to the study of artifacts in museums, historiography, and relevant artistic images. During his reported visits to the Tretiakov Gallery in early 1941 as he prepared for the Ivan films, he undoubtedly spent time contemplating Repin's canvas.[59] Significantly, Repin's name came up several times in the director's early mass-press articles about the project. In April and May 1941, in articles in *Ogonek* and *Izvestiia*, Eisenstein announced that his film would correct the views of earlier historians and artists who had disparaged Ivan, singling out as polemical opponents, with all due respect, the achievements of "Antokolskii's chisel, Repin's brush, and A. K. Tolstoi's pen."[60]

The director's memoirs and unpublished materials provide further evidence of the importance of Repin's painting for the films. Some months before the press announcements cited above, on January 23, 1941, Eisenstein jotted in his private notebooks that "Repin's *Ivan* came to him under the influence of Rimskii-Korsakov's *Vengeance*." Clearly, the director was musing on Repin's canvas precisely as part of a tradition of interrelated representations.[61] He continued to think in these terms in the years to come: in the late summer of 1944, as he was editing the first Ivan film, he began an essay in which he cited at length the interview Repin had granted in the aftermath of Balashov's attack on the painting, in which the artist had linked inspiration for the work to Rimskii-Korsakov and the assassination of Alexander II. Significantly, Eisenstein's essay in general concerns the relation of Soviet film to the "iron arsenal" of the prerevolutionary cultural tradition that entered "our minds and hearts in childhood." As he explains immediately following his citation of Repin, the key to the power of Soviet art is not only "the October revolution, which [. . .] freed the intelligent mind, equipping it with the ultimate weapon for exposing secrets and lifting veils of agnosticism," but also "the fact that

---

59. See Iurenev, *Sergei Eizenshtein*, 2:211.
60. "Beseda s S. M. Eizenshteinom," *Ogonek*, May 15, 1941, 19; see also S. M. Eizenshtein, "Ivan Groznyi," *Izvestiia*, April 30, 1941, 3.
61. See Iurenev, *Sergei Eizenshtein*, 2:212.

the new generation [. . .] stood on the terra firma of Russian cultural traditions, an inexhaustible wealth of original and national talent."[62]

Eisenstein's archives include as well photos of Chaliapin in his signature role of Ivan the Terrible from *The Maid of Pskov*, at the end of which the great basso recreated the Repin canvas as a *tableau vivant* (see fig. 14).[63] There is no hard evidence that Eisenstein attended any performance of the opera by Chaliapin. However, at the conclusion of his work on Ivan in May 1946, the director noted that at some point in 1915 he had seen the silent film *Ivan the Terrible*, based on Rimskii-Korsakov's opera, in which Chaliapin again recreated Repin's painting in a long static shot (see fig. 15).

In brief, then, the available evidence confirms not only that Eisenstein was musing on Repin's canvas as he embarked on his Ivan project in 1941, but that the director had personally observed the tradition of interlinked representations of Ivan as a filicidal father to which the painting belonged. Moreover, he explicitly connected his thoughts on earlier representations to the question of his own relationship to the prerevolutionary tradition per se. Eisenstein's own climactic scene, then, should be seen as a self-conscious and deliberate response to Repin's painting and the series of other representations of the Terrible Tsar to which it belongs and a key to the response of these films to that earlier tradition generally.

In the 1944 essay mentioned above, Eisenstein misnames Repin's painting as *Ivan the Terrible Murdering His Child*.[64] As a member of "the new generation," what "secrets" did the director "expose," what "veils" did he "lift" in shaping his response to the prerevolutionary canon? To put the metapoetical and metahistorical implications of these questions plainly, how did Eisenstein challenge his cultural fathers on the topics of intergenerational violence, private pain and public goods, state imperatives and personal sacrifice? Any attempt to answer this question must first recognize that, for all the static qualities of the restaging of Repin's work in the scene of Efrosiniia's downfall, Eisenstein's use of the painting is filmic and dynamic, a pervasive figural citation that recurs several times in the course of part 2 of the project.

Let us examine some of these other shots. In the earliest portions of the film, Ivan recounts the trials of his orphaned youth at the hands of abusive and power-hungry courtiers. In a flashback sequence, Eisenstein shows the death of Ivan's mother, Elena, who has been poisoned. The young Ivan cradles her in his arms in the *Pietà* pose, as she warns him of the treachery of the boyars (fig. 19). Later, we see Efrosiniia, plotting to assassinate Ivan, holding her son Vladimir in her arms as she sings the lullaby she will reprise in the climactic scene (fig. 20). Then, at the royal banquet, Ivan in turn cradles Vladimir in a similar pose as he elicits the drunken Vladimir's foolishly frank admissions of the plot

62. S. M. Eisenstein [Eizenshtein], "Beyond the Stars," in his *Selected Works*, 4:346–47.
63. See Iurenev, *Sergei Eizenshtein*, 2:212.
64. Eisenstein [Eizenshtein], "Beyond the Stars," 4:346.

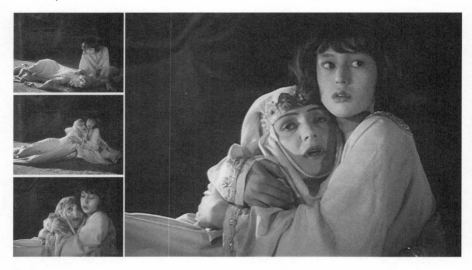

Figure 19: Ada Voitsik and Erik Pyrev as Elena Glinskaia and the young Ivan IV in Sergei Eisenstein's film *Ivan the Terrible*, part 2, 1944.

Figure 20: Serafima Birman and Pavel Kadochnikov as Efrosynia Staritskaia and Vladimir Staritskii in Sergei Eisenstein's film *Ivan the Terrible*, part 2, 1944.

to set him in Ivan's place (fig. 21). Finally, the film returns to the *Pietà* pose in the scene of Efrosiniia holding Vladimir's corpse (fig. 18).

Each of these shots shows an intergenerational pair from the ruling family in which the upright figure is responsible—in indirect manner related to the dynamics of royal power—for the death of the reclining one: Ivan's mother is killed *because* he is the tsar; Efrosiniia, as we have seen, unwittingly engineers

Figure 21: Nikolai Cherkasov and Pavel Kadochnikov as Ivan IV and Vladimir Staritskii in Sergei Eisenstein's film *Ivan the Terrible*, part two, 1944.

Vladimir's death in her hunger for power; and Ivan organizes Vladimir's death in his prescient substitution of fool for tsar. As other commentators have noted—even without reference to the Repin composition—the shots in question are linked to one another in various ways, both compositionally and interpretatively. Efrosiniia's two lullaby shots obviously mirror each other. The scene of Ivan's mother's death is a mirror image of the scene of Vladimir's death, up to the conclusion of the shot, at which point the corpse of Elena is dragged out of Ivan's arms to the left while the corpse of Vladimir is dragged out of Efrosiniia's grasp to the right.[65] Finally, one of Eisenstein's production sketches shows side by side the scene of Vladimir's admission as a mirror of the scene of Efrosiniia's plotting.[66] The stylized, posed quality of Eisenstein's use of the human figure in his later historical films is often noted. However, as this example demonstrates, for Eisenstein the pose was an element in a dynamic interrelation of shots. In short, in distinction from Petrov's arid "succession of poses" and "checklist of traits," Eisenstein creates his plot as an "organism" by means of a dispersed montage of related figural compositions.

In this montage of *tableaux vivants* we see the response of the new expressive potentials of film—as a plastic art across time—to the static limitations of

65. Tsivian, *Ivan the Terrible*, 78–79.
66. In Tsivian's account of the notations jotted on this sketch, the director viewed the congruence of the poses in these scenes and the positioning of Ivan above and behind Vladimir in the terms of Reichian psychoanalytic theories concerning bodily memory—and therefore as motivating Vladimir to "blurt out" the truth about the conspiracy to murder Ivan (*Ivan the Terrible*, 73–76).

previous media. Eisenstein's game is one of permutation and combination, variations on the fundamental motifs of Repin's work and of nineteenth-century dramatic representations of Ivan in general: tsaricide; the unintended or mediated filicidal parent; the ironic consequences of the violence of Russian autocracy and the challenge and hope of coordinating love of the state with private, individual affections. Note that the film picks up on many of the allegorical inconsistencies and surprises of Repin's historical painting: the pattern of unexpected substitutions and convergences of dead parents (Alexander II, Elena) with dead children (Tsarevich Ivan, Vladimir); the odd gender reversal of the painting, that equates Ivan with the Virgin Mary, which is repeated in Eisenstein's mix and match of genders in the four shots under discussion. Even in the last shot, where the gender distribution of the *Pietà* is reestablished, one must observe that Efrosiniia is a masculinized woman—a castrating mother rather than the Virgin Mother of God.

These variations on Repin's motif formulate an answer to the myth of history and power inherent in the earlier tradition of historical representation. In that tradition, reaching from Aleksei K. Tolstoi's *Death of Ivan the Terrible* forward through the many other operatic and stage representations to Chaliapin's performances of *The Maid of Pskov*, the figure of Ivan had been used to instruct audiences about an ancient cycle in which the powerful father inflicts a violent discipline on the weak children, yet in so doing ironically brings about his own downfall, the fall of his dynasty even, and unwittingly sets the conditions for the repetition of the same pattern—as Alexander III did with his violent response to unrest and revolutionary violence.

This is the tragic pattern of progressive reform or revolution achieved through coercion, which founds a new order on the very principles that it set out to overcome. As Repin's and Rimskii-Korsakov's works insist, the only way out of this tragic "anti-Oedipal" cycle is through repentance and redemption, rendering the dead a sacrificial double of Christ in the interests of familial and national salvation. To ignore this path is to risk perpetuating the "genetically encoded" pattern of autocratic violence and the national bloodshed that results from it.

Eisenstein's work offers a different resolution of historical myth, however. To be more precise, it presents a calculated equivocation between alternate readings of the Russian past—ultimately necessitating a sophisticated historical hermeneutics. The film's play with the *Pietà* composition can be interpreted as an orthodox Stalinist rewrite of the imperial myth of Ivan—akin to Petrov's transformation of Ge's painting but far more sophisticated in effect. The violence inflicted on Ivan as a child, both directly and indirectly through the murder of his mother, indeed pulls him into the pattern of intergenerational conflict that is his birthright. In his mature years, animated by his great progressive project, Ivan strikes back against the forces that once terrorized him. Yet these are powerful opponents, and Ivan is in danger of either falling victim to the violence he has unleashed or sinking into senselessly cruel despotism. Then, through his mystical ability to anticipate his own fate, Ivan sidesteps the cyclic logic of the bloodline, becoming in the climactic scene of part 2 neither victim nor perpetrator—blood flows around, and not through him.

The apologetic implications of this reading of Eisenstein's revision of Repin and the tradition to which he belonged are plain: Efrosiniia's betrayal leads inevitably to her downfall. Staritskii's death is justified by his participation in the conspiracy against Ivan and his progressive mission. In the past, and by analogy in the Stalinist present, violence constitutes a necessary and natural element of the age-old struggle for social progress; its victims are not sacrifices but vanquished enemies who are themselves responsible for their own condemnation and execution. This reading of the film resonates with the Soviet myth of revolution—envisioning a non-Christian transcendence of history made possible by the October revolution's leap outside of time. Ivan is a "historical hero," in precisely the terms Stalin used to explain Peter, Lenin, and himself to Ludwig in 1931: that rare individual who understands the forces of history and therefore can rise up and direct them into new paths. In Eisenstein's version, instead of being the unwitting conduit of history's violence, Ivan is its choreographer. His loneliness is the tragic isolation of the great man—one more sacrifice that Ivan must make to his great historical cause.

Yet this reading tells only half of the story. For one may just as certainly read Eisenstein's homage to the Repin painting not as a polemical response but as a respectful reference. Although the tsar is not himself the agent of murder, he is nevertheless morally culpable for Vladimir's death, which stands in for the many other deaths wrought by Ivan's revolution. By this reading, Ivan, who was a victim of reactionary violence in his youth and in part 1, learns the cruel lesson of the dependence of Russian greatness on mayhem in part 2 and shows his willingness to sacrifice anything and anyone to achieve grand ends. Yet in killing Vladimir, his blood relative and his double, Ivan has merely managed a "coverup" of his murder both of his own humanity and of his progressive goals—remember that Repin's painting, lurking beneath Eisenstein's frame, depicts Ivan's murder of his own son, Ivan, and of the future of the dynasty with him.

The moral of Efrosiniia's story may be that you can never know whom you are going to kill when you reach for ultimate power—perhaps it will turn out to be those whom you most love. And if Efrosiniia herself is villainous and unsympathetic, Vladimir is a lamb led to the slaughter—and a pretty compelling Christ figure, as the final *Pietà* shot stresses emphatically. In such a way, the myth of Christian repentance and redemption remains a powerful alternative to the revolutionary transcendence of history. This interpretation leads to the contrasting conclusion that Ivan's aspirations are deluded, that the mayhem of his reign is simply the transmission of the violence of the boyars who preceded him in power. Allegorically projected against Eisenstein's day, this reading of the film reveals the irrepressible resurgence of historical trauma, precisely at the moment when it was to have been transcended, echoing uncontrollably forward up to the Stalinist era, which is caught in a frozen gaze into an ancient mirror.

The tightly wound logic of each of these two readings corresponds to the widely contrasting responses and debates the films elicited from contemporaries and future commentators alike. This approach is the interpretative analogue to the "unity of opposites" in Eisenstein's image of Ivan—and it is most reminiscent of Pushkin's studied ambivalence in *The Bronze Horseman*. Yet Eisenstein's work, with its pointed intervention into the nineteeth-century tradition of representations of the Russian past, takes Pushkin's musings on the inconclusive nature of Petrine history to a deeper level of insight. The key to a synthetic interpretation of Eisenstein's films lies in approaching them not as a war between allegories but rather as a critique of historical allegory per se. Such an approach allows us to view the repeated deployments of the *Pietà* as more than a brilliant resolution of a technical challenge—that of creating a dynamic, filmic response to Repin's static image. They are also as a means to model the fluidity of historical truth as it itself devolves in time: each revision and reappearance of the image adds new momentum to a growing set of interpretational possibilities. According to this interpretation, Eisenstein's play on the *Pietà* is neither a reference nor a response to Repin's allegory but rather an evocation of the repeated *historical* deployments of Ivan and his dead children, who surface and resurface over the many works and decades of the cultural tradition to which both the painting and the films belong.

Eisenstein's films go beyond historical allegory to offer an allegory of historical allegory. They place Ivan's and Stalin's eras into allegorical equivalence while casting Eisenstein's use of this historical allegory into an allegorical equivalence with the uses of this "same" allegory by Chaliapin, Repin, Karamzin, and others. In addition to projecting the present as a repetition of the deep past, whether we see this repetition in the key of trauma or in the key of greatness, Eisenstein's work projects the present as a repetition of previous episodes of precisely this sort of historical allegorization. In so doing, the film offers a trenchant critique of Stalinist and imperial historical myth alike, reminding us that the two traditions are not so easy to separate after all. How many times can one call for a transcendence of history before repetition itself renders the futility of the project obvious? Eisenstein's allegory of historical allegory, in some sense, uncovers a sinkhole of irony similar to those glimpsed in earlier meditations on the self-defeating linkage of progress to coercion in Russian history of Aleksei K. Tolstoi, Repin, Rimskii-Korsakov, Merezhkovskii, and Miliukov. But even though these predecessors grasped this problematic of Russian history, they all fell prey to the hope that their own era would resolve the pattern in a final moment of historical transcendence or revolutionary conflagration—a hope that time and again proved illusory.

Eisenstein avoids this superordinate irony. As Pushkin had done in his *Bronze Horseman*, the Soviet director refuses to resolve his allegory of history: his Ivan is both despot and hero. And with his allegory of historical allegory he steps beyond Pushkin's precedent. By showing the embeddedness of historical allegory in its own history, he calls viewers to recognize that the Achilles' heel of any vision of history is the blindness of those who are trapped in human time, attempting to grasp the true meaning and consequences of their actions, the true significance of their own allegorical readings of their past and present, when these meanings are themselves temporary, historical constructs.[67] Just as in Eisenstein's account, Ivan's triumph over historical fate (or fall back into it) is uncertain, each allegorical restaging of Ivan's reign over the preceding century had called for a transcendence of the Russian history of terror and greatness that might just as easily be read, in retrospect, as a repetition of that violence, reiterated in the very act of disavowing a corrupt and unwanted past.

In this way, Eisenstein articulates an allegory for Stalinist historiography and the sins it inherited from its imperial predecessors—an allegory for chosen but disavowed trauma. Rather than mapping Ivan and his deeds onto those of present-day actors, the film maps Repin's placement in time onto Eisenstein's, which no longer lays claim to any exceptional status or special access to "objective" knowledge. Rather than being the mythic origin for an ancient pattern of either national heroism or trauma, Eisenstein's Ivan the Terrible has no "inner truth." Instead, he is the occasion for a history of allegories that since the nineteenth century has undergirded the Russian cultural tradition of terror and greatness, intertwined.

—m—

In 1946, only weeks after awarding Stalin Prizes to Aleksei N. Tolstoi and Vladimir A. Solovev for their works on Ivan and to Eisenstein for part 1 of his film project, the party's Central Committee banned the release of part 2.[68] This event marked the beginning of the end not only of the campaign to rehabilitate Ivan the Terrible but of most new attempts at revisionist history of the tsarist era in general. To be sure, no special effort would be made to dismantle the vision of history generated in the late 1930s until after Stalin's death, when Soviet educational curricula moved by gradual steps away from the primacy of the Shestakov textbook and when, more spectacularly, the "idealization of Ivan the Terrible" was denounced as a distorting reflection of Stalin's "cult of

---

67. By one classic account, the perpetual lapse between partial, temporal knowledge and "full" knowledge, or truth, lies at the base of all irony. See de Man, "Rhetoric of Temporality."

68. The Stalin Prizes for 1943–44 were publicly announced on January 27, 1946. Part 1 of *Ivan the Terrible* earned first prizes for Eisenstein, as well as for the film's lead actor Cherkasov, its composer Sergei Prokofev, and its cinematographers Andrei Moskvin and Eduard Tisse. A first prize also went to Tolstoi, posthumously. The prizes for 1945 were announced on June 29, 1946: Solovev won a second prize for his play, while its production at Tbilisi's Rustaveli Theater earned first prizes for its director Akakii Khorava and the actors Akakii Vasadze and Georgii Davitashvili. Kostylev and Selvinskii were also nominated but did not win prizes—see RGASPI, f. 17, op. 125, d. 399, ll. 1–11. For the banning of part 2 of *Ivan the Terrible*, see RGASPI, f. 17, op. 116, d. 249; Zhdanov's undated handwritten draft is at f. 77, op. 3, d. 179, ll. 73–75; Central Committee resolution of 4 September 1946 "O kinofil'me 'Bol'shaia zhizn'.'"

personality."[69] Yet suddenly, in the aftermath of the war, the heyday of film epics on great tsarist figures and mass-press campaigns celebrating their centenaries was over.

The causes of this shift were diverse. The scandal that engulfed Eisenstein may have focused awareness on the equivocal successes of revisionist history, and although there was some discussion of reshooting and completing the trilogy, Eisenstein's death in 1948 and the lack of enthusiasm for various proposed replacements foreclosed this possibility. The other titan of Stalinist history, Aleksei N. Tolstoi, had died in 1945, his novel on Peter still incomplete. Peter the Great himself came to be viewed in a less positive light as a result of postwar campaigns against western influence.[70] Perhaps more important were changes in the priorities of Soviet mobilizational propaganda and the sudden availability of a new and compelling source of historical myth: the sacrifices and heroism of the war itself, the primary source of rousing patriotic plots in literature, drama, and film for the remainder of the Soviet era.[71]

A commonplace in accounts of the banning of part 2 of Eisenstein's *Ivan the Terrible* is the assumption that Stalin and his lieutenants objected to the film's portrayal of Ivan's bloody elimination of his political opponents when what they had ordered up was a whitewash of the Terrible Tsar that could serve to suppress, by allegorical extension, the memory of contemporary excesses and executions. Nothing could be farther from the reality of this event or from the propagandistic priorities of an era that had for decades been awash with bloodshed. As Stalin explained in a well-documented interview with Eisenstein and Cherkasov in the wake of the banning of *Ivan the Terrible,* part 2, Ivan's fatal shortcoming was not his taste for violence but his restraint in not killing enough boyars.[72]

The official objection to the film was, in fact, that Ivan and his comrades-in-arms were not shown in sufficiently heroic light as they carried out the death sentences imposed by history itself. As Stalin informed the director and the actor: "Ivan the Terrible was very cruel. It is fine to show that he was cruel.

---

69. On the Shestakov textbook's demise, see Brandenberger, *National Bolshevism*, 251–60. For the "dethroning" of the Stalinist Ivan the Terrible, see Dubrovskii, "Protiv idealizatsii"; Kurmacheva, "Ob otsenke deiatel'nosti Ivana Groznogo"; and Sheviakov, "K voprosu ob oprichnine." On this episode, see "Iz dnevnikov Sergeia Sergeevicha Dmitrieva"; Sidorova, "Anna Mikhailovna Pankratova"; and the epilogue to Perrie, *Cult of Ivan the Terrible*, esp. 179–86.

70. See Stalin's disparaging reference to Peter in his conversation with Eisenstein and Cherkasov in 1946, reproduced in the third epigraph to Chapter 5 (B. N. Angarov, "Zapis' besedy," in Stalin, *Sochineniia*, 18:443–40, here 434).

71. Weiner, *Making Sense of War*, 7–39.

72. See Cherkasov, *Zapiski sovetskogo aktera*, 379–81; "Stalin, Molotov i Zhdanov o vtoroi serii fil'ma *Ivan Groznyi*: Zapis' Sergeia Eizenshteina i Nikolaia Cherkasova," *Moskovskie novosti*, August 7, 1988, 8; and Angarov, "Zapis' besedy."

But what is needed is to show why it is necessary to be cruel."[73] According to the party resolution of September 1946, Eisenstein had been guilty of "ignorance in his depiction of historical facts, presenting Ivan the Terrible's *oprichniki* as a band of degenerates along the lines of the American Ku Klux Klan, and Ivan the Terrible, a man of strong will and character, as weak and irresolute, like some sort of Hamlet."[74]

This resolution, which echoes what we know of Stalin's immediate reaction to the film and of the private discussions of the Soviet cultural establishment surrounding its banning, reveals that one of its chief flaws related not to what Eisenstein depicted of Ivan's tale but to his shaping of that tale as a tragedy. Here the campaign stumbled against a feature of the era's cultural works that the officials who oversaw the Ivan campaign had apparently failed to anticipate and foreclose: the tragic plot that was key to the Terrible Tsar's dramatic potential not only in Eisenstein's films but also in the commissioned dramatic works of Tolstoi, Solovev, and Selvinskii. In this respect, these Stalinist renditions of Ivan's story echoed the dramatic tradition of the imperial era, which almost without exception had represented Ivan as a tragic figure.

Most likely, the playwrights and filmmakers of Stalin's time did not fully think through this inheritance—accepting it as axiomatic for dramatic portrayals of the Terrible Tsar. Nevertheless, this tragic narrative diverged greatly from the romance story of battles won and progressive goals achieved that the party hierarchy had envisioned. In Shcherbakov's view, Ivan had "completed the establishment of a centralized Russian state, [. . . and] fundamentally eliminated the country's feudal fragmentation, successfully crushing the resistance of representatives of the feudal order." To tell such a tale as a tragedy was nothing short of a falsification of history.[75]

In short, the rehabilitations of Ivan and Peter and Stalinist historical revisionism as a whole foundered on the insurmountable difficulty of coordinating the campaign's many professional contexts and hermeneutic imperatives. This unprecedented, state-directed effort to resolve once and for all the significance of the Russian past instead gave rise to intractable interpretive flux. Intended to generate a monumental and inspiring official history, Stalinist revisionism bogged down in endless bickering among historians, cultural figures, and party authorities, who were powerless to reconcile or to adjudicate between myth and history,

---

73. "Stalin, Molotov i Zhdanov o vtoroi serii fil'ma *Ivan Groznyi*." Eisenstein was well aware of this interpretation of Ivan's violence as he worked on the film, putting similar thoughts to paper himself in 1945. See S. M. Eizenshtein, "Ivan Groznyi," in his *Izbrannye proizvedeniia*, 1:193.

74. "O kinofil'me *Bol'shaia zhizn'*," in *O partiinoi i sovetskoi pechati*, 575–76.

75. The discussion in this and the next paragraph is derived from mine and David Brandenberger's more extensive account of interprofessional and interinstitutional discoordination, drawing on Hayden White's model of metahistorical analysis, in our "Terribly Romantic." Also see White, *Metahistory*, 1–42.

allegory and dialectic, romance and tragedy. As we have seen, their debates derived from the campaign's more fundamental inconsistencies—from its antihistorical aspiration for interpretative finality given the essential openness of human
time, and from the cleavage between the campaign's stated ambitions and its social and psychic functionality. Ultimately, the Stalinist attempt to remake the
Imperial Russian myths of Ivan and Peter was but one more turn in the folding
and refolding of trauma within greatness, one more instrumental application of
the perverse functionality of liminal figures in the Russian mythology of history.

In the early nineteenth century, the submersion of the violence of Peter's
reign in the story of Russia's rise to imperial greatness masked but also depended on the significance of Petrine history as a site of chosen trauma. The
resulting, stridently triumphant historical myth fed off the psychic urgency of
disavowed pain, presenting a vision in which ancient wounds justify and demonstrate the necessity of present ones. Stalinist historical mythology illustrates
this same mechanism in its new iterations of the historical myths of both Peter
and Ivan, whose cruel and bloody reigns in the service of history's march forward were to offer Soviet men and women a plot for comprehending the violence and glory of the present. Just as in the nineteenth century, although this
strategy proved instrumentally effective, it retained at its base the interpretational irresolution of the liminal figure, which always admits of a reading in
which political and historical greatness is haunted by the trauma that supports
it. As Eisenstein's masterwork reveals, rediscovering in Ivan the implications
Pushkin had revealed in Peter a century earlier, too concerted a contemplation
of such a historical mythology in the end arrives at comprehension not only of
the resurgence of ancient pain in the very texts that were intended to erase it
but also of the ambivalence and indecipherability of Russian history, as represented in the works that were meant to pin it down, once and for all.

In a 1941 letter to Olga Freidenberg, Boris Pasternak remarked on the rise
of Ivan as a subject of Soviet historical myth: "To our benefactor [i.e., Stalin—
K.M.F.P.] it seems that up until now we have been too sentimental and that it
is time to come to our senses. Peter the Great no longer appears to be an appropriate parallel. The new enthusiasm, openly professed, is for the Terrible
Tsar, the *oprichnina*, and cruelty. New operas, plays, and film scripts are being
written on this topic. No joke."[76]

Pasternak's sarcasm is palpable. Yet the letter is striking for its restrained
expressive means: truly, all the poet is doing here is stating the obvious. In a
certain sense, something comparable may be said about Eisenstein's *Ivan the
Terrible*. Returning, for a moment, to the question of the director's possibly
subversive intent, one must question how effective a critique of Stalinism, per
se, his films can be said to have accomplished if that critique was so well camouflaged that it is still debated six decades later, after exhaustive archival research and elaborate interpretative maneuvers. At the same time, perhaps the

76. Pasternak, *Sobranie sochinenii*, 5:392.

key to the films' subversive potential is as simple as Pasternak's statement of the obvious. Truly, more than anything else, Eisenstein demonstrated that the insertion of a critique of Stalinism into the Soviet myth of Ivan the Terrible—or of Peter the Great, for that matter—was always already a *fait accompli*, ensured by the prehistory of representations of these figures and the interpretive implications of the campaign itself.

Here we may distinguish between Tolstoi's and Eisenstein's differing approaches to hermeneutic ambivalence. Whereas Tolstoi had used the slippage of tradition and revisionism from one representation to the next as a mechanism to conceal his own creative and political maneuvering, Eisenstein's work laid bare the entire tradition of revision and disavowal, the nested-doll construction of Russian representations of history. As the director shows, in the end, there was no need for a special articulation of critique, since it was an obvious and logical outcome of the deployment of Ivan and Peter as allegories for present leaders in the first place.

As Eisenstein's masterwork demonstrates, the attempt to overcome or erase past representations of history is futile: disavowal of historical trauma was itself at the base of the historical myth that the Soviet era inherited from the imperial. The Stalinist urge to transcendence was merely a hypertrophied version of imperatives inherent from the beginning in the Russian myth of greatness and terror intertwined. The ambition to forget the past gave rise, ironically, merely to its repetition. In retrospect, Pasternak's dry evocation of the irony of Stalin's "passion" for Ivan represents not only the private thoughts of many informed members of the Soviet elite in the 1930s and 1940s. It also captures the angle of vision of all who came after Stalinism or viewed it from afar: later generations of Soviets and Russians as well as foreign observers who could not but remark on the irony of Stalin's attachment to the tsars, and to these tsars in particular.

In retrospect, it is clear that the Ivan campaign in particular was guilty of the most egregious oversights regarding history's own placement in history. The Stalinist cult of Peter the Great has been indicted for misappropriating the first emperor's historical myth, but things are not so simple with the Stalinist Ivan. In imperial historical myth a vision of Ivan as a cruel despot had predominated. As a result, his Stalinist apotheosis as a visionary, heroic leader served both to demonstrate the error of imperial commentators and to achieve current propagandistic goals. Yet for this very reason, it became in subsequent decades a favorite piece of evidence for critics of Soviet history and the Stalinist legacy of all stripes—a pithy means to demonstrate that Stalin, who had endorsed the campaign, was therefore by his own admission as monstrous as his sixteenth-century forebear. This stock irony of Stalinist history appears in works from Alexander Yanov, who wrote that "given all his ignorance of Russian history, Stalin nevertheless, intuitively yet completely correctly identified among the multitude of Russian tsars his historical doubles,"[77] to Robert

---

77. Yanov [Ianov], *Ten' groznogo tsaria*, 174.

Tucker, who wrote that the Terrible Tsar had served Stalin as a "role model" in the Great Purge.[78] In the end, blinded by historiographical hubris, Stalinist revisionism, which sought to create an apologetic myth of collective greatness, instead forged a hackneyed tool for the critique of Stalinism as a resurgence of ancient Russian terror.

78. Tucker, *Stalin in Power*, 7, 52, 319–22, 481–86, 557.

Redux

Our country is divided between state and subjects, which is to say that the people is not identified with the state. The state is a separate machine, a sort of idol, to which one must pray and in the name of which one must sacrifice oneself. It seems to me that it was precisely the *oprichnina* that played the leading role in the formation of such a state structure in the national consciousness. The *oprichnina* was a very fateful and very Russian phenomenon.

—Vladimir Sorokin, in an interview concerning his novella
A Day in the Life of an Oprichnik, 2007

4.4 Who stands at the head of the Russian state?
Students are asked to look at the portraits of heads of state and think about their contributions to the development of the state. (Ivan IV, Peter I, V. V. Putin)
Students offer their responses. (Ivan IV was the first Russian tsar; Peter I was the first Russian Emperor; V. V. Putin is the current president of Russia.)

—A. E. Kambulova, excerpt from a lesson plan for
Russian fourth-graders, 2004

—Interviewer: In your view, the specter of Ivan the Terrible is growing more distant from us. But many, in contrast, are dreaming of the rise to power of a contemporary analogue who could gather together again everything that fell apart or was destroyed in the years of reform. For, as historians confirm, it was precisely in the Terrible Tsar's day that the principality of Moscow was transformed into the state of Muscovy.
—Lungin: This is one of the secrets of Rus. All of them—all the dictators, each one who is tied in one way or another with violence and who poured out a sea of his own people's blood—are for Russia the objects of a strange, somewhat masochistic love.

—Interview with Pavel Lungin about his film *Tsar*, 2008

In 1998, a curious little soft-cover book was published in Moscow, bearing two separate titles and the names of two authors. The titles, however, were identical: *Ivan the Terrible* (Ivan Groznyi). This was a joint reprint edition in one volume of two monographs on the Terrible Tsar, both of them written in the 1920s, by the historians Robert Iu. Vipper and Sergei F. Platonov. In many ways, this volume's appearance in the late 1990s is symptomatic of the continuing dynamism up to the present day of the complex of historical myth and political and cultural life described in this book, as well as of its continuing potential for unforeseen transformations in new circumstances. Let us briefly retrace the history of Vipper's *Ivan the Terrible*. This work, perhaps the most effusively celebratory history of Ivan ever written, elicited an impossibly broad range of responses when it was first published in 1922: did it express anti-Bolshevik nostalgia for tsarism's absolute law and order (the most likely reading), or was it an allegorical eulogy to revolutionary culture and bloody methods of social transformation? In any case, Vipper himself was no Bolshevik insider, and he emigrated to Riga in independent Latvia in the 1920s. During the 1930s, however, the historian came to view the Soviet state as a legitimate successor to the tsarist empire.[1] When Soviet troops annexed Latvia in 1940, Vipper was morally prepared to be drafted into state service, inducted into the Academy of Sciences, and set to work as a leading authority on the Russian past. In a startling reversal of interpretive fortune, his monograph had now come to seem monumentally solid in its allegorical projection of Ivan and his deeds as mythic protoimages of the leaders of Stalinist society and their triumphs. Vipper's book, in new editions, as well as his lectures and articles, became centerpieces of the campaign to rehabilitate the Terrible Tsar as the great predecessor of the Soviet leadership.

Vipper died in 1954, a year after the death of his patron, Stalin. A coordinated critique of the "idealization" of Ivan the Terrible in 1956 dethroned his views, seemingly for good.[2] In subsequent decades, his work on Ivan was largely forgotten, referenced as an example of Stalinist distortions of history only in dissident circles and in the west (and finally in the USSR during the glasnost era).[3] Fast-forward to the post-Soviet era, and Vipper's monograph resurfaces alongside the work of his almost exact contemporary, Platonov. Produced by the house press of the University of the Russian Academy of Education, the publisher's blurb advertised it as material suitable "for undergraduates and advanced elementary-school students, as well as for all those interested in the history of the fatherland."[4] In his introduction, the historian Dmitrii Volodikhin, the volume's editor, described the two monographs as divergent but equally valid interpretations of Ivan. Vipper's monograph was reprinted from its first edition, and Volodikhin gave almost no hint of the Stalinist history of the book and its author, informing readers that both Vipper and Platonov were Russian patriots opposed to the Soviet regime. Vipper, the reader learns, was forced to

1. Such positions were common among émigré Russian intellectuals and characteristic of members of the Change-of-Landmarks and Eurasianist movements. See Raeff, *Russia Abroad*, 84–85; and Hardemann, *Coming to Terms with the Soviet Regime*.

2. See Dubrovskii, "Protiv idealizatsii"; and Kurmacheva, "Ob otsenke deiatel'nosti Ivana Groznogo."

3. See, for instance, the dissident émigré journalist Alexander Yanov's remarks on Vipper in his *Origins of Autocracy*, 291–98. For glasnost discussions of Vipper, see Kobrin, *Ivan Groznyi*, 9–10.

4. Front matter of Vipper, "Ivan Groznyi," in *Ivan Groznyi: 1530–1584/Ivan Groznyi*, 2.

flee the country in 1924; and Platonov perished after his arrest and exile to Samara at the end of the 1920s.[5]

These few details are already enough to make this publication's peculiarity plain. From what vantage point, one wonders, did this foundational text of the Stalinist Ivan campaign appear "suitable" for schoolchildren in 1998? And anyhow, the notion that the two works wield equivalent authority is preposterous. Platonov's interpretation of Ivan IV was founded on a long career of research in late premodern Russian history. Although some specialists dispute his fundamental claim that Ivan should be seen as a rational (albeit cruel) political actor, Platonov's work undoubtedly contributed to the contemporary historiographic consensus on the Terrible Tsar.[6] Vipper, in contrast, was writing outside his area of specialization and in a tradition of historical interpretation that after the Stalin era was completely discredited. Platonov himself, comparing his own monograph to Vipper's in 1928, more or less panned his contemporary's work: "Vipper's book is not only an apology for the Terrible Tsar but his apotheosis. In contrast, I take Ivan in his local, national significance and strive to establish the true and actual features of his personality and activity, in as much as they are revealed by the sum of reliable sources."[7] Nevertheless, in 1998, for some, all these historical and professional contexts could be overlooked or forgotten to grant Vipper's work a lease on interpretive authority for a new reading public. And in a final chapter in this story of memory, forgetting and re-membering, as the taboo on the legacy of the Stalin era has faded in

---

5. Volodikhin mentions Vipper's triumphal return to Moscow on the eve of World War II only in a footnote, reporting that the monograph "was reprinted in 1942 and 1944 with substantial revisions in the spirit of the analogy of the two cults of personality—of Ivan the Terrible and I. V. Stalin"—a statement that suggests that Vipper himself had nothing to do with the republication of his book and might lead an uninformed reader (e.g., the high-school students for whom the book is intended) to conclude that its second and third editions articulated a *critique* of Stalin, rather than a eulogy. Volodikhin's revision of Vipper's biography reflects a trend in republications of his works during the 1990s, which framed the historian's writings as a rediscovered treasure of prerevolutionary culture. For instance, the preface to a 1997 edition of Vipper's textbook *Modern History* (Istoriia Novogo vremeni) proclaims that the volume is a first reprinting for "more than seventy years" and that Vipper's name has, "unfortunately, been unknown for many years to a wider audience." No mention is made of the mass audience he enjoyed in the 1940s. See "Ot redaktsii," in R. Iu. Vipper, *Istoriia Novogo vremeni: Uchebnoe posobie*, 3. Volodikhin is the prime mover in a veritable cottage industry of publications concerning Vipper—including not only the reprint edition of his *Ivan the Terrible* but also an article in a leading Russian historical journal and a monograph—all of which appear to take as their goal the task of transforming Vipper back into a Great *Russian* historian and of raising up his work on Ivan as the culmination of his profound historical thought. See Volodikhin, *Ochen' staryi akademik*; and Volodikhin, "Kritika teorii progressa."

6. For an assessment of the scholarly authority of Platonov's work on Ivan the Terrible, see Hellie, "In Search of Ivan the Terrible."

7. Platonov, "Aftobiograficheskaia zapiska," 285–86. Platonov, one imagines, would hardly consent to a joint publication of the two works.

more recent years, the suppression of Vipper's Stalinist past has become irrelevant: the 1944 edition of the work is now freely available as an electronic resource on an Internet site devoted to military history.[8] As the century-long story
of the interpretation and reinterpretation of Vipper's monograph illustrates, one
good rehabilitation sometimes demands another.

The post-Soviet republication of Vipper's *Ivan the Terrible* demonstrates once
again the complex imbrication of history, trauma, memory, and forgetting in
modern Russia. Volodikhin and his publishers likely comprehend their undertaking as an effort to correct the abuses of Stalinism—an attempt to overcome
the trauma of twentieth-century history. Certainly, they may reason, Vipper's
monograph, in its original edition, cannot be accused of complicity in the evils of
the Bolshevik regime—how could it be, when the historian was apparently writing against this very regime and was coopted by it only twenty years later? If
Stalin and his henchmen abused a defenseless and aged academic by transforming him into their spokesman, this cannot compromise the original value of his
works. Here the situation regarding Vipper's entanglement in Stalinism mirrors
the more familiar cases of other nineteenth- and twentieth-century cultural figures who were either adopted or coopted by the Stalinist and Nazi regimes—
Nietzsche, Wagner, Heidegger, Gorkii, de Man, and so on. Yet the interpretive
challenges presented by such figures are magnified in Vipper's case, in which an
effort to promulgate a purportedly valid representation of the past is itself predicated on a nontrivial falsification of history, and in which an attempt to overcome historical trauma involves forgetting rather than memory.

In fact, this latest refashioning of Vipper from a Stalinist historian into an
Imperial Russian one in many ways retraces the path marked out by his first,
Stalinist retrofitting. Both episodes were, in essence, efforts to redeploy a vision of Russian history while effacing the history of that very historical vision.
Both recover a triumphal version of the Russian past by burying a traumatic
one. In the case of Vipper's latest rehabilitation, the basic irony of this dependence of memory on forgetting, of greatness on the disavowal of terror, is dou-
bled, for Vipper's most recent handlers erased not only a given portion of the
historian's biography but previous and different episodes of erasure. And ultimately, one must not forget that this ironic double erasure of history was in
the service of the multiple rehabilitations of another traumatic figure, that of
Ivan the Terrible—a process that is pulled out into a sea of irony by a parallel
undertow of fabrications in the service of "truth." One recalls Renan's oft-quoted
remark: "For the essence of the nation is that all its members hold many things
in common, but also that they have all forgotten many things."[9] In the Russian
case, one may add: several times over. At the same time, these acts of dis-

---

8. The site is "Voennaia literatura," at http://militera.lib.ru. Vipper's book is republished
at http://militera.lib.ru/bio/vipper_ru/index.html (accessed December 15, 2009).

9. Ernest Renan, "Qu'est-ce qu'une nation?" in his *Oeuvres Complètes*, 1:887–906,
here 892.

avowal vividly exemplify how each time a "given" representation of the past comes to the fore in public discourse, it is substantially new, by virtue not only of its novel ideological context but also by virtue of its peculiar encrustation with prior contextual meaning, its own past, that grows thicker each time the book is cited, read, circulated from the library.

In his novel *The History of the Siege of Lisbon*, Jose Saramago remarks that the norms of historical truth are "founded on consensus and authority, although it is obvious that any change in authority is reflected in a corresponding change in consensus."[10] The tricky bit here is the relationship—"reflection," Saramago calls it—which ties together authority and historiographical consensus, and the further linkage of this dyad to the constitution of historical truth. As Vipper's case reminds us yet again, there is perhaps no better natural laboratory for work on these problems than the history of representation and interpretation of Ivan the Terrible and Peter the Great in Russia. As my study shows, Russia's complex history of changing authorities and consensuses has driven the representation of these figures, their "truths," from one extreme to another, as schools of historiography, political generations, and regimes have risen and fallen. The "reflective" relationship linking successive representations of these figures—historiographic, allegorical, or mythic—to the consensuses and purposes that they have been made to serve has been multiply mediated: by the institutions that have articulated them, by state efforts at cultural management, by artistic and literary invention and possibility, and by the dynamics of a collective identity based in trauma—its witnessing and overcoming and/or its disavowal and reinscription.

Finally, each of these mediating contexts has itself been mediated by its own history of becoming—the history of genres, of political generations or of institutional development. The representation of history is embedded in the history of representation, so that each "new" vision of Ivan or Peter has contributed to a growing, unstable system of meaning accreted around these figures—a growing history of voice and clamor—of debate, competition, dialogue, and miscommunication across time. It is perhaps an obvious truth that every successive generation, historian, political leader, and artist adopts some stance toward history—even if it is one of rejection or inattention. Perhaps more subtle is the insight that they also necessarily stand in some definite relation to history's own history—ranging from self-conscious inheritance and redeployment of past historiographical traditions to quixotic efforts to break free from history's own history or step outside of its stream and sophisticated attempts to model or manage the ironic dependence of historical knowledge on the passage of time.

It may be that this last, the attempt to manage the imbrication of history in its own historical becoming, is the best one can hope for. For recognition of the low place of historical knowledge, mired in its own history, cannot arrest

10. Saramago, *History of the Siege of Lisbon*, 267.

the unending accumulation of signification around historical figures, poses, and events. As we have seen, this process of accumulation grants some visions of the past unforeseen roles in future cultural and political contexts—Ge's vision of Peter, critiqued in Repin's representation of Ivan, then turned on its head in Aleksei N. Tolstoi and Petrov's film, and echoing once more in Eisenstein's revision of Repin's figural composition; Kavelin's vision of Ivan the state builder, startlingly reflected in Stalinist historiography and then rendered, ironically, as "evidence" in later anti-Stalinist critiques; and Vipper's study of Ivan, which has been cardinally reinterpreted to suit changing ideological contexts (twice and counting). In other cases, the dependence of historical "truths" on the accrual or management of past "truths" has granted long-term cultural significance precisely to those works that deflate historical meaning in general by means of a critique of their overburdened, overdetermined historical objects, such as Pushkin's *Bronze Horseman* or Eisenstein's *Ivan the Terrible*.

This highly inflected, unpredictable feedback loop between the representation of the past and the history of the representation of the past has left its mark on the core of significances associated with these two rulers—the amalgam of contradictory meanings that supports their function as condensation points for collective identity. Celebrated from at least the beginning of the nineteenth century as liminal figures, symbolic of epochal and institutional transformation of one idea of Russia into another, therefore susceptible to interpretations ranging from the traumatic to the heroic, the convoluted history of use and reuse of these figures, of attempts to erase or supersede trauma with a story of heroic greatness, has embedded the psychic urgency of trauma into the civic celebration of heroic patriotism and the luster of greatness into submission to an inscrutable victimhood. The resulting complex of meanings has contributed to formulations of collective and national identity in which greatness is predicated on the paradoxical conjunction of memorialization and disavowal of state violence and on the infliction of a violent discipline on the self. History has become dependent most of all on forgetting, and collective trauma appears as a mythically fated path to national greatness. Ultimately, the inscription and reinscription of Ivan and Peter has made them supremely versatile myths, an indispensable symbolic reserve for every occasion and political initiative but a supremely unstable one. These myths have the potential to signal precisely the opposite of what those who attempt to deploy them intend.

—⁊⁊⁊—

As the case of Vipper's many afterlives indicates, the story I have told does not come to an end following Stalin's death in 1953, the renunciation of the "idealization" of Ivan and the fading of the Stalinist historiography of Peter. Although a thoroughgoing account of these figures' significance in the later Soviet and post-Soviet periods lies beyond the scope of this book, I conclude with a quick sketch of subsequent developments. Despite the fading of the Stalinist Ivan and Peter from cultic prominence, the historical mythmaking of the 1930s and 1940s left the significance of these figures radically altered for later Soviet generations. Both in cases that enact a forgetfulness of the Stalinist legacy and in contrasting cases that accept and investigate this legacy, the allegorical linkage of the events and figures of the Russian national past to those of the twentieth century remains a looming interpretive context. This is especially the case with Ivan, the linkage of whose name to Stalin's has become nearly proverbial in accounts of despotic rulers of Russia. How, indeed, could one invoke Ivan or Peter in any context in the decades after Stalin's death without raising the Soviet leader's specter? Yet it should also be said that the cultural life and historiography of the late Soviet period largely attempted to do just that, reflecting the imperative to disavow the Stalinist past. Professional historical scholarship, free of the overt weight of the mobilizational campaigns of the 1930s and 1940s, conducted forays into the history of Ivan and Peter that in general declined to recognize their mythic significance.[11] Only occasionally, the public discourse and cultural life of the late Soviet era self-consciously exploited the allegorical potential of the two figures: Peter the Great appeared as a tool to stoke submerged if tacitly encouraged, Russian nationalist sentiments in the 1970s; Ivan the Terrible cropped up intermittently as a vehicle for Aesopean critiques of Stalinism.[12]

The exception to the general rule of silence was émigré writing of the period, which insistently reminded audiences that Stalin was a "self-conscious" heir to the mayhem and terror of Ivan and Peter. During the perestroika reforms of the late 1980s and the first post-Soviet years, however, a number of works of professional history took off the hermeneutic gloves and enlisted the two figures in rethinking Russian and Soviet political history. Prominent examples of the "return of the repressed" during these years include Evgenii Anisimov's popularizing monographs on Peter and Vladimir Kobrin's and Ruslan Skrynnikov's on Ivan, which used their distant eras as springboards for strident critique of Russia's traditions of progress through coercion, with overt allegorical reference to the Soviet history of revolution and social engineering.[13] Anisimov, in the introduction to a 1989 volume, baldly pronounced Peter's era to be the "apotheosis of etatism" and the "moment of the founding of totalitarian society" that Russians must now renounce: "To realize reforms conceived on bases other than those of Peter, let us look back once again at the

---

11. See, for example, Zimin, *Oprichnina Ivana Groznogo*, 479.

12. Regarding Peter's resonance in late Soviet nationalist circles, consider, for example, Viktor Chalmaev's characterizations of him in his manifesto ("Filosofiia patriotizma"). Examples of Ivan's late Soviet resonance include the discussions of Eisenstein's film among the characters of Aleksandr I. Solzhenitsyn's *One Day in the Life of Ivan Denisovich* (Odin den' Ivana Denisovicha, 1962), which serve to broadcast the character's relationships to Stalin and Stalinism more generally, and Iurii N. Grigorovich's ballet *Ivan the Terrible* (Ivan Groznyi, 1975), based on Prokofev's music for Eisenstein's film, which was widely viewed as an apology for Stalin.

13. Anisimov, *Vremia petrovskikh reform*; Skrynnikov, *Tsarstvo terrora*; Kobrin, *Ivan Groznyi*.

gigantic figure of Russia's great reformer, looming in the past, so that we may learn once and for all the lessons he taught us."[14] Kobrin, in his 1989 book *Ivan the Terrible*, devotes his conclusion to a discussion of the Stalin-era cult of Ivan, noting, "even if parallels between Ivan and Stalin are inappropriate, the responsibility for their appearance lies not with publicists and historians but with Stalin himself, who insistently propagandized the Terrible Tsar as an example for emulation." This allows Kobrin to conclude that "taking Ivan as a case study, one may study certain common specificities of the mechanism of personal power," applicable to both Stalin and his sixteenth-century predecessor.[15] Similarly, the first line of Skrynnikov's 1992 *Kingdom of Terror* (Tsarstvo terrora) ensured that readers would not miss his title's allegorical resonance with the Stalinist past: "In the history of Russia, profound social crisis and unsuccessful reforms have many times been followed by periods of bloody terror. Ivan IV, called 'the Terrible,' was the first Russian leader to use terror as a method of rule."[16]

Yet ultimately, this late burst of Stalinist historical myth, turned inside out, did not prove definitive for the post-Soviet historical imagination. Some circles of post-Soviet historical scholarship maintained the largely critical approach to Ivan and Peter and their eras signaled, for instance, in Anisimov's formula "progress through coercion," while backing away from these historians' overt, anachronistic projection of Russia's early modern legacy into its more recent past and present.[17] Yet Anisimov's and Skrynnikov's efforts to support a new liberal consensus with critical antimyths of Ivan, Peter, and Stalin ultimately had no real success in Russian political discourse or public life. The dominant metaphors governing the historical consciousness of the early to mid-1990s cast the Soviet years as a disastrous renunciation of tsarist politics, society, and culture and saw the post-Soviet era as the scene of the "undoing" or "reversal" of the distortions and anomalies of the preceding seventy years. In this light, it is perhaps unsurprising that the political establishment of the Russian Federation was from the start inclined to view the tsars, and especially Peter, as one of its primary symbolic resources, capable of granting to the new state the legitimacy and gravitas that only a glorious history can endow. Just to mention a few examples, Yeltsin was regularly granted the moniker "Boris the First" in the press; Moscow Mayor Iurii Luzhkov backed the erection of a monstrous, celebratory maritime monument to Peter I on the banks of the Moscow River in 1996; and Prime Minister Viktor Chernomyrdin addressed the Parliament of the Netherlands on the tercentennial of Peter the Great's diplomatic mission to Europe in 1997, announcing that he strove to "learn from Peter," whose

14. Anisimov, *Vremia petrovskikh reform*, 11–14.

15. Kobrin, *Ivan Groznyi*, 159–66, here 163.

16. Skrynnikov, *Tsarstvo terrora*, 5. In the same vein, the first line of chapter 1 uses a term commonly applied to the Stalinist period with reference to Ivan's: the "Great Terror of the sixteenth century."

17. For a review of recent work on Peter, see Zitser, "Post-Soviet Peter." Besides works by American historians, Zitser reviews works by D. M. Serov and V. M. Zhivov.

reforms were clearly justified, for they allowed Russia to "overcome autarky" and "to establish its geopolitical priorities from the Baltic to the Black Sea, to engage as an active and equal participant in all of Europe's affairs."[18] The general aspiration to erase or reach past the Soviet era, to return like a prodigal son to a tsarist fold, led to a different fate for Ivan, who largely dropped from view—as unwelcome in Russia's first generation of post-Soviet reformers' genealogy of power as he had been in the Romanovs'. The few exceptions include a postage stamp issued in 1997 as part of the commemoration of the founding of Moscow (fig. 22), as well as some indications of communist politicians' continuing attachment to the Terrible Tsar—for instance, their evocation of his supposedly red battle standards as part of a rationale for the readoption of the red flag during a 1997 Duma debate.[19]

Nevertheless, we should also note that the official political establishment was rather incoherent and halting in its mobilization of history during the first post-Soviet decade.[20] Furthermore, political discourse was far from the most productive site of historical representation during the 1990s. As the weight of state oversight lifted from a rapidly privatizing publishing industry and from research and educational institutions, a flood of publications on iconic eras and names of the Russian past, including Ivan and Peter, swept over Russian readers. Reminiscent of the historiographical climate of the 1920s, the political and institutional conditions of the 1990s initiated a new "open season" on Ivan and Peter that allowed for a proliferation of competing images, myths and allegories but also enormous interpretational looseness. In distinction from that earlier period, however, the most prominent representations of the Russian national past of the 1990s consisted of republications of the classics of historiography and historical fiction. This is the context that brought about the joint reprint edition of Vipper's and Platonov's monographs—conflicting interpretations of the Terrible Tsar that together signal precisely the combination of mythic, allegorical potential and hermeneutic incoherence that had characterized the reception of Vipper's book in the 1920s.

In the early post-Soviet years, Russian publishers, in a rush to derive profit from the tsarist past's renewed luster, printed anything they could lay their hands on in cheap editions, often lacking in even the most elementary commentary or critique. As a result, shoppers could find the works of classic Soviet authors like Aleksei N. Tolstoi and the works of his imperial predecessor Aleksei K. Tolstoi side by side on the shelves of bookstores or bound into a single volume—suspended, as it were, in an informational vacuum and a collapse of

18. Vladimir Abarinov, "Sud'by zapadnichestva v Rossii skladyvaetsia neprosto," *Russkii telegraf*, October 4, 1997, 3.

19. See Petr Zhuravlev, "Khochu nazad serpok i molotok," *Itogi*, April 8, 1997, 17–18.

20. Consider, for instance, the failed project to formulate a "Russian national idea" in the mid-1990s or the drawn-out debates concerning symbols of state and the hymn of the Russian Federation. See Smith, *Mythmaking in the New Russia*, 160–61, 181–84; and Daughtry, "Russia's New Anthem."

chronology.[21] Beyond the bookstores, the iconic significance of Ivan and Peter cropped up in other novel discursive arenas. Peter the Great's name and likeness graced chocolate bars, boxes of tea, and no fewer than three brands of cigarettes (fig. 23). Ivan found himself on the label of "Tsar Ivan" vodka—advertisements asked: "Why not lose your head?" (fig. 24).

Most surprisingly, in the late 1990s Russia witnessed a religious revival that called for the canonization of Ivan the Terrible as an Orthodox saint.[22] If, as I have proposed, the history of history unfolds as an accumulation of competing and inter-

21. Consider, for example, the numerous series pumped out by the Moscow publishing house Armada in the late 1990s, including hundreds of classic and forgotten novels under the rubrics "History in Novels," "The Time of Troubles," "The Romanovs," "Allies and Favorites," "Russian Generals," "Leaders of Russia," etc.

22. The most important historical statement connected with the canonization movement was published by Metropolitan Ioann of St. Petersburg and Ladoga, the proponent of an extreme religious nationalism. Among other things, he explained that "the *oprichnina* was a tool by means of which the tsar winnowed the entirety of Russian life, the whole of Russia's order and mode, separating out the good seeds of the Russian Orthodox spiritual community and great-power statehood from the chaff of heretical sophistry, perversity in morals, and forgetfulness of religious duty" (Snychev, *Samoderzhavie dukha*, 151). The church hierarchy quashed the canonization movement in 2004.

Figure 22: Stamp commemorating the 850th anniversary of the founding of Moscow in 1997, depicting the crowning of Ivan IV as tsar.

Figure 23: Tea, cigarettes, and chocolate bearing Peter the Great's name and image, mid-1990s. Author photo.

related images, representations, and interpretations, the 1990s magnified the resulting hermeneutic complexity to the point of white noise, in which the iconic figures of Russia's past meant everything to everybody, or perhaps nothing definite at all. In spite of the continuing potential for significance demonstrated in these many appearances of Ivan and Peter, the extraordinary profusion of divergent redactions of their myths leads one to wonder whether their capacity for symbolic meaning may simply be buried under an excess of conflicting significances or worn away like a coin that has passed through too many hands.

The answer, I think, is no. Quite to the contrary, the cacophony of diverse and contradictory historical visions of the 1990s illustrates the extent to which the representation of national pasts is a conservative process that preserves long-dead voices, seemingly defunct interpretive positions, and obsolete formulations of collective identity alongside novel and innovative stances. Historians are used to considering the development of historical knowledge as a linear process, in which better information and more refined techniques lead toward ever more precise and interpretively sound comprehensions of the past. But outside the discipline of historiography, modern cultural life and its institutions—libraries, literary canons, performance repertoires, museums, and commercial trademarks—are like time capsules that allow for the reanimation and reappearance of obsolescent visions of the past when least expected.

Recent events efficiently demonstrate this point and show the undiminished capacity for political and cultural significance remaining in the mechanisms of historical memory and collective identity described in this book. With the

Figure 24: Advertisement for "Tsar Ivan" vodka in
Moscow, 1997. The caption asks "Why not lose your
head?" Author photo.

turn of the new century the chaos that had characterized Russian political
life and historical consciousness in the immediate post-Soviet years began to
fade. Beginning in 2003, the Putin administration made concerted efforts to
bring representation of history in the Russian Federation under tighter political control, with the stated goal of reducing the interpretational flux of preceding years to turn Russian and Soviet history into a basis for patriotic
sentiment. As Putin explained at a meeting with history educators in 2003:
"Contemporary textbooks for schools and institutions of higher education
must not become a stage for new political and ideological battles. The facts
of history should be related in these textbooks. They should foster a sense of
pride in one's history, in one's country."[23] The history of the twentieth century and of the very recent past has been at the center of official attention:
one of the first fruits of the Kremlin's renewed interest in actively managing his-

23. "Putin: shkol'nye uchebniki—ne ploshchadka dlia politicheskoi bor'by, s istorii 'nado
sniat' vsiu shelukhu i penu,'" www.newsru.com (originally published November 27, 2003;
accessed August 24, 2007).

tory was the banning from schools of a textbook of twentieth-century history that reproduced characterizations of Russia under Putin as a "police state."[24]

These processes have gone far beyond such straightforward political infighting. Putin's statements on history have called for a more "uplifting" interpretation of Russian and Soviet history as a whole: "At a certain point, historians were emphasizing the negative, in keeping with the task of destroying the previous system. But now we have a different, constructive task."[25] Voicing what is perhaps the official view of these matters, the Kremlin insider Gleb Pavlovskii has called for a concerted public relations effort to create a positive politics of memory for Russia.[26] The Medvedev administration has continued in the footsteps of Putin, with the adoption in May 2009 of a presidential decree coordinating efforts at a variety of levels to "counteract falsifications of history that are detrimental to the interests of Russia."[27]

Since 2003, the Ministry of Education has repeatedly called for textbooks that fulfill the "new task" of inculcating patriotism and has urged teachers to "emphasize the positive" in the national past. Some teachers have responded with lessons that return not only to Peter the Great but to Ivan the Terrible as well the status of heroic leadership and lofty precedent that they have not enjoyed together for fifty years.[28] A sample lesson plan, submitted to a teachers' conference in Moscow in 2007, calls for a child to dress up as Ivan and recite the following doggerel (of the teacher's own composition):

I ruled Russia for a long time.
And obstinately fought with enemies.
I carried out the reforms of the Select Council
Which did not please all of the common people.
But I always defended Russia's independence.
Which is why I will remain forever in your hearts.

Following this performance, other children dressed as Peter the Great, Boris Yeltsin, and Vladimir Putin offer similarly inspiring readings.[29] At a 2007 con-

24. The textbook in question was Dolutskii, *Otechestvennaia istoriia.* This work was first published in 1994 in a single volume—this edition was an expanded, two-volume version.

25. "Putin: shkol'nye uchebniki—ne ploshchadka."

26. See Pavlovskii's article, "Plokho s pamiat'iu—plokho s politikoi," *Russkii zhurnal,* December 9, 2008, http://russ.ru/pole/Ploho-s-pamyat-yu-ploho-s-politikoj (accessed December 10, 2009).

27. "Ukaz Prezidenta Rossiiskoi Federatsii ot 15 maia 2009g. no. 549 'O Komissii pri Prezidente Rossiiskoi Federatsii po protivodeistviiu popytkam fal'sifikatsii istorii v ushcherb interesam Rossii," www.rg.ru/2009/05/20/komissia-dok.html (accessed May 20, 2009).

28. A. E. Kambulova, "Konspekt uroka; Predmet: 'Okruzhaiushchii mir'; 4-i class; Tema: 'My zhivem v Rossiiskom gosudarstve; Gosudarstvennaia simvolika Rossii,'" materials presented at the 2004–2005 teachers conference "Open Lesson" ["Otkrytyi urok"], http://festival.1september.ru (accessed October 4, 2007).

29. V. V. Milovanova, "Razrabotka klassnogo chasa iz predpolagaemoi sistemy klassnykh chasov na temu 'Patriotizm segodnia,' priurochennyi k 12 dekabria,'" materials presented

ference on education in the humanities, again attended by Putin, a teacher's handbook offering what has been interpreted as the new official line on Russian history was introduced. *Modern Russian History, 1945–2006* (Noveishaia istoriia Rossii, 1945–2006) is credited to the authorship of Aleksandr Filippov, the assistant director of the National Laboratory of Foreign Policy, and is rumored to have been composed to meet specific demands articulated at the highest level of the Kremlin hierarchy.[30] The handbook suggests, for example, that in teaching the Stalin era emphasis should be divided between matter-of-fact discussion of repressions and purges, and attention to the successes of the USSR in modernization and military conflict. Attempting to place Stalin in a historical context, the work cites, of all people, Winston Churchill:

> Among the most prominent assessments of the historical role of Stalin is that
> of [. . .] Winston Churchill, who cannot easily be described as one of
> Stalin's supporters: "He took over a Russia still using the wooden plow, and
> left it equipped with atomic weapons." [. . .] The authority of the ruler of
> the state in Russia has traditionally been omnipotent, uniting all resources
> and subordinating all political forces to itself. The difficult circumstances of
> the evolution of the Russian state demanded a concentration of resources,
> including political resources, in a single center and their centralized alloca-
> tion in key areas. [. . .] In this connection, one must note the anomalies that
> have regularly accompanied this centralization. Chief among these is the
> transformation of the actual necessity for a strong state power into an
> exaggerated preference far in excess of any need. Such an analysis is equally
> applicable to the rule of Ivan the Terrible, Peter the Great, and Joseph Stalin.
> [. . .] Stalin considered himself the heir of his predecessors on the Russian
> throne. He knew Russian history well and respected the historical figures
> mentioned above, considering them to be his teachers.[31]

Filippov's book evoked heated debate in the Russian press and in Internet discussions, including a great deal of consternation at its minimization of Stalinist abuses. Even so, it has found a great many supporters. The official Kremlin position appears to be that while the Soviet past was the scene of regrettable bloodshed, Russians should by and large avert their eyes from these aspects of the historical record and attend instead to Russia's triumphs, past and present.

In the wake of this official renovation of the Russian past, mass culture has reinvested in patriotic history and its critique as well. Perhaps the most spec-

---

at the 2007–2008 teachers conference "Open Lesson" ["Otkrytyi urok"], http://festival
.1september.ru (accessed October 4, 2007).

30. Filippov, *Noveishaia istoriia Rossii*. On the involvement of the Putin administration
in this work's composition, see Anna Kachurovskaia, "Istoricheskii pripadok," *Vlast'*, July
16, 2007, www.kommersant.ru (accessed August 24, 2007). On this publication in general,
see the forum published in *Kritika* 10, no. 4 (2009): 825–68.

31. Cited at Shamil' Idiatullin, "Po obrazu i posobiiu," *Vlast'*, July 16, 2007, www.kom
mersant.ru (accessed August 24, 2007).

tacular illustration to date of the resurgence of the patterns of historical representation treated in this book has been the "Name of Russia" (Imia Rossiia) undertaking of 2008. This project, either in sympathy with the Kremlin's politics of memory or in response to an official directive, began as an extensive Internet site in which Russians were able to participate in an "all-national election" of the "most valuable, remarkable, and symbolic personality of Russian history," selecting their choice from any of five hundred historical figures.[32] Based on the results of this exercise, the project launched a television show in which the twelve finalists were each treated in a separate installment before a final vote for the ultimate winner. Among the twelve were Ivan the Terrible, Peter the Great, and Joseph Stalin. The Internet site and television programs devoted to these figures presented a newly refurbished version of Russian history as a chain of interrelated epochs of state-sponsored mayhem that was nevertheless necessary to ensure collective greatness. The "winner" of the "Name of Russia" contest was ultimately Aleksandr Nevskii. Widespread rumors, however, claimed that Stalin had actually won the vote and that the organizers had falsified voting data to avoid this too apologetic outcome.

There has also been resistance in Russian cultural life to the new official and mass history. In 2007, the *enfant terrible* author Vladimir Sorokin published his *A Day in the Life of an Oprichnik* (Den' oprichnika), a novella set in 2027 in a Russia where a "new *oprichnina*" surpasses the violence and iniquity of the original. As Sorokin makes plain in the interview cited in the epigraph, he intended the work as an allegorical warning against the resurgence of ancient cycles of violence in the authoritarian course plotted by current Russian elites.[33]

As of this writing, the leading Russian director Pavel Lungin has just released his film *Tsar*. As the director's many interviews have announced, this work, too, presents an allegorically charged meditation on state-sponsored violence.[34] Focused on the story of Ivan's relationship with Metropolitan Filipp, the friend and ally whom the tsar eventually martyred for his public criticisms (fig. 25), Lungin's film presents Ivan mired in animalistic violence, the dupe of venal and evil advisors and of his vicious "eastern" wife Maria Temriukovna, motivated by a combination of paranoia, misguided religiosity, and desire for national greatness. Filipp, in contrast, is a classic Russian holy man who resists Ivan's evil with nonviolent means—love of truth and readiness to submit to Ivan's divinely sanctioned authority, no matter how unjustly he wields it. Filipp's martyrdom, accompanied by what purport to be "actual" miracles, instructs viewers in submission to a common trauma as the path to transcendence in a

---

32. From the subpage "O proekte" on the "Name of Russia" (Imia Rossiia) Web site, www.NameOfRussia.ru (accessed March 20, 2009).

33. "Vladimir Sorokin: oprichnina—ochen' russkoe iavlenie," www.grani.ru (accessed October 4, 2007).

34. Pavel Lungin, "Ivan Groznyi—vechnoe iskushenie Rossii," *Argumenty i fakty*, April 16, 2008, www.aif.ru (accessed April 18, 2008).

Figure 25: Petr Mamonov and Oleg Iankovskii as Ivan the Terrible and Metropolitan Filipp in Pavel Lungin's film *Tsar*, 2009.

superindividual, collective identity—a lesson familiar to Russian audiences since the time of Karamzin.

This eerie resurgence of the sort of state management of historical knowledge familiar from the Soviet 1930s, accompanied by the rise of allegorical critique in the cultural arena, provides a fitting scene with which to conclude. As these recent developments illustrate, forms of triumphal collective identity based on the disavowal of chosen historical traumas linked to figures of despotic power— figures who continue to accumulate in an allegorically interlinked series—persist in Russian political and cultural life with seemingly undiminished potential to support the rise of new candidates for the lists of Russia's great and bloody dictators. There is no telling where the contemporary revival of these figures will lead. Certainly, the political conditions of the present are not really comparable to those of the Stalin era, and in this age of Internet and desktop publishing no modern society can return to the condition of total state management of public discourse and cultural life of the early Soviet period. Just as certainly, these developments can lead only to new and unpredictable turns in the representation and significance of Peter the Great and Ivan the Terrible, rather than to their obsolescence. How, indeed, may one imagine an exit from the traditions in political culture, historical interpretation, and collective identity represented by these figures when each attempt at reinterpretation is already encoded in their supremely capacious hermeneutic potential, and when forgetting or transcendence immediately reveals itself to be disavowal and repetition?

SELECTED BIBLIOGRAPHY

Archives Consulted

Abbreviations used in notes and captions are listed in parentheses

Gosudarstvennyi fond kinofil'mov Rossiiskoi Federatsii (Gosfilmofond)
Gosudarstvennaia tret'iakovskaia galereia (State Tretiakov Gallery)
Rossiiskii gosudarstvennyi arkhiv literatury i iskusstva (RGALI)
Rossiiskii gosudarstvennyi arkhiv sotsial'no-politicheskoi istorii (RGASPI)
Sankt-Peterburgskii gosudarstvennyi muzei teatral'nogo i muzykal'nogo iskusstva
 (SGMTMI)
Tsentral'nyi gosudarstvennyi arkhiv istoriko-politicheskikh dokumentov (TsGAIPD)

Works Cited

The following represents a list of major primary and secondary sources cited in this
book. Items of lesser significance, such as newspaper articles, are not listed here. Full
bibliographical information for those items is contained in the notes.

Adibekov, G. M., K. M. Anderson, and L. A. Rogovaia. *Politbiuro TsK RKP(b)-
 VKP(b): Povestki dnia zasedanii 1919–1952 v trekh tomakh. Katalog.* 3 vols.
 Moscow: Rosspen, 2000–2001.
Adrianova-Peretts, V. P., ed. *Poslaniia Ivana Groznogo.* Text prepared by D. S.
 Likhacheva and Ia. S. Lur'e. Moscow: Izdatel'stvo Akademii nauk, 1951.
Aksakov, K. S. *Polnoe sobranie sochinenii.* 3 vols. Moscow: Tipografiia P. Bakhme-
 teva, 1861–80.
Al'tshuller, Mark. *Epokha Val'tera Skotta v Rossii: Istoricheskii roman 1830–kh
 godov.* St. Petersburg: Akademicheskii proekt, 1996.
Amiantov, Iu. N., ed. "Stenogramma soveshchanii po voprosam istorii SSSR v TsK
 VKP(b) v 1944 g." *Voprosy istorii,* 1996, no. 2: 47–86; 1996, no. 3: 82–112;
 1996, no. 4: 65–93; 1996, no. 5/6: 77–106; 1996, no. 7: 70–87; 1996, no. 9:
 47–77.
Anderson, Benedict. *Imagined Communities: Reflections on the Origin and Spread of
 Nationalism.* Rev. ed. New York: Verso, 1991.
Anderson, Perry. *Lineages of the Absolutist State.* London: Verso, 1979.
Anisimov, Evgenii V. *Vremia petrovskikh reform.* Leningrad: Lenizdat, 1989.
Annenskii, I. F. *Izbrannoe.* Moscow: Pravda, 1987.

Apor, Balázs, Jan C. Behrends, Polly Jones, and E. A. Rees, eds. *The Leader Cult in Communist Dictatorships: Stalin and the Eastern Bloc.* Houndmills, U.K.: Palgrave Macmillan, 2004.

Babichenko, D. L., ed. *"Literaturnyi front": Istoriia politicheskoi tsenzury, 1932–1946 gg.—Sbornik dokumentov.* Moscow: Entsiklopediia rossiiskikh dereven', 1994.

Barsukov, Nikolai P. *Zhizn' i trudy M. P. Pogodina.* 22 vols. St. Petersburg: Tipografiia M. M. Stasiulevicha, 1888–1910.

Barzun, Jacques. "Romantic Historiography as a Political Force in France." *Journal of the History of Ideas* 2, no. 3 (1941): 318–29.

Becker, Seymour. "Russia and the Concept of Empire." *Ab Imperio,* 2000, no. 3/4: 329–42.

Bedford, C. Harold. *The Seeker: D. S. Merezhkovskiy.* Lawrence: University Press of Kansas, 1975.

Beliakova, M. M., and T. V. Chertoritskaia. "Krug chteniia staroobriadtsa-spasovtsa pervoi poloviny XX v., ili tri biblioteki Dorofeia Utkina." In *Traditsionnaia dukhovnaia i material'naia kul'tura russkikh staroobriadcheskikh poselenii v stranakh Evropy, Azii i Ameriki,* edited by N. N. Pokrovskii and R. Morris, 306–12. Novosibirsk: Nauka, 1992.

Belinskii, V. G. *Sobranie sochinenii v deviati tomakh.* 9 vols. Moscow: Khudozhestvennaia literatura, 1976–82.

Belyi, Andrei. *Peterburg.* Kiev: Dnipro, 1990.

——. *Ritm kak dialektika i Mednyi vsadnik.* Moscow: Federatsiia, 1929.

Bestuzhev-Riumin, K. N. *Russkaia istoriia.* 2 vols. St. Petersburg: Tipografiia A. Transhelia, 1885; repr., The Hague: Mouton, 1969.

Bethea, David M. "The Role of the *Eques* in Puškin's *Bronze Horseman.*" In *Puškin Today,* edited by David M. Bethea, 99–118. Bloomington: Indiana University Press, 1993.

——. *The Shape of Apocalypse in Modern Russian Fiction.* Princeton, N.J.: Princeton University Press, 1989.

Blagoi, D. D. *Tvorcheskii put' Pushkina, 1926–1930.* Moscow: Sovetskii pisatel', 1967.

Bol'shaia sovetskaia entsiklopediia. 65 vols. Moscow: Sovetskaia entsiklopediia, 1926–47.

Bol'shaia sovetskaia entsiklopediia. 2d ed. 51 vols. Moscow: Sovetskaia entsiklopediiia, 1950–58.

Borozdin, A. K. *Iz pisem i pokazanii dekabristov: Kritika sovremennogo sostoianiia Rossii i plany budushchego ustroistva.* St. Petersburg: Izdanie M. V. Pirozhkova, 1906.

Brandenberger, David. *National Bolshevism: Stalinist Mass Culture and the Formation of Modern Russian National Identity, 1931–1956.* Cambridge, Mass.: Harvard University Press, 2002.

Brandenberger, David, and Karen Petrone. " 'Vse cherty rasovogo natsionalizma...': internatsionalist zhaluetsia Stalinu (ianvar' 1939 g.)." *Voprosy istorii,* 2000, no. 1, 128–33.

Briggs, Asa. *Collected Essays.* 2 vols. Sussex, U.K.: Harvester Press, 1985.

Briusov, V. Ia. *Sobranie sochinenii v semi tomakh.* 7 vols. Moscow: Khudozhestvennaia literatura, 1973–75.

Brooks, Jeffrey. "From Folklore to Popular Literature: A Changing View of the Autocrat and the Empire." *Russian History/Histoire russe* 14, nos. 1–4 (1987): 37–46.

——. *"Thank You, Comrade Stalin": Soviet Public Culture from Revolution to Cold War.* Princeton, N.J.: Princeton University Press, 1999.

———. *When Russia Learned to Read: Literacy and Popular Literature, 1861–1917*. Princeton, N.J.: Princeton University Press, 1985.

Broyde, Stephen. *Osip Mandel'shtam and His Age*. Cambridge, Mass.: Harvard University Press, 1975.

Brubaker, Rogers, and Frederick Cooper. "Beyond 'Identity.'" *Theory and Society* 29, no. 1 (2000): 1–47.

Bukharin, N. I. *Tsezarism pod maskoi revoliutsii*. Moscow: Pravda, 1925.

Bulgarin, F. V. *Vospominaniia*. 6 vols. St. Petersburg: Tipografiia D. M. Ol'khina, 1846–49.

Burdei, G. D. *Istorik i voina: 1941–1945*. Saratov: Izdatel'stvo Saratovskogo universiteta, 1991.

Burke, Kenneth. *On Symbols and Society*. Edited by Joseph R. Gusfield. Chicago, Ill.: University of Chicago Press, 1989.

Bushkovitch, Paul. "Power and the Historian: The Case of Tsarevich Aleksei 1716–1718 and N. G. Ustrialov 1845–1859." *Proceedings of the American Philosophical Society* 141, no. 2 (1997): 177–212.

Byrnes, Robert. *V. O. Kliuchevskii: Historian of Russia*. Bloomington: Indiana University Press, 1995.

Bystriantseva, L. A. "Mirovozzrenie i obshchestvenno-politicheskaia deiatel'nost' N. V. Ustrialova (1890–1937)." *Novaia i noveishaia istoriia*, 2005, no. 5: 162–90.

Carlyle, Thomas. *On Heroes, Hero-Worship, and the Heroic in History: Six Lectures, Reported, with Emendations and Additions*. New York: J. Wiley, 1861.

Caruth, Cathy. *Unclaimed Experience: Trauma, Narrative, and History*. Baltimore: Johns Hopkins University Press, 1996.

Cassedy, Steven. "Bely's Theory of Symbolism as a Formal Iconics of Meaning." In *Andrei Bely: Spirit of Symbolism*, edited by John Malmstad, 285–312. Ithaca, N.Y.: Cornell University Press, 1987.

Cavanagh, Clare. *Osip Mandelstam and the Modernist Creation of Tradition*. Princeton, N.J.: Princeton University Press, 1995.

Chaadaev, P. Ia. *Philosophical Letters and Apology of a Madman*. Translated by Mary-Barbara Zeldin. Knoxville: University of Tennessee Press, 1969.

Chalmaev, V. A. "Filosofiia patriotizma." *Molodaia gvardiia*, 1967, no. 10: 272–93.

Cherkasov, N. K. *Zapiski sovetskogo aktera*. Moscow: Iskusstvo, 1953.

Cherniavsky, Michael, ed. *The Structure of Russian History: Interpretive Essays*. New York: Random House, 1970.

Chistov, K. V. *Russkie narodnye sotsial'no-utopicheskie legendy XVI–XIX vekov*. Moscow: Nauka, 1967.

Christensen, Peter G. "*Christ and Antichrist* as Historical Novel." *Modern Language Studies* 20, no. 3 (1990): 67–77.

Christoff, Peter K. *An Introduction to Nineteenth-Century Russian Slavophilism; A Study in Ideas*. 4 vols. The Hague, Mouton, 1961, 1972; Princeton, N.J.: Princeton University Press, 1982; Boulder, Colo.: Westview, 1991.

Clark, Katerina. *The Soviet Novel: History as Ritual*. 2d ed. Chicago: University of Chicago Press, 1985.

Corney, Frederick. *Telling October: Memory and the Making of the Bolshevik Revolution*. Ithaca, N.Y.: Cornell University Press, 2004.

Croce, Benedetto. *History: Its Theory and Practice*. Translated by Douglas Ainslie. New York: Russell and Russell, 1960.

Crummey, Robert O. "Eastern Orthodoxy in Russia and Ukraine in the Age of Counter-Reformation." In *Eastern Christianity, The Cambridge History of Christianity* 5, edited by Michael Angold, 302–24. Cambridge: Cambridge University Press, 2006.

Dal', V. I. "Vospominanie o Pushkine." In *Pushkin v vospominaniiakh sovremennikov*, 2: 258–61. 3d ed. 2 vols. St. Petersburg: Akademicheskii proekt, 1998.

Dalton, Margaret. *A. K. Tolstoi*. New York: Twayne, 1972.

Daughtry, J. Martin. "Russia's New Anthem and the Negotiation of National Identity." *Ethnomusicology* 47, no. 1 (2003): 42–67.

David-Fox, Michael. *Revolution of the Mind: Higher Learning among the Bolsheviks, 1918–1929*. Ithaca, N.Y.: Cornell University Press, 1997.

De Man, Paul. "The Rhetoric of Temporality." In *Blindness and Insight: Essays in the Rhetoric of Contemporary Criticism*, Theory and History of Literature 7, 2d ed., 187–228. Minneapolis: University of Minnesota Press, 1983.

Derzhavin, G. R. *Sochineniia Derzhavina*. 5 vols. St. Petersburg: Tipografiia Shnora, 1808–16.

Deutscher, Isaac. *Stalin: A Political Biography*. Rev. ed. London: Penguin, 1990.

Dimitrov, Georgi. *Diary of Georgi Dimitrov, 1933–1949*. Edited by Ivo Banac. Translated by Jane T. Hedges, Timothy D. Sergay, and Irina Faion. New Haven, Conn.: Yale University Press, 2003.

Dobrenko, Evgeny. *The Making of the State Reader*. Translated by Jesse M. Savage. Stanford, Calif.: Stanford University Press, 1997.

——. *Stalinist Cinema and the Production of History: Museum of the Revolution*. Translated by Sarah Young. New Haven: Yale University Press, 2008.

Dolgorukii, V. G., and V. I. Anofriev. *Putevoditel' po Moskve i okrestnostiam*. Moscow: T. Ris, 1872.

Dolinin, Alexander. "Historicism or Providentialism? Pushkin's *History of Pugachev* in the Context of French Romantic Historiography." *Slavic Review* 58, no. 2 (1999): 291–308.

Dolutskii, I. I. *Otechestvennaia istoriia, XX vek, uchebnik dlia 10–11 klassov*. 2 vols. Moscow: Mnemozina, 2001–2.

Dostoevskii, F. M. *Polnoe sobranie sochinenii v tridtsati tomakh*. 30 vols. Leningrad: Nauka, 1972–90.

Doyle, Peter. "Bulgakov's *Ivan Vasil'evich*: Light-Hearted Comedy or Serious Satire?" *Journal of Russian Studies*, no. 43 (1982): 33–42.

Drizen, N. V. *Dramaticheskaia tsenzura dvukh epokh, 1825–1881*. Petrograd: Prometei, 1917.

Duara, Prasenjit. *Rescuing History from the Nation: Questioning Narratives of Modern China*. Chicago: University of Chicago Press, 1995.

Dubrovskii, A. M. *Istorik i vlast': Istoricheskaia nauka v SSSR i kontseptsiia istorii feodal'noi Rossii v kontekste politiki i ideologii (1930–1950-e gg.)*. Briansk: Izdatel'stvo Brianskogo gosudarstvennogo universiteta im. Akad. I. G. Petrovskogo, 2005.

Dubrovskii, A. M., and D. L. Brandenberger. "Itogovyi partiinyi dokument soveshchaniia istorikov v TsK VKP(b) v 1944 g. (Istoriia sozdaniia teksta)." *Arkheograficheskii ezhegodnik za 1998 g.*, 148–63. Moscow: Nauka, 1999.

Dubrovskii, S. M. "Protiv idealizatsii deiatel'nosti Ivana IV." *Voprosy istorii*, 1956, no. 8, 121–29.

Eidel'man, N. Ia. *Gertsen protiv samoderzhaviia: Sekretnaia politicheskaia istoriia Rossii XVIII–XIX vekov i Vol'naia pechat'*. Moscow: Mysl', 1973.

——. *Poslednii letopisets*. Moscow: Vagrius, 2004.

Eisenstein [Eizenshtein], S. M. *Selected Works*. Edited by Richard Taylor. Translated by William Powell. 4 vols. London: BFI Publishing, 1988–96.

Eizenshtein, S. M. *Izbrannye proizvedeniia*. 6 vols. Moscow: Iskusstvo, 1964.

Emerson, Caryl. *Boris Godunov: Transpositions of a Russian Theme*. Bloomington: Indiana University Press, 1986.

——. "Pretenders to History: Four Plays for Undoing Pushkin's *Boris Godunov*." *Slavic Review* 44, no. 2 (1985): 257–79.

Emmons, Terence. "Kliuchevskii's Pupils." In *Historiography of Imperial Russia: The Professional Writing of History in a Multinational State*, edited by Thomas Sanders, 118–45. Armonk, N.Y.: M. E. Sharpe, 1999.

Enteen, George M. *The Soviet Scholar-Bureaucrat: M. N. Pokrovskii and the Society of Marxist Historians*. University Park: Pennsylvania State University Press, 1978.

Evdokimova, Svetlana. *Pushkin's Historical Imagination*. New Haven, Conn.: Yale University Press, 1999.

Ewers, Johann Philipp Gustav von. *Das älteste Recht der Russen in seiner geschichtlichen Entwickelung*. Dorpat: August Sticinsky, 1826.

Fedotov, G. P. *Sviatoi Filipp, mitropolit moskovskii*. Paris: YMCA Press, 1928.

Feinberg, I. L. *Nezavershennye raboty Pushkina*. 5th ed. Moscow: Sovetskii pisatel', 1969.

Feuer, Kathryn B. *Tolstoy and the Genesis of "War and Peace."* Edited by Robin Feuer Miller and Donna Tussing Orwin. Ithaca, N.Y.: Cornell University Press, 1996.

Filippov, A. V. *Noveishaia istoriia Rossii, 1945–2006 gg.: Kniga dlia uchitelia*. Moscow: Prosveshchenie, 2007.

Fitzpatrick, Sheila. *The Cultural Front: Power and Culture in Revolutionary Russia*. Ithaca, N.Y.: Cornell University Press, 1992.

Fleishman, Lazar. *Boris Pasternak i literaturnaia zhizn' 1930-kh godov*. 2d ed. St. Petersburg: Akademicheskii proekt, 2003.

——. *Boris Pasternak v dvadtsatye gody*. 2d ed. St. Petersburg: Akademicheskii proekt, 2003.

Gasiorowska, Xenia. *The Image of Peter the Great in Russian Fiction*. Madison: University of Wisconsin Press, 1979.

Gasparov, Boris. "The 'Golden Age' and Its Role in the Cultural Mythology of Russian Modernism." In *Cultural Mythologies of Russian Modernism: From the Golden Age to the Silver Age*, edited by Boris Gasparov, Robert P. Hughes, and Irina Paperno, 1–16. Berkeley: University of California Press, 1992.

Gertsen, A. I. [A. I. Herzen]. *Sobranie sochinenii v tridtsati tomakh*. 30 vols. Moscow: Izdatel'stvo Akademii nauk, 1954–66.

Gossman, Lionel. "History as Decipherment: Romantic Historiography and the Discovery of the Other." *New Literary History* 18, no. 1 (1986): 23–57.

Grabar', I. E. *Il'ia Efimovich Repin: Monografiia v dvukh tomakh*. 2 vols. Moscow: Gosudarstvennoe izdatel'stvo izobrazitel'nykh iskusstv, 1937.

——. *Repin*. Zhizn' zamechatel'nykh liudei 21–22. Moscow: Zhurnal'no-gazetnoe ob'edinenie, 1933.

Graham, Hugh. "R. Iu. Vipper: A Russian Historian in Three Worlds," *Canadian Slavonic Papers* 28, no. 1 (1986): 22–35.

Greenfeld, Liah. *Nationalism: Five Roads to Modernity*. Cambridge, Mass.: Harvard University Press, 1992.

Greenleaf, Monika. *Pushkin and Romantic Fashion: Fragment, Elegy, Orient, Irony.* Stanford, Calif.: Stanford University Press, 1994.

Greenleaf, Monika, and Stephen Moeller-Sally, eds. *Russian Subjects: Empire, Nation, and the Culture of the Golden Age.* Evanston, Ill: Northwestern University Press, 1998.

Grekov, B. D., ed. *Protiv istoricheskoi kontseptsii M. N. Pokrovskogo: Sbornik statei.* 2 vols. Moscow: Izdatel'stvo Akademii nauk SSSR, 1939–40.

Gumbrecht, Hans Ulrich. *Making Sense in Life and Literature.* Edited by Wlad Godzich. Translated by Glen Burns. Minneapolis: University of Minnesota Press, 1992.

Gur'ianova, N. S. *Krest'ianskii antimonarkhicheskii protest v staroobriadcheskoi eskhatologicheskoi literature perioda pozdnego feodalizma.* Novosibirsk: Nauka, 1988.

Gutsche, George J. "Puškin and Nicholas: The Problem of 'Stanzas.'" In *Puškin Today*, edited by David M. Bethea, 184–200. Bloomington: Indiana University Press, 1993.

Hamburg, Gary M. "Inventing the 'State School' of Historians, 1840–1995." In *Historiography of Imperial Russia: The Profession and Writing of History in a Multinational State*, edited by Thomas Sanders, 98–117. Armonk, N.Y.: M. E. Sharpe, 1999.

Hardemann, Hilde. *Coming to Terms with the Soviet Regime: The "Changing Signposts" Movement among Russian Emigres in the Early 1920s.* DeKalb: Northern Illinois University Press, 1994.

Hegel, Georg Wilhelm Friedrich. *The Philosophy of History.* Translated by J. Sibree. New York: Dover, 1956.

Hellie, Richard. "In Search of Ivan the Terrible." In *Ivan the Terrible*, by S. F. Platonov, edited and translated by Joseph L. Wieczynski, ix–xxiv. Gulf Breeze, Fla.: Academic International Press, 1974.

Hill, Christopher. *Puritanism and Revolution: Studies in the Interpretation of the English Revolution of the Seventeenth Century.* 2d ed. New York: St. Martins Press, 1997.

Hobsbawm, Eric J. *Nations and Nationalism since 1780: Programme, Myth, Reality.* Cambridge: Cambridge University Press, 1990.

Hobsbawm, Eric J., and Terence Ranger, eds. *The Invention of Tradition.* Cambridge: Cambridge University Press, 1992.

Hoffmann, David. *Stalinist Values: The Cultural Norms of Soviet Modernity, 1917–1941.* Ithaca, N.Y.: Cornell University Press, 2003.

Hosking, Geoffrey. "Mozhet li Rossiia stat' natsional'nym gosudarstvom?" *Ab Imperio*, 2000, no. 1: 33–50.

Hroch, Miroslav. "From National Movement to the Fully-Formed Nation: The Nation-Building Process in Europe." *New Left Review* 1/198 (March-April 1993): 3–20.

——. *Social Preconditions of National Revival in Europe: A Comparative Analysis of the Social Composition of Patriotic Groups among the Smaller European Nations.* Cambridge: Cambridge University Press, 1985.

Iablonskii, S. "Pokushenie na 'Ioanna Groznogo.'" In *Novoe o Repine*, edited by I. A. Brodskii and V. N. Moskvinov, 332–35. Leningrad: Khudozhnik, 1969.

"Itogovyi partiinyi document soveshchaniia istorikov v TsK VKP(b) v 1944 g. (Istoriia sozdaniia teksta)." *Arkheograficheskii ezhegodnik za 1998 g.*, 148–63. Moscow: Nauka, 1999.

Iurenev, R. N. *Sergei Eizenshtein: Zamysly, fil'my, metod.* 2 vols. Moscow: Iskusstvo, 1985–88.

Ivanov, V. I. *Cor Ardens.* 2 vols. Moscow: Skorpion, 1911–12.

Ivanov-Razumnik, R. *Pisatel'skie sud'by.* New York: Literaturnyi fond, 1951.

"Iz dnevnikov Sergeia Sergeevicha Dmitrieva." *Otechestvennaia istoriia,* 2000, no. 1: 164–71.

Izbrannye stsenarii sovetskogo kino. 6 vols. Moscow: Goskinoizdat, 1949–50.

Jakobson, Roman. *Pushkin and His Sculptural Myth.* Translated by John Burbank. The Hague: Mouton, 1975.

Kantorowicz, Ernst H. *The King's Two Bodies: A Study in Medieval Political Theology.* Princeton, N.J.: Princeton University Press, 1957.

Karamzin, N. M. *Istoriia gosudarstva rossiiskogo.* 5th ed. 12 vols. in 4. St. Petersburg: Tipografiia Eduarda Pratsa, 1842–44; repr., Moscow: Kniga, 1988.

———. *Izbrannye sochineniia v dvukh tomakh.* Edited by P. Berkov. 2 vols. Moscow: Khudozhestvennaia literatura, 1964.

———. *Zapiska o drevnei i novoi Rossii v ee politicheskom i grazhdanskom otnosheniiakh.* Edited by Iu. S. Pivovarov. Moscow: Nauka, 1991.

Kavelin, K. D. *Sobranie sochinenii.* 4 vols. St. Petersburg: Tipografiia M. M. Stasiulevicha, 1897–1900.

Keenan, Edward L. *The Kurbskii-Groznyi Apocrypha: The Seventeenth-Century Genesis of the "Correspondence" Attributed to Prince A. M. Kurbskii and Tsar Ivan IV.* Cambridge, Mass.: Harvard University Press, 1971.

———. "Putting Kurbskii in His Place, or: Observations and Suggestions Concerning the Place of the *History of the Grand Price of Muscovy* in the History of Muscovite Literary Culture." *Forshchungen zur osteuropaschen Geschichte* 24 (1978): 132–61.

Kireevskii, I. V. *Polnoe sobranie sochinenii v dvukh tomakh.* Edited by M. Gershenzon. 2 vols. Moscow: Tipografiia Moskovskogo gosudarstvennogo universiteta, 1911.

Kliuchevskii, V. O. *A History of Russia.* Translated by C. J. Hogarth. 5 vols. New York: E. P. Dutton, 1911–31.

———. *Sochineniia v vos'mi tomakh.* 8 vols. Moscow: Gosudarstvennoe izdatel'stvo politicheskoi literatury, 1956–59.

Kobrin, V. B. *Ivan Groznyi.* Moscow: Moskovskii rabochii, 1989.

Koselleck, Reinhart. *Futures Past: On the Semantics of Historical Time.* Translated by Keith Tribe. New York: Columbia University Press, 2004.

———. *The Practice of Conceptual History: Timing History, Spacing Concepts.* Translated by Todd Presner, Kerstin Behnke, and Jobst Welge. Stanford, Calif.: Stanford University Press, 2002.

Kostomarov, N. I. *Istoricheskie monografii i issledovaniia.* Moscow: Kniga, 1989.

———. *Russkaia istoriia v zhizneopisaniiakh ee glavneishikh deiatelei.* Moscow: Kniga, 1990.

Kozlov, Leonid. "The Artist and the Shadow of Ivan." In *Stalinism and Soviet Cinema,* edited by Richard Taylor and Derek Spring, 109–30. London: Routledge, 1993.

Kramskoi, I. V. *Ivan Nikolaevich Kramskoi: Ego zhizn' perepiska i khudozhestvenno-kriticheskie stat'i, 1837–1887.* Edited by V. V. Stasov. St. Petersburg: Tipografiia A. S. Suvorina, 1888.

Kraus, Tamash [Tamás Krausz]. *Sovetskii termidor: Dukhovnye predposylki stalinskogo povorota (1917–1928).* Budapest: Vengerskii institut rusistiki, 1997.

Kriukov, A. M. *A. N. Tolstoi i russkaia literatura: Tvorcheskaia individual'nost' v literaturnom protsesse.* Moscow: Nauka, 1990.

Kujundžic, Dragan. *The Returns of History: Russian Nietzscheans after Modernity.* Albany: State University of New York Press, 1997.

Kurmacheva, M. D. "Ob otsenke deiatel'nosti Ivana Groznogo." *Voprosy istorii,* 1956, no. 9: 195–203.

Kutateladze, L., ed. *F. Stravinskii: Stat'i, pis'ma, vospominaniia.* Leningrad: Muzyka, 1972.

Kuznetsova, Marina. "Petr Pervyi." In *Rossiiskii illiuzion,* edited by L. M. Budiak, 171–76. Moscow: Materik: 2003.

LaCapra, Dominick. *Writing History, Writing Trauma.* Baltimore: Johns Hopkins University Press, 2001.

Lane, Christel. *The Rites of Rulers: Ritual in Industrial Society—the Soviet Case.* Cambridge: Cambridge University Press, 1981.

Lawton, Anna, ed. *Russian Futurism through Its Manifestoes, 1912–1928.* Translated by Anna Lawton and Herbert Eagle. Ithaca, N.Y.: Cornell University Press, 1988.

Lazhechnikov, I. I. *Sochineniia v dvukh tomakh.* 2 vols. Moscow: Khudozhestvennaia literatura, 1963.

Lebed'ev. V. I., B. D. Grekov, and S. V. Bakhrushin, eds. *Istoriia SSSR,* vol. 1: *S drevneishikh vremen do kontsa XVII v.* Moscow: Gosudarstvennoe Sotsial'no-ekonomicheskoe izdatel'stvo, 1939.

Lednicki, Waclaw. *Pushkin's "Bronze Horseman": The Story of a Masterpiece.* Berkeley: University of California Press, 1955.

Lemke, M. K. *Nikolaevskie zhandarmy i literatura 1826–1855: Po podlinnym delam Tret'ego otdeleniia Sobstvennogo Ego Imperatorskogo Velichestva Kantseliarii.* 2d ed. St. Petersburg: S. V. Bunin, 1909.

Lenin, V. I. *Polnoe sobranie sochinenii.* 5th ed. 55 vols. Moscow: Izdatel'stvo politicheskoi literatury, 1958–70.

Levi-Strauss, Claude. "The Structural Study of Myth." In *Structural Anthropology,* translated by Claire Jacobson and Brooke Grundfest Schoepf, 206–31. New York: Basic Books, 1963.

Liaskovskaia, O. A. *Il'ia Efimovich Repin.* Moscow: Iskusstvo, 1982.

Lomonosov, M. V. *Polnoe sobranie sochinenii.* 11 vols. Moscow and Leningrad: Izdatel'stvo Akademii nauk, 1950–83.

Losev, V., and L. Ianovskaia, eds. *Dnevnik Eleny Bulgakovoi.* Moscow: Knizhnaia palata, 1990.

Lotman, Iu. M. *Izbrannye stat'i.* 3 vols. Tallinn: Aleksandra, 1992–93.

——. *Karamzin; Sotvorenie Karamzina; Stat'i i issledovaniia, 1957–1990; Zametki i retsenzii.* St. Petersburg: Iskusstvo-SPB, 1997.

——. "Neskol'ko dobavochnykh zamechanii k voprosu o razgovore Pushkina s Nikolaem 18 sentiabria 1826 goda." In *Pushkinskie chteniia,* edited by S. G. Isakov, 41–43. Tallinn: Eesti Raamat, 1990.

——. *Pushkin: Biografiia pisatelia; Stat'i i zametki; "Evgenii Onegin"—kommentarii.* St. Petersburg: Iskusstvo-SPB, 1995.

Lur'e, A. N. "Poema A. S. Pushkina 'Mednyi vsadnik' i sovetskaia poeziia 20-kh godov." In *Sovetskaia literatura: Problemy masterstva,* Uchenye zapiski 322, edited by A. N. Shishkina, 42–81. Leningrad: Institut imeni A. I. Gertsena, 1968.

Lur'e, Ia. S. "Ivan Groznyi i drevnerusskaia literatura v tvorchestve M. Bulgakova." *Trudy Otdela drevnerusskoi literatury* 45 (1992): 315–21.

———. *Povest' o Drakule*. Moscow: Nauka, 1964.

Lur'e, Ia. S., and Iu. D. Rykov, eds. *Perepiska Ivana Groznogo s Andreem Kurbskim*. Leningrad: Nauka, 1979.

Maguire, Robert A., and John Malmstad. "Petersburg." In *Andrei Bely: Spirit of Symbolism*, edited by John Malmstad, 96–144. Ithaca, N.Y.: Cornell University Press, 1987.

Maikov, A. N. *Polnoe sobranie sochinenii*. Edited by P. V. Bykov. 9th ed. 4 vols. St. Petersburg: Tipografiia A. F. Marksa, 1914.

Malaia sovetskaia entsiklopediia. 10 vols. Moscow: Sovetskaia entsiklopediia, 1928–31.

Manchester, Laurie. "Contradictions at the Heart of Russian Liberalism: Pavel Miliukov's Views of Peter the Great and the Role of Personality in History as an Academic, a Politician, and an Émigré." *Russian History/Histoire russe* 37, no. 2 (2010): 102–32.

Markov, P. A. *O teatre*. 4 vols. Moscow: Iskusstvo, 1974–77.

Markovin, N., ed. *Sovetskii istoricheskii fil'm: Sbornik statei*. Moscow: Goskinoizdat, 1939.

Marks [Marx], Karl, and Fridrikh Engel's [Friedrich Engels]. *Arkhiv Marksa i Engel'sa*. Moscow: Partiinoe izdatel'stvo, 1932–.

Martin, Terry. *The Affirmative Action Empire: Nations and Nationalism in the Soviet Union, 1923–1939*. Ithaca, N.Y.: Cornell University Press, 2001.

Matich, Olga. "The Merezhkovskys' Third Testament and the Russian Utopian Tradition." In *Russian Culture in Modern Times*, Christianity and the Eastern Slavs 2, California Slavic Studies 17, edited by Robert P. Hughes and Irina Paperno, 158–71. Berkeley: University of California Press, 1994.

Mazour, Anatole G. *Modern Russian Historiography*, 2d ed. Princeton, N.J.: D. Van Nostrand, 1958.

———. *The Writing of History in the Soviet Union*. Stanford, Calif.: Hoover Institution Press, 1971.

McCannon, John. *Red Arctic: Polar Exploration and the Myth of the North in the Soviet Union, 1932–1939*. Oxford: Oxford University Press, 1998.

Mei, L. A. *Izbrannye proizvedeniia*. Biblioteka poeta, Bol'shaia seriia. Leningrad: Sovetskii pisatel', 1972.

Meilakh, B. S. "Iz istorii politicheskoi liriki Pushkina ('Stansy' i 'Druz'iam')." In *Iz istorii russkikh literaturnykh otnoshenii XVIII–XX vekov*, edited by S. V. Kastorskii, 96–107. Moscow: Izdatel'stvo Akademii nauk, 1959.

Merezhkovskii, D. S. *Akropol': Izbrannye literaturno-kriticheskie stat'i*. Moscow: Knizhnaia palata, 1991.

———. *Polnoe sobranie sochinenii*. St. Petersburg: Izdanie tovarishchestva M. O. Vol'f, 1911–13.

———. *Sobranie sochinenii v chertyrekh tomakh*. Edited by O. N. Mikhailov. 4 vols. Moscow: Pravda, 1990.

———. *Tsarstvo Antikhrista: Stat'i perioda emigratsii*. Edited by A. N. Nikoliukin. St. Petersburg: Izdatel'stvo Russkogo khristianskogo gumanitarnogo universiteta, 2001.

Mikhailovskii, N. K. *Sochineniia*. 6 vols. St. Petersburg: Russkoe bogatstvo, 1896–97.

Miliukov, P. N. *Ocherki istorii istoricheskoi nauki*. Moscow: Nauka, 2002.

———. *Ocherki po istorii russkoi kul'tury*. Pt. 1. 4th ed. St. Petersburg: Tipografiia I. N. Skorokhodova, 1900.

——. *Ocherki po istorii russkoi kul'tury*. Pt. 3. 2 vols. 1st ed. St. Petersburg: Tipo-grafiia I. N. Skorokhodova, 1901–3.

——. *Ocherki po istorii russkoi kul'tury*. 3 vols. Jubilee edition. Paris: Sovremennye zapiski, 1930–37.

——. *Vospominaniia*. 2 vols. Moscow: Sovremennik, 1990.

Miller, Alexei. *The Romanov Empire and Nationalism: Essays in the Methodology of Historical Research*. English ed. rev. and enl. Budapest: Central European University Press, 2008.

Miller, David B. "Official History in the Reign of Ivan Groznyi and Its Seventeenth Century Imitators." *Russian History/Histoire russe* 14, nos. 1–4 (1987): 333–60.

Miller [Mller], G. F. "Kratkoe izvestie o nachale Novagoroda i o proiskhozhdenii rossiiskogo naroda, o novogorodskikh kniaz'iakh i znatneishikh onogo goroda sluchaiakh." In *Selected Works*, edited by S. S. Ilizarov, 100–157. Moscow: Janus-K, 2006.

Mut'ia, Natal'ia. *Ivan Groznyi: istorizm i lichnost' pravitelia v otechestvennom iskusstve xix–xx vekov*. St. Petersburg: Aleteiia, 2010.

Naiman, Eric. *Sex in Public: The Incarnation of Early Soviet Ideology*. Princeton, N.J.: Princeton University Press, 1997.

Nechkina, M. V., and V. I. Lebedev. *Istoriia SSSR*. 2 vols. Moscow: Gosudarstvennoe Sotsial'no-ekonomicheskoe izdatel'stvo, 1939.

Neuberger, Joan. *Ivan the Terrible*. KINOfiles Film Companion 9. London: I. B. Tauris, 2003.

Nikitin, A. L. "O pol'ze al'ternativnykh vzgliadov v istoricheskoi nauke." In *Kogo boialsia Ivan Groznyi? K voprosu o proiskhozhdenii oprichniny*, edited by G. L. Grigor'ev, 3–6. Moscow: IGS, 1998.

Nikitina, Z. A., and L. I. Tolstaia. *Vospominaniia ob A. N. Tolstom: Sbornik*. Moscow: Sovetskii pisatel', 1973.

Nivat, Georges. "Alexis Tolstoi et le roman historique." *Lettres nouvelles*, 1977, no. 1: 183–87.

Nora, Pierre, ed. "Between History and Memory." Translated by Marc Roudebush. *Representations* 26 (1989): 7–24.

——. *Realms of Memory: Rethinking the French Past*. Translated by Arthur Gold-hammer. New York: Columbia University Press, 1996.

"Novye dokumenty o soveshchanii istorikov v TsK VKP(b) (1944 g.)." *Voprosy istorii*, 1991, no. 1: 188–204.

O partiinoi i sovetskoi pechati: Sbornik dokumentov. Moscow: Pravda, 1954.

Ol'ga Nikolaevna, Grand Princess. "Son iunosti." In *Nikolai I: Muzh, otets, impera-tor*, edited by Diana Tevekelian, 174–329. Moscow: Slovo, 2000.

Ospovat, A. L., and R. D. Timenchik. *"Pechal'nu povest' sokhranit'...' "*: Ob avtore i chitateliakh "Mednogo vsadnika." Moscow: Kniga, 1985.

Panchenko, A. M., and B. A. Uspenskii. "Ivan Groznyi i Petr Velikii: Kontseptsii pervogo monakha." In *Iz istorii russkoi kul'tury*, edited by V. Ia. Petrukhin, 5 vols., 2:457–78. Moscow: Iazyki slavianskikh kul'tur, 1996–2002.

Pankratova, A. M. "Pis'ma." *Voprosy istorii*, 1988, no. 11: 54–78.

Parker, Fan, and Stephen Jan Parker. *Russia on Canvas: Ilya Repin*. University Park: Pennsylvania State University Press, 1980.

Pasternak, B. L. *Pis'ma B. L. Pasternaka k zhene Z. N. Neigauz-Pasternak*. Edited by K. M. Polivanov. Moscow: Dom, 1993.

——. *Sobranie sochinenii v piati tomakh.* 5 vols. Moscow: Khudozhestvennaia literatura, 1989–92.

Pasternak, E. B. *Boris Pasternak: Biografiia.* Moscow: Tsitadel', 1997.

Perrie, Maureen. *The Cult of Ivan the Terrible in Stalin's Russia.* Houndmills, U.K.: Palgrave, 2001.

——. *The Image of Ivan the Terrible in Russian Folklore.* Cambridge: Cambridge University Press, 1987.

——. "Nationalism and History: The Cult of Ivan the Terrible in Stalin's Russia." In *Russian Nationalism Past and Present,* edited by G. Hosking and L. Service, 1–20. New York: Macmillan, 1997.

——. "The Terrible Tsar as Comic Hero: Mikhail Bulgakov's 'Ivan Vasil'evich.'" In *Epic Revisionism: Russian History and Literature as Stalinist Propaganda,* edited by Kevin M. F. Platt and David Brandenberger, 143–56. Madison: University of Wisconsin Press, 2006.

Pervyi vsesoiuznyi s'ezd sovetskikh pisatelei, 1934: Stenograficheskii otchet. Moscow: Khudozhestvennaia literatura, 1934.

Petelin, Viktor. *Sud'ba khudozhnika: Zhizn', lichnost', tvorchestvo Alekseia Nikolaevicha Tolstogo.* Moscow: Khudozhestvennaia literatura, 1982.

Pipes, Richard. *Karamzin's Memoir on Ancient and Modern Russia: A Translation and Analysis.* Cambridge, Mass.: Harvard University Press, 1959.

Platonov, S. F. "Aftobiograficheskaia zapiska." In *Akademicheskoe delo 1929–31 gg.: Dokumenty i materialy sledstvennogo dela, sfabrikovannogo OGPU,* edited by V. P. Zakharov, M. P. Lepekhin, and E. A. Fomina, 1:256–88. Two parts in three volumes. Saint Petersburg: Biblioteka Rossiiskoi akademii nauk, 1993.

——. *Ivan Groznyi, 1530–1584.* Petrograd: Brokgauz-Efron, 1923.

——. *Ivan the Terrible.* Edited and translated by Joseph L. Wieczynski. Gulf Breeze, Fla.: Academic International Press, 1974.

——. *Petr Velikii: Lichnost' i deiatel'nost'.* Paris: Izdanie Tovarishchestva N. P. Karabasnikov, 1927.

Platt, Kevin M. F. "Antichrist Enthroned: Demonic Visions of Russian Rulers." In *Russian Literature and Its Demons,* edited by Pamela Davidson, 87–124. Oxford: Berghahn Books, 2000.

——. "History and Despotism, or: Hayden White vs. Ivan the Terrible and Peter the Great." *Rethinking History* 3, no. 2 (1999): 247–69.

——. *History in a Grotesque Key: Russian Literature and the Idea of Revolution.* Stanford, Calif.: Stanford University Press, 1997.

——. "History, Inertia, and the Unexpected: Recycling Russia's Despots." *Common Knowledge* 10, no. 1 (2004): 130–50.

——. "Pushkin's *History of Peter the Great*: Interpretation by Triangulation." In *Collected Essays in Honor of the Bicentennial of Alexander S. Pushkin's Birth,* edited by Juras T. Ryfa, 141–63. Lewiston, U.K.: Edwin Mellen Press, 2000.

Platt, Kevin M. F., and David Brandenberger, eds. *Epic Revisionism: Russian History and Literature as Stalinist Propaganda.* Madison: University of Wisconsin Press, 2006.

——. "Terribly Romantic, Terribly Progressive, or Terribly Tragic: Rehabilitating Ivan IV under I. V. Stalin." *Russian Review* 58, no. 4 (1999): 635–54.

Pocock, J. G. A. *The Ancient Constitution and the Feudal Law: A Study of English Historical Thought in the Seventeenth Century.* 2d ed. Cambridge: Cambridge University Press, 1987.

Poe, Marshall. *A People Born to Slavery: Russia in Early Modern European Ethnography, 1476–1748.* Ithaca, N.Y.: Cornell University Press, 2000.

Pogodin, M. P. *Sud nad tsarevichem Alekseem Petrovichem: Episod iz zhizni Petra Velikogo.* Moscow: Tipografiia A. Semena, 1860.

Pokrovskii, M. N. *Izbrannye proizvedeniia v chetyrekh knigakh.* 4 vols. Moscow: Mysl', 1965–67.

——. *Russkaia istoriia s drevneishikh vremen.* 5 vols. Moscow: Mir, 1913–14.

——. *Russkaia istoriia s drevneishikh vremen.* 4 vols. Moscow: Gosudarstvennoe sotsial'no-ekonomicheskoe izdatel'stvo, 1933–34.

Pokrovskii, N. N. "Sledstvennoe delo i vygovskaia povest' o tsarskikh sobytiiakh 1722 g." In *Rukopisnaia traditsiia XVI–XIX vv. na vostoke Rossii,* edited by N. N. Pokrovskii and E. K. Romodanovskaia, 46–70. Novosibirsk: Nauka, 1983.

Polevoi, N. A. *Dramaticheskie proizvedeniia.* Edited by V. I. Shemiakin. St. Petersburg, Tipo-litografiia M. P. Frolovoi, 1899.

Polnoe sobranie zakonov Rossiiskoi imperii. St. Petersburg: Tipografiia II-go otdeleniia Sobstvennogo Ego Imperatorskogo Velichestva Kantseliarii, 1830–1916.

Polosin, I. I. "Zapadnaia Evropa i Moskoviia v XVI veke." In *O Moskve Ivana Groznogo: Zapiski nemtsa oprichnika,* by Genrikh Staden (Heinrich von Staden), 9–53. Leningrad: Izdatel'stvo imeni M. i S. Sabashnikovykh, 1925.

Powelstock, David. *Becoming Mikhail Lermontov: The Ironies of Romantic Individualism in Nicholas I's Russia.* Evanston, Ill.: Northwestern University Press, 2005.

Prokopov, T. F., ed. *Tainyi pravitel' Rossii: K. P. Pobedonostsev i ego korrespondenty.* Moscow: Russkaia kniga, 2001.

Pushkin, A. S. *Polnoe sobranie sochinenii v desiati tomakh.* 4th ed. 10 vols. Leningrad: Nauka, 1977–79.

Ragussis, Michael. "Writing Nationalist History: England, the Conversion of the Jews, and *Ivanhoe.*" *ELH* 60, no. 1 (1993): 181–215.

Raeff, Marc. "An Early Theorist of Absolutism: Joseph of Volokolamsk." In *Readings in Russian History,* edited by Sidney Harcave, 1:177–87. 2 vols. New York: Crowell, 1962.

——. *Russia Abroad: A Cultural History of the Russian Emigration, 1919–1939.* New York: Oxford University Press, 1990.

Raikova, Irina. *Petr I: Predaniia, legendy, skazki i anekdoty.* Moscow: Izdatel'stvo imeni M. i S. Sabashnikovykh, 1993.

Renan, Ernest. *Oeuvres complètes.* 10 vols. Paris: Calmann-Lévy, 1947–61.

Repin, I. E. *Dalekoe blizkoe,* 6th ed. Moscow: Akademiia khudozhestv, 1961.

——. *Izbrannye pis'ma v dvukh tomakh.* 2 vols. Moscow: Iskusstvo, 1969.

Riasanovsky, Nicholas V. *The Image of Peter the Great in Russian History and Thought.* New York: Oxford University Press, 1985.

——. *Nicholas I and Official Nationality in Russia.* Berkeley: University of California Press, 1961.

——. "The Norman Theory of the Origin of the Russian State." *Russian Review* 7, no. 1 (1947): 96–110.

Riha, Thomas. *A Russian European: Paul Miliukov in Russian Politics.* Notre Dame, Ind.: University of Notre Dame Press, 1969.

Rimskii-Korsakov, N. A. *The Maid of Pskov: An Opera in Four Acts.* Melville, N.Y.: Belwin Hills, 1982.

——. *My Musical Life.* Translated by Judah A. Joffee. Edited by Carl Van Vechten. 3d ed. New York: Knopf, 1942.

Rosenthal, Bernice Glatzer. "Stages of Nietzscheanism: Merezhkovsky's Intellectual Evolution." In *Nietzsche in Russia*, edited by Bernice Glatzer Rosenthal, 69–93. Princeton, N.J.: Princeton University Press, 1986.

Rosovetskii, S. K. "Oral Prose of the 16th–17th Centuries about Ivan the Terrible as a Ruler." *Soviet Anthropology and Archeology* 23, no. 3 (1984–85): 3–49.

Rubinshtein, N. L. *Russkaia istoriografiia*. Moscow: Gospolitizdat, 1941.

Russkaia istoriia v dvadtsati-chetyrekh kartinkakh. St. Petersburg: Obshchestvennaia pol'za, 1866.

Ryleev, K. F. *Polnoe sobranie sochinenii*. Moscow: Academia, 1934; repr., The Hague: Europe Printing, 1967.

Safronov, B. G. *Istoricheskoe mirovozzrenie R. Iu. Vippera i ego vremia*. Moscow: Moscow University Press, 1976.

Samarin, Iu. F. *Sochineniia*. 12 vols. Edited by D. Samarin. Moscow: Tipografiia A. I. Mamontova, 1877–1911.

Samuels, Maurice. *The Spectacular Past: Popular History and the Novel in Nineteenth-Century France*. Ithaca, N.Y.: Cornell University Press, 2004.

Saramago, José. *The History of the Siege of Lisbon*. Translated by Giovani Pontiero. New York: Harcourt Brace, 1996.

Scherr, Barry P. "Poet and Tsar: History, Lineage, and Lyric Identity in Pushkin." In *Word, Music, History: A Festschrift for Caryl Emerson*, Stanford Slavic Studies 29–30, edited by Lazar Fleishman, Gabriella Safran, and Michael Wachtel, 1:93–109. 2 vols. Stanford, Calif.: Berkeley Slavic Specialties, 2005.

Serman, Il'ia. *Mikhail Lermontov: Zhizn' v literature*. Jerusalem: Slavisticheskii tsentr Gumanitarnogo fakul'teta Evreiskogo universiteta, 1997.

Sevost'ianov, G. N., and L. T. Mil'skaia, eds. *Portrety istorikov: vremia i sud'by*. Moscow: Universitetskaia kniga; Jerusalem: Gesharim, 2000.

Shaliapin, Fedor. *Stranitsy iz moei zhizni*. Edited by E. A. Grosheva. Kaliningrad: Kaliningradskoe knizhnoe izdatel'stvo, 1996.

Shcherbina, V. R. *A. N. Tolstoi: Tvorcheskii put'*. Moscow: Sovetskii pisatel', 1956.

Shenk, Frit'of Ben'iamin [Schenk, Frithjof Benjamin]. *Aleksandr Nevskii v russkoi kul'turnoi pamiati: Sviatoi, pravitel', natsional'nyi geroi (1263–2000)*. Moscow: Novoe Literaturnoe Obozrenie, 2007.

Shestakov, A. V., ed. *Kratkii kurs istorii SSSR: Uchebnik dlia 3-go i 4-go klassov*. Moscow: Gosudarstvennoe uchebno-pedagogicheskoe izdatel'stvo, 1937.

Sheviakov, V. N. "K voprosu ob oprichnine pri Ivane IV." *Voprosy istorii*, 1956, no. 9: 71–77.

Shil'der, N. K. *Imperator Nikolai I: Ego zhizn' i tsarstvovanie*. Moscow: Eksmo, 2008.

Shklovskii, V. B. *Za 60 let: Raboty o kino*. Moscow: Iskusstvo, 1985.

Shneiderman, E. "Benedikt Livshits: Arest, sledstvie, rasstrel." *Zvezda*, 1996, no. 1: 82–126.

Shul'gin, Ivan. *Izobrazhenie kharaktera i soderzhaniia istorii trekh poslednikh vekov*. 2d ed. St. Petersburg: N. Grech, 1833.

Sidorova, L. A. "Anna Mikhailovna Pankratova." In *Istoricheskaia nauka Rossii v XX veke*, 429–33. Moscow: Skriptorii, 1997.

Siljak, Ana. "Christianity, Science, and Progress in Sergei M. Solov'ev's *History of Russia*." In *Historiography of Imperial Russia: The Professional Writing of History in a Multinational State*, edited by Thomas Sanders, 215–38. Armonk, N.Y.: M. E. Sharpe, 1999.

Simmons, Clare A. *Reversing the Conquest: History and Myth in Nineteenth-Century British Literature*. New Brunswick, N.J.: Rutgers University Press, 1990.

Skrynnikov, R. G. *Tsarstvo terrora*. St. Petersburg: Nauka, 1992.

Slezkine, Yuri. "The USSR as a Communal Apartment, or How a Socialist State Promoted Ethnic Particularism." *Slavic Review* 53, no. 2 (1994): 414–52.

Smith, Kathleen E. *Mythmaking in the New Russia: Politics and Memory during the Yeltsin Era*. Ithaca, N.Y.: Cornell University Press, 2002.

Snychev, Ioann, Metropolitan. *Samoderzhavie dukha: Ocherki russkogo samosoznaniia*. St. Petersburg: Tsarskoe delo, 1995.

Solov'ev, S. M. *Istoriia Rossii s drevneishikh vremen*. 15 vols. Moscow: Sotsial'no-ekonomicheskaia literatura, 1960–66.

——. *Izbrannye trudy; Zapiski*. Moscow: Izdatel'stvo Moskovskogo universiteta, 1983.

——. *Publichnye chteniia o Petre Velikom*. Edited by V. I. Buganov. Moscow: Nauka, 1984.

Solov'ev, V. S. *Literaturnaia kritika*. Moscow: Sovremennik, 1990.

Stalin, I. V. *Sochineniia*. 18 vols. Moscow: Gosudarstvennoe izdatel'stvo politicheskoi literatury, 1949–53 (vols. 1–13); Moscow: Pisatel', 1997 (vols. 14–16); Tver: Severnaia korona, 2004–6 (vols. 17–18).

Stallybrass, Peter, and Allon White. *The Politics and Poetics of Transgression*. Ithaca, N.Y.: Cornell University Press, 1986.

Stasov, V. V., ed. *Ivan Nikolaevich Kramskoi: Ego zhizn', perepiska i khudozhestvenno-kriticheskie stat'i, 1837–1887*. St. Petersburg: Tipografiia A. S. Suvorina, 1888.

——. *Nikolai Nikolaevich Ge: Ego zhizn', proizvedeniia i perepiska*. Moscow: Tipografiia I. N. Kushnereva, 1904.

——. *Sobranie sochinenii*. 4 vols. St. Petersburg: Tipografiia M. M. Stasiulevicha (vols. 1–3); St. Petersburg: Energiia, 1906 (vol. 4).

Stockdale, Melissa Kirschke. *Paul Miliukov and the Quest for a Liberal Russia, 1880–1918*. Ithaca, N.Y.: Cornell University Press, 1996.

Suny, Ronald G. "The Empire Strikes Out: Imperial Russia, 'National' Identity, and Theories of Empire." In *A State of Nations: Empire and Nation-Making in the Age of Lenin and Stalin*, edited by Ronald G. Suny and Terry Martin, 23–66. Oxford: Oxford University Press, 2001.

——. *The Revenge of the Past: Nationalism, Revolution, and the Collapse of the Soviet Union*. Stanford, Calif.: Stanford University Press, 1993.

Taruskin, Richard. "The Present in the Past: Russian Opera and Russian Historiography, ca. 1870." Chap. 3 in his *Musorgsky: Eight Essays and an Epilogue*. Princeton, N.J.: Princeton University Press, 1993.

Terras, Victor, ed. *A Handbook of Russian Literature*. New Haven, Conn.: Yale University Press, 1985.

Timasheff, Nicholas. *The Great Retreat: The Growth and Decline of Communism in Russia*. New York: E. P. Dutton, 1947.

Todd, William Mills III. *Fiction and Society in the Age of Pushkin*. Cambridge, Mass.: Harvard University Press, 1986.

Tolstoi, A. K. *Sobranie sochinenii v chetyrekh tomakh*. 4 vols. Moscow: Pravda, 1980.

——. *Polnoe sobranie stikhotvorenii v dvukh tomakh*. Biblioteka poeta, Bol'shaia seriia. 2d ed. 2 vols. Leningrad: Sovetskii pisatel', 1984.

Tolstoi, A. N. *Polnoe sobranie sochinenii*. 15 vols. Moscow: Khudozhestvennaia literatura, 1946–53.

——. *Sobranie sochinenii v desiati tomakh.* 10 vols. Moscow: Khudozhestvennaia literatura, 1958–61.

Tolstoi, L. N. *Sobranie sochinenii v dvadtsati-dvukh tomakh.* 22 vols. Moscow: Khudozhestvennaia literatura, 1978–85.

Tomashevskii, B. V. *Pushkin: Kniga vtoraia, materialy k monografii (1824–1837).* Moscow: Izdatel'stvo Akademii nauk SSSR, 1961.

Tsivian, Yuri. *Ivan the Terrible.* London: British Film Institute, 2002.

Tucker, Robert C., ed. *The Marx–Engels Reader.* 2d ed. New York: Norton, 1978.

——. *Stalin in Power: The Revolution from Above, 1928–1941.* New York: Norton, 1990.

Tumarkin, Nina. *Lenin Lives! The Lenin Cult in Soviet Russia.* Cambridge, Mass.: Harvard University Press, 1983.

Turner, Victor. *The Ritual Process: Structure and Anti-Structure.* New York: Aldine, 1968.

Uhlenbruch, Bernd. "The Annexation of History: Eisenstein and the Ivan Groznyi Cult of the 1940s." In *The Culture of the Stalin Period,* edited by Hans Gunther, 266–87. New York: St. Martin's Press, 1990.

Ulam, Adam B. *Stalin: The Man and His Era.* Boston: Beacon, 1973.

Uspenskii, B. A. "Historia sub specie semioticae." In *Kul'turnoe nasledie drevnei Rusi (istoki, stanovlenie, traditsii),* 286–92. Moscow: Nauka, 1976.

——. "Tsar and Pretender: Samozvančestvo or Royal Imposture in Russia as a Cultural-Historical Phenomenon." Translated by David Budgen. In *The Semiotics of Russian Culture,* edited by Ann Shukman, 259–92. Ann Arbor: Dept. of Slavic Languages and Literatures, University of Michigan, 1984.

Ustrialov, N. G. *Istoriia tsarstvovaniia Petra Velikogo.* Vols. 1–4, 6. St. Petersburg: Tipografiia II-go otdeleniia Sobstvennogo Ego Imperatorskogo Velichestva Kantseliarii, 1858–63.

——. *Russkaia istoriia.* 5th ed. 2 vols. St. Petersburg: Tipografiia Appolona Fridrikhsona, 1855.

Ustrialov, N. V. *Pod znakom revoliutsii: Sbornik statei.* Harbin: Russkaia zhizn', 1925.

Uvarov, S. S. *Desiatiletie Ministerstva narodnogo prosveshcheniia, 1833–1843.* St. Petersburg: Tipografiia Imperatorskoi akademii nauk, 1864.

Valkenier, Elizabeth Kridl. "Politics in Russian Art: The Case of Repin." *Russian Review* 37, no. 1 (1978): 14–29.

——. *Russian Realist Art: The State and Society, the Peredvizhniki, and Their Tradition.* Ann Arbor, Mich.: Ardis, 1977.

——. "The Writer as Artist's Model: Repin's Portrait of Garshin." *Metropolitan Museum Journal* 28 (1993): 207–16.

Van Os, Hek, and Sjeng Scheijen. *Ilya Repin, Russia's Secret.* Zwolle, The Netherlands: Waanders Publishers, 2001.

Verkhoven', B. G. *Rossiia v tsarstvovanii Ivana Groznogo.* Moscow: Gospolitizdat, 1939.

Vernadsky, George. "The Death of the Tsarevich Dmitry: A Reconsideration of the Case." *Oxford Slavonic Papers* 5 (1954): 1–19.

Vipper, R. Iu. *Istoriia Novogo vremeni: Uchebnoe posobie.* Kiev: Nika-tsentr, 1997.

——. "Ivan Groznyi." *Prepodavanie istorii v shkole,* 1946, no. 1: 3–29.

——. *Ivan Groznyi.* 3d ed. Moscow: Gosudarstvennoe izdatel'stvo politicheskoi literatury, 1944.

——. "Ivan Groznyi." In *Ivan Groznyi, 1530–1584/Ivan Groznyi*, edited by D. M. Volodikhin, 101–211. Moscow: Universitet Rossiiskoi akademii obrazovaniia, 1998.

——. *Stenogramma publichnoi lektsii akademika Vipper R. Iu., prochitannoi 17 sentiabria 1943 goda v Kolonnom zale Doma Soiuzov v Moskve* (Moscow: Lektsionnoe biuro pri Komitete po delam vysshei shkoly pri Sovet narodnykh komissarov SSSR, 1943).

Volkan, Vamik D., and Norman Itzkowitz. "Modern Greek and Turkish Identities and the Psychodynamics of Greek-Turkish Relations." In *Cultures under Siege: Collective Violence and Trauma*, edited by Antonius C. G. M. Robben and Marcelo M. Suarez-Orozco, 227–47. Cambridge: Cambridge University Press, 2000.

Volodikhin, D. M. "Kritika teorii progressa v trudakh R. Iu. Vippera." *Voprosy istorii*, 1999, no. 2: 153–62.

——. *"Ochen' staryi akademik": Original'naia filosofiia istorii R. Iu. Vippera.* Moscow: Universitet Rossiiskoi akademii obrazovaniia, 1997.

Voloshin, M. A. *O Repine.* Moscow: Ole-Lukoe, 1913.

——. *Stikhotvoreniia i poemy.* Edited by B. A. Filippov. 2 vols. Paris: YMCA Press, 1982–84.

Wachtel, Andrew Baruch. *An Obsession with History: Russian Writers Confront the Past.* Stanford, Calif.: Stanford University Press, 1994.

Walicki, Andrzej. *A History of Russian Thought: From the Enlightenment to Marxism.* Translated by Hilda Andrews-Rusiecka. Stanford, Calif.: Stanford University Press, 1979.

Weeks, Theodore R. "Russification: Word and Practice, 1863–1914." *Proceedings of the American Philosophical Society* 148, no. 4 (2004): 471–89.

Weiner, Amir. *Making Sense of War: The Second World War and the Fate of the Bolshevik Revolution.* Princeton, N.J.: Princeton University Press, 2001.

Werth, Alexander. *Russia at War, 1941–1945.* New York: Carroll and Graf, 1984.

White, Hayden. *The Content of the Form: Narrative Discourse and Historical Representation.* Baltimore: Johns Hopkins University Press, 1987.

——. *Metahistory: The Historical Imagination in Nineteenth-Century Europe.* Baltimore: Johns Hopkins University Press, 1973.

Wolfe, Bertram D. *Revolution and Reality: Essays on the Origin and Fate of the Soviet System.* Chapel Hill: University of North Carolina Press, 1981.

Wortman, Richard S. *Scenarios of Power: Myth and Ceremony in Russian Monarchy.* 2 vols. Princeton, N.J.: Princeton University Press, 1995–2000.

Yanov [Ianov], Alexander. *The Origins of Autocracy: Ivan the Terrible in Russian History.* Translated by Stephen Dunn. Berkeley: University of California Press, 1981.

——. *Ten' groznogo tsaria: Zagadki russkoi istorii.* Moscow: Kruk, 1997.

Yaresh, Leo. "The Role of the Individual in History." In *Rewriting Russian History: Soviet Interpretations of Russia's Past*, edited by C. E. Black, 78–106. New York: Praeger, 1956.

Zelnik, Reginald E. *Perils of Pankratova: Some Stories from the Annals of Soviet Historiography.* Seattle, Wash.: Herbert J. Ellison Center for Russian, East European, and Central Asian Studies, 2005.

Zhivov, V. M. "Ivan Susanin i Petr Velikii: o konstantakh i peremenakh v sostave istoricheskikh personazhei," *Novoe literaturnoe obozrenie* 38 (1999): 51–65.

Zhivov, V. M., and B. A. Uspenskii. "Tsar' i bog: Semioticheskie aspekty sakralizatsii monarkha v Rossii." In *Iazyki kul'tury i problemy perevodimosti*, edited by B. A. Uspenskii, 47–153. Moscow: Nauka, 1987.

Zhukov, D. A. *Aleksei Konstantinovich Tolstoi*. Moscow: Molodaia gvardiia, 1982.

Zimin, A. A. *Oprichnina Ivana Groznogo*. Moscow: Mysl', 1964.

Zitser, Ernest A. "Post-Soviet Peter." *Kritika* 6, no. 2 (2005): 375–92.

Zograf, N. Iu., ed. *Nikolai Nikolaevich Ge: Pis'ma, stat'i, kritika, vospominaniia sovremennikov*. Moscow: Iskusstvo, 1978.

Zorin, Andrei. *Kormia dvuglavogo orla . . . : Literatura i gosudarstvennaia ideologiia v Rossii v poslednei treti XVIII–pervoi treti XIX veka*. Moscow: Novoe literaturnoe obozrenie, 2001.

INDEX

Note: The letter "f" following page numbers indicates reference to a figure; "n" references a note; italicized page numbers refer to an in-depth treatment.